The African Diaspora

CRITICAL AND CULTURAL MUSICOLOGY
VOLUME 3
GARLAND REFERENCE LIBRARY OF THE HUMANITIES
VOLUME 1995

Critical and Cultural Musicology

The African Diaspora
A Musical Perspective

EDITED BY

INGRID MONSON

Garland Publishing, Inc.
A MEMBER OF THE TAYLOR & FRANCIS GROUP
NEW YORK AND LONDON / 2000

Published by Garland Publishing, Inc.
A member of the Taylor & Francis Group
29 West 35th Street
New York, New York 10001

Library of Congress Cataloging-in-Publication Data

The African diaspora : a musical perspective / edited by Ingrid Monson.
     p. cm. — (Garland reference library of the humanities ; v. 1995.
  Critical and cultural musicology ; v. 3)
  Includes bibliographic references and index.
  ISBN 0-8153-2382-4 (alk. paper)
    1. Blacks—Music—History and criticism. 2. Music—Africa—
History and Criticism. I. Monson, Ingrid T. (Ingrid Tolia)

ML3760.1 .A37 2000
780'.89'9621—dc21   99-045341

Printed on acid-free, 250-year-life paper
Manufactured in the United States of America
10 9 8 7 6 5 4 3 2

Contents

CRITICAL AND CULTURAL MUSICOLOGY

Series Editor's Foreword

Martha Feldman

Musicology has undergone a seachange in recent years. Where once the discipline knew its limits, today its boundaries seem all but limitless. Its subjects have expanded from the great composers, patronage, manuscripts, and genre formations to include race, sexuality, jazz, and rock; its methods from textual criticism, formal analysis, paleography, narrative history, and archival studies to deconstruction, narrativity, postcolonial analysis, phenomenology, and performance studies. These categories point to deeper shifts in the discipline that have led musicologists to explore phenomena that previously had little or no place in musicology. Such shifts have changed our principles of evidence while urging new understandings of existing ones. They have transformed prevailing notions of musical texts, created new analytic strategies, recast our sense of subjectivity, and produced new archives of data. In the process they have also destabilized canons of scholarly value.

The implications of these changes remain challenging in a field whose intellectual ground has shifted so quickly. In response to them, this series offers essay collections that give thematic focus to new critical and cultural perspectives in musicology. Most of the essays contained herein pursue their projects through sustained research on specific musical practices and contexts. They aim to put strategies of scholarship that have developed recently in the discipline into meaningful exchanges with one another while also helping to construct fresh approaches. At the same time they try to reconcile these new approaches with older methods, building on the traditional achievements of musicology in helping to forge new disciplinary idioms. In both ventures, volumes in this series also attempt to press new associations among fields outside of musicology, making aspects of what has often seemed an inaccessible field intelligible to scholars in other disciplines.

In keeping with this agenda, topics treated in the series include music and the cultures of print; music, art, and synesthesia in nineteenth-century Europe; music in the African diaspora; relations between opera and cinema; Marxism and music; and music in the cultural sensorium. Through enterprises like these, the series hopes to facilitate new disciplinary directions and dialogues, challenging the boundaries of musicology and helping to refine its critical and cultural methods.

The African Diaspora

CHAPTER 1

Introduction

Ingrid Monson

To speak of *diaspora* evokes many interrelated ideas: dispersion, exile, ethnicity, nationalism, transnationalism, postcolonialism, and globalization among them. *African* in front of the term adds the concept of race and racism, conjuring debates about Pan-Africanism, black nationalism, essentialism, and hybridity, as well as invoking issues of history, modernity, and cultural memory. If the Jewish diaspora was the quintessential example of diaspora before the 1960s (Tölölyan 1996), the African diaspora has surely become the paradigmatic case for the closing years of the twentieth century. If the fact of dispersion, exile, and migration has been the traditional point of departure for defining diaspora (Tölölyan 1996), then the continuing experience of racial oppression has been crucial in the emergence of the transnational identities and ideologies of the African diaspora.

This volume offers ten essays, organized in three parts, exploring the relationship of music to the emergence of African diasporic sensibilities in the twentieth century. The first part, *Traveling Music and Musicians,* explores the globalization of African diasporic musics with particular attention to exchanges between African America, Europe, and the Black

Atlantic. *Beyond Tradition or Modernity,* the second part of the volume, explores the redefinition of tradition and modernity through music in contemporary Africa, with particular emphasis on gender, urban popular theater, and the selling of "traditional experience" on the international market. The third part, *Contradictory Moments,* explores aspects of particular musics that do not conform to idealized notions of African diasporic music as fully resistant to Western hegemony and a source of unambiguous black cultural pride. The aims of the volume are to address why music claims such pride of place in the African diasporic imaginary and to provide particular case studies of the interweaving of the local and global in the lives of musicians and their audiences.

Musical-Centrism?

Music, more than any other cultural discourse, has been taken as the ultimate embodiment of African and African diasporic cultural values and as prima facie evidence of deep cultural connections among all peoples of African descent. One reason for this perception of the centrality of music surely lies in its ability to coordinate several culturally valued modes of expression, including song, verbal recitation, dance, religious worship, drama, and visual display. The participatory, egalitarian, and spiritual qualities of African diasporic musics have frequently been idealized in the ethnomusicological literature (Chernoff 1979; Keil 1995), with scant attention to intracultural power stratifications and processes of contestation. In contemporary African diasporic cultural sensibilities, music is often a place where black trumps white, providing a sweet sense of cultural triumph, a vision of black power in its cultural, moral, ethical, and embodied dimensions. To the extent that the recognized achievements of black people are confined to music, however, this very point of cultural pride also serves to fuel stereotypical notions of the essential black subject, whose "natural" intuitive, emotional, and rhythmic gifts define her or his possibilities.

As attractive as the idea that music holds a special place in the cultural definition of the African diaspora may be, in other words, the claim is not without its problems and complications. Just as racism, slavery, and colonialism were crucial to the construction of the idea of Africa (Mudimbe 1988), and the very idea of blackness (with its simplifying synthesis of many African ethnicities) was forged in a dialectic with white supremacy, so the idea of a transnational black music has been synthesized in opposition to racial subjugation. The idea of a unified black musical ethos, consequently, is partially dependent on the continuing experience of racism. The forging of a collective identity through opposition to a common enemy contributes, in turn, to the ease with which the complexities of the African diaspora dissolve into a binary opposition between black and white. As Faye Harrison (1998: 617) has noted: "This construct is difficult to uproot, even in the current context of an increasingly multicolored and multicultural society in which racial formation assumes a multiplicity of forms, many of which vigorously contest the hegemonic constructs of whiteness and blackness." The continuing structural quality of racism, with its enduring set of economic, political, ideological, and color hierarchies that place black on the bottom, is the ultimate context reinforcing this tendency to binarism.

Nevertheless, claims for an idealized "Africanness" articulated and transmitted through music, often a subtext of the literature on the African diaspora, are sometimes disquietingly similar to twentieth-century nationalist assertions of an opposite political valence. Pamela Potter's (Potter 1998) fascinating study of how a German sense of musical superiority was used to uphold ideologies of racial superiority in the Third Reich, for example, reveals that claims for music's embodiment of the collective character of a people cannot be evaluated independent of the political and historical use to which such claims are put. In an African diasporic literature that frequently celebrates musicality, spirituality, and emotional depth as obviously counterhegemonic, it is important to remember that German National Socialists of the early twentieth century also claimed to be an especially musical people, given to passionate depth and spiritual transcendence through art (Potter 1998: 200–234). This is not to suggest that African diasporic assertions of the centrality of music are equivalent to those of the National Socialists, but to underscore the importance of placing the emotional and spiritual dimensions of music within the context of concrete historical and social practice.

Establishing the particular network of the linkages made between music, cultural identities, and globalizing economic, historical, and political forces thus is crucial to the larger project of analyzing African diasporic musical sensibilities in the twentieth century. The essays in this volume generally reject the idea of a static African essence in favor of a more continuously redefined and negotiated sense of cultural authenticity that emerges from generation to generation in response to larger geopolitical forces.

Gilroy's Legacy

Since Paul Gilroy's Black Atlantic (1993) has been critical in defining both the cultural studies debate about the African diaspora and arguing for the centrality of music in the construction and maintenance of contemporary transnational identities, a review of his principal arguments is in order. As the title suggests, Gilroy is interested not simply in the interchange between Africa and the New World—a binary relationship between those exiled and the "homeland." Rather, Gilroy addresses the multiplicity of cultural flows between and among the Caribbean, Britain, the African continent, and North America. Ships, chosen for their symbolic ability to evoke the middle passage, provide his visual image for the transatlantic interaction, but it is music to which he returns to make his case again and again.

Gilroy identifies three principal positions regarding the relationship between race and cultural meaning: (1) ethnic absolutism, (2) antiessentialism (or pluralism), and (3) anti-antiessentialism. Positions on black music, he believes, are divided between those "who see the music as the primary means to explore critically and reproduce politically the necessary ethnic essence of blackness and those who would dispute the existence of any such unifying, organic phenomenon" (100). *Ethnic absolutism* is the term he uses to describe the first position, while the second view (antiessentialism) implies a social constructionist and ideological view of race. The problem with the antiessentialist position, in Gilroy's view, is that it is often "insufficiently alive to the lingering power of specifically racialised forms of power and subordination" (32). For Gilroy this is tantamount to "forsaking the mass of black people who continue to comprehend their lived particularity through what it does to them" (101). The third position, "anti-antiessentialism," is the least discussed, but is centrally important. Here Gilroy invokes Foucault's notion of the "technology of power" to suggest that racialized subjectivity be seen "as the product of social practices that supposedly derive from it" (102). Here Gilroy holds to a social constructionist view of race, but takes exception to the idea that racial identity is simply an ideological effect. A deeply real difference emerges, he argues, as a product of racialized power exercised over black people. Since Gilroy's viewpoint is often confused with the second notion of antiessentialism, this point deserves emphasis. For Gilroy, despite his frontal assault on essentialism, race is not an imagined community, something that can be infinitely deconstructed so as to neutralize the importance of black power and experience, but a condition produced through coping with the historical legacy and contemporary reality of what Cornel West calls "white supremacist abuses." If West defines blackness as minimally involving being subject to these assaults and "being part of a rich culture and community that has struggled against such abuse" (1998: 155), for Gilroy (and many other commentators on the African diaspora) the centrality of black music emerges from the fact that "the self-identity, political culture, and grounded aesthetics that distinguish black communities have often been constructed through their music" (1993: 102).

Gilroy's book is refreshing, in part, because he addresses intradiasporic stratifications of power, especially of the apparent African American dominance in black diasporic culture in Britain. His charge of "ethnic absolutism" is most usually directed at African American ideological leaders, who, from Gilroy's vantage point, forsake the global in claiming elements of diasporic cultures as signs of a specifically African American cultural authenticity. The Caribbean antecedents of hip hop, transported to New York from Jamaica, which frequently go unacknowledged, are a particular sore point for Gilroy, who asks "what is it about black America's writing elite which means that they need to claim this diasporic cultural form in such an assertively nationalist way?" (1993: 34). Jacqueline Brown, who has documented the role of African American culture on black Liverpool and its specifically gendered effects, suggests that a central question that must be asked is "how particular black communities outside of the United States are affected by the global dominance of American culture." When, she wonders does the "unrelenting presence of black America actually become oppressive, even as it inspires?" (1998: 297).

The first part of this volume addresses many of the questions posed by Gilroy's *Black Atlantic* (1993)—issues of identity, ritual, aesthetics, and globalization. Proceeding from Gilroy's call for greater attention to the "rituals of performance," Travis Jackson's "Jazz Performance As Ritual" argues that jazz performance is driven by both an encompassing blues aesthetic and a sense of performance as a sacred ritual of transcendence. Drawing much from the work of Albert Murray (1970, 1976) and the community of contemporary jazz musicians with whom he conducted ethnographic research, Jackson develops a nonessentialized concept of blues aesthetic and demonstrates its implementation in performance. For Jackson, the notion of a blues aesthetic implies both a shared set of normative and evaluative criteria and Steven Feld's (Feld 1994) notion of an "iconicity of style"—where music becomes a "cross-modal homology" linking many different modes of cultural expression, such that its metaphoric power becomes "feelingfully synonymous" from one cultural domain to another. Indeed, music's ability to link several expressive modalities—including language (lyrics or recitation), dance, and visual display (clothing and personal style), as well as present idealized ethical and social sensibilities—seems central to its symbolic power across diasporic settings. The coordinating function of sound in this expressive integration should be especially noted.

The ethical and spiritual aspects of jazz performance are also central to Jackson's argument. If improvisation requires several ingredients, including an individual voice, the ability to play with multiple musical parameters during performance, and an understanding of the cultural foundations of the music, then the ultimate ethical goal of the music as expressed by musicians is to take the music to the "next level." This includes the transcendence of self and the establishment of a seemingly effortless musical flow, simultaneously hitting a musical and spiritual groove. This transcendence, Jackson argues, is not about escape but deep involvement in an art form that metaphorically encodes deep cultural values and "strategies for survival." In Jackson's view, the linkages between jazz and other musics of the African diaspora are ultimately to be found in musical performance, which provides a means of integrating these local cultural values with strategies for coping with racism that are shared widely across the African diaspora.

In "Communities of Style" Veit Erlmann follows several versions of the song "The Lion Sleeps Tonight" through recordings made at various diasporic locations. This classic of South African Zulu migrant workers' music was composed by Solomon Linda and recorded under the title of "Mbube" in 1939. Erlmann is interested in the musical alterations made as the song was revised and reinterpreted by a succession of groups including the Weavers in 1952, the Tokens in 1961 (both American groups), and a collaboration between Ladysmith Black Mambazo and the Mint Juleps (an Anglo-African group) in 1990 on Spike Lee's compilation album *Do It A Cappella*. At stake here is the construction of black diasporic identities through music, a process Erlmann calls "endotropic performance." The term emphasizes the intraracial construction of identity through a shared experience of style. These diasporic identities have emerged under the increasingly globalized and mediatized conditions of social life since the late nineteenth century. This is a "strange situation in which a person's understanding of himself or herself and their sense of the social world no longer coincide with the place in which they take place." Like Gilroy (1993: 76), Erlmann views music as "essentially phatic"[1]—that is, not about meaning or representation but about the process of communication itself. Critically assessing applications of Henry Louis Gates Jr.'s (1988) concept of Signifyin(g) to musical contexts, Erlmann proposes to extend a specific aspect of Signifyin(g)—that which focuses on repetition as a means of foregrounding the signifier itself.

At first Erlmann's denial that music is about "meaning" may confuse readers familiar with the broader ethnomusicological literature on music and meaning (see, e.g., Feld 1981, 1984). Erlmann does not deny that musical sound has indexical—that is, relational—meaning (and thus plays a role in the construction of globalized cultural identities) but wishes to emphasize that black diasporic musics are less about communicating a racial signified (a denotational meaning) than a metacommunicative play of signifiers that is crucial to producing a "shared experience of style." Reaching a position similar to Gilroy's antiantiessentialism, Erlmann emphasizes the endless process of redefining and reinventing identities in a globalized world characterized by "inescapable relatedness." In the end, "even though communities may seek to establish themselves around markers of racial identity, such coalescence of sound and society is never stable."

Traveling

Diaspora studies have historically emphasized the exile and migration from a homeland and the longing for return. Jacqueline Brown (1998: 293) credits Gilroy with developing a framework for diasporic analysis in which "all roads do not point to Africa," a perspective she argues is important in analyzing the relationship of Britain's black communities to the broader locales of a transnational African diaspora, especially African America and the Caribbean. Brown's discussion of the pull of African America in Britain, especially its music and its civil rights and black power movements, emphasizes the importance of African American travel to Europe as a source of diasporic crossfertilization. The implications of musicians as travelers for issues of globalization have not been sufficiently analyzed.

The expansion of the recording and broadcasting industries in the twentieth century has not only allowed musical performances to be circulated in virtual form but has also created demand for live performances in widely dispersed locations. For this reason, musicians' lives have been even less tied to place than other citizens of globalized modernity. From the 1930s to the 1950s, travel for jazz musicians often took the form of extended tours of one-nighters, and African American musicians traveled most of all, since Jim Crow shut them out of more stable engagements (of a week or longer) (DeVeaux 1997: 236–60). Many jazz bands, including Duke Ellington's and Count Basie's, spent far more time on the road than in any "home" location. Since the late nineteenth century international travel for top African American musicians has been commonplace, and their early destinations included not only Europe but also South Africa (Erlmann 1991). Europe remains an important travel destination for American jazz musicians, although other locations, especially Japan and Hong Kong, have emerged in the past twenty years.

Jerome Harris's essay, "Jazz on the Global Stage," provides an insider's analysis of the globalization of jazz, based on his twenty years of professional involvement as a guitarist and bassist and on research he conducted with promoters, journalists, editors, managers, and other musicians. Harris describes what he calls an "ecology of jazz," a web of interrelationships among three types of agents: art makers, art users, and mediators (broadcasting, record companies, promoters, and managers). By describing six basic activities of these agents—touring, recording, broadcasting, criticism and pedagogy, governmental support, and incorporating cross-cultural influence—Harris provides a rich portrait of jazz performance and reception, particularly in Europe, which remains the primary international destination for American jazz musicians. In so doing, Harris provides the most comprehensive portrait currently available of jazz outside the United States.

After completing this description of the structure of the jazz industry, Harris turns his attention to the issue of identity and aesthetics "on the global stage." Organized by the twin questions of who owns jazz and what is the appropriate aesthetic for the music, Harris delineates the tensions between an African American sense of ownership of the music and the increasing participation of non–African American musicians in the music, both here and abroad. Taking the international jazz industry as evidence that "prerogatives of ownership are loosening," Harris suggests that one explanation for why "some African Americans have become invested in a definition of jazz (also held by some whites) as a cultural form in which no non–African American can validly participate" is a collective sense of loss engendered by the dismantling of cohesive black communities in the post–civil rights era. These protectionist sentiments are also fueled by an expansion in the European jazz scene that, Harris suggests, may at some point rival the North American jazz community.

Harris identifies two basic aesthetic orientations through which musicians cope with these structural dilemmas: the "canon" aesthetic and the "process" aesthetic. Harris chose these terms to provide an alternative framework to the classic dichotomies of tradition/innovation and mainstream/avant-garde. Both sides of this debate, in his view, may properly lay claim to respecting tradition and emphasizing innovation in the music. The "canon" position emphasizes connections to the historical past and the cultural basis of the music, while the "process" position validates risk and surprise and actively incorporates outside influences that advocates of the canon reject. The canon position attempts to ward off encroaching globalization of jazz and the disempowering of the African American jazz legacy, while the process point of view often embraces a heterogeneous palette of musical sounds incorporated into jazz aesthetic through its incorporative principles of improvisation. In the end Harris views the globalization and hybridization of jazz as posing painful issues of identity and cultural ownership for African Americans but also as offering exciting new musical possibilities as players interact with the rest of the world's music.

Beyond Tradition or Modernity

If black versus white has been the defining binary in discussions of African diasporic musics of the black Atlantic, then tradition versus modernity has been the paradigmatic opposition shaping discussion of African musics themselves. Karin Barber (1997) links the emergence of this heuristic to colonialism and the "extension of global capitalism" on the one hand and the "assertion of cultural nationalism by African elites" on the other (1). In visual art Europeans prized "authentic" examples of tribal art, particularly those that could be detached from ritual contexts and placed in familiar Euro-American categories such as "sculpture." Ethnomusicologists valued indigenous traditional music and regarded the infusion of Western sounds and instruments as contamination. In literature, on the other hand, Western critics devoted most of their attention to Europhone texts, often unaware of the extent of popular literatures written in African languages. African elites, on the other hand, celebrated traditional art forms in order to assert the cultural worth of the precolonial African past, while at the same time claiming indigenous Europhone literatures, uniquely shaped by African oral traditions, as an emblem of modernity. Barber argues that "what this binary paradigm has obscured is the cultural activities, procedures, and products of the majority of people in present-day Africa. There is a vast domain of cultural production which cannot be classified as either 'traditional' or 'elite,' as 'oral' or 'literate,' as 'indigenous' or 'Western' in inspiration, because it straddles and dissolves these distinctions" (1–2).

The second part of this volume comprises four essays exploring in detail the processes of sustaining, remaking, and transforming "traditional" culture through time in particular locations and popular genres in West Africa: Mali, Guinea, Nigeria, and Ghana. If we may take as a point of departure the idea that all cultural systems, even in the absence of external influences, are inevitably engaged in processes of reproducing themselves through time that include not only duplication but also contestation and synthesis (often intergenerational), then we may consider how cultural authenticity is necessarily redefined and renegotiated in each generation at the nexus of changing local, regional, national, and global conditions.

Lucy Durán's "Women, Music, and the 'Mystique' of Hunters in Mali" provides a fascinating account of *wassoulou* music, a genre made internationally popular in recent years by the singer Oumou Sangare. Durán explains how women have come to dominate music performance in Mali in the postindependence years through the creative recontextualization of their traditional role as singers and their appropriation of the symbolism, instruments, and mystique of the hunter, an idealized figure embodying deep Malian cultural and moral values. In the postcolonial years, nonhereditary musicians have undermined the traditional dominance of the *jeliw,* the hereditary musicians who have historically carried the most prestige and dominated public performance in Mande society. *Wassoulou* music, as Durán argues, "occupies an interesting space between global and local, popular and traditional." On the one hand, *wassoulou* singers legitimate themselves through contextualizing themselves in the locally valued image of the generous, brave, honest, and spiritually powerful hunter and, on the other, use these songs to articulate issues of particular concern to Malian women and youth. Duran's thick description illustrates how these women deploy traditional imagery to legitimate their renegotiation of gender norms in a modern African society, use their traditional role as singers as a point of leverage, and have in the process become an important force in the popular music of the Black Atlantic. Sangare's lyrics, as Durán points out, are rarely confrontational, but Mande listeners "understand the implied criticism through their knowledge of the social context in which she has composed her songs."

Embedded in Durán's account is also an analysis of the role of the postcolonial state in the modernizing tradition through state-sponsored ensembles, a national television network, and national radio. In the course of the story, Durán helps us understand where internationally known musical figures such as the Super Djata Band, the Rail Band, Salif Keita, and Bembeya Jazz National fit into the musical context of contemporary Mali. She includes a discussion of how female *jeli,* such as Kandia Kouyate and Ami Koita, make use of hunters' imagery, while clearly illustrating the difference between hereditary and nonhereditary musicians. Since, as Durán emphasizes, "there has been a tendency by non-Malian writers to paint them all with the same brush and misunderstand the social spheres they represent," her account is of particular help in clarifying just who is and is not a *jeli.*

"*Mamaya,*" the essay by Lansiné Kaba and Eric Charry, explores a particular genre and composition from the repertory of the *jeli* (*jeliya*) that gained great popularity in Guinea in the 1930s and 1940s. *Mamaya* describes both a type of joyful music and dance event, and a particular composition of the same name that has a special place in the repertory of the *jeli.* Associated with the musical preferences of youth and the cosmopolitan culture of the city of Kankan, the music of *Mamaya* represented a modernization and recontextualization of traditional Maninnka praise singing to urban circumstances. Unlike most *jeliya, Mamaya* was associated with a specific dance. *Mamaya* was also linked to a particular age set, known as *san diya.* Kaba and Charry argue that age groups, which collectivize people born between three and four years apart and carry specific names, are just as significant as the more familiar sociological variables of ethnicity, class, and national identity in describing the cultural dynamics of Maninnka society.

Akin Euba's chapter on "Concepts of Neo-African Music As Manifested in the Yoruba Folk Opera" provides a detailed account of a genre that embodies Karin Barber's assertion that much of contemporary African cultural production collapses the boundaries between traditional or elite and indigenous or Western. The Yoruba dance-drama known as folk opera or traveling theater applies many dramatic conventions of Western theater to the performance of narratives enacting Bible stories, historical narrative, encounters with the *orishas,* and/or social

commentary. The performance conventions, however, have been decidedly non-Western. Ethnomusicology has often avoided hybridized genres like the Yoruba traveling theater, which are not "traditional" and for
this reason have been termed inauthentic. But as Wole Soyinka has
recently written:

> Most Nigerians of my generation were weaned on opera, complete
> with every structural component, from overture to stand-and-
> ·deliver arias to tragic climaxes. The overture went by a different
> name, of course; it was called the Opening Glee, which meant that
> our opera went one better than others in that it also boasted a Clos-
> ing Glee. The idea of "cloture" in European Romantic opera
> would be a near profanity: ruin the climax, dissipate the catharsis
> and curb those interminable curtain calls? (1999: 1)

Biodun Jeyifo has argued that the Yoruba traveling theater (or folk
opera) is truly a theater of the masses, including in its audience "the
entire range of occupational and socioeconomic groups and classes"
(1984: 1). Akin Euba takes us through the stories and music of three
major plays from the folk opera repertory: *The Palmwine Drinkard, Ọba
Kò So,* and *Ọbalúayé.* Interaction with the Yoruba spiritual world and
tensions between Christianity and Yoruba spirituality are prominently
featured. The musical accompaniment often includes a complement of
Yoruba percussion.

In many discussions of the African diaspora taking place in the
United States, Britain, the Caribbean, and Latin America, Africa is constructed as the ultimate location of cultural authenticity and purity, the
counterweight to the various cultural "dilutions" produced through the
legacy of the diaspora. The prominence of theatrical forms like Yoruba
folk opera carries an implied lesson: that the diasporic desire to "return
to authentic roots" might better be focused on examining the social and
cultural processes through which contemporary Africans revise and
reinvent notions of cultural legitimacy from generation to generation
rather than on an original cultural baseline to be reclaimed. As Andrew
Apter argues in his critical reexamination of Melville Herskovits,
processes of cultural revision and negotiation through time suggest that
"West Africa's contribution to the African diaspora lies not merely in
specific ritual symbols and forms, but also in the interpretive practices
that generate their meanings" (1991: 256).

If African tradition and purity has been especially important to

Africans of the diaspora and Westerners anxious to escape the stultifications of industrial and postindustrial society, it is not surprising that enterprising Africans have found ways to market the "traditional" to Western consumers. Steven Cornelius's "They Just Need Money: Goods and Gods, Power and Truth in a West African Village" provides an account of the Dagbe Cultural Institute in the village of Kopeyia, Ghana, an institution devoted to teaching traditional Ewe music to foreigners in a traditional village setting. Cornelius argues that "it has been the reconstitution and repackaging of traditional music itself that has been, both consciously and unconsciously, largely responsible for that village's ever widening relationship with the West." This expanding relationship, in turn, precipitated an incident of *juju* directed against the center's founder, Godwin Agbeli, an Ewe master drummer, dancer, and choreographer, who died in 1998. Agbelli had taught Ewe traditional music at several American universities and was formerly the senior drum and dance coach of Ghana's National Folkloric Company. Agbelli's commitment to traditional life resulted in his decision to found the Dagbe Cultural Institute in Kopeyia, a village without electricity or running water or much visible incursion of modern life. The flow of foreign students, however, has brought money and prestige to the village, and the Agbelli family became one of the most prosperous in the village. Agbelli's wealth in turn prompted a demand for money from a group of devotees of the god Koku (the Kokushio), who disguised the demand through traditional means—offering to locate and neutralize an evil *juju* packet planted on Agbelli's property for a fee (comprising cash and in-kind payments). Cornelius's fascinating account of the negotiations between Agbelli and the Kokushio illustrate how both sides used traditional belief systems to support their position in the debate over the "truth" of the *juju* and its management. This is an excellent example of the use of traditional interpretive practices to generate new meanings in a social context in increasing dialogue with the West.

Contradictory Moments

If the tendency toward a black-white racial binarism in African diasporic sensibility is structurally reinforced through the continued existence of implicit and explicit ideologies of white supremacy, then one response to this structural condition has been to invert the racial hierarchy by figuring Africa and blackness as morally and spiritually superior to the technological West. If white Western capitalism is exploitative and greedy, then true blackness is spiritual and communitarian; if the West is militaristic and violent, then African tradition is peace loving; if the West is oppressive and stultifying, then blackness is resistant and liberatory. The idea of the African personality, used by both Leopold Senghor and Kwame Nkrumah, was built on this line of reasoning.

As attractive as the idea of black moral superiority may be to the victims of racism, and to outsiders who idealize them, no society or social grouping is without its contradictions, inconsistencies, and hypocrisies. To hold that the African diasporic subject must be perfectly consistent and above reproach, or that the black subject must be "better than" the white subject in order to be considered fully human, is dehumanizing. Nevertheless, the revelation that an African diasporic music or political movement has been anything less than "resistant" to Western hegemony is disappointing to those who view African diasporic cultural values as offering a possible model for a utopian redemption of humankind. Any weakness in Africa or the diaspora, many fear, may be used to undermine the validity of demands for racial justice. For this reason diasporists often refrain from acknowledging aspects of African diasporic cultural systems that do not conform to their high expectations, emphasizing instead the importance of "positive" celebratory images. Yet the richness of the diasporic experience is lost without examining the complex interplay between power, cultural goals, human fallibility, and structural dilemmas.

Gage Averill and Yuen-Ming David Yih's "Militarism in Haitian Music"—the first essay in Part III, *Contradictory Moments*—addresses a topic that they acknowledge many readers may find "counterintuitive": the role of militarism in Haitian social and cultural life. Work on the African diaspora has been more accustomed to associating military power exclusively with the repressive colonialism of the West, but Averill and Yih assert that militarism has played "a more serious role in structuring African diasporic consciousness than is commonly attributed to it." The authors identify several factors that explain the importance of the military legacy in Haiti: (1) the military backgrounds of the first generation of Creole slaves, especially escaped slaves (maroons) and those who formed African "national" organizations; (2) the involvement of enslaved Africans in the colonial military; (3) the length of the military struggle for independence; and (4) the postcolonial dominance of the Haitian army.

Military imagery is particularly striking in Haitian vodou, which is divided into two principal rites known as Rada and Petwo, commonly coded as "civilian" and "military," respectively. Since military struggle was essential to the slave uprising of 1791 (which is said to have begun at a vodou ceremony), it is not surprising that enslaved Africans would celebrate military prowess. Averill and Yih describe three other musical genres laden with military imagery, instruments, and organization that borrow not only from African military traditions but also from the French military: *ochan* and *rasanble* drumming, which draw heavily from French signal drumming; *kò mizik mennwat,* a small ensemble tradition from the southern peninsula; and the bands associated with *rara* and Carnival.

Militarism in Haitian cultural life, according to Averill and Yih, is multifaceted and sometimes paradoxical. On the one hand, military legacy in expressive culture reveals "the residue of struggles against slavery, colonialism, and marginalization; and the covert self-organization of the African slave society in the Americas." On the other hand, the celebration of military music of European provenance in *ochan* and *rasanble* reveals the complex operations of power in the colonial experience. As Averill and Yih conclude, in a country where most traditional music draws on African aesthetics, "the preservation of a European-derived repertory and performance practice within genres that refer to power and hierarchy is an intriguing legacy of colonization and a window into the contradictions of the postcolonial experience."

Julian Gerstin's chapter, "Musical Revivals and Social Movements in Contemporary Martinique: Ideology, Identity, Ambivalence," addresses music and politics in Martinique from an unusual angle. Noting the proliferation of multiple musical styles on the island, Gerstin asks why, unlike virtually every other island in the Caribbean, does the public sphere in Martinique fail to make a strong correlation between indigenous Martinican musical genres and national or ethnic identity? Gerstin uses New Social Movement (NSM) theory to address the interrelationship of art in politics in Martinique, a perspective that he argues has considerable potential for ethnomusicology. NSM theory is interested in groups that no longer follow class, racial, or ethnic divisions exclusively but are characterized by myriad interwoven alliances that complicate the achievement of political mobilization. Through a close look at two genres—*bèlè,* a traditional rural dance/drum style revitalized during the 1980s and 1990s by politically motivated urban performers, and Carnival, also revitalized during the 1980s and 1990s but without appreciable political intent—Gerstin's ultimate goal is to map the local and global conditions that limit the possibility of oppositional social movements in Martinique. The ascendance of the ideology of *créolité* (which empha- sizes Martinican identity as a mixture of races) rather than Aimé Césaire's African-identified *négritude* partially explains the paucity of oppositional movements in Martinique. Martinique's national identity, in Gerstin's analysis, is characterized by a great deal of ambivalence. On the one hand, there is much resentment of the island's dependence on France; on the other, there is a fear of independence and an attraction to French global culture and the material goods it provides. Although Mar- tinicans experience a deep sense of racial and cultural difference in rela- tionship to France, the particular circumstances on the island have led to a standoff between a "resented dependence" and an "ambiguous" oppo- sition that is articulated in its cultural expressions. If the literature on music and politics has stressed the oppositional nature of African dias- poric musical forms, then Gerstin adds the possibility that Martinicans may simultaneously resist and accommodate.

The final chapter, my essay on "Art Blakey's African Diaspora," examines the rather large disjunction between what jazz drummer Art Blakey *said* about his relationship to Africa and African music and the music he actually *played*. During the black power era and after (when the jazz community increasingly embraced the idea that jazz had deep connections to Africa), Blakey was often quoted as denying any rela- tionship between jazz and African music. Blakey's one year stay in Ghana and Nigeria in the late 1940s, as well as several albums recorded at the time of Ghana's independence in collaboration with Afro-Cuban musicians, however, reveal Blakey's more complicated relationship to the idea of an African diaspora. Contextualizing Blakey's contradictory moments requires an examination of three prinicipal cultural and histor- ical contexts: (1) the impact of anticolonialism, Pan-Africanism, and Islam on the African American community from the 1920s through the1940s; (2) the musical invocation of Africa via Afro-Cuban percus- sion at the time of Ghanaian independence in 1957; and (3) Blakey's masterful articulation of a diasporic "jazz message" through indexical musical signification.

Blakey was among several jazz musicians who converted to Islam through the Ahmadiyya movement in the 1940s and 1950s, including Sahib Shihab, Ahmad Jamal, and McCoy Tyner. His travels to Africa, as he repeatedly emphasized, were motivated more by religious than musi- cal interests. Examining the relationship of the multiethnic Ahmadiyya movement to Garveyism, the Moorish Science Temple of America, and the Nation of Islam undermines any simplistic association of Islam in the African American community with racial separatism, yet reveals the close connection between Pan-Africanist political interests and Pan-Islamic spiritualism. At the same time, a look at the musical means through which Blakey articulated an African diasporic consciousness illustrates the centrality of Afro-Cuban musical traditions in triangulating between Africa and African America in the 1950s.

Collectively these essays underscore the importance of ethnographic and historical case studies of particular musical practices for understanding the construction of African diasporic sensibilities in the twentieth century. Since it is commonplace to speak of the globalization of popular musics in the late twentieth century and quite tempting to make facile generalizations about commodification, resistance, race, hegemony, gender, and musical power, the particular constellations of interconnection provided by empirical work that traces the vantage point of a particular genre, person, or point in time contributes to undermining lingering transhistorical correlations between sound and culture.

If traditional studies of the African diaspora have stressed first and foremost the condition of dispersion and exile, then the essays in this volume additionally emphasize the importance of developing a more informed understanding of music and mediation in contemporary Africa. A deeper understanding of the way in which notions of cultural authenticity and legitimacy are necessarily reinvented in each generation through a process of intergenerational negotiation, contestation, and synthesis points to the enduring importance of notions of authenticity and tradition in music of the African diaspora, without reducing them to a racial essence, a standard of purity that is impossible to achieve, or the whipping boy of poststructural cultural theories that are suspicious of any implictly color-coded boundary. The enduring character of white supremacy, after all, is one of the principal generators of the need and longing for a specifically black unity.

Examining that which is taken for authentic and legitimate in particular locations and at particular times, itself constructed against the backdrop of larger forces of globalization, also leaves space open for the inevitably contradictory and fallible aspects of human cultural practice. Indeed, points of contradiction in a particular genre, culture, or person may reveal most clearly the larger constellation of forces in which a culture is embedded. Imperfect attempts to cope with these contradictions do not point to a lack of principle or character but to the ongoing difficulty of improvising one's way through a minefield of global forces.

If music holds a special place in this process, it is likely in the way it models the creative work of coping and contending. Music in the African diaspora both creates a context in which various kinds of expressive modalities can be coordinated, contested, or enjoyed (e.g., dance, song, costume, cutting contests), while at the same time pointing to larger historical and cultural contexts of power. African diasporic sensibilities have emerged and sustained themselves in the twentieth century to the degree that people recognize themselves in this ongoing critical process.

Notes

[1]"Phatic" is one of the six functions of language defined by Roman Jakobson: emotive, conative, referential, poetic, phatic, and metalingual. For an explanation of these terms see Duranti 1997: 284–86.

References

Apter, Andrew. 1991. "Herkovits's Heritage: Rethinking Syncretism in the African Diaspora." *Diaspora* 1(3): 235–60.

Barber, Karin. 1997. "Introduction." In *Readings in African Popular Culture,* edited by Karin Barber, 1–12. Bloomington: Indiana University Press.

Brown, Jacqueline Nassy. 1998. "Black Liverpool, Black America, and the Gendering of Diasporic Space." *Cultural Anthropology* 13(3): 291–325.

Chernoff, John Miller. 1979. *African Rhythm and African Sensibility: Aesthetics and Social Action in African Musical Idioms.* Chicago: University of Chicago Press.

DeVeaux, Scott. 1997. *The Birth of Bebop: A Social and Musical History.* Berkeley: University of California Press.

Duranti, Alessandro. 1997. *Linguistic Anthropology.* Cambridge: Cambridge University Press.

Erlmann, Veit. 1991. *African Stars: Studies in Black South African Performance.* Chicago: University of Chicago Press.

Feld, Steven. 1981. " 'Flow Like a Waterfall': The Metaphors of Kaluli Music Theory." *Yearbook for Traditional Music* 13: 22–47.

———. 1984. "Communication, Music and Speech about Music." *Yearbook for Traditional Music* 16: 1–18.

———. 1994. "Aesthetics As Iconicity of Style (Uptown Title); or, (Downtown Title) 'Lift-Up-Over Sounding': Getting into the Kaluli Groove." In *Music Grooves: Essays and Dialogues,* edited by Charles Keil and Steven Feld, 109–50. Chicago: University of Chicago Press.

Gates, Henry Louis, Jr. 1988. *The Signifying Monkey: A Theory of African-American Literary Criticism.* New York: Oxford University Press.

Gilroy, Paul. 1993. *The Black Atlantic: Modernity and Double Consciousness*. Cambridge: Harvard University Press.

Harrison, Faye V. 1998. "Introduction: Expanding the Discourse on 'Race.' " *American Anthropologist* 100(3): 609–31.

Jeyifo, Biodun. 1984. *The Yoruba Popular Travelling Theatre of Nigeria*. Lagos: Nigeria Magazine.

Keil, Charles. 1995. "The Theory of Participatory Descrepancies: A Progress Report." *Ethnomusicology* 39(1): 1–19.

Mudimbe, Valentin Y. 1988. *The Invention of Africa: Gnosis, Philosophy and the Order of Knowledge*. Bloomington: Indiana University Press.

Murray, Albert. 1970. *The Omni-Americans: Some Alternatives to the Folklore of White Supremacy*. New York: Da Capo.

————. 1976. *Stomping the Blues*. New York: Da Capo.

Potter, Pamela. 1998. *Most German of the Arts: Musicology and Society from the Weimar Republic to the End of Hitler's Third Reich*. New Haven, CT: Yale University Press.

Soyinka, Wole. 1999. "African Traditions at Home in the Opera House." *New York Times,* 25 Apr., Arts and Leisure: 1, 26.

Tölölyan, Khachig. 1996. "Rethinking Diaspora(s): Stateless Power in the Transnational Moment." *Diaspora* 5(1): 3–36.

West, Cornel. 1998. "Moral Reasoning versus Racial Reasoning." In *African Philosophy: An Anthology,* edited by Emmanuel Chukwudi Eze, 155–59. Oxford: Blackwell.

PART I

Traveling Music and Musicians

CHAPTER 2

Jazz Performance as Ritual: The Blues Aesthetic and the African Diaspora

Travis A. Jackson

The African American music known as jazz generally merits little mention in discussions of the musics of the African diaspora. One could perhaps account for its absence by examining the contexts in which it has been discussed and researched. Those who have written about jazz have typically understood Western concert music—if indeed they understood any music—better than they did jazz (Gennari 1991; Gabbard 1995). Moreover, they have frequently tried to fit jazz into modernist discourses on art and aesthetics (Gioia 1988 furnishes a good example; for a critique, see Johnson 1993). Jazz's relation to other forms of African American music is minimal in their analyses (Starks 1981, 1993), surfacing only in cursory mentions of jazz's seemingly passive "mixture" of European and African elements (Gridley 1997). Indeed, jazz is separated from other African American musics to emphasize its status as art and its expansive "Americanness" at the expense of its ritual functions and seemingly less expansive *African*-Americanness. Thus, alongside musics associated with *santería, candomblé,* and *vodou,* as well as *samba, salsa,* and *konpa,* it might be seen as one of the most "European" and least "African" of all African-derived musics in the Americas.[1]

23

In this regard, its low level of "Africanness" is a function of the sur-face features of musical sound—discernible Africanisms in musical form or melodic or rhythmic patterning. As a number of commentators have argued, such an evaluative framework, freighted as it is with assumptions about what "sounds African" and what "sounds European," fails to distinguish between the expressive medium of musical sound and the conceptual bases that inform its production (Olly Wilson 1974, 1985, 1992; Reyes Schramm 1986; Logan 1984; Monson 1990; Floyd 1995). In other words, such evaluation privileges form over concept in determining the cultural meaning of a particular performance for its par-ticipants.

Still, a diaspora perspective is not without its difficulties. Gilroy (1994) pointedly raises some of the questions that complicate this view:

> How are we to think critically about artistic products and aesthetic codes which, though they may be traceable back to one distinct location, have somehow been changed either by the passage of time or by their displacement, relocation or dissemination through wider networks of communication and cultural exchange? (94)

Indeed, the scholar conducting work that tries to link the cultural prac-tices of those in diaspora with one another or with Africans risks having her/his work dismissed as "essentialism or idealism or both" (94). Gilroy suggests that scholars think critically about the relationships between cultural identity and performative acts:

> If . . . a style, genre, or performance of music is identified as expressing the absolute essence of the group that produced it, what special analytical problems arise? What contradictions appear in the transmission and adaptation of this cultural expression by other diaspora populations and how will they be resolved? How does the hemispheric displacement and global dissemination of Black music get reflected in localised traditions of critical writing and, once the music is perceived as a world phenomenon, what value is placed upon its origins in opposition to its contingent loops and fractal trajectories? (96)

Gilroy, unfortunately, does a better job of raising such questions than he does answering them. Perhaps the strength of his writing is its theoreti-cal suggestiveness. More than suggestive is the ethnomusicological literature that shows how these questions are being answered among diaspora populations (Mensah 1971–72; Coplan 1985; Collins 1987; Waterman 1990; Erlmann 1991; Guilbault et al. 1993).

But taking up Gilroy's challenge and focusing on practices shared by Black Atlantic populations opens up interesting avenues of inquiry, particularly the relationship of musical performance to ritual and the meanings that obtain in ritual settings. As he observes, in black diaspora cultures, records (or songs) lose privileged status as objects, becoming instead tools for creative improvisation. Thus recast, these objects become "central to the regulation of collective memory, perception and experience in the present, to the construction of community by symbolic and ritual means in dances, clubs, parties, and discos" (Gilroy 1991b: 211).

In this essay, I will explore jazz's performance rituals and the aesthetic that informs them, later posing connections to ritual and aesthetic in other Black Atlantic musics. I will begin by comparing a number of works by selected scholars interested in accounting for meanings in African American musics (Baraka 1963; Ellison 1964; Murray 1970; 1976; Levine 1977; Small 1987; Floyd 1995). The conclusions of that survey will be placed in relief against the ideas and attitudes of the individuals interviewed during fieldwork conducted in New York City in the mid-1990s. Through such a juxtaposition, I will show that one of the primary forces driving the creation and making possible the interpretation of African American musics and, in particular, jazz is concern both with the blues as an aesthetic or sensibility and with performance as a sacred, ritual act.

Scholarly Views of Meaning in African American Music

Much of the writing and criticism of jazz prior to the early 1960s was predicated on conceptions of musical style and performance that had very little to do with how practitioners of the music thought and acted (Starks 1993: 150–56). The hobbyists, discographers, critics, and historians who devoted themselves to jazz wrote from vantage points that saw it and jazz performers primarily as primitive, libidinal, rebellious, or "artistic" (for overviews, see Welburn 1987; Gioia 1988; Gennari 1991). Those writers expressing the artistic view typically concerned themselves with the culture and attitudes of musicians, but their work had its clearest analogues in the work of text-based music scholars (Gennari 1991).

Amiri Baraka's *Blues People* (1963)[2] was perhaps the first book-length study to attempt sustained theoretical argument about the relations between African American culture and African American musical forms.[3] In the book's introduction, Baraka presents his main premise: "if the music of the Negro in America, in all its permutations, is subjected to socio-anthropological as well as musical scrutiny, something about the essential nature of the Negro's existence in this country ought to be revealed, as well as something about the essential nature of this country, *i.e.,* society as a whole" (x, see also 137 and 153).[4] His concern throughout is examining the progression of social and historical forces that brought the first African captives to the colonies of North America and, through the experiences of slavery and the years following emancipation, helped transform them into African Americans with distinct world-views and attendant cultural forms. The theoretical underpinning for Baraka's tracing of this progression is Melville Herskovits's theory of acculturation and its companion concept syncretism (Herskovits 1990).[5] In his discussion of the differing forms and styles of African American music (32–94), Baraka's view of meaning in African American music is one that sees it as purely derived from or expressive of social conditions.

He believes that one must understand the blues in order to understand jazz: "Blues is the parent of all legitimate jazz" (17). He is not merely attempting to police the boundaries of "legitimate" jazz, to see the presence or absence of the blues, however defined, as a sort of litmus test. He is asserting, additionally, that all music that would be called jazz has to negotiate and maintain a close relationship with the blues, that it must somehow trace its lineage through the blues. In that sense, he sees the development of jazz performance in terms of what Charles Keil has called an "appropriation-revitalization" process (Keil 1991: 43–48)[6]: in successive waves, blues-based jazz forms are appropriated and have their blues content diluted by whites and the recording industry. In response, black musicians in each generation—such as bebop pioneers like Charlie Parker and Dizzy Gillespie or musicians from the early 1960s like John Coltrane and Ornette Coleman—find ways to revitalize the music by reaffirming the centrality of blues-based practices (225).

He intensifies his view of the relationship between blues and jazz when he glosses "jazz" as "purely instrumental blues" (71) and explains that "although jazz developed out of a kind of blues, blues in its later popular connotation came to mean *a way of playing jazz*" (71; emphasis in original). Blues, in relation to jazz, then, functions not only as a noun denoting a musical progenitor and a higher level of musical categorization, but also as one describing modifiable musical forms (8-, 12-, and 16-bar I–IV–V progressions: see Koch 1982) and an approach to playing derived from performance on such forms. One major facet of that approach was a way of adapting sounds, techniques, and concepts to the playing of jazz: "In order for the jazz musician to utilize most expressively any formal classical techniques, it is certainly necessary that these techniques be subjected to the emotional and philosophical attitudes of Afro-American music—that these techniques be used not canonized" (230, cf. Levine 1977: 195–96).

While writers like Ralph Ellison would not quarrel with Baraka's insistence on the importance of the blues, they would disagree about the way in which Baraka arrived at his conclusions. In a now famous review of *Blues People,* Ellison takes issue with the statement previously quoted from Baraka's introduction: "The tremendous burden of sociology which [Baraka] would place upon this body of music is enough to give even the blues the blues" (1964: 249). He is also highly critical of Baraka's facile linking of social status and racial purity with forms of musical expression, explaining that from Baraka's account, "One would get the impression that there was a rigid correlation between color, education, income and the Negro's preference in music."

Beyond his critique of Baraka, Ellison's comments on the importance of the blues are instructive. Near the end of his review, he writes eloquently about the role that the blues and the sensibility that informs them have played in African American culture:

> The blues speak to us simultaneously of the tragic and the comic aspects of the human condition[,] and they express a profound sense of life shared by many Negro Americans precisely because their lives have combined these modes. This has been the heritage of a people who for hundreds of years could not celebrate birth or dignify death and whose need to live despite the dehumanizing pressures of slavery developed an endless capacity for laughing at their painful experiences. This is a group experience shared by many Negroes, and *any effective study of the blues would treat them first as poetry and ritual . . .* There are levels of time and function involved here, and the blues which might be used in one place as entertainment . . . might be put to a ritual use in another. Bessie Smith might have been a "blues queen" to the society at large, but within the tighter Negro community where the blues were part of a total way of life, and a major expression of an attitude

toward life, she was a priestess, a celebrant who affirmed the values of the group and man's ability to deal with chaos . . . [The] blues are not concerned with civil rights or obvious political protest; they are an art form and thus a transcendence of those conditions created within the Negro community by the denial of social justice. As such they are one of the techniques through which Negroes have survived and kept their courage. (256–57, emphasis added; cf. Ellison 1964: 78–79)

What Ellison adds to Baraka's view is the notion that the blues function not only as individual expression but as part of a ritual involving words, music, and trappings of spirituality. The ritual itself crystallizes some of the most essential values of African Americans with regard to survival and daily living. Ellison is also careful to divorce his explication of the functions of the blues from one that simply equates them with protest. For him, they and the music they inspire constitute, in Albert Murray's borrowed phrase, "equipment for living."[7]

More than Baraka, Ellison delves into the nature of that ritual by exploring its larger implications. In short, each performance helps each individual performer to negotiate his or her identity vis-à-vis other musicians, the larger community, and the history of the music:

[T]rue jazz is an art of individual assertion within and against the group. Each true jazz moment (as distinct from the uninspired commercial performance) springs from a contest in which each artist challenges all the rest; each solo flight, or improvisation, represents (like the successive canvases of a painter) a definition of his identity: as individual, as member of a collectivity and as a link in the chain of tradition. Thus because jazz finds its very life in an endless improvisation upon traditional materials, the jazzman must lose his identity even as he finds it. (1964: 234)

He elaborates in another essay: "The delicate balance struck between strong individual personality and the group during those early jam sessions was a marvel of social organization. I had learned too that the end of all this discipline and technical mastery was the desire to express an affirmative way of life through [a] musical tradition and that this tradition insisted that each artist achieve his creativity within its frame. He must learn the best of the past, and add to it his personal vision" (1964: 189). In this sense, each jazz performance takes on meaning through the interactions of the performers with one another and with the music's history. For Ellison, even the nonperforming participant in a musical event also partakes of those interactions with history (1964:197).

Ellison's ideas about the nature of jazz performance have been extended, elaborated, and refined[8] by his younger classmate from Tuskegee Institute, Albert Murray. In a series of essays and fictional works since 1970, Murray has continually returned to the blues, using it not only as the basis for aesthetic theorization but also as a way of characterizing the nature of the American experience. For him, Ellison's writing about ritual, affirmation, and interaction with tradition are subsumed under the rubric of the blues.

In his first collection, *The Omni-Americans* (1970), Murray borrows from Constance Rourke the notion that American culture is hybrid, choosing himself to see it as a "mulatto culture" (3, 13–22, 78–85). The blues is a particular response to adversity within that mulatto culture, the response of African American people. He echoes something of Baraka's relating of sound structure to social structure when he says,

> [W]hat is represented in the music, dance, painting, sculpture, literature and architecture of a given group of people in a particular time, place, and circumstance is a conception of the essential nature and purpose of human existence itself. More specifically, an art style is the assimilation in terms of which a given community, folk, or communion of faith embodies its basic attitudes toward experience. (55)

What is different, however, is his emphasis on expression, rather than determination. Social and cultural circumstances do not so much predict or shape the forms that artistic expressions will take as they provide raw materials that might be transformed according to individual and group proclivities (cf. Gilroy 1991a: 154).

For African Americans, working primarily within what he refers to as the "blues idiom," the element of "play" (cf. Hall 1992) and its potential for making existence meaningful are paramount. The blues come to constitute equipment for living through their modeling of the way in which individuals confront the difficulties they face in daily life; the most successful individuals will see the necessity of playing with the materials and situations before them as essential:

> The definitive statement of the epistemological assumptions that underlie the blues idiom may well be the colloquial title and opening declaration of one of Duke Ellington's best-known dance tunes

from the mid-thirties: "It Don't Mean a Thing if It Ain't Got That Swing." In any case, when the Negro musician or dancer swings the blues, he is fulfilling the same existential requirement that determines the mission of the poet, the priest, and the medicine man. . . . Extemporizing in response to the exigencies of the situation in which he finds himself, he is confronting, acknowledging, and contending with the infernal absurdities and ever-impending frustrations inherent in the nature of existence *by playing with the possibilities that are also there.* Thus does man the player become man the stylizer and by the same token the humanizer of chaos; and thus does play become ritual, ceremony, and art; and thus also does the dance-beat improvisation of experience in the blues idiom become survival technique, esthetic equipment for living, and a central element in the dynamics of U.S. Negro lifestyle. (58; emphasis in original)

Like Baraka and Ellison, Murray is concerned with the multivalence of the blues. They work not only on the level of musical form, technique, or style, but also on the level of prevailing ethos, as an approach to dealing with the exigencies of daily life. Or put more simply, what works in the context of musical performance is extensible to the performances that are our daily interactions with other people, institutions, and situations (cf. Goffman 1959).

Murray also delves into the specific kinds of dynamics that character-ize the blues-based ritual of performance. He carries out this work most exhaustively in *Stomping the Blues* (1976), a book that some individuals have referred to as one the best books ever written about jazz.[9] Blues and jazz for him are synonymous both in style and function: "[T]he fun-damental function of the blues musician (also known as the jazz musi-cian) . . . is not only to drive the blues away and hold them at bay at least for the time being, but also to evoke an ambiance of Dionysian revelry in the process. . . . [E]ven as [a performer and entertainer, he was] at the same time fulfilling a central role in a ceremony that was at once a purification rite and a celebration the festive earthiness of which was tantamount to a fertility ritual" (17).

Murray foregrounds the amount of skill and preparation that go into performing effectively and creatively in the blues idiom:

After all, no matter how deeply moved a musician may be, whether by personal, social, or even aesthetic circumstances, he must always play notes that fulfill the requirements of the context, a feat which presupposes far more skill and taste than raw emotion. . . . [Such skill and taste] represent . . . not natural impulse but the refinement of habit, custom, and tradition become second nature, so to speak. Indeed on close inspection what was assumed to have been unpremeditated art is likely to be largely a matter of conditioned reflex, which is nothing other than the end product of discipline, or in a word, training. . . . That musicians whose sense of incantation and percussion was conditioned by the blues idiom in the first place are likely to handle its peculiarities with greater ease and assurance than outsiders of comparable or even superior conventional skill should surprise no one. (98; cf. Berliner 1994)

Such training is deployed in a ritual all of whose musical and performative parameters can be "refined, elaborated, extended, abstracted, and otherwise played with" (106). And the techniques through which musicians extend, elaborate, and refine those parameters can be described as "intermusical" (Monson 1994: 303–7) in that their most immediate references are other musical events: "[M]uch goes to show that what musicians are always most likely to be mimicking (and sometimes extending and refining and sometimes counterstating) are the sounds of other musicians who have performed the same or similar compositions" (Murray 1976: 125). Blues playing, therefore, "is not a matter of having the blues and giving direct personal release to the raw emotion brought on by suffering. It is a matter of mastering the elements of craft required by the idiom. It is a matter of idiomatic orientation and of the refinement of auditory sensibility in terms of idiomatic nuance. It is a far greater matter of convention, and hence tradition, than of impulse. . . . It is not so much what blues musicians bring out of themselves as what they do with existing conventions" (126).

   Writers following Murray in writing about African American musics have also recognized the centrality of blues in the interpretation of musical meaning. In *Black Culture and Black Consciousness* (1977), Lawrence Levine focuses on the constant interaction between the forms of music making that have been called gospel, blues, and jazz (179–85), noting that social function may be the only criterion that could definitively distinguish them from one another (186). And he sees the importance of African American music in its ability to affirm and reaffirm the values of African Americans and to reinforce their most basic conceptions of themselves (189). Drawing on the work of Charles Keil and

John Szwed, he argues that African American musical performances typically have ritual significance and that, in them, musicians serve a shamanistic function—blending elements of the sacred and the secular (234–37). He contends as well that jazz partakes of the same impulses and can be described in the same terms as blues: "it is clear that for both its partisans and its detractors, jazz came to symbolize many of the very qualities we have found central to the blues" (293, cf. 238).

Christopher Small sees all of African American music as having ritual significance. The subtitle of *Music of the Common Tongue* (1987a)—*Survival and Celebration in Afro-American Music*—makes clear what the function of that ritual is for him. Understanding the role of music in ritual requires an explanation first of what music means to him. He writes that music

> *is not primarily a thing or a collection of things, but an activity in which we engage.* One might say that it is not properly a noun at all, but a verb. . . . I define the word to include not only performing and composing . . . but also listening and even dancing to music; all those involved in any way in a musical performance can be thought of as musicking. (50, emphasis in original)

And by extension African American music is "an approach to the act of music making, a way of playing and responding to music" (14). The most expressive moments in or performances of music, he argues, will be those that "most subtly, comprehensively and powerfully [articulate] the relationships of our ideal society—which may or may not have any real, or even possible, existence beyond the duration of the performance" (70). It is in its capacity to articulate ideal relationships that music—from any society—has a ritual significance informed by performance practice, performance context, and the relationships between the participants in a musical event. African American music is thus configured as a ritual concerned with survival under hostile, changing conditions and with the celebration of triumphs and occasional good fortune.

Small accords a high place to the blues sensibility in these rituals: "The blues style of performance, which pervades almost the whole of the Afro-American tradition as a colour, an emotional tinge, has also given rise to a poetic and musical form, which is to say a definitive way of organizing a performance, of simplicity, clarity and seemingly infinite adaptability" (198). And through developing a blues-based sensibility, through learning to play with form, pitch, rhythm, timbre, and any of a number of other musical, interactive, and performative parameters, the performer becomes a model for how one can "play" with living, within the constraints of culture:

> But while the players are free to engage in dialogue with one another, to explore, affirm and celebrate their various identities and their relationship . . . they are still bound by the requirements of the idiom; there are ways in which they may respond to one another and ways in which they may not. They are caught in the ancient and creative paradox of all human social life: that relationships can be established between people only through the acceptance of some kind of common language. (302)

Moreover, he does not draw the lines between black and white performance styles so strictly within the jazz idiom. For any musician playing jazz, he suggests, the act of performance is an exploration of African American identities.

Samuel A. Floyd Jr.'s *The Power of Black Music* (1995) is an expansive attempt to mine the insights of Sterling Stuckey's *Slave Culture* (1987) and Henry Louis Gates Jr.'s *The Signifying Monkey* (1988) for African American musical scholarship. Floyd says that his book "is based on the assumption that African musical traits and cultural practices not only survived but played a major role in the development and elaboration of African American music" (5). He also asserts that he will demonstrate that

> African survivals exist not merely in the sense that African-American music has the same characteristics as its African counterparts, but also that the musical *tendencies,* the mythological beliefs, assumptions, and the interpretive strategies of African Americans are the same as those that underlie the music of the African homeland, that these tendencies and beliefs continue to exist as African cultural memory, and that they continue to inform the continuity and elaboration of African-American music. (5)

He focuses much of his attention on applying Gates's concept of signifyin(g) to African American music, pointing out the ways in which African American musics signify on one another as well as other forms.

Within the world of signifyin(g) African American musical practices, he accords great importance to the blues, suggesting that "[s]ince the blues appears to be basic to most forms of black music, and since it seems to be the most prominent factor in maintaining continuity between most of them, we might think of it as the Urtrope of the tradition" (79). For jazz performance practice, he explains the importance of the blues as bedrock for bebop's experimentation and expanded harmonic conception; its more "highly syncopated, linear rhythmic complexity" and "melodic angularity"; its reemphasis on percussiveness and "ring-centered" values; and its extension of the improvising vocabulary beyond paraphrase to melodic invention based on "running changes" (138). And through performance practice, jazz becomes linked to cultural memory, signifyin(g) and ritual:

> The technique, knowledge of structure and theory, and the external ideas that facilitate and support improvisation, then, must be called on to convey, in coherent and effective presentation, what emerges from cultural memory. It is this dialogical effectiveness that jazz musicians strive for as they create and re-create, state and revise, in the spontaneous manner known as improvisation; it is this Signifyin(g) revision that is at the heart of the jazz player's art; and it is this Signifyin(g) revision that debunks the notion that jazz is merely a style, not a genre, for in meeting the substantive demands of Signifyin(g) revision, it is not merely the *manner* in which attacks, releases, sustainings, tempi, and other technical-musical requirements are rendered that makes jazz. On the contrary, it is the dialogical *substance,* the content *brought to* and *created in* the experience that determines a genre. Style is a given. But as with any genre, it is the substance and its structures that make the difference—the Signifyin(g) difference—in jazz. . . . The similarity of the jazz improvisation event to the African dance-possession event [is] too striking and provocative to dismiss, but in the absence of a provable connection, it can only be viewed as the realization of an aspect of ritual and of cultural memory. (140–141)

Like the other writers, then, Floyd shares a preoccupation with the importance of the blues for African American music making. Moreover, he posits performance as the central arena in which the blues and African American musics make their impact. Those performances, however, cannot be interpreted solely on the basis of sound: one must be attentive to what is brought to each musical encounter and its relationship to African American culture.

The writers just surveyed can be broadly characterized as being concerned with jazz performance as a blues-based, ritual activity. In different ways, they emphasize the roles of cultural background, skill, and training, and individual and group expression. Moreover, they see the power of jazz in its ability to communicate through the practices of performers and listeners African American views of the world and ways of organizing and responding to experience. The musical performance has meaning because it assumes a metaphoric or synecdochic relationship to other aspects of African American culture: it comments on, reflects, and articulates actual and idealized visions of existence.[10] A survey of the interviews I conducted with various musicians for this project shows that similar concerns have been verbalized by musicians active on the New York scene.

Musicians' Normative Views of Jazz Performance

In their normative statements about jazz performance and jazz audiences, the musicians I interviewed reveal a number of concerns that, taken cumulatively, express a considered vision of how one has to approach the varied facets of "musicking." Those concerns can be characterized as the importance of having an individual voice; developing the ability to balance and play with a number of different musical parameters in performance; understanding the cultural foundations of the music; being able oneself to "bring something to the music"; creating music that is "open enough" to allow other musicians to bring something despite or because of what has been provided structurally or contextually; and being open for transcendence to "the next level" of performance, the spiritual level. All are important for the ability of the musician to communicate with listeners and other performers, individually and collectively. Below, I discuss each of those concerns and how they have been explained by the musicians consulted.

Perhaps the chief concern of every musician I interviewed is having an immediately distinguishable, individual sound. The word *sound* refers not only to the timbre of one's playing but also to particular usages of harmonic, rhythmic, and textural resources in performance and composition. The way in which such individual sounds are achieved varies from instrument to instrument, musician to musician, but a number of variables as well as motivated and unmotivated decisions enter into the process. For players of wind instruments, for example, the embouchure (the way in which the mouth touches the instrument), the type of mouthpiece, the manufacturer of the instrument, and the amount of air blown into it are among the factors that determine the timbral aspects of an individual's sound. Players of string instruments like the guitar write their timbral signatures through their methods of producing sound (plucking with fingers or plectra made of various materials), the size and type of strings they use, the manufacturer and materials of one's guitar of choice, as well as through one's preferred amplifier(s) and settings for equalization and electronic effects (like reverb and chorus).

Players interested in achieving such distinctive sounds play and practice diligently to determine what type of sound pleases them or expresses their particular attitude(s) toward music. Pianist Bruce Barth says that he is constantly listening to and absorbing ideas and techniques from the playing of other musicians. When he sits down to practice, however, he focuses on those ideas and techniques that seem "unique to him"—that is, most appealing to him—and tries to "amplify them and develop them" (Barth 1994). Similarly, the saxophonists interviewed tend to start their practice routines with "long tones," playing each note in a scale or in the instrument's range as long and as evenly as possible, paying attention to the way the sound exits the horn and the way the vibrations feel in their mouths.[11]

Steve Wilson (1995) explains the importance of working on individual sound in discussing his teaching methods. He notes that many students come to him wanting to know how to play "the hippest stuff on the changes"—that is, the most sophisticated material in terms of harmony and rhythm. He redirects their energies toward sound production, asking whether they could play a particular whole note in a tune the way alto saxophonist Johnny Hodges might have and hoping they will understand the skill required to produce such a sound:

That's the litmus test. That's how you can identify Lester Young, Johnny Hodges, Coleman Hawkins, Sonny Rollins, Coltrane: *by one note.* Because they knew how to play a whole note. And, um, I remember being in college and hearing cats, some of the older cats, saying, you know, "Baby, a whole note is sure the hardest thing in the world to play." And for years I didn't understand that. Like, "Man, what are they talking about?!" And I understand that now, you know. If I can play one good note, that's it. And that's the way I try to approach my teaching. It's to really have your own sound, after all is said and done, after studying everybody. *Have your own identity,* you know.

Or as saxophonist Antonio Hart (1995) says, "If cats want to be identified, they need [their own] identities."

Having an individual sound also includes the use that a player makes of other musical resources expressed through preferences for certain kinds of harmonies, harmonic substitutions, or voicings; regular use of certain melodic phrases (sometimes formulaically); methods of constructing a solo or writing a composition; along with approaches to rhythm, texture, and interaction. A musician like Thelonious Monk, therefore, is recognizable not only for the way in which he produces each individual sound, but also for the way in which he chains those sounds together in performance or composition. Sam Newsome (1995) believes that playing in the quintet of trumpeter Terence Blanchard for three years was quite important in his own development because

[Blanchard] kinda went against like the whole trend that was, I think, that was happening around New York [in the late 1980s and early 1990s], this kind of "retrospective" approach to playing. 'Cause his whole thing was just like getting in, you know, getting in touch with yourself and just, uh, just trying to develop your *own personality* on the instrument. You know, still remaining true to the tradition, just as far as like keeping the, the, the swing element and the blues element in the playing, but not really, just not really taking everything so verbatim. 'Cause I always kinda looked at it as like, it's like I would treat, I try to treat music like a, as like I would treat a proverb [laughs]. You know, it's like you don't, you don't take it— if someone says "Don't put all of your eggs in one basket"—you don't take that literally. I mean, you kind of look at it that way musically, too. It's like if I hear someone play, like if I were to take Trane [John Coltrane], it's like if I just took, uh, the way, the *three-tonic*[12] system of Trane, it's like I, I wouldn't, I wouldn't think of playing it the way he would play it. It's like I would just use it as, um, as a *harmonic* device that he introduced. . . . [I]t's up to the, it's up to the individual to *interpret* it any way that they want to.[13]

Newsome, like Barth in a previously cited comment, underscores the importance of taking whatever resources one gets from elsewhere and giving them a personal spin, an individual interpretation. He later amplifies his point and Wilson's previous one by asserting that one's sound should be consistent regardless of the tune serving as a vehicle for improvisation. Musicians without distinctive sounds tend to place the emphasis in the wrong place, having the attitude that

> You know, if you play, I don't know, if you play "Impressions," [you should] play like Trane [John Coltrane]. And if you're playing a ballad, try to play like Ben Webster. And if you're playing "Confirmation," you know, try to play like Bird [Charlie Parker], rather than just have *one approach* which is you and just keep that.[14]

Musicians who do not possess their own sounds, who seemingly mimic the sound of other musicians, are singled out for particularly harsh criticism, sometimes referred to as "clones" who sound "just like" Miles Davis, John Coltrane, Herbie Hancock, Betty Carter, or other well-known musicians. The point of the criticism is not so much that one should be "innovative" or do something *novel* in terms of sound or approach, but that one should strive for something *different* and *distinctive*. Bruce Barth (1995), for example, stresses the importance of

> *saying something* that's *original*. I'm not saying necessarily *ground-breaking* or *revolutionary,* but something that isn't just . . . like a, like a generic *rehashing* of things that you've heard before. Where you put that record on and you say, "That sounds exactly like *this*. This piano player sounds like such-and-such a player. This tune sounds like such-and-such a tune," you know.[15]

The ability to balance and deal with a number of different musical parameters in the course of performance follows from having an individual sound, for the possession of an identifiable musical persona is the product of having considered a number of approaches and synthesized them into a "concept." Steve Wilson praised alto saxophonist Kenny Garrett precisely for his ability to play well in and adapt to the demands of a variety of contexts—from his work in traveling shows like *Sophisticated Ladies* in the early 1980s to that in groups led by Freddie Hubbard, Woody Shaw, and Miles Davis. Garrett's concept, according to Wilson, works precisely because it balances a number of different elements and approaches, but it does so in a way that identifies their usage as "Kenny Garrett's." While a student at the Berklee School of Music, Sam Newsome learned about the need for balance from pianist Donald Brown. Brown told Newsome that most musicians know more harmony than they actually need for performing. According to Newsome (1995), Brown asserted that

> "If you use *too much* [harmony], it's going to sound mechanical." 'Cause he, 'cause he always, he told me, he felt [there] wasn't enough *room* . . . if he wanted to be *musical* . . . to have too much harmony 'cause that doesn't leave much room for *melody* or, or dealing with rhythmic ideas. It doesn't leave room for, for maybe if you wanted to *develop* ideas, you know, that doesn't leave room for, for dealing with *blues,* the *blues aspect* of harmony. So I mean . . . there are so many *elements* that, that go into producing like a, a good, a good *solo,* that if you were to incorporate too much of *one* thing, it's, you know, it's gonna sound mechanical and unmusical.

These musicians work on being balanced in their practice routines, which, according to their performance, recording, and touring schedules, can vary considerably. Because their time is often limited—as little as a couple of hours per day, and sometimes less—they frequently apply themselves to practical problems, focusing attention on the technical demands of their instruments, on improving their abilities to hear and respond to harmonies, substitutions, and chord scales, on playing well at different tempos, and on ways of developing melodic, harmonic, or rhythmic ideas. Sometimes, those sessions involve listening to recordings of their own performances or going over difficulties they have encountered in performing. Joshua Redman (1995) says that his focus at such times is on "trying to learn tunes I don't know, play through the melodies, play them in different keys. As a general rule, I try to work on things that don't come naturally. The general concept is to stretch and grow." Both Antonio Hart (1994) and Sam Newsome (1995) speak of having notebooks full of harmonic concepts that they have not fully incorporated into their playing, concepts that will require extensive practice to internalize and make effective in performing contexts. Newsome, for example, has been interested in applying John Coltrane's three-tonic system to improvising over minor chords, while Hart, inspired by the music of Eric Dolphy, has been working out ways to apply "incorrect" harmonic substitutes and scales to harmonic progressions in improvisation—for example, superimposing a B-major scale over an F dominant-seventh chord.[16] Guitarist Peter Bernstein stressed the importance of using practice time to internalize standard forms and harmonic schemes in the jazz repertoire. But those specific materials and activities are only part of practice routines that vary depending on what a musician feels she or he has neglected, has failed to do well, or needs to improve. Those lacunae are revealed when a player feels the elements of individual style to be improperly balanced.

Mention has to be made here of another issue raised in one of Newsome's previously cited statements—where he refers to the "blues aspect of harmony." He partially defines traditional jazz playing with reference to "the blues" and rhythmic swing. In that way, he summarizes many conversations I have had with musicians and fans, most of whom considered developing the ability to play the blues or to play with blues feeling essential skills for playing jazz. The integration and mastery of such skills is precisely what allows performers such as pianist Wynton Kelly, tenor saxophonist Hank Mobley, and guitarist Grant Green to be considered important figures in the music's history from the standpoint of knowledgeable players and listeners (Rosenthal 1992; Starks 1993: 149). While historians rarely mention them because they were not decidedly "innovative" in terms of their technical or harmonic conceptions, their playing is suffused with the blues sensibility via phrasing, rhythms, and pitch choices.[17] Pianist Bruce Barth (1995), for example, took Wynton Kelly and Herbie Hancock as models for learning how to "comp," partially because of their occasional and compelling use of "blues licks" and melodic phrases in place of chords.[18] And, as Newsome asserted, playing with "blues feeling" is also an essential component in performance on tunes not using one of the variants of blues form. Indeed, in the field of rhythmic, harmonic, melodic, and timbral conceptions, the blues-based conception is thought to be of integral importance in "making a connection" with audiences, in expressing a type of "soulfulness."

Joshua Redman (1995) credits his study of the playing of saxophonist Stanley Turrentine with having taught him about that soulfulness and its roots in the blues:

> I think any kind of music has its own soul, and you can have, you know, you can play from the soul in any style of music. I mean, I think that *Pat Metheny* is a very soulful player. That['s one] definition of soul. There's another definition of soul which is more of a specific kind of, has more specific stylistic connotations, you know. A certain kind of emoting. Soulfulness which is associated with the blues, you know, the blues idiom and blues expression.

And under that definition, Pat Metheny wouldn't, doesn't play with that, you know, that type of soul. . . . That's not pejorative. Whereas someone like Stanley Turrentine to me is exemplary of that. I mean, he is just an incredibly bluesy, soulful player. . . . And, um, I think the thing I've gotten from him more than anything else is, you know, by listening to him I really learned a lot about playing the blues, and, and . . . that kind of "soul" style of tenor playing. Um, I've learned, I've learned a lot about, you know, how important the *strength* of your sound is, you know. Before you even worry about what notes, or what combination of notes, just the *power* you put into your sound and the *strength* of each attack, you know, and the way you play a note, whatever the note is. What you can do with that note, the kind of passion you can put into that note. Because, you know, if you broke down and ana . . . , if you broke down Stanley Turrentine's improvisations and analyzed them, you know, from a harmonic standpoint, they wouldn't be what you would call particularly complex, you know. Even some of the combinations of notes that he plays, some of the licks that he plays, are in some ways very standard. I mean, you can get those combinations out of any, you know, book on bebop. Bebop textbook. But the *way* in which he plays them, the way in which he phrases them, is *so unique* that there's no one who's, I mean, he has *such* an identifiable style. I can literally from two notes [snaps fingers] [know that it's] Stanley Turrentine.

Blues-derived playing and expression, then, become not a function of harmonic or rhythmic complexity. Neither, however, are they merely a function of simplicity. Rather, they are concerned with the projection of "strength" and "power" through the way in which one approaches whatever rhythmic, harmonic, or timbral resources are being utilized.[19] Implicit in Redman's statement is the assumption that other participants in a musical event know such "strength" and "power" when they hear it.

To some degree, Redman's assertions are borne out by the evaluative commentary of audience members at musical events. On numerous occasions, I heard musicians, critics, and other participants disparage musicians whose playing was marked by an inability to play compellingly on blues-based compositions or with convincing blues feeling. The major criticism was that these players weren't "saying anything," that their playing was cold or mechanical. Peter Bernstein informed me in July 1994 that saxophonist Lou Donaldson, an elder musician with whom he performs frequently, refers to such musicians as "sad mother-fuckers." What is implied in Donaldson's criticism is that the blues feeling is a sine qua non in jazz performance. The balance that Donald Brown advocates, therefore, includes a blues sensibility among the parameters to be balanced. The importance of blues feeling for the evaluations made by differing participants will be illustrated later in this essay, where I note how often positive responses to performances come at those moments that are expressive via blues-derived performance practices.

To a large degree, the necessity of having an individual sound, the notion of balance, and the importance of the blues are seen as products of a larger *African American* musical or performative sensibility. Interestingly, none of the questions in my interview schedule specifically addressed issues of race or culture. Each African American musician brought issues of race into the interviews at many points,[20] and I infer the importance of African American sensibilities from non–African American musicians' frequent references to African American musics and musicians as influential and inspirational.

Peter Bernstein did so, for example, by citing as his early, nonjazz influences folk and rock singer Bob Dylan, rock and blues guitarists Jimi Hendrix and Eric Clapton, blues guitarists B. B. King and Freddie King, and the heavy rock group Led Zeppelin. With Bob Dylan as a notable exception, almost all of the musicians he named—African American or not—were heavily involved in playing blues and blues-derived musics. In discussing his jazz influences, he constructed a list consisting largely of African American musicians. His list included guitarists Wes Montgomery, Grant Green, Kenny Burrell, Joe Pass, John Abercrombie, and Pat Metheny; trumpeter Miles Davis; pianists Duke Ellington, Wynton Kelly, and Keith Jarrett; saxophonists John Coltrane, Cannonball Adderley, Wayne Shorter, and David Murray; and bassist Paul Chambers.[21]

Some musicians and some scholars argue that it is impossible to understand the music without understanding African American culture.[22] Older musicians such as Duke Ellington and Dizzy Gillespie articulated such ideas in published writings and interviews (Ellington 1939; for Gillespie's statements, see Taylor 1993: 126–27), the latter lamenting the "whitewashing" of writing about jazz.[23] In stating their belief in similar principles, younger musicians frequently cite a specific historical vision that is not always put forward in educational settings. They see African American musicians as those whose contributions have been picked up and studied most extensively by other musicians.[24] That particular vision, however, is not the one they see educational institutions promulgating. As Sam Newsome (1995) says:

> I feel a lot of times with the, when you institutionalize jazz, it takes it, in a way, it takes it from the culture. And a lot of institutions don't like to deal with that. It's like I, I heard very little about jazz coming from the black culture when I was at, at Berklee. . . . A lot of times you end up getting like a watered-down version of jazz, where it's like, you know, you're gonna talk some about, you know, they're like, "Well, here's Louis Armstrong and *also Bix Beiderbecke.*" And then it just goes, you know, it's like . . . "Here's [Charlie Parker]." Then, "Oh, okay. We also have, uh, *Lee Konitz and Paul Desmond.*" You know, it's always you have, they have to always put that, put that other like perspective on it, which in a lot of cases isn't really that necessary. I mean, it's like these, all of those players, they, they could play, but if you just really want to deal with like the, the *definitive* sound and the people who, who made like the, the real contributions to jazz, you know, I think you, you have to give credit where it's due.

Similarly, saxophonist Donald Harrison expressed disappointment when I told him of a debate that took place in a New York University classroom where I had lectured. The students passionately questioned whether jazz was "African American music" or "American music." Harrison invoked the wisdom of drummer Art Blakey, who said he did not care what the music was called as long as everyone "gave credit to the music's creators and innovators" (Fieldnotes, 12 October 1994), thus keeping the relationship between the music and African American culture in the foreground.

In the formal interviews I conducted, issues of race and culture were most frequently mentioned in response to a question about the effectiveness of jazz education.[25] Unanimously, musicians felt that jazz education was good for teaching technique and specific ways to use harmony, but noted a gap between what could be taught in a conservatory setting and what one needed to know to play the music well (cf. Ellison 1964: 209). Donald Harrison, Antonio Hart, Gregory Hutchinson, Sam Newsome, James Williams, and Steve Wilson all suggested that young musicians had to engage with African American culture and be apprenticed to master musicians—the majority of whom in their estimation are African

American—to be effective performers of the music. Hart (1995), for example, sought and was sought by older musicians on his arrival in New York. He has performed extensively with Nat Adderley, Slide Hampton, and Jimmy Heath. Those experiences, he believes, allowed him to tap "some of that spirit, some of that fire, of what the music is really about." Hutchinson feels that he has grown enormously as a musician through working with Betty Carter and Ray Brown, while Donald Harrison and James Williams say the same of their time with Art Blakey.[26] Even musicians from outside the United States who want to be good players on the New York scene—like pianist Jacky Terrasson—were encouraged to work with seasoned African American performers like Betty Carter and Arthur Taylor in order understand the concepts that underlie the technical demands of jazz performance.

In that sense, African Americans who have been socialized in communities that transmit values similar to those that have nurtured some of the most influential musicians have an advantage over others of whatever ethnicity or cultural background. They conceivably have less distance to travel to tap into "what the music is really about." Both Barth and Newsome expound on this idea in describing different audience responses to jazz performance. Each of them relates anecdotes comparing gigs in other countries with those in United States African American communities. Barth (1995) feels jazz has a certain "romantic appeal" for European (and some American) audiences. He contrasts their responses to performance with those of African Americans in North Philadelphia: "[Europeans] love the idea of jazz; they respect the tradition, that it's an American music, that it's a black music. And sometimes I feel that . . . especially like a younger audience in Europe, you won't necessarily have the kind of audience that knows the music the way [they do in Philadelphia]. Like you'll find, like you go to an audience, you play a club in Philly, and you'll . . . , there are a lot of people in the audience who knew McCoy [Tyner], you know. People who knew Lee Morgan and McCoy [and John Coltrane] when he lived there. Who know the music . . . who have just a very close, *personal* connection with the music." And, more pointedly, Sam Newsome (1995) asserts ("N" designates Newsome's words, while "J" designates mine):

N: I think . . . a black person that's . . . , you know, familiar with the music can relate to something that comes from the black culture on a much deeper level than someone who doesn't. I mean, it's, um, I mean, even if it's someone that's [not familiar] maybe . . . they can hear like the *soulful* side of soloing. It's like, uh, I don't know, I think someone black can relate to *that* on a deeper level . . . than someone who doesn't, doesn't really come from the culture.

J: And, um, how can you tell?

N: They . . . respond in the right places. 'Cause I remember I did this thing in Japan, and it's like they would start clapping at the most bizarre places during a solo. It's like places that were not meant to excite them [laughing]. Whereas like the, the experiences I've had with black audiences, it's like, you know, it's like where you may peak your solo at a certain place, and it's like you're . . . exuding like a certain amount of emotions, and it's like you can feel like you're connected. Where with someone else, you . . . may *not* be able to, it's more . . . maybe more intellectual. *Not to say that other people can't connect spiritually,* but it's, I don't think, on the same . . . deeper level.

Note here that Newsome is emphasizing certain forms of learned cultural knowledge that are deployed in responding to music, particularly those related to soulfulness and blues feeling that Joshua Redman described previously.

The cultural component of performing, along with having an individual identity and balancing a number of musical elements in performance, is linked to what Steve Wilson referred to as "bringing something to the music" (cf. Floyd 1995: 140–41). Wilson (1995) connects the depth and variety of one's nonmusical experiences to that capacity when he explains: "The music is only what you bring to it, you know. And if your life condition is not . . . set, or if it, if it's not, if your life condition doesn't have a solid foundation, um, more often than not, your music won't." He continues by noting that what made a musician like Duke Ellington so important was his connection to tradition and his understanding of African American culture:

I mean, let's take a look at tradition. What is tradition, you know? I mean, you cannot discard, uh, you cannot take out or pick and choose out of our experience what you want, you know. It's just like if you look at, if you look at the emancipation of black people in America, you can't, you can't, uh, say, "Okay, well I'll take Frederick Douglass, but I'll delete the Emancipation Proclamation," you know. That's all a part of our experience, too, you know.

So, it's just . . . hey, man, all that comes into the music, you know.
All of our experiences, music or any artistic endeavor or expression, you know, be it by word of mouth or painting or dance or
whatever. All of it is there. And, and, uh, I think that that's what
they were doing in the Harlem Renaissance, man. . . . [T]hey were
taking a look at all of our experiences, and that's why Duke Ellington was such a, such a master, man. He took . . . all of our experiences and put 'em into his art form.[27]

Other musicians expressed similar sentiments, though all were largely
silent on the processes whereby the experiences of daily life are translated into or expressed in musical performance. The silence, however, is
an indicator not of the illegitimacy of the concept, but of the difficulty of
verbalizing experiential and musical concepts (Feld 1994b) that are
deeply felt.

The complexity of "bringing something" as a metaphor was under-
scored near the end of my interview with Wilson. I routinely concluded
sessions with an invitation for the interviewee to raise questions that had
occurred to him or her during the course of the interview but had not
been asked. Wilson pointedly asked what I, as a young African American listener, brought to the music. What emerged from that question was
a lengthy discussion about modes of listening, musical preferences, performing experiences, and criteria for evaluating music. I explained that I
brought a set of experiences from listening to various forms of African
American and African-derived musics beginning in my childhood, feeling the most contact with the work of musicians like Stevie Wonder,
Marvin Gaye, Al Green, Bobby Womack, and Bob Marley. In addition, I
brought a specific knowledge of jazz history and current jazz practice to
each performance as well as a desire to *listen* to the kinds of interactions
taking place in a performance. In the ensuing dialogue, Wilson stressed
the interconnectedness of forms of African American music, the necessity of understanding tradition (see the previous quotation), and the
importance of communicating with audiences. All of the other musicians felt as well that one had to bring something to the music to be able
to communicate, to say something to audiences. The "something" that
one brings to the music is the sum of his or her experiences—musical
and nonmusical—as well as his or her individuality, musical skill, taste,
and ability to empathize with other musicians.

The necessity of bringing something to the music has implications as
well for the way that jazz musicians structure their compositions and

performances. By necessity, jazz's musical structures have to be somewhat "open." In addition to allowing room for improvisation, they have to be the kinds of vehicles that facilitate interaction among the participants in a musical event. Guitarist Peter Bernstein (1995) discussed the alternatives he considered in preparing for the recording session for his CD *Signs of Life*:

> with *jazz,* the thing that's been hard is to, like, 'cause really when you write a jazz kind of thing, it's really about letting people bring something to it. And that's what I learned, especially doing this last record, like, keeping the tunes so, you know, someone could just look at [them and play them], and you have to have enough of yourself in the tune, but you don't want to restrict the player, the individuality of the player from coming out. 'Cause that's when . . . when you get a good bass player [Christian McBride] and good drummer [Gregory Hutchinson], you know, it's not about telling them what to play, having them read eighteen pages of written music because . . . why have them? Why not have the guy from the, from the, you know, you know, Philharmonic, you know. I mean, it's like jazz is, is individual music. It's really about, you know, it's about egos and, like, making the egos work together, but you need the ego[s], you know.

So while one of his tunes ("Minor Changes") may require that the musicians stick with notated harmonies and accents during the head, the structure on which they improvise, a minor blues progression, is a more open structure with only the key and tempo of the performance dictated.[28] The musicians are free, after the head, to play harmonic substitutes[29] and to blur the boundaries of the form.

The ways in which bandleaders interact with sidemen are equally subject to the requirement that there be a certain amount of "space" for each musician to make a contribution. When asked about the leadership styles of bandleaders with whom they had worked, each musician said that openness and adaptability were marks of great leaders. Steve Wilson (1995) noted that individuals like Miles Davis and Duke Ellington were great precisely because they "let the personalities shape the music." About leading his own groups, Wilson says, "I have a concept about what I want to do, but I realize it's the personalities of the other players that are really going to bring it to fruition." In a sense, then, such openness is a way of dealing with the materials at hand (structure, sound, skill, personalities, performing context) and fashioning them into viable and meaningful expression. They are also a direct outgrowth of the other factors discussed thus far. Flexible frameworks for improvisation and flexible leadership strategies have the potential to work well precisely because it is expected that each musician is knowledgeable and skillful enough to fill in what is not explicitly arranged.

All of these criteria ultimately work in the service of reaching a state of transcendence, of getting to "the next level."[30] This next level has been described as being the "spiritual" level of the music, the level during which participants in the musical event are in a state akin to what psychologist Mihaly Csikszentmihaly (1982, 1988) refers to as "flow"[31] or what others might refer to as trance or possession. In those situations performance takes place seemingly on its own. Musicians speak of their being outside of themselves, of their being completely in tune with all that is going on around them musically, of instruments playing themselves. While their descriptions of being in such a state could only approximate the experience, they are clear about what conditions are necessary for them to reach that level.

Steve Wilson notes that each musician must bring to the performance all that he or she can. In other words, each musician must come to a gig or recording session prepared to play, prepared to listen, and prepared to respond to other musicians and participants. Wilson describes the drummer Ralph Peterson, very much influenced by Art Blakey, as someone who puts all of his energy into making every performance—whether it is a live gig, a recording session, or even a rehearsal—the best it possibly can be. For Peterson, the aim is putting the maximum into the music, knowing what he wants from it, and always pushing it to the edge, for that is the only way to get the maximum out of it, to tap into the music's spiritual side. Peter Bernstein (1995) learned from his study with guitarist Kevin Eubanks that one has to "be serious about music[, for e]very thing you play counts." Bernstein explained that such a feeling could equally be applied to practice and performance. Part of reaching that spiritual level, then, is coming to each musical situation prepared and ready to engage and be engaged by the process of performing with others.

Audiences are also responsible for whether the music reaches the next level. They, too, have to bring something to the performance. In addition to knowledge of the music's history and the work of individual performers, Wilson (1995) feels that they must be willing to listen attentively and to respond to musical events:

It's kinda like . . . in a sense going to church, you know, as they say, "You have to be ready to receive," you know. . . . I don't even go to hear music if I'm not in the frame of mind to listen to it. I don't go just to be hanging, you know. If I'm really not in the frame of mind to go and support my peers and really listen to what they have to say musically, I don't go because that's a disservice to them. So, uh, when I do go to hang out, I really not only go to hang out for the social part, but for that too. And I think it should be the same for the audience.

He continues by specifying the conditions necessary for musicians to get to that next level:

Once each musician can focus on the purpose at hand, and when you get the sense that each musician is focused on the purpose at hand, that will, uh, that will allow or facilitate that to happen, you know, that, that spiritual level to happen. I know particularly with bassist Buster [Smith]'s band, it was the use of space that everybody allowed, you know, and that, uh, you knew that you didn't have to, you weren't just *boxed in,* musically speaking, you know. . . . Once you get the sense that you are allowed to use, um, your imagination and, um, to tune in with all of the other, uh, players, then *really* that sets the stage . . . for, for it to really, you know, to go to another level spiritually. And we had a few of those nights when it was just . . . , you know, it really went *beyond* what, you know, at least what I felt, um, [was] just a musical performance, you know. . . . Because everyone has to be in tune. Yeah. Everyone has to be *subservient* to that.

And when a musician or group of musicians reach that level, they sometimes make inexplicable strides in their playing, feel themselves carried by the flow of the music, and transported by the varied sounds and activities constituting a musical event. They frequently find themselves unable to recall exactly what happened immediately after a performance. (It is also interesting to observe the spiritually tinged language employed by Wilson, particularly his references to "receiving" and "subservience.")

As an example of what happens in such moments, I include here an excerpt from my fieldnotes for 5 September 1994. The excerpt describes a performance by saxophonist Antonio Hart, pianist Benny

Green, and bassist Ed Howard at Bradley's on the night of 4 September 1994, 12:00 A.M. set:

> During the second tune ["91st Miracle"], Hart . . . initiated some stimulating metric and rhythmic activity, most notably the super-imposition of patterns in 3/8 over a 4/4 metric framework. He really got hot in this solo, getting lots of good, encouraging, sympathetic audience response. At one point, after playing some particularly intricate and long phrases that kept building in intensity, he stopped playing. What was most interesting about his stopping was that previously he had started to rock back and forth with the peaks and accents in his phrases. When he stopped playing, he continued to rock back and forth with the horn out of his mouth and with a look of intense concentration or absorption or pain or intensity (almost a pain-filled frown) on his face. After about eight seconds of rocking back and forth [without playing a note], he put the horn back into his mouth and resumed playing. I wonder what was running through his head at that moment. Did he have too much to say? Nothing to say? No way to say what he wanted to?

When I asked him about this performance in an interview in December 1994, he said the following:

> I do that all the time, man. I, you know, I'm gone. When I'm play-ing, when the situation's right, I'm usually gone. I'm not even on Earth anymore, you know. I'm really not here. So, um, a couple of . . . People tell me I do that all the time. I'll stomp my feet or I'll scream, you know. 'Cause I'm like in a trance, man. I'm, I'm not there. I remember doing stuff like that probably because [there's] something saying, "Stop. Breathe. Leave some space, leave some air." So um, that's what I do. And you, you pretty much hit it on the nose, man, I just . . . I didn't know what to do, so I just stopped and cleared my head and tried to get my thoughts back together and tr[ied] to come back and say something 'cause I am trying to talk. You know, I'm *trying* to. It doesn't always work, man.
>
> It's a blessing just to *play* music. . . . It's just a blessing, and I try to take it that way. Every day, I try to think of it that way. . . . It's not me that's playing. I'm just a tool that the music's coming through, the compositions are coming through, that's why when you see me going off and I'm rocking and shit, it's not me. At that

particular point, I'm there, but I'm not there. The more spiritual
I become—I've been laying low on that—but the more spiritual I
become, the further my music is gonna go. I know that already.

Not every transcendent moment is as intense as this one, nor is every
response the same. But the connection between stimulating jazz performance and feelings that are best described as spiritual becomes more
apparent through this example. Hart's mention of being a tool—along
with Wilson's use of the words *receive* and *subservient*—suggests that at
those and similar moments, the individual's sense of self is temporarily
suspended, and he or she becomes part of something else. What happens
at those moments is the core of what is meaningful about jazz performance for performers and other knowledgeable participants. It is one of
the major shared understandings of what jazz performance is supposed
to be "about." Those shared understandings emerge from performance
and the importance in it of having an individual voice, balancing a number of musical and performative parameters, understanding the cultural
foundations of the music, bringing something to each performance,
allowing other musicians and participants to bring something, and, in
the end, being open toward moving to the next level.

Toward a Blues Aesthetic

On the basis of my survey of scholarly literature and of musicians' normative views of jazz performance—from which one can infer ways of
evaluating it as well—I want to posit the existence of an integrating and
encompassing aesthetic. Because of the emphasis that musicians place
on blues feeling, particularly as something that must guide the use of
other resources,[32] this aesthetic might be called the blues aesthetic. I use
term *aesthetic* to denote a set of shared normative and evaluative criteria. It is also used as a label for a certain "iconicity of style." As Steven
Feld (1994a: 131–32) writes, when a style term (in musical performance, for example) becomes a "cross-modal homology" connecting
differing modes of interpersonal expression, its metaphoric force leads
us to view it as "naturally real, obvious, complete, and thorough." That
is, because of its versatility and applicability across modes, it takes on a
force that makes it seemingly part of everything in the world. As a result,
what could be considered a metaphor—like the blues[33]—becomes
iconic, a symbol that stands for itself and is experienced "as feelingfully

synonymous from one domain or level of image and experience to another" (Feld 1994a: 132). Surveying the comments of scholars and musicians makes it clear that blues-based performance, as synonym for jazz performance, is metaphorically linked to other realms of experience: it is an ethos that informs African American visual art (Powell 1989: 19–35), literature (Baker 1984; Gates 1988), and daily living (Ellison 1964; Murray 1970, 1976; Small 1987; Floyd 1995; Steve Wilson 1995), in addition to music. And in the popular imagination, blues are associated with "realness," soulfulness, honesty, and sincerity.

Other scholars have proposed the existence of a "Black Aesthetic," undergirded by analyses of African American art, literature, and music. Their concept of blackness is, as the term indicates, intimately tied to phenotypic and socially constructed notions of race.[34] Many of their pronouncements started as description but quickly became programmatic, connecting expression by genetically or visibly "black" artists and writers to a unique essence possessed by all black people and dictating the kinds of expression that would qualify existing and future works as "black" (Fuller 1971; Welburn 1971; for critiques, see Baker 1984: 72–91; Jarab 1985). More recent writers have sought to maintain the spirit that originally motivated work on the black aesthetic, choosing, however, to privilege culture, learning, and practice over race. They have focused on describing an "African American aesthetic" (Starks 1993), in some ways synonymous with a blues aesthetic (Andrews 1989; Powell 1989, 1994; Baraka 1991 conflates the two). Each of these writers, however, stops short of describing a blues aesthetic. They restrict their arguments to characteristics of the blues and what must precede the formulation of that aesthetic, such as consideration of the views of African American musicians as well as poets, novelists, and painters (Starks 1993: 152).

The blues aesthetic, as such, is the sum of the reflective and normative assertions that musicians have made regarding processes of performance, interaction, and evaluation. In the simplest terms, it is constituted by (learned) practices derived from and continually fed by African American musics and culture. It is not, however, racially based, nor is it "coded" in the genes of any group of individuals. Rather, it is learned through the engagement of individuals with those musics and that culture—to the degree that one could view them as separable entities—through their close attention to the practices of African Americans and those in African American musics (cf. Olly Wilson 1985, 1992).[35] Participants in musical events, using the blues aesthetic as a performative and evaluative framework (cf. Marshall 1982), place a premium on individual expression within established frames for performance (Hymes 1964; Bauman 1975; Bauman and Briggs 1990) and on equally patterned interaction with other performers and participants. Such events are oriented toward each performer "saying something" (cf. Barth 1995; Monson 1996) about how to take the materials at hand (e.g., instruments, compositions, forms, harmony, venues, musicians, listeners) and spontaneously exploit their expressive potential. This aesthetic is another manifestation of a diasporic musical trace or awareness, what composer Olly Wilson has described as an African-derived "conceptual approach" to music making (1974, 1992). Novelty is not among the primary concerns of the participant motivated by the blues aesthetic; creativity, distinctiveness, and interactivity are. These concerns manifest themselves in the ways in which performers sometimes reinforce and sometimes push against the frames that surround jazz performance.[36] Even more, the blues aesthetic is a statement of the egalitarian, enabling myth of jazz performance, a myth that says that any musician who understands and actualizes the normative criteria can be seen as a good performer. The aesthetic is the shared conceptual underpinning for what musicians do when they perform and what performing and nonperforming participants call on in evaluating performance.

There are, of course, other discourses and evaluative frameworks that can be brought to bear in the analysis of jazz. In this extended world of discourse, the blues aesthetic has a related but alternate function. While it grows out of African American culture and the interaction between participants on the jazz scene, it also uses terms and concepts derived from the discourses on Western concert music.[37] Jazz scene participants, like many other people, are aware of the ways in which the discourses surrounding classical music have historically been used by educators and critics to denigrate other musical styles, to deny their specificity and cultural significance. The musicians' knowledge of Western classical music, for example, encouraged by training at institutions like the New England Conservatory or the Berklee School of Music, surely contributes to a desire to see the music they perform recognized as being on par with classical music in terms of artistry and complexity. Indeed, their knowledge of and engagement with discourses on European "art music" help them strategically to call on those same discourses to "elevate" jazz in the eyes of its detractors. Moreover, they can strategically employ those discourses to attract audiences whose understandings of music and strivings for social and cultural capital (Bourdieu 1984) lead them to evaluate and choose music on its "artistic merit."

When musicians like Donald Harrison describe jazz by analogy to classical music, therefore, they frequently do so with a specific intent that does not contradict their belief that blues aesthetic criteria are paramount in evaluating musical performance. Harrison ended a performance at Iridium in May 1995 by thanking the audience for coming to hear his group and encouraging them to continue supporting "America's classical music" by buying recordings and going to live shows. The use of the label "America's classical music" can appeal to any of a number of social actors, regardless of their racial, ethnic, or cultural backgrounds. Those who respond to it as a positive label constitute a self-selected group, perhaps allying themselves with an "American" version of classical music that is distinct from the European one. To the degree that musicians like Harrison believe that jazz is a music on par with Western classical music, they do not see as a corollary that the music must be analyzed or understood in the same way as classical music. At other times—as in Harrison's previously related anecdote about giving credit to the music's African American "creators and innovators"—they foreground the African Americanness of the music. The choice to describe jazz as American or African American is frequently a strategic one. African American musicians, for example, can describe jazz as "American" when it is to their advantage, that is, when it serves to include the widest possible number of potential audience members or attract potential listeners. Alternately, they can emphasize its African Americanness when a focus on its supposedly universal characteristics threatens to erase what they see as its cultural roots. Non–African Americans, likewise, can use the term *America's classical music* to escape the feeling that a term like *African American music* questions their participation in or erases their contributions to jazz (cf. Monson 1996: 200–203).

Like some of their "classical" counterparts, however, either group can describe jazz in nontechnical, nonacademic terms without mentioning (African American) culture for other strategic reasons. In such situations, they are arguing for separating jazz from an overly cold and analytical paradigm that seems concerned only with harmony, melody, rhythm, and other notable aspects of performance. In that case, they are moving closer to a classical notion of "transcendence." Joshua Redman's liner notes from his 1994 recording *Mood Swing* are instructive here:

> Jazz is music. And great jazz, like all great music, attains its value not through intellectual complexity, but through emotional expres-

sivity. True, jazz is a particularly intricate, refined, and rigorous art form. Jazz musicians must amass a vast body of idiomatic knowledge and cultivate an acute artistic imagination if they wish to become accomplished creative improvisers. Moreover, a familiarity with jazz history and theory will undoubtedly enhance a listener's appreciation of the actual aesthetics. Yes, jazz *is* intelligent music. Nevertheless, extensive as they might seem, the intellectual aspects of jazz are ultimately only means to its emotional ends. Technique, theory, and analysis are not, and should never be considered, ends in themselves.

Jazz is not about flat fives or sharp nines, or metric subdivisions, or substitute chord changes. Jazz is about feeling, communication, honesty, and soul. Jazz is not supposed to boggle the mind. Jazz is meant to enrich the spirit.

All the key words are there: "all great music," "refined," "art." Redman is at great pains to indicate the ways in which those descriptors apply to jazz, even as he wants to distinguish their use with regard to jazz from that with classical music. Classical music aficionados may make similar claims about the disservice analysis does to music, but Redman's assertions proceed differently from those that see the musical experience as communicative or expressive in and of itself (see Kivy 1990). His attempt to deemphasize the intellectualism of musical response foregrounds notions of communication, soulfulness, and expressivity. But those terms are to be understood via their connection with the blues aesthetic and the way in which notions like soulfulness and communication are configured within it. Redman *learned* about that soulfulness from listening to Stanley Turrentine (as well as Stevie Wonder, Otis Redding, and Aretha Franklin) and from working with master musicians.

The foundations of the blues aesthetic are found in various domains of activity: in African American musical practices, in African American religious worship, and in other aspects of African American culture. Musicians and other scene participants become acquainted with the aesthetic through their engagment with and understanding of African American musics and African American culture as well their interactions with parallel and competing discourses. Through verbal and performative communication, record listening, and reading, participants tap into different aspects of the aesthetic, learning how to make, interpret, and respond to the sounds and other stimuli in musical events.

Jazz as Ritualized Performance

The scene and the blues aesthetic constitute two related ways of framing musical events as jazz and as performance. The scene can be said to provide space and place for jazz performance, while the blues aesthetic provides a way to negotiate space and place. Other forms of music or performance can be framed or understood via their positioning in other scenes and/or via the normative and evaluative criteria of other aesthetics. Within the scene and working within the blues aesthetic, the emphasis placed by musicians on "taking it to another level," their many mentions of spirituality, and participants' church-derived responses to jazz performance suggest a ritualized view of jazz performance.

Anthropologists, scholars of comparative religion, and even literary scholars have long emphasized the importance of ritual in structuring human experience (e.g., van Gennep 1960; Kluckhohn 1942; Eliade 1959; Turner 1969; Asad 1983; Comaroff 1985; Combs-Schilling 1989; Seremetakis 1991).[38] Explicit attempts have been made as well to apply insights from the study of ritual to African American musics including jazz (Marks 1974; Burnim 1985, 1988; Leonard 1987; Small 1987b; Salamone 1988). The meanings of *ritual* have been debated, with one view tending to dominate: "the definitions of ritual that have been offered have tended to share a presupposition about their object . . . indigenously represented as 'ancient' and unchanging, [connected] to 'tradition,' the sacred, to structures that have generally been represented in stasis" (Kelly and Kaplan 1990: 120). In this view, rituals are essentially conservative and devoted to maintaining the status quo. They have an established, unchanging structure from which deviations can be dangerous.

This view of ritual has been challenged in anthropological theory since the late 1970s, particularly on the grounds that not all rituals are seasonal, calendrical, or concerned with healing rites. Just as researchers studying identity and ethnicity have come to see those concepts as plastic and negotiable—concerned more with policing boundaries than with specifying content (Barth 1969)—so have anthropologists begun to view ritual in ways that see it as possessing varying degrees of and responses to formalization (Irvine 1979; Schieffelin 1985; Kelly and Kaplan 1990), characterized less by rote repetition than by performative negotiations with structure. Indeed, even the seminal work of Victor Turner (1969) allowed room for the performative in the study of ritual, though later scholars seem to have ignored that dimension of his work.[39]

Regardless of whether one sees ritual as conservative or performative, there are still common themes regarding ritual's role in individual and social transformation and its power to organize experience. Jean Comaroff (1985), for example, sees the power of ritual in its ability to play "most directly upon the signifying capacity of symbols, using them as the means through which to grasp, condense, and act upon qualities otherwise diffused in the social and material world" (78). African Zionists in South Africa, she notes, "construct rituals so as to reform the world in the image they have created, to reestablish a dynamic correspondence between the self and the structures that contain it" (198). In this sense, ritual escapes the everyday association it has with meaningless routine. It not only informs the interactions that one has with the surrounding world, but provides a forum in which one can intervene directly in that world to change its structures or, at least, one's relation to them.

Similarly, in her book *Sacred Performances: Islam, Sexuality, and Sacrifice* (1989), M. E. Combs-Schilling stresses ritual's ability to combine images or ideas metaphorically in such a way that participants must search for "their points of likeness and opposition" (248). But such use of metaphor does not allow for free association. Rather, it "demands imagination and creativity and yet . . . is highly constraining in the kinds of understandings it allows to be built, for it defines the parameters of comparison" (248), linking present actors with the past and other ritual practitioners. Ritual at once makes possible the perception of meaning but constrains the operations whereby one comes to apprehend it. In the process, ritually constructed meanings become iconic representations, "truths" that are not easily destroyed:

> Ritual's fullness, independence, and capacity to orchestrate experience [enable] it to build definitions that impact upon all others. . . . Other definitions and experiences exist, definitions that can be quite oppositional to the ones that are ritually built. . . . Yet, when effective, the ritual definitions come to dominate, for they are experienced as essential definitions—definitions in purest form. Their cultural worth enables them to overshadow all others. (253)

Issues of selfhood and cultural identity thus find perhaps their strongest articulation in rituals, for such events provide definitions that not only extend into daily life but help to determine its very fabric.

What a ritual framework allows the scholar of jazz is a way to integrate the flux and mutability of the scene with the attitudes toward performance, participation, and evaluation that achieve iconicity in blues-based performance. It becomes a single figure that contains the structure provided by the scene and musical style and the negotiations of that structure via blues aesthetic criteria, at once making possible the interpretation of meaning, but constraining its possible forms. Scholars of music and history have proposed that African American musical forms, including jazz, are ritualistic or ritualized.[40] Though each of them states the purpose of ritualized musics differently, they agree that their focus is stomping out the blues and giving participants metaphoric "equipment for living," different ways of seeing and reacting to the world around them. The parallel with anthropological literature on ritual is too strong here to be missed. Understanding the ritual nature of performance, particularly as it is suggested by statements and actions of scene participants, allows one to see more clearly that, in addition to its function as entertainment, jazz can have expressive and transformative potential (cf. Burnim 1985: 160).

Christopher Small's commonsense notion of ritual (1987a) provides a point of departure for discussion of the ways in which jazz performance is ritualized activity. In noting several aspects of Western art music performance that can be characterized as "ritualistic," Small explicitly details the following: (1) that performance takes place in a space specifically set aside for that purpose; (2) that the space is constructed in such a way as to focus attention on the performers; (3) that there are workers charged with maintaining and ensuring the sacredness of the space; (4) that there are conventions regarding the dress of performers and other participants; and (5) that there are strict behavioral expectations for both performers and participants (8–11). He goes on to note that "most concerts consist mainly of a limited number of works which get played over and over again, with minute variations in interpretation, and that audiences become extremely skilled in perceiving these variations and comparing them" (13–14).

It is quite apparent that jazz as performed in bars, nightclubs, festivals, and concert halls shares many of the previously mentioned ritual characteristics: there are spaces in New York City that are set aside for jazz performance. The performers are central in those spaces, often being the reason why nonperformers are present. The layout of many venues, as noted previously, focuses the attention of other participants on performers, who typically are in an area raised above floor level. To varying degrees, those spaces are maintained for the presentation of music with images of jazz musicians, instruments, and other memorabilia adorning the walls and sound systems amplifying and projecting the sound(s) of the performers. Owners and managers make more or less committed efforts to maintain performance spaces, keeping pianos in tune and even improving or modifying the appearance of a space over time.

There are, moreover, conventionalized, though variable, expectations regarding the dress and behavior of performers and other participants alike. The "quiet policies" of various venues seem intended, for example, not to prohibit all verbal activity, only that which is not in response to the music. Shouts of encouragement are prohibited only to the degree that their excessiveness interferes with the ability of others to hear or see what the performers are doing (cf. Racy 1991: 15–16). Finally, there is a more or less unvarying repertoire of compositions known as "standards" that will often be performed or that can serve as models or springboards for new compositions (cf. Monson 1991; Jackson 1992). All of these elements and behaviors link jazz performance in such venues to ritual activity.

Whereas Small is attentive to details of context, Frank Salamone focuses on the negotiation of structure within the context described by Small. In his essay "The Ritual of Jazz Performance" (1988), Salamone treats jazz as a sacred form that creates and renews itself through ritual. Like Small, he pays considerable attention to the conventions of jazz performance that make it similar to repeated ritual activity. He sees preperformance agreements about solo order, chord progressions, and so on, as part of the repeated ritual of performance. And like Neil Leonard (1987), he recognizes the degree to which conventions of song form and interaction make possible "spontaneous performance": "Only when a musician thoroughly understands musical structure is exceptional improvisation possible. The individual's seemingly featured status, therefore, is based only on the strength of the group's internal cohesiveness" (Salamone 1988: 96). In that sense, the openness of musical structure previously discussed by Peter Bernstein and Steve Wilson can be conceived as an "enabler" (Jackson 1992) or frame that allows interactions to take place, for it allows musicians to bring something to a performance. While each individual must say something, each does so with the explicit support of other participants in the musical event.

Within ritualized scene- and blues-aesthetic–based performances, there is a specific governing structure, a ritual structure, if you will.

There are, of course, variations depending on whether the performance takes place "live" in front of an audience or in a recording studio before a more limited set of participants (just as a wedding or funerary ritual might have contextual differences). In either event, musicians must come into a space having prepared themselves through rehearsals specifically geared toward that event or through cumulative preparation and study from their engagement with musical performance over time. They must also bring a willingness to listen to and interact with other performers and participants. Nonperformers are also expected to come to the performance with specific kinds of knowledge of how performance normatively proceeds and how to listen to and evaluate performance as it is occurring. As Steve Wilson put it, all must be "ready to receive." When listeners come with other expectations—such as to have conversation or conduct an informal meeting—a critical mass of other participants, musicians or even management can censure them through polite requests for silence or less polite calls for their immediate departure.[41] Similarly, at recording sessions observers are required to be quiet and unobtrusive, literally speaking only when addressed by someone with a more central role in the recording process.

The contours of the ritualized structure of jazz performance can be sketched by reference to a musical event in a nightclub. Its beginning is framed by lights being dimmed and/or by the introduction of the performers. Depending on their own personal preferences, the performers or the bandleader may further frame the performance by addressing the audience with talk about the occasion or the tunes they are going to play. If the order of tunes has not been set prior to the performers' entrance into the performance space, the leader will quickly communicate verbally to the other musicians what tune will be played, perhaps also indicating the key, dynamics, and other information. She or he then indicates the tempo through visual and aural means: with motions like finger snapping or foot tapping combined with *sotto voce* counting. This framing of the performance is extremely important. While a particular tune can be played at any of a number of tempos, finding one that will ensure that the musicians fall into a groove is considered an art unto itself. For that reason, a leader may clap or snap several pulses before cueing the band to start to ensure that the right pulse will be used.

Once the tune has begun (and this scheme applies for recording sessions as well), a group will tend to follow a scheme used by small jazz groups since at least since the mid-1940s. The progression of events is generally similar to that presented in Figure 2-1. The scheme presented

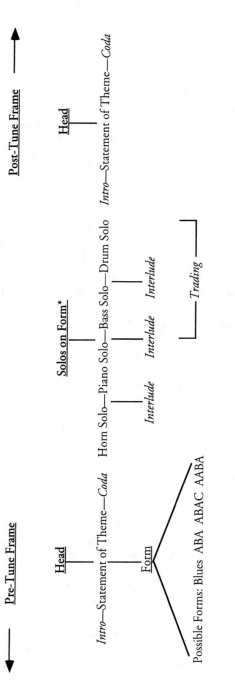

FIGURE 2-1. Typical progression of events in a tune.

is merely a guide. While the italicized items can generally be omitted, any of the others can be removed or modified in some way.

The head consists of all musical material prior to the beginning or after the end of improvised solos. At the beginning of a tune, it can be referred to as the "head in." Correspondingly, it would be the head-out at the end, though the term *out-chorus* is used more frequently. The head can include a prearranged introduction or an improvised one. In some cases, the material for the introduction comes from the coda or from the statement of the theme, particularly the last portion of a sectional form—for example, the last "A" of an AABA form, the "C" of an ABAC form, or the last four measures of a twelve-bar blues progression. Likewise, the introduction can consist of a vamp on a two- or four-measure harmonic progression. (Some bandleaders, like saxophonist Lou Donaldson, frequently dispense with this aspect of framing. In such situations, Donaldson simply begins to play, expecting the other members of his ensemble—like organist Dr. Lonnie Smith, guitarist Peter Bernstein, and drummer Fukushi Tanaka—to know the tune and to infer tempo and key from what and how he plays.) The statement of the theme follows the introduction (or begins the tune when the introduction has been omitted). This portion of the head most clearly allows other participants in the musical event (or record listeners) to identify the tune if it is one already known to them. Otherwise, it provides them the opportunity to hear and grasp the form of an unfamiliar composition.

Forms are harmonic/rhythmic structures that serve as a basis for improvisation. Sections within them are generally four, eight, or sixteen measures in length. Such designations as "AABA" or "blues" mark the organization of a particular form. An AABA form has two sections at its beginning and one at its end that are of equal lengths and have identical or nearly identical harmonic progressions. The B section of such a form generally modulates to a contrasting key area or through a series of contrasting keys that eventually lead back to the key area that begins the A section. George and Ira Gershwin's "I Got Rhythm" is a popular and frequently used example of an AABA form, in which each section is eight measures in length.[42] A blues form is typically twelve measures in length, though there are numerous variants (as Koch 1982 indicates). Short forms, like blues forms or sixteen-bar ones, tend to be played twice during the head, while longer forms are played only once. Indeed, while such forms may seem structurally simple, they can contain enormous variety in terms of harmonic, melodic, rhythmic, and textural activity. From section to section, there may be changes of feel,[43] meter, or any other musical parameter. In composing and improvising on tunes, jazz musicians can treat form in a highly elastic manner, taking well-known tunes or forms and extending or truncating sections to make the listening and performing experience more challenging. In some cases, the statement of the theme is so intricate that the performers choose a less complicated form for solos.[44]

For participants, recognizing and understanding form is essential to comprehending the musical event. Visual/spatial metaphors (from written notation) help them to describe some portions of the form. The top of a form or of a section, for example, is its beginning. The B section in an AABA tune is known as a bridge or a channel because it connects the A sections to one another. Performers who frequently lose their way in a form[45] are harshly criticized, for understanding and being able to perform effectively on a number of forms is a basic skill that precedes the ability to improvise effectively.

Once the statement of the theme is complete, the performers may move into the next frame—solos on the form—or delay its arrival with transitional material or a coda. As with the introduction, such material may be precomposed or improvised, for example, on a vamp. In some cases, the material for the coda and the introduction may be identical. The head-in and head-out, in any event, frame the group improvisational activity of the solo sections in the same way that verbal introductions and setting the tempo frame the performance of a tune.

The harmonies, feels, textures, meter, and tempo of the form furnish the given material that the performers work with during the solo sections of the performance (Tirro 1967; Byrnside 1975).[46] Each cycle through the form is referred to as a chorus.[47] As Figure 2-1 indicates, the order of solos generally proceeds from the solos of "horns" (brass and reed instruments), to those of chording instruments (e.g., piano, organ, guitar), then to bass, and drums. Individual ensembles or band leaders may modify those parameters from tune to tune for contrast, omitting bass and drum solos, for example, or changing the order of solo slots. Composed interludes[48] or improvised vamps may fill the space between individual solos.

In some cases, a leader or a group of soloists may "trade eights" or "fours" with one another or with the drummer (in lieu of or prior to a drum solo). Each performer solos for the specified number of measures, generally completing a phrase on the first beat of the measure after the designated grouping, and is followed by the next performer who observes the same procedure. In trading fours with a drummer, for example, a saxophonist will solo for four measures accompanied by the entire ensemble (including the drummer), finishing his or her first section of trading on the first beat of the fifth measure. The drummer will begin a four-measure solo passage at that same moment and, on the first beat of the ninth measure, will resume an accompanying role as the saxophonist begins soloing again. This procedure continues until a visual, verbal, or musical cue at the end of a chorus signals that the drummer will take an extended solo on the form or that the ensemble should play the head-out.[49] Trading passages can often generate considerable excitement, particularly when performers turn them into competition (which musician can play the fastest or most registrally extreme phrases) or manipulate the terms of trading in process (starting by trading eights, cutting down to fours, then twos, single measures, half measures, and finally beats, for example).

When the solos are finished, the leader of the group cues the band to play the head again. Introductory materials from the head-in may be reused to signal the head's return. Or the band may simply play the theme statement without introductory material and then use what was the introduction as a coda. In some cases, the final statement of the theme is followed by more solos (on a vamp) or a cadenza played by the leader of the group. When the tune is done, and typically before the last sounds have decayed, the performers frame the end of the performance by slightly bowing their heads and acknowledging audience applause. In a studio setting, the performers maintain silence for several seconds until the recording engineer or producer informs them that they have stopped rolling tape.

This scheme characterizes the playing on most tunes in a nightclub set, in a concert hall, or on a festival stage. When one tune ends, the performers begin framing the next tune, agreeing to follow a preset arrangement or to depart from it, perhaps taking time to introduce the band members to the audience, to acknowledge other musicians or important people in the audience, to remind listeners about currently available recordings of theirs, or to announce the previous tune or the next one. Afterwards, the leader again sets the tempo, and the performers enter the tune frame. The pre- and post-tune framing differs in the context of rehearsals or recording sessions, but what happens within the tune frame is typically the same, with the important exception that the performers have the option of stopping a tune in rehearsals or in a recording session if they are not satisfied with it.

After four or five tunes, a typical nightclub set ends. The performers leave one temporal frame (see Figure 2-2). If there is another set to be

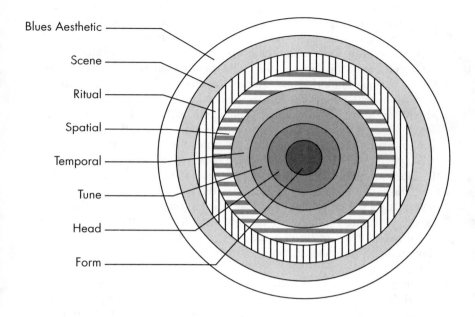

Blues Aesthetic
Scene
Ritual
Spatial
Temporal
Tune
Head
Form

FIGURE 2-2. Frames around jazz performance.

played that evening, they remain within a spatial frame and may invite the participants to attend later sets. The performers might also seek ways to relax and dissipate the energy amassed during the previous set and to prepare themselves for the next one through conversation with other participants, concentration, or practice (cf. Berliner 1994: 453). Or they may remove themselves from the venue, only to reenter the spatial frame before the next set begins. If they have finished an evening's final set, the performers or venue personnel invite the other participants to come again for an engagement later in the week. And if the performers have finished the last set of a week-long engagement, then they leave that frame as well. Venue personnel focus their energies on informing other participants of other engagements. Likewise, in a recording session or rehearsal, the studio or apartment is the spatial frame within which musical performance takes place.

These different frames, graphically represented in Figure 2-2,[50] are different areas in which participants in musical events can creatively manipulate and respond to the materials they have.[51] These frames also furnish the differing arenas into which all participants are expected to bring something. They adapt themselves to the performance space, taking into account the "vibe"—the "general atmosphere" (Berliner 1994: 449)—of a particular venue, studio, or rehearsal space. They adjust themselves to the temporal demands placed on them by the space within which they perform—set lengths, engagement lengths, allotted studio time, and so on. Once those adjustments are made—and they are all subject to renegotiation—the performers enter the frames in which they most specifically grapple with the performative and evaluative criteria of the blues aesthetic. Here, they find creative ways to play the head of a tune, through the way they introduce it, the ways in which they play the materials presented to them as the head of a tune (harmonies, rhythms, melodies, timbres, dynamics), and the ways in which they adhere to or obscure the form. Likewise, in the solo passages, each performer ideally plays with all the musical parameters that make up a composition and its form.

When performers successfully synthesize and work with all of the materials of a performance (space, time, tune, form, other performers, and other participants), that is when a performance is likely to proceed to the next level. Performers and other participants experience sensations or series of feelings that they describe, like Antonio Hart, as being literally "out of this world." Every element of a performance seems to fit, and each individual appears to be making a contribution to what is occurring. Some of the feelings associated with possession or ecstasy lead to an apparent nullification of time outside of the performance and of space outside the venue. In process, the musical event is said to be "swinging," "burning," "on," or some similar phrase that indicates positive motion, activity, and good feeling (cf. Monson 1990: 35).

The responses of participants attending such events are variable and sometimes virtually indistinguishable from those that might accompany stirring sermons in African American Baptist and Pentecostal churches. At a performance by trumpeter Nicholas Payton, pianist Mulgrew Miller, bassist Peter Washington, and drummer Lewis Nash at the Village Vanguard in March 1995, the shared nature of response to impressive musical performance was foregrounded via silent, visually perceived actions. In the middle of the tune "Maria's Melody," Washington and Nash played an intense groove over which Miller soloed—playing riff-based figures alternating with long, intricate single-line passages with his right hand. One of my table companions, Bess Weatherman, was moving her head up and down in time with the groove in the same fashion that I was. As the interaction between the rhythm section members intensified, I looked across the room and made eye contact with Sharon Blynn, who opened her mouth as if silently to say, "Wow," nodded her head in the direction of the stage, and looked back at me in awe. I nodded in agreement, smiled, and turned my gaze back toward the stage.

In some cases, responses are clearly verbalized and spur the performers on to greater performative heights. One could assert that when the performers have "said something" to nonperforming participants, those nonperformers feel free literally to say something in response (cf. Burnim and Maultsby 1987: 132–33). This kind of interactive response, not generally encouraged in some performance venues, is essential to jazz performance and connects it, again, to other forms of African American music. The way in which Keil (1991) describes the reactions of African American audiences to blues performances in Chicago, or in which Haralambos (1970) and Ward (1998) describe reactions to soul and rhythm and blues are strikingly similar to what sometimes happens in jazz performances. A clear example comes from a performance by pianist James Williams, singer Kevin Mahogany, and bassist Curtis Lundy at Bradley's in October 1994. It also highlights the degree to which blues-inflected performance can generate positive audience response. Near the end of a set, the musicians performed the song "Since I Fell for You." Some of the participants seated at the bar were urging Mahogany on as he sang the melody and lyrics at the beginning of the tune. They shouted encouragement to him at every bluesy turn of phrase and every decoration of the tune's standard melody. Most interestingly, one shouted, "Go on, Kevin! Sing the blues!" right before the word "blues" came up in the text. Perhaps in response, but definitely on cue, Mahogany caressed the word by descending pentatonically from the initial pitch on that syllable. He also mirrored the pitch descent by gradually decreasing dynamics. One could argue here that performance is truly participatory and dialogic with performers and nonperforming participants contributing to and influencing the emergent shape of a musical event.

Jazz performers ideally take the materials at their disposal, what is provided and what they bring, and attempt to "say something" with them, to become like one (Jackson 1992) with one another and with other participants in the musical event. The blues aesthetic shapes the way they approach those materials, and the materials themselves—framed by space, time, tune, and form—are part of ritualized jazz performances. The scene and the aesthetic provide conditions that allow the participants in the musical event to go to the next level, to remove them temporarily from all concerns beyond those of the performance, and to give them metaphoric tools for seeing and relating the world differently once the performance has ended. Each musician who shows him or herself capable of responding creatively, distinctively, and interactively at the same time shows other musicians and participants ways of seeing what is possible within the structures of musical performance and the varied structures within which individuals live their lives.

It is in this sense that jazz performance is a kind of social action that intervenes in the daily lives of those who listen to and perform it. It does not merely reflect the events and circumstances that frame it. Rather, within those frames, musical items or other sound terms (Meyer 1956)—phrases, rhythms, voicings, approaches, compositions, and techniques—become symbols, associatively and connotatively linked via the shared "interpretive moves" (Feld 1994b) of performers and other participants with other performances, performers, and musics. They are not so much symbols *of* something that can be categorized and classified, but symbols that can be *linked* to something. Meanings emerge from the linkages and oppositions between juxtaposed musical sounds and their interpretations by listeners.

Each musical item and its creative use becomes a way of connecting with some of the most deeply held values of African Americans toward performance, toward living, and toward who they are as people, values that stress tolerance of individual variation and group cooperation in the service of survival (see the introduction of Gwaltney 1993; see also Roberts 1989). It is not merely a music of resistance—a term closely associated with social action; it is a music of survival as well for those, regardless of racial, cultural, or ethnic background who understand the ways in which various conventions are or can be manipulated in performance. Jazz performance therefore assumes a synecdochic relationship to African American culture: one brings to the musical event those ideals that should motivate daily living—as in music, so in life. As Joshua Redman noted in discussing playing with older musicians, one hopes that from playing with them, he or she will internalize something of their spirit and wisdom in order to become not just a better musician but a more mature person.

Similar processes can be observed in a number of other musics created and performed by Black Atlantic populations. In a much-overlooked article, Morton Marks (1974) makes similar claims regarding a number of different African-derived performance traditions in the African diaspora. Noting that performance itself models social behavior and refelcts adaptive strategies (cf. Whitten and Szwed 1970: 220), his aim is to show how "the patterned use of sounds, both linguistic and musical . . . reflect and/or actually bring about changes from one social or psychological state to another" (67). He examines, in turn, Afro-Brazilian Carnival, Latin popular music in New York performed by *santeros,* and African American gospel performance. In the second of those examinations, he details how a commercially released song performed by Justi Barretto, "El Santo en Nueva York," is framed as sacred through the use of verbal and musical elements from a *toque* for Yemaya, one of the *santos* for practitioners of *santería,* when it begins. Immediately afterwards, the performance switches to a dance-band format with words in Spanish and a standard harmonic progression that one might find in a typical jazz composition. As it unfolds, however, the performers "switch" musical and linguistic codes: changes of harmony are simplified, alternating only between a tonic and dominant-seventh chord every two measures; call and response patterning becomes the dominant mode of presentation; and the singer gradually shifts from singing in Spanish to singing in Lucumí, the Yoruba language in Cuba. The importance of such switching, he argues, lies in its preservation of essential group values:

> What this shift signifies is that even though drastic changes have taken place in the *natural* setting which render the practices of *santería* difficult, the *cultural* forms which pay homage to the deities are still intact. . . . The opening dance-band format might be seen as a masking device which hides the real content of the song. The code-switching near the end is a type of de-masking, which symbolically reaffirms the ritual by moving away from the "acculturated" format and[,] symbolically, from the problems created in the transplant of the religion to the United States. (86–87)

In a sense, therefore, changes in performance and the specific content of performance (in terms of structures and what happens within those structures) support a normative vision of the relationship that one must have with the *santos.* They communicate how one is to live under new circumstances: through mastering several musical and linguistic codes and using them creatively and expressively in performance. Marks's discussions of Afro-Brazilian and African American practices come to similar conclusions.[52]

Similarly, in his writings about tradition and cultural identity in modern-day Nigeria, Christopher Waterman (1990) shows that one can find clear correspondences between musical and social orders despite Western analytical frameworks that separate reified musical structures from music's more expressive, qualitative parameters. The relational processes that build individual and group identity among the Yoruba in Nigeria are mirrored in ritualized transactions—involving money, status, and the management of meaning—and uses of metaphor in musical performance (217–19). These processes become understandable when he describes the composition and performance of larger ensemble:

> The larger bands in Ibadan, based on the Sunny Ade and Ebenezer Obey paradigms . . . are comprised of three semiautonomous units. The guitar section includes a lead or solo player (generally not the band captain) supported by interlocking tenor guitars, Hawaiian guitar, and bass guitar. The senior talking drummer improvises on a rhythmic base created by the cumulative interaction of supporting drums. The praise singer is flanked and supported by his chorus. Thus, the fundamental relationship between *elé* (lead part, call, "that which drives ahead of or into something") and *ègbè* (subordinate part, choral response, "supporters" or "protectors") is reproduced in each section of the band. The aural gestalt generated by the intersection of these micro-hierarchies metaphorically predicates an idealized social order: a congeries of localized networks focused on big men. (219)

"An effective performance of jùjú," he continues, "predicates not only the structure of the ideal society, but also its interactive ethos or 'feel': intensive, vibrant, buzzing, and fluid" (220). Such performance "externalizes, comments upon, metaphorically grounds, and helps to reproduce the hegemonic values that guide behavior at secular urban secular rituals. . . . Put simply, jùjú performances advance the following arguments concerning the relationship of the individual to culture and community: (1) 'We're all Yoruba'; (2) 'Our values are intact'; and (3) 'Keep working' " (227). Indeed, jùjú peformance achieves its power and impact precisely through its "metaphoric correlation of social-structural, ideological, and aural patterns" (227), through its ability to communicate in the ritual context the kinds of behaviors and interactions that will be most effective in daily life.

There are numerous other examples that could be marshaled to underscore the importance and ritual nature of music making in the African diaspora outside those already mentioned. Paul Gilroy's writing about black music in Britain in the 1980s (1991a); Stephen Stuempfle's (1995) work on music in Trinidad; various writings concerning reggae and politics (Bones 1986; Waters 1985; Hebdige 1979); Karen McCarthy Brown's study of Haitian *vodou* (1991); Jocelyne Guilbault's book on zouk (1993); and Veit Erlmann's (1991) and David Coplan's (1985) writings on the history and meanings of South African music are just a few examples of works that concern themselves with musical performance by African diaspora populations and the ways in which those performances and their attendant rituals can become, as Gilroy (1991a: 211) has observed, central to the regulation of collective memory and experience, as well as the construction of community. Each of those works notes how important the elasticity and flexibility of musical performance is, the kinds of negotiations with structure and setting that make performance meaningful. The meaning is never solely in the sound; rather, it is in the interactions that make the sound possible and the ongoing adjustments of the sound to the context.

It is in this sense that jazz performance, conceived as ritual and motivated by the blues aesthetic, is connected to other musics in the African diaspora. Just like the other musics of the diaspora, and in many similar ways, it privileges interaction, participation, and formal flexibility in the service of transcendence and communication of normative values and cultural identity. Musical performance does not merely serve to reproduce or express the hierarchies or frames that surround it. It is also concerned with transcending them through metaphoric encodings of deeply held values and strategies for survival.

Notes

[1]Describing jazz in such a fashion recalls the scale of intensities that was part of Herskovits's syncretic paradigm. See Herskovits (1990). For critiques, see Apter (1991) and Scott (1991).

[2]See also Gilroy (1991a, b, 1993, 1994, 1995).

[3]Gilroy, however, is not the first to propose such a perspective for viewing and understanding African-derived musics. Indeed, the "black-music cultural sphere"

described by Olly Wilson (1974) has boundaries that mark it as coterminous with Gilroy's area. More will said about Wilson's work later.

[4]Baraka was known as Leroi Jones at the time of the book's release.

[5]Some aspects of Herskovits's ideas and methods have come under criticism in recent years. See Harrison (1988), Apter (1991), and Scott (1991).

[6]Keil's notion is drawn at least partially from his reading of *Blues People*.

[7] See Burke (1964).

[8]In *Stomping the Blues* (1976), Murray repeatedly encapsulates the spirit of what bluesmen do with the words "extension, elaboration, and refinement."

[9]See, for example, Crouch (1990: 47). During the course of my fieldwork, critic Peter Watrous and pianist Eric Reed, among others, expressed similar views.

[10]Note that the use of the term *African American culture* does not presuppose homogeneity in that culture. Indeed, what defines the culture are its ways of looking at and adapting to changing situations rather than the specific responses to them. Culture, in this sense, is conceived as a number of strategies or practices for responding to and making sense of experience.

[11]A good sound has not only to sound good but also to feel good.

[12]Coltrane's three-tonic system, reportedly influenced by his practicing with Nicolas Slonimsky's *Thesaurus of Scales and Melodic Patterns* (1947), was a system that allowed the substitution of chord scales a major third away from a dominant chord's root in improvisation or composition. On a G-dominant chord, for example, one could typically use pitches from a Mixolydian scale starting on G. In the three-tonic system, Mixolydian scales starting on E♭ and B are permissible substitutes for the G-based scale (though each may require some chromatic alteration to "fit"). This system is employed most famously on "Giant Steps" from *Giant Steps* (compact disc, Atlantic 1311–2, recorded 4 May 1959).

[13]One way in which Blanchard forced his musicians to break old habits was to write compositions relying heavily on nonfunctional tonal progressions, particularly using the sonority of the minor-seventh chord with a flattened sixth. With C as root, the pitches contained in a closed-position voicing of the chord would be C–E♭–G–A♭–B♭.

[14]"Impressions" can be found on John Coltrane's *Impressions* (MCA/Impulse MCA-5887, recorded 26 November 1961). An example of a late Ben Webster ballad is his recording of "How Long Has This Been Going On?" from Ben Webster and "Sweets" Edison, *Ben and "Sweets"* (Columbia CJ 40853, recorded 7 June 1962). "Confirmation" can be found on Charlie Parker's *Bird's Best Bop on Verve* (Verve 314 527 452–2, recorded 30 July 1953).

[15]This statement has interesting correspondences with ideas developed by Mikhail Bakhtin (1981). The meaning of a particular word or utterance, for him, is not static but is intimately tied to previous meanings and emerging from the social and material circumstances of its use: "The word in language is half someone else's. It becomes 'one's own' only when the speaker populates it with his own intention, his own accent, when he appropriates the word, adapting it to his own semantic and expressive intention" (293–94). As with Barth and Newsome's statements, the emphasis is not on novelty or revolutionary usage, but on making the word (sound) "one's own" through deploying it in specific contexts with specific, personal intentions.

[16]The substitution is "incorrect" because the E natural in the B-major scale creates a clash with E♭, the seventh of the F dominant chord. Jazz harmonic theory gen-

erally forbids chord extensions or embellishments that create minor-ninth intervals with respect to lower-voiced chord tones (except with the root of a dominant chord).

[17]William Tallmadge (1984) discusses the definitions and applicability of the terms *blue note* and *blue tonality,* particularly as they relate to harmonic progressions, whether categorized as "blues progressions" or not. In short, blue tonality is characterized by certain kinds of pitch play in specific harmonic contexts. So that a blue note on a C dominant-seventh chord, such as E♭, might not be a blue note in another harmonic context, such as over an F dominant-seventh chord (an E♭ is part of the dominant chord).

[18]To comp is to provide rhythmic/harmonic/textural accompaniment for instruments playing melodies.

[19]This line of argument has continuity with Gates's understanding of "signifyin(g)": one does not signify *something,* one signifies *in some way.* The centrality of the blues is confirmed as well by the staggering number of compositions based on its 8-, 12-, and 16-bar forms throughout the history of the music. For a discussion of those forms and their various transformations, see Koch (1982). Wynton Marsalis paid tribute to the music with his 1989 recording *The Majesty of the Blues* (Columbia CK 45091, recorded 27–28 October 1988, New York, New York).

[20]Compare those responses with the negation of the importance of race when the researcher is non–African American (Monson 1990: 38–39).

[21]Burrell, Pass, Abercrombie, Metheny, and Jarrett are non–African Americans on the list. Wynton Kelly (1931–71) was black and born in Jamaica, but his family moved to New York when he was 4 years old.

[22]Reyes Schramm (1986) notes that analysts frequently confuse a music's "content system"—that is, its meaning to culture bearers—with its expressive system, sound. The latter is a way of getting to the former, with innovations in the expressive system usually helping to preserve the traditions that constitute the content system. Traditional musicological analysis focuses attention on the expressive system but tends to ignore (or take for granted) the context system. See also Higgins (1991).

[23]The Ellington essay is reprinted in Mark Tucker's *The Duke Ellington Reader* (1993: 132–35). A number of African American musicians with whom I talked expressed dismay over the place accorded African American musicians and culture in the writing of history and criticism, fearing that too much concentration on the artistic complexity of the music would eclipse its role as a form of African American cultural expression/communication.

[24]For example, musicians like Louis Armstrong, Duke Ellington, Lester Young, Billie Holiday, Charlie Parker, Dizzy Gillespie, Miles Davis, John Coltrane, Wayne Shorter, Herbie Hancock, Woody Shaw, Kenny Garrett, and Mulgrew Miller are more frequently cited as influential by musicians of differing backgrounds than are non–African American musicians like Bix Beiderbecke, Gil Evans, Bill Evans, Scott LaFaro, Dave Holland, Joe Zawinul, or Michael Brecker. Those in the latter group are most often cited only by European American musicians. Based on what African American musicians and audience members say, it would seem that the reason for the continued importance of African American musicians might be located in the connections between wider African American cultural practices and musical performance. This argument is often thought to be essentialist, when, in fact, it stresses learning and enculturation.

[25]Antonio Hart saw as problematic the segregation of different groups of musicians at the Berklee School of Music in Boston in the late 1980s, observing that

racial and cultural differences mapped onto stylistic ones. Sam Newsome confirmed the same for his experiences there, starting a few years prior to Hart's arrival. Newsome asserted that the majority of white—European and European American—students were interested in musicians like Gary Burton, while many of the African American musicians were interested in learning "how to swing."

[26]So pervasive is Blakey's influence that a number of musicians who had played with him spent nearly an hour discussing his wisdom and his foibles during and after a break at the second evening of recording for James Williams's CD *Truth, Justice, and the Blues* (Fieldnotes, 12 December 1994).

[27]Note here an apparent difference between Wilson's understanding of tradition and that usually espoused by scholars. Whereas scholars have recently viewed traditions as selective constructions and "inventions" (Hobsbawm and Ranger 1983), Wilson seems to be contradicting that view. He is saying, in effect, that one does not "invent" tradition; rather, it is already "there," and one must negotiate a relationship to it. Obviously, this view of tradition is still one that is constructed and invented, though his emphasis is on selecting a whole corpus of materials from the cultural matrix rather than valorizing some and passing over others.

[28]Herbie Hancock's composition "Eye of the Hurricane" (*Maiden Voyage,* compact disc, Blue Note CDP 7 46339 2, recorded 17 May 1965) is a similar but more complicated example. Hancock's tune has a difficult head with abrupt metric and harmonic shifts, but the form for solos is blues in F minor.

[29]For a discussion of substitute harmonies, see Steven Strunk's entry on harmony in the *New Grove Dictionary of Jazz* (1988).

[30]Note that this next level is not so much a transcendence of place or circumstance, but a form of communion in which participants share aspects of their identities and understandings in the context of musical performance. In other words, it is less a form of escape than it is a form of deep involvement.

[31]In a flow situation, the individual does not feel or recognize the passage of time or other items that normally register in his or her consciousness. Moments of flow are most likely to occur when the challenge of a particular activity and the skills possessed by an individual are nearly matched. When the challenge outweighs one's skill, anxiety about one's skill is the result. When one's skills exceed what is required by a certain challenge, then boredom is highly likely.

[32]Scholars writing about African American musics have often seen the blues as musical form and/or as ethos as pivotal to an understanding of all African American musics.

[33]Its metaphoric quality is immediately apparent through its description of the aural via the visual.

[34]See Fields (1982) for a discussion of race as a social and ideological construct.

[35]Indeed, I prefer *blues aesthetic* to *African American aesthetic* because the term *African American* has a tendency to be equated with biological and ideological constructions of race, even though its meaning has more to do with cultural practice (cf. Powell 1989: 20–21).

[36]This argument has some continuity with studies of hegemony and resistance that note that any act that resists hegemony also serves in some ways to reinforce it. Likewise, there is a suggestive relationship to Pierre Bourdieu's notion of *habitus,* defined as "a system of lasting, transposable dispositions which, integrating past experiences, functions at every moment as a *matrix of perceptions, appreciations,*

and actions, and makes possible the achievement of infinitely diversified tasks" (Bourdieu 1977: 82–83).

[37]For a more extensive discussion of the epistemological foundations of this aesthetic, see Jackson (1998: 122–30).

[38]Van Gennep's book was originally published in 1908 as *Les rites de passage.* Some of the literary scholars who have focused on ritual include Gilbert Murray, Jane Ellen Harrison, and Lord Raglan. I thank Robert O'Meally for bringing them to my attention, particularly because they were influential for Ralph Ellison.

[39]Turner writes in his introduction: "in order to live, to breathe, and to generate novelty, human beings have had to create—by structural means—spaces and times in the calendar or in the cultural cycles of their most cherished groups[,] which cannot be captured in the classificatory nets of their quotidian routinized spheres of action. These liminal areas of time and space—rituals, carnivals, dramas, and latterly films—are open to *the play of thought, feeling, and will;* in them are generated new models, often fantastic, some which may have sufficient power and plausibility to replace eventually the force-backed political and jural models that control the centers of society's ongoing life" (vii, emphasis added). Turner's turn toward the performative became more pronounced as he came to view ritual as dramaturgical and to focus on the theatrical aspects of daily living. See Turner (1974a, b; 1982).

[40]See, for example, Ellison (1964: 256–57), Keil (1991: 164), Murray (1970: 58; 1976: 17), Levine (1977: 234–37), Leonard (1987: 23, 53–55, 61–64, 71–75), Small (1987a: 70, 302), Salamone (1988), and Floyd (1995: 140–41).

[41]The responses to such requests are highly variable. The privileges that some individuals ascribe to having paid admission fees complicate such situations when they assert their "right" to do whatever they want because they are "paying customers." The disdain reserved for such audience members is quite similar to that engendered by the increasing number of European tourists visiting Harlem churches in recent years. As tourists, they disrupt services by taking photographs, for example, as times that are disrespectful. See Lii (1995), Bruni (1996), and Gomes (1996).

[42]That is, as the tune is frequently performed by jazz musicians. Gershwin's published version of the tune is a thirty-four bar structure with the last section comprising ten measures. Indeed, in the same way that one can say "Blues in F minor" and count off a tempo and have other musicians play along, one can also say "Rhythm changes in F"—indicating the harmonic progression from the Gershwin tune and a key—and get a similar result.

[43]*Feel* refers to the rhythmic/accentual/textural patterning of or approach to playing a tune or section thereof based on conventional understanding. Several different feels exist; among the most common named ones are Latin, bossa, samba, ballad, two-beat, and swing, each of which carries with it expectations about how rhythm section members (piano, bass, and drums, in particular) are supposed to play.

[44]Herbie Hancock's previously cited "Eye of the Hurricane" is a good example. The form for the solos is a blues progression. David Sanchez's composition "Ebony" (1994, *The Departure,* compact disc, Columbia CK 57848, recorded 23–24 November and 7 December 1993, New York, New York) is a thirty-two-bar form divided into eight-, six-, eight-, and ten-bar sections, respectively. There are also marked changes of feel, as when the ensemble switches to a Latin feel in the second eight-bar section.

⁴⁵For example, in an AABA tune, one plays three A sections in succession between each B section. Some performers unwittingly drop one of the A sections from time to time. The resultant harmonic and rhythmic clashes can be embarrassing for the performer and other participants in the musical event (cf. Monson 1991: 245–52).

⁴⁶In a sense, the term *solo* is misleading, for multiple performers are improvising during the "solo" sections of a performance. The term *feature* might be more appropriate.

⁴⁷If a soloist plays through the form four times, she or he has taken a four-chorus solo.

⁴⁸Under different circumstances, these interludes might be called "sendoffs" or "shout choruses."

⁴⁹See Jackson (1992) for more discussion of communication and cueing.

⁵⁰By nesting the scene frame within the blues aesthetic frame, I am leaving open the possibility of examining other African American music scenes through the prism of a blues aesthetic.

⁵¹Performances not framed by blues aesthetic criteria, such as "pit bands" for Broadway shows, will of course proceed in different ways.

⁵²One might also favorably compare some of the conclusions Frances Aparicio (1998) makes regarding salsa for modern-day Puerto Ricans in the United States and elsewhere.

References

Andrews, Dwight D. 1989. "From Black to Blues." In *The Blues Aesthetic: Black Culture and Modernism,* edited by Richard J. Powell, 37–41. Washington, DC: Washington Project for the Arts.

Aparicio, Frances R. 1998. *Listening to Salsa: Gender, Latin Popular Music, and Puerto Rican Cultures.* Hanover, NH: Wesleyan University Press.

Apter, Andrew. 1991. "Herskovits's Heritage: Rethinking Syncretism in the African Diaspora." *Diaspora* 1: 235–60.

Asad, Talal. 1983. "Notes on Body Pain and Truth in Medieval Christian Ritual." *Economy and Society* 12: 287–327.

Baker, Houston A., Jr. 1984. *Blues, Ideology, and Afro-American Literature: A Vernacular Theory.* Chicago: University of Chicago Press.

Bakhtin, M. M. 1981. *The Dialogic Imagination: Four Essays.* Edited by Michael Holquist. Austin: University of Texas Press.

Baraka, Amiri (LeRoi Jones). 1963. *Blues People: Negro Music in White America.* New York: Morrow.

———. 1991. "The 'Blues Aesthetic' and the 'Black Aesthetic': Aesthetics As the Continuing Political History of a Culture." *Black Music Research Journal* 11(2): 101–9.

Barth, Bruce. 1994. Interview by author. Brooklyn, NY. 14 December.

———. 1995. Interview by author. New York, NY. 22 February.

Barth, Fredrik. 1969. "Introduction." In *Ethnic Groups and Boundaries: The Social Organization of Culture Difference,* edited by Fredrik Barth, 9–38. Boston: Little, Brown.

Bauman, Richard. 1975. "Verbal Art As Performance." *American Anthropologist* 77: 290–311.

Bauman, Richard, and Charles L. Briggs. 1990. "Poetics and Performance As Critical Perspectives on Language and Social Life." *Annual Review of Anthropology* 19: 59–88.

Berliner, Paul F. 1994. *Thinking in Jazz: The Infinite Art of Improvisation*. Chicago: University of Chicago Press.

Bernstein, Peter. 1995. Interview by author. New York, NY. 31 January.

Bones, Jah. 1986. "Reggae Deejaying and Jamaican Afro-Lingua." In *The Language of the Black Experience: Cultural Expression through Word and Sound in the Caribbean and Black Britain,* edited by David Sutcliffe and Ansel Wong, 52–68. Oxford: Basil Blackwell.

Bourdieu, Pierre. 1977. *Outline of a Theory of Practice*. Cambridge: Cambridge University Press.

———. 1984. *Distinction: A Social Critique of the Judgement of Taste*. Cambridge: Harvard University Press.

Brown, Karen McCarthy. 1991. *Mama Lola: A Vodou Priestess in Brooklyn*. Berkeley: University of California Press.

Bruni, Frank. 1996. "Drawn to Gospel, If Not Gospels, Foreigners Arrive by Busload." *New York Times,* 24 Nov.: 37.

Burke, Kenneth. 1964. "Literature As Equipment for Living." In *Perspectives by Incongruity,* edited by Stanley Edgar Hyman, 100–109. Bloomington: Indiana University Press.

Burnim, Mellonee V. 1985. "The Black Gospel Music Tradition: A Complex of Ideology, Aesthetic, and Behavior." In *More Than Dancing: Essays on Afro-American Music and Musicians,* edited by Irene V. Jackson, 147–67. Westport, CT: Greenwood Press.

———. 1988. "Functional Dimensions of Gospel Music Performance." *Western Journal of Black Studies* 12(2): 112–21.

Burnim, Mellonee V., and Portia Maultsby. 1987. "From Backwoods to City Streets: The Afro-American Musical Journey." In *Expressively Black: The Cultural Basis of Ethnic Identity,* edited by Geneva Gay and Willie L. Baber, 109–36. New York: Praeger.

Byrnside, Ronald. 1975. "The Performer As Creator: Jazz Improvisation." In *Contemporary Music and Music Cultures,* edited by Bruno Nettl, Charles Hamm, and Ronald Brynside, 233–51. Englewood Cliffs, NJ: Prentice-Hall.

Collins, Edmund John. 1987. "Jazz Feedback to Africa." *American Music* 5: 176–93.

Comaroff, Jean. 1985. *Body of Power, Spirit of Resistance: The Culture and History of South African People*. Chicago: University of Chicago Press.

Combs-Schilling, M. E. 1989. *Sacred Performances: Islam, Sexuality, and Sacrifice*. New York: Columbia University Press.

Coplan, David. 1985. *In Township Tonight! South Africa's Black City Music and Theatre*. London: Longman.

Crouch, Stanley. 1990. "Chitlins at the Waldorf: The Work of Albert Murray." In *Notes of a Hanging Judge: Essays and Reviews, 1979–89,* 42–48. New York: Oxford University Press.

Csikszentmihalyi, Mihaly. 1982. "Toward a Psychology of Optimal Experience." *Review of Personality and Social Psychology* 3: 13–36.

————. 1988. "The Flow Experience and Its Significance for Human Psychology." In *Optimal Experience: Psychological Studies of Flow in Consciousness,* edited by Mihaly Csikszentmihalyi and Isabella Selega Csikszentmihalyi. Cambridge: Cambridge University Press, 15–35.

Eliade, Mircea. 1959. *The Sacred and the Profane: The Nature of Religion.* New York: Harcourt Brace.

Ellington, Duke. 1939. "Duke Says Swing Is Stagnant!" *Down Beat,* February: 2, 16–17.

Ellison, Ralph. 1964. *Shadow and Act.* New York: Random House.

Erlmann, Veit. 1991. *African Stars: Studies in Black South African Performance.* Chicago: University of Chicago Press.

Feld, Steven. 1984. "Sound Structure As Social Structure." *Ethnomusicology* 28: 383–409.

————. 1994a. "Aesthetics As Iconicity of Style (Uptown Title); or, (Downtown Title) 'Lift-Up-Over Sounding': Getting into the Kaluli Groove." In *Music Grooves: Essays and Dialogues,* edited by Charles Keil and Steven Feld, 109–50. Chicago: University of Chicago Press.

————. 1994b. "Communication, Music, and Speech about Music." In *Music Grooves: Essays and Dialogues,* edited by Charles Keil and Steven Feld, 77–95. Chicago: University of Chicago Press.

Fields, Barbara J. 1982. "Ideology and Race in America." In *Region, Race, and Reconstruction: Essays in Honor of C. Vann Woodward,* edited by J. Morgan Kousser and James M. McPherson, 143–77. New York: Oxford University Press.

Floyd, Samuel A., Jr. 1995. *The Power of Black Music: Interpreting Its History from Africa to the United States.* New York: Oxford University Press.

Fuller, Hoyt W. 1971. "Towards a Black Aesthetic." In *The Black Aesthetic,* edited by Addison Gayle Jr., 3–12. Garden City, NY: Doubleday.

Gabbard, Krin. 1995. "Introduction: The Jazz Canon and Its Consequences." In *Jazz among the Discourses,* edited by Krin Gabbard, 1–28. Durham, NC: Duke University Press.

Gates, Henry Louis, Jr. 1988. *The Signifying Monkey: A Theory of African-American Literary Criticism.* New York: Oxford University Press.

Gennari, John. 1991. "Jazz Criticism: Its Development and Ideologies." *Black American Literature Forum* 25: 449–523.

Gilroy, Paul. 1991a. *"There Ain't No Black in the Union Jack": The Cultural Politics of Race and Nation.* Chicago: University of Chicago Press.

————. 1991b. "It Ain't Where You're From, It's Where You're At: The Dialectics of Diasporic Identification." *Third Text* 13: 3–16.

————. 1993. *The Black Atlantic: Modernity and Double Consciousness.* Cambridge: Harvard University Press.

————. 1994. "Sounds Authentic: Black Music, Ethnicity, and the Challenge of a *Changing* Same." In *Imagining Home: Class, Culture and Nationalism in the African Diaspora,* edited by Sidney J. Lemelle and Robin D. G. Kelley, 93–117. London: Verso.

————. 1995. "Roots and Routes: Black Identity As an Outernational Project." In *Racial and Ethnic Identity: Psychological Development and Creative Expres-*

sion, edited by Herbert W. Harris, Howard C. Blue, and Ezra E. H. Griffith, 15–30. New York: Routledge.

Gioia, Ted. 1988. *The Imperfect Art: Reflections on Jazz and Modern Culture.* Oxford University Press.

Goffman, Erving. 1959. *The Presentation of Self in Everyday Life.* New York: Doubleday.

Gomes, Peter J. 1996. "Religion As Spectator Sport." *New York Times,* 28 Nov.: 29.

Gridley, Mark C. 1997. *Jazz Styles: History and Analysis.* 6th ed. Upper Saddle River, NJ: Prentice-Hall.

Guilbault, Jocelyne, et al. 1993. *Zouk: World Music in the West Indies.* Chicago: University of Chicago Press.

Gwaltney, John Langston. 1993. *Drylongso: A Self-Portrait of Black America.* New York: New Press.

Hall, Edward T. 1992. "Improvisation as an Acquired, Multilevel Process." *Ethnomusicology* 26: 223–35.

Haralambos, Michael. 1970. "Soul Music and Blues: Their Meaning and Relevance in Northern United States Black Ghettos." In *Afro-American Anthropology: Contemporary Perspectives,* edited by Norman E. Whitten Jr. and John F. Szwed, 367–84. New York: Free Press.

Harrison, Faye V. 1998. "Introduction: An African Diaspora Perspective for Urban Anthropology." *Urban Anthropology* 17: 111–41.

Hart, Antonio. 1994. Interview by author. Brooklyn, NY. 22 December.

———. 1995. Interview by author. Brooklyn, NY. 17 February.

Hebdige, Dick. 1979. *Subculture: The Meaning of Style.* London: Routledge.

Herskovits, Melville J. 1990. *The Myth of the Negro Past.* Boston: Beacon Press.

Higgins, Kathleen Marie. 1991. *The Music of Our Lives.* Philadelphia: Temple University Press.

Hobsbawm, Eric, and Terence Ranger, eds. 1983. *The Invention of Tradition.* Cambridge: Cambridge University Press.

Hymes, Dell. 1964. "Introduction: Toward Ethnographies of Communication." *American Anthropologist* 66(6): 1–34.

Irvine, Judith T. 1979. "Formality and Informality in Communicative Events." *American Anthropologist* 81: 773–90.

Jackson, Travis A. 1992. "Become Like One: Communication, Interaction, and the Development of Group Sound in Jazz Performance." Master's thesis, Columbia University.

———. 1998. "Performance and Musical Meaning: Analyzing 'Jazz' on the New York Scene." Ph.D. diss., Columbia University.

Jarab, Josef. 1985."Black Aesthetic: A Cultural or Political Concept." *Callaloo* 8(3): 587–93.

Johnson, Bruce. 1993. "Hear Me Talkin' to Ya: Problems of Jazz Discourse." *Popular Music* 12(1): 1–12.

Keil, Charles. 1991. *Urban Blues.* Chicago: University of Chicago Press.

Kelly, John D., and Martha Kaplan. 1990. "History, Structure, and Ritual." *Annual Review of Anthropology* 19: 119–50.

Kivy, Peter. 1990. *Music Alone: Philosophical Reflections on the Purely Musical Experience.* Ithaca, NY: Cornell University Press.

Kluckhohn, Clyde. 1942. "Myths and Rituals: A General Theory." *Harvard Theological Review* 35: 45–79.

Koch, Lawrence O. 1982. "Harmonic Approaches to the Twelve-Bar Blues Form." *Annual Review of Jazz Studies* 1: 59–71.

Leonard, Neil. 1987. *Jazz: Myth and Religion.* New York: Oxford University Press.

Levine, Lawrence W. 1977. *Black Culture and Black Consciousness: Afro-American Folk Thought from Slavery to Freedom.* New York: Oxford University Press.

Lewis, Alan. 1987. "The Social Interpretation of Modern Jazz." In *Lost in Music: Culture, Style and the Musical Event,* edited by Avron Levine White, 33–55. London: Routledge & Kegan Paul.

Lii, Jane H. 1995. "God, Gospel and the Camcorder." *New York Times,* 26 Mar.: 3.

Logan, Wendell. 1984. "The Ostinato Idea in Black Improvised Music: A Preliminary Investigation." *Black Perspective in Music* 12: 193–215.

Lomax, Alan. 1959. "Folk Song Style." *American Anthropologist* 61: 927–54.

———. 1976. *Cantometrics: An Approach to the Anthropology of Music.* Berkeley: University of California Extension Media Center.

Marks, Morton. 1974. "Uncovering Ritual Structures in Afro-American Music." In *Religious Movements in Contemporary America,* edited by Irving I. Zaretsky and Mark P. Leone, 60–134. Princeton: Princeton University Press.

Marshall, Christopher. 1982. "Towards a Comparative Aesthetics of Music." In *Cross-Cultural Perspectives on Music,* edited by Robert Falck and Tim Rice, 162–73. Toronto: University of Toronto Press.

Mensah, Atta Annan. 1971–72. "Jazz—The Round Trip." *Jazzforschung* 3–4 : 124–37.

Meyer, Leonard B. 1956. *Emotion and Meaning in Music.* Chicago: University of Chicago Press.

Monson, Ingrid. 1990. "Forced Migration, Asymmetrical Power Relations and African-American Music: Reformulation of Cultural Meaning and Musical Form." *World of Music* 32(3): 22–45.

———. 1991. "Musical Interaction in Modern Jazz: An Ethnomusicological Perspective." Ph.D. diss., New York University.

———. 1994. "Doubleness and Jazz Improvisation: Irony, Parody, and Ethnomusicology." *Critical Inquiry* 20: 283–313.

———. 1996. *Saying Something: Jazz Improvisation and Interaction.* Chicago: University of Chicago Press.

Murray, Albert. 1970. *The Omni-Americans: Some Alternatives to the Folklore of White Supremacy.* New York: Da Capo.

———. 1976. *Stomping the Blues.* New York: Da Capo.

Newsome, Sam. 1995. Interview by author. Brooklyn, NY. 5 February.

Pareles, Jon. 1996. "Jelly Roll and the Duke Join Wolfgang and Ludwig." *New York Times,* 2 July: C11, 15.

Powell, Richard J. 1989. "The Blues Aesthetic: Black Culture and Modernism." In *The Blues Aesthetic: Black Culture and Modernism,* edited by Richard J. Powell. Washington, DC: Washington Project for the Arts, 19–35.

———. 1994. "Art History and Black Memory: Toward a 'Blues Aesthetic.' " In *History and Memory in African-American Culture,* edited by Robert G. O'Meally and Geneviève Fabre, 228–43. New York: Oxford University Press.

Racy, Ali Jihad. 1991. "Creativity and Ambience: An Ecstatic Feedback Model from Arab Music." *World of Music* 33(3): 7–27.

Redman, Joshua. 1994. *Mood Swing*. Compact disc. Recorded New York, NY, 8–10 March 1994: Warner Brothers 9 45643-2.

———. 1995. Interview by author. New York, NY. 27 February.

Reyes Schramm, Adelaida. 1986. "Tradition in the Guise of Innovation: Music among a Refugee Population." *Yearbook for Traditional Music* 18: 91–101.

Roberts, John W. 1989. *From Trickster to Badman: The Black Folk Hero in Slavery and Freedom*. Philadelphia: University of Pennsylvania Press.

Rosenthal, David H. 1992. *Hard Bop: Jazz and Black Music, 1955–1965*. New York: Oxford University Press.

Salamone, Frank A. 1988. "The Ritual of Jazz Performance." *Play and Culture* 1: 85–104.

Schieffelin, Edward L. 1985. "Performance and the Cultural Construction of Reality." *American Ethnologist* 12: 707–24.

Scott, David. 1991. "This Event, That Memory: Notes on the Anthropology of African Diasporas in the New World." *Diaspora* 1: 261–84.

Seeger, Charles. 1977. "The Musicological Juncture: 1976." *Ethnomusicology* 21: 179–88.

Seremetakis, C. Nadia. 1991. *The Last Word: Women, Death, Divination in Inner Mani*. Chicago: University of Chicago Press.

Slonimsky, Nicolas. 1947. *Thesaurus of Scales and Melodic Patterns*. New York: Scribner's.

Small, Christopher. 1987a. *Music of the Common Tongue: Survival and Celebration in Afro-American Music*. New York: Riverrun Press.

———. 1987b. "Performance As Ritual: Sketch for an Enquiry into the True Nature of a Symphony Concert." In *Lost in Music: Culture, Style and the Musical Event*, edited by Avron Levine White, 6–32. London: Routledge & Kegan Paul.

Starks, George L., Jr. 1981. "The Performance Context and Sociocultural Perspective: Avenues to the Understanding of African American Music." *Proceedings of NAJE Research* 1: 100–105.

———. 1993. "Jazz Literature and the African American Aesthetic." In *The African Aesthetic: Keeper of the Traditions*, edited by Kariamu Welsh-Asante, 143–57. Westport, CT: Greenwood Press.

Strunk, Steven. 1988. "Harmony (i)." In *New Grove Dictionary of Jazz*, edited by Barry Kernfeld. New York: Macmillan.

Stuckey, Sterling. 1987. *Slave Culture: Nationalist Theory and the Foundations of Black America*. New York: Oxford University Press, 1987.

Stuempfle, Stephen. 1995. *The Steelband Movement: The Forging of a National Art in Trinidad and Tobago*. Philadelphia: University of Pennsylvania Press.

Tallmadge, William. 1984. "Blue Notes and Blue Tonality." *Black Perspective in Music* 12: 155–65.

Taylor, Arthur. 1993. *Notes and Tones: Musician-to-Musician Interviews*. New York: Da Capo.

Tirro, Frank. 1967. "The Silent Theme Tradition in Jazz." *Musical Quarterly* 53: 313–34.

Tucker, Mark, ed. 1993. *The Duke Ellington Reader*. New York: Oxford University Press.

Turner, Victor. 1969. *The Ritual Process: Structure and Anti-Structure*. Ithaca, NY: Cornell University Press.

————. 1974a. *Dramas, Fields, and Metaphors: Symbolic Action in Human Society.* Ithaca, NY: Cornell University Press.

————. 1974b. "Liminal to Liminoid, in Play, Flow, and Ritual: An Essay in Comparative Symbology." *Rice University Studies* 60(3): 53–92.

————. 1982. *From Ritual to Theatre: The Human Seriousness of Play.* New York: PAJ Publications.

van Gennep, Arnold. 1960. *The Rites of Passage.* Chicago: University of Chicago Press.

Ward, Brian. 1998. *Just My Soul Responding: Rhythm and Blues, Black Consciousness, and Race Relations.* Berkeley: University of California Press.

Waterman, Christopher Alan. 1990. *Jùjú: A Social History and Ethnography of an African Popular Music.* Chicago: University of Chicago Press.

Waters, Anita M. 1985. *Race, Class, and Political Symbols: Rastafari and Reggae in Jamaican Elections.* New Brunswick, NJ: Transaction Books.

Welburn, Ron. 1971. "The Black Aesthetic Imperative." In *The Black Aesthetic,* edited by Addison Gayle Jr., 132–49. Garden City, NY: Doubleday.

————. 1987. "Jazz Magazines of the 1930s: An Overview of Their Provocative Journalism." *American Music* 5: 255–70.

Whitten, Norman E., and John F. Szwed., eds. 1970. *Afro-American Anthropology: Contemporary Perspectives.* New York: Free Press.

Wilson, Olly. 1974. "The Significance of the Relationship between Afro-American Music and West African Music." *Black Perspective in Music* 2: 3–22.

————. 1985. "The Association of Movement and Music As a Manifestation of a Black Conceptual Approach to Music Making." In *More Than Dancing: Essays on Afro-American Music and Musicians,* edited by Irene V. Jackson, 9–23. Westport, CT: Greenwood Press.

————. 1992. "The Heterogeneous Sound Ideal in African-American Music." In *New Perspectives on Music: Essays in Honor of Eileen Southern,* edited by Josephine Wright and Samuel A. Floyd Jr., 327–38. Warren, MI: Harmonie Park Press.

Wilson, Steve. 1995. Interview by author. New York, NY. 2 March.

CHAPTER 3

Communities of Style: Musical Figures of Black Diasporic Identity

Veit Erlmann

Spike Lee is now widely acclaimed as one of America's leading film-makers. But critics also reckon with him as a major intellectual force, prominently intervening in such films as *Do the Right Thing, Jungle Fever,* and *Malcolm X* in some of the most heated debates over issues of race, morality, and gender. One of the less celebrated of Lee's interventions is *Do It A Cappella,* a "filmic tour" of mostly black vocal harmony styles that premiered in the PBS *Great Performances* series in 1990 and was subsequently released on compact disc. The show involved a number of well-known and also less well known African American acts such as hip-hoppers True Image, the veteran Persuasions, and the six-piece gospel group Take 6. Equally represented are the white doo-woppers Rockapella and, no doubt in recognition of the globality of black musical intercommunication, the Anglo-African female sextet Mint Juleps and Ladysmith Black Mambazo from South Africa. As for the latter group's participation, it consisted of a rousing performance of the South African national anthem "Nkosi Sikelel IAfrika," the song "Nansi Imali" from the 1981 album *Phansi Emgodini* (In the mines), and a joint performance with the Mint Juleps of "The Lion Sleeps Tonight" (Lee

1990, Ladysmith 1981). It is a reading of the latter that I would like to concentrate on here.

The fact that an Anglo-African and a black South African choral group teamed up under the auspices of one of America's most controversial filmmakers is not accidental. Spike Lee's cinematographic work and political vision, as most critics seem to agree, is tainted by a strong dosage of racial exclusivism and neonationalism, by what Michael Eric Dyson (1993) calls "a static conception of racial identity." It is hard to disagree with Dyson and other critics, but a glance at a piece of work such as *Do It A Cappella* might also reveal a more nuanced, if also somewhat indefinite picture: an attempt, namely, to account for the more dynamic, messy aspects of black diasporic identity. For, as I shall argue, what we can see taking place in many of the songs assembled on Lee's compilation is what I would call endotropic performance, the sonic construction of a black diasporic identity by way not of tightly bound ideological constructs but through the shared experience of style. Performances such as "The Lion Sleeps Tonight" create a black ecumene of listeners not by delineating crisply separated, racially defined orders of meaning but by focusing attention on the act of communication as such. Such performances are essentially phatic; they do not concern themselves with a meaning but with what goes on when black people converse with one another in certain ways and thereby mark themselves as different.

My hypothesis comes out of the context of a larger project in which I am concerned with bringing together a set of phenomena arising from what I call the global imagination: the fact that beginning in the late nineteenth century, in the West and Africa, a complex play of absences and presences inscribes itself in the very syntax of all kinds of discourses of racial, ethnic, national, and sexual identity (Erlmann 1999). Autobiographies, Christian hymns, travel diaries, colonial shows, Michael Jackson concerts and music videos—all in one way or another register the strange situation in which a person's understanding of himself or herself and their sense of the social world no longer coincide with the place in which they take place and are increasingly being shaped by other people's understandings elsewhere. And, as I found, as varied as the "contents"of all these discourses may be, they do not exist independently of the forms the new media of the modern age impose on them. One of the areas in which this seemed particularly crucial and perhaps also instructive in a more general sense was the tense forms of "double consciousness" that W. E. B. Du Bois saw as the central figure of twentieth-century black American culture, and I would add, of black diasporic culture as well.

The argument that I am sketching here in part intersects with the intriguing attempts by Henry Louis Gates Jr. to broaden the concept of signifying from a form of verbal abuse in black American folklore and everyday practice to a general principle of African American aesthetics. Signifyin(g), according to Gates, is more than the dozens, capping, or naming. It is a pervasive mode of communication under which are subsumed several other rhetorical tropes, including metaphor, metonymy, metalepsis, hyperbole, and also irony and parody. Although transcending the realm of politics, signifyin(g) is a language of blackness that enables the black person to communicate behind masks, in a linguistic universe shielded from white control. In short, signifyin(g) is "the black trope of tropes, the figure for black rhetorical figures" (Gates 1988: 51).

Gates's notion of signifyin(g) includes occasional references to music and thus, not surprisingly, has found ready acceptance among scholars of African American music, informing work on funk, pop, on parody and irony in jazz, and also techniques of troping in the blues (Brown 1994; Brackett 1995: 108–56; Monson 1994; Floyd 1995: 212–26). While I do not deny the importance of irony and parody in a great many African American performance traditions, I am reluctant to grant signifying in music the same general status as a governing aesthetic principle as in Gates's theory of African American literary criticism. The principal reason for this is the fact that distinctions between, say, ordinary and figurative uses are much more problematic and much less clear-cut in music than they are in language. Regardless of the specific meanings of figuration in Western music, no apparent case can be made for a general rhetoric of music. Indirection, in its most general sense, is the very essence of musical performance.

Despite its limited applicability, then, outside the literary field, the point where Gates's concept may be usefully applied to musical analysis is in the more extended and "thicker" meaning of signifyin(g) as repetition that aims at foregrounding the signifier itself. For signifyin(g), as Gates suggests, self-consciously advertises its rhetorical status. By organizing its syntagmatic structure around repetition, refiguration, and variation, signifying discourses foreground styling rather than the mimetic representation of novel content (Gates 1988: 79). Or, put another way, while in standard English usage signification denotes meaning, in the black tradition it denotes *ways of meaning* (81). In a broader sense, one might even argue that what signifyin(g) constitutes is a black semiotics proper, a vernacular science of the sign and the paradigm. But whereas Gates seems to limit this definition of signifyin(g) to relations between texts, to the kinds of double-voiced shifts and displacements that obtain when one text tropes another, I would suggest that this formal principle is also key to black performance even within the same piece of music or within a single performance.

What does this mean? At the broadest level, African performance and all diasporic musical styles that flow from it are characterized by repetition. There is a wide spectrum of forms in which repetition occurs, from the cyclical recurrence of short patterns to the polyrhythmic interlocking of several such contrasting cycles and larger call-and-response structures.[1] The most important characteristic, however, of the cyclic structure of African music and the main point where it differs from Western types of repetition lies in the fact that repetition must be thought of here as *practice*. The cycles of African music focus attention on how things are being done rather than on what externalities are being signaled and pictured by them. African music works by implication, not by explication. It emphasizes manner rather than matter, and temporal flow is more important to it than static representation. Or, as ethnomusicologist and drummer John M.Chernoff puts it in what is still one of the best discussions of African rhythm and musical aesthetics:

> African music is a cultural activity which reveals a group of people organizing and involving themselves with their own communal relationships . . . The aesthetic point of this exercise is not to reflect a reality which *stands behind* it but to ritualize a reality that is *within* it (Chernoff 1979: 36).

Yet these features of African musical performance exceed purely technical or aesthetic concerns. Embedded in them are some of the cardinal principles of African ethics and social conduct. Repetition in African (or, for that matter, any non-Western) performance does not aim at a loss of the subject. Contrary to the massive misinterpretations of "primitive" music in Western philosophical dogma and pop ideology, African music in and of itself is seldom trance inducing, and it does not as a rule serve to remove the social inhibitions that supposedly weigh down individual spontaneity like in the West. Quite to the contrary, the repetitiveness of much African performance calibrates and stabilizes; it fosters mediated involvement and community building. The cycles and recurring patterns of African music require and effectively promote composure rather than self-abandonment and ecstasy. Music making in Africa, in Chernoff's phrase, "is above all an occasion for the demonstration of character" (151).[2]

I am not stressing these distinctions idly here. It has not been my intention to compare two idioms that are in themselves rather incompatible. Nor did I wish to dispute the fact that in Western music, too, repetition plays a significant role. Rather, what I want to describe is the discursive field in which musical differences become associated with certain notions of racial exclusivity; how, for instance, the question of repetition has been reduced by authors such as James Snead and Tricia Rose to a sine qua non of black identity or, alternatively, is seen by Theodor W. Adorno and other Marxist critics as the mark of cultural regression and commodification (Snead 1984; Rose 1994: 71f; Adorno 1941). There are several implications of this for my contention that black ecumenes are communities of style. The most important of these is the notion that the "blackness" of iterative musical structures, their unique status as a vernacular semiotics of sorts, is determined by complex notions of personhood and communal ethos and by historically determined practices of intercultural exchange. Critical differences between black and European musics are never given. They must be placed in the dialogic relationships between Africa, the diaspora, and also Europe (Middleton 1986). In other words, even though communities may seek to establish themselves around markers of racial identity, such coalescence of sound and society is never stable. Central to my argument, then, is the question of how such aesthetic differences and definitions of personal identity are historically determined, sonically mediated, and infallibly caught up in a vortex of racial ambiguity. I want to explore how specific uses of repetition frequently come to reflect and sustain a dialectic of racial feeling, a slippery politics of cross-racial desire and repulsion. Most of all, I am fascinated by the shifts and revisions that arise from cross-racial handlings of repetition and from the layering of different modes of reiteration in crossover musical styles.

One example of the kind of codings across racial lines I have in mind is Eric Lott's incisive discussion of mid-nineteenth-century minstrel sheet music in his book *Love and Theft* (1995). Drawing on the findings of earlier scholars that from the 1840s multiple repetitions of brief phrases had become the chief structural principle of minstrel music, Lott argues that these willed attempts to approximate the effects found in slave songs were more than "handicraft" devices deployed by the burgeoning music industry to disguise the alienated character of its product.

They were performing "fairly direct kinds of cultural work," he says, "of both class and race." Although tied to heterogeneous audiences, by using racial meanings as a cover for class conflict minstrel music helped to "represent" plebeian theatergoers (180). At the same time, this potentially "insurgent" impulse, by girding itself with a chimerical, performed "blackness," was channeled into a kind of "bland, albeit racialized, gentility." In the final analysis, what the repetition found in minstrel music represented amounted to a "plundering of black music," as Lott puts it, an act of dispossession whose outcome was a "hesitation between types, a tension between circularity and teleology, a wink at the counterfeit alongside a nod toward 'blackness' " (182).

Lott's hypothesis would deserve careful ethnographic substantiation, I believe, especially with regard to the way these different types of repetition together constituted a variable field in which different "racial effects" were being brought forth. For instance, it may be worth testing Lott's assertion that the minstrel show staged conflicted (white) racial subjectivities by vacillating between what he calls the "libidinal" and "ego" functions of musical repetition. The emptying out of the self achieved by the rapturous, cyclic motion of short repeated phrases in the minstrel show immersed white spectators in blissful experiences of boundary crossing into realms of racial otherness. Intermeshed with these were the more extended strophic structures associated with European folk music and the concomitant enjoyment of selfhood, both of which translate feelings of racial mastery (184). Lott's main concern is of course with a specific, historically determined set of racial subjectivities turning on the power imbalances of slave-holding antebellum America and attendant white crises of identity. But by attending to the discourses and logic of racial exchange, his analysis also usefully tackles the more general question of how performance provides an arena for the construction of precarious racial identities.

In any case, returning to "Mbube" or, rather, to "The Lion Sleeps Tonight," what an intervention in black diasporic cultural politics such as Lee's compilation illustrates is how a parallel set of black racial feelings is girded by the ambiguities of cultural and musical form and how the construction of black ecumenes can be and inevitably is complicated by a jumbling of racial signifiers that simultaneously negate and call forth exclusivist, essentialist views of black difference. The musical shifts that underlie "The Lion Sleeps Tonight" configure tropes of blackness as well as whiteness and through these index the social constellations they encompass. In order to gain a sense of these complicated reversals and inversions, and before entering into a detailed structural analysis, a few words about the song's origins are in order. "The Lion Sleeps Tonight" is based on one of the great South African classics of all time: the 1939 hit record "Mbube." Its composer, Solomon Linda, is recognized as one of the great figures in the history of black South African music, his work (he and his choir, the Evening Birds, recorded slightly more than forty songs between 1938 and 1954) representing the apex of what should be properly called the golden era of Zulu migrant workers' music and of a genre bearing the name of his most celebrated composition, *mbube*.[3]

Readers familiar with the history of American popular music are perhaps more likely to associate "Mbube" with Pete Seeger and the Weavers, the folk revival of the 1960s, and perhaps also the Tokens. And indeed, as we shall see, it was the cover versions of "Mbube" by these two groups that later had a considerable impact on endotropic black reworkings of Linda's song. But before I go into some of these, let me quickly review some of the song's main structural elements.

First, the distribution of vocal parts. There are four parts called soprano, *altha* (alto), *thena* (tenor), and *bhes* (bass). The soprano part is sung by the leader, while alto and tenor are sung by one singer each. The bass part is taken by the remaining singers and consists of a fairly busy ostinato pattern—repeated seventeen times—whose strong triadic structure suggests the harmonic framework of the song (Figure 3-1). Alto and tenor, for their part, frequently provide filling-in parts, sometimes moving in parallel thirds or fourths (Figure 3-2). The soprano, finally, sings three distinct melodic patterns, each with their own variations (Figures 3-3, 3-4, and 3-5).

The second element is the multipart organization of the vocal parts, here especially the responsorial relationship between the chorus and the leader. What is striking here is the absence of what has been identified as one the main principles of African vocal polyphony: the nonsimultaneous entry of the vocal parts (Rycroft 1967: 90). There exists in the recording under consideration a fit between the solo vocal line and the chorus so closed and fixed that it is impossible to consider this synchronism as the complete overlapping of "call" and "response." The reason

FIGURE 3-1. "Mbube," bass pattern.

FIGURE 3-2. "Mbube," *altha* and *thena.*

FIGURE 3-3. "Mbube," pattern A.

FIGURE 3-4. "Mbube," pattern B.

FIGURE 3-5. "Mbube," pattern C.

for this is that the lead singer's part, in the terms of Western functional harmony, is contingent on the chordal movement of the chorus. Throughout the seventeen cycles the beginnings of Linda's solo phrases coincide with the first notes of the choral response, and in all cases it is the tonic that is being stated or implied in all four parts.

The regularity exhibited by the responsorial structure moving in synchrony with the basic harmonic framework is enhanced by the third and last feature of "Mbube": the pairing of basic phrases and their syntactic arrangement in an overall symmetry. For instance, each cycle consists of four bars, and each bar contains one chord. Moreover, two of the three melodic patterns sung by the lead singer are grouped in strict binary fashion, while the third pattern occurs only once at the end, thus somehow forming the symmetrical counterpart to the silent cycle one. Thus, the overall architecture of the song presents itself as shown in Figure 3-6.

The point hardly needs to be labored. None of the features I have pinpointed here qualifies "Mbube" as the founding text of a genre that is now generally accepted as belonging to the Zulu traditional core. And, clearly, Linda's song is not, as one observer of the 1939 recording session echoed white mythology, the fortuitous result of an on-the-spot improvisation, "with that natural feel for harmony inherent in the African" (Trewhela 1980: 138).

But how can one hear a song such as this with an intraracial, endotropic ear when obviously so much of it appears to be so different from anything commonly associated with African musical traditions? One way of tackling this question would be to listen for traces in "Mbube" of Zulu musical tradition. And indeed, on closer inspection, we find that there are several elements in Linda's recording that disrupt the non-African regularity exhibited in the three areas of musical organization I have just mentioned. Thus, with the exception of the first occur-

Introduction	
solo, chorus	bass pattern

1	2	3	4
A	A	B	B

5	6	7	8
A	A	B	B'

9	10	11	12
A	A'	B''	B''

13	14	15	16	finis
A'	A''	C	B	rit, chord

FIGURE 3-6. Overall architecture of "Mbube" by Solomon Linda.

rence of the lead singer's solo, Linda always anticipates the main beat of his line by a fraction. Other features include the timbral textures of booming basses and male falsetto voice that, apart from indexing a Western mixed choir, in an endotropic perspective, suggest specific— and not necessarily gendered—notions of emotional intensity and active participation.

By far the best way, however, of tracing these specifically African elements is by considering the fine grain of the temporal organization, the minute spaces, displacements, and "participatory discrepancies," to use Charles Keil's terminology, that disrupt the closure of Western harmonic form and phrase structure. Of fundamental importance here is a tension between the squareness of the repetitive groundwork and a certain laggard motion that toward the end of the recording seems to slow the overall tempo, as if trying to hold back the cyclic iteration.

Clearly, then, "Mbube" exhibits a number of ambiguities, if not antagonisms, that do not permit us to comfortably link the song to a specific African essence or to view it as the product of black submission under the dominant culture. But what is the song really? A parody of Western music? An acceptance of the dominant culture and the music industry? Answers to these questions are crucial to an understanding of black diasporic interpolations of "Mbube," but they are difficult to give on the basis of a structural analysis alone. Rather, a genre of migrant workers' performance such as *mbube* in itself offers a medium for working through the complex experience of moving in and out of multiple social contexts and identities while at the same time offering a symbolic universe for the construction of personal identity and character.

Linda's "Mbube" reflects all these conflicting strands of the migrant experience in ways that are located within its very syntax and, more important perhaps, in the chain of signifiers it brings to the fore. Here it becomes apparent why in examining hybrid forms it is fruitless to concern ourselves with determining "parent cultures" or degrees of acculturation and authenticity and why instead we should focus on the ways in which such permutations create a realm of discursive complicity, a sphere of inclusive exclusivity in which the terms of primal reference, mimetic representation, and longing are inextricably jumbled. "Mbube," then, is not concerned with setting up a separate code or with ironically counterposing its own universe of authentic truth against the dominant code. Although such signifyin(g) techniques are not entirely absent from black South African performance, Linda does not parody the rigidity of Western mass-produced musical forms. Rather, his song subtly inflects the received structure and uses it as a mask behind which to focus on the chain of signifiers. The repetitiveness of "Mbube," its sameness, even where it seems to be cast in a Western mold, underscores a statement of black difference, and thus it conforms with the way in which black performers in general draw attention to the process of signification, rather than meaning itself.

To what extent does all this apply to the recording by the Mint Juleps and Ladysmith Black Mambazo heard at the beginning? In order to answer this question, another, more prolonged digression will be necessary. We have to consider some of the cover versions that emerged after Linda's 1939 recording, especially two early U.S. versions that proved particularly influential in determining later black South African and African American handlings of Linda's song. The first version is a Decca recording made in 1952 under the title "Wimoweh" by Pete Seeger's Weavers, accompanied by a big band under Gordon Jenkins. Seeger claimed that the Weavers had learned the song from Linda's record and that he played the notes "almost as I learned them" (Seeger 1992: 576). Problematic as such claims to authenticity undoubtedly on many levels are, in the case of the second cover version, "The Lion Sleeps Tonight" by the Tokens, they are almost impossible to sustain. Backed by Neil Sedaka's band and sung to new lyrics by producers Hugo Peretti and Luigi Creatore, the Tokens' version not only topped the charts for three consecutive weeks in 1961 but also turned Linda's original song into a pop song along the lines of Tin Pan Alley, and, as we shall see, subjected "Mbube" to yet another, this time even more ambiguous process of racial interpretation (Bronson 1985: 102; Shapiro and Pollack 1985: 2058).[4]

Let me briefly compare these two cover versions with "Mbube." To begin with the first feature of Linda's song—the distribution of parts—both the Weavers and the Tokens retain the basic quaternary structure of a bass providing some sort of ground pattern, two middle voices, and the falsetto lead singer. Similarly, both the Weavers and the Tokens make use of middle parts singing the familiar pattern of three eighth notes, though with the words changed from the three-syllabled *i-mbu-be* to the four-syllabled *e-wi-mo-weh,* the rhythm shifts to a brisker upbeat pattern.

Similarly, like in Linda's original, there is in both the Weavers' and the Tokens' version a high-registered or falsetto lead vocalist singing a combination of the three melodic patterns. Although the overall ratio of permutations and variations is greatly reduced, it is the third pattern that becomes subject to the most far-reaching revision, a revision that must be seen in close relationship with the third and last feature I singled out

FIGURE 3-7. "The Lion Sleeps Tonight," enlarged pattern C.

in my analysis of Linda's "Mbube": the overall architecture of the song and its pop song–like division into binary phrases. It is in this area that the Tokens' version diverges most prominently from the 1939 recording. As in most cover versions, the third melodic pattern becomes the central element, a hook that is repeated with little or no variation at all. Moreover, the Tokens rework the pattern so as to expand it to a Western eight-bar phrase divided into two sections, the second of which typically begins on the dominant—thereby suggesting "narrative" flow—before it reverts to the sameness of the first four bars (Figure 3-7).

Equally in keeping with Western models is the typical Tin Pan Alley ABABCB format. The Tokens divide the song into four cycles of sixteen bars each, with a "bridge" of eight bars after the third cycle (played by soprano sax and the obbligato voice) and a "fade-out" of eight bars after the fourth cycle (Figure 3-8). Each of these cycles is further subdivided into two sections of eight bars separated by a voice shouting "hop-hop," thus creating the impression of contrast or of solo and refrain.

My brief analysis leads to two conclusions. First, it is clear that in the hands of Western mainstream pop musicians, the microdynamics of African repetitive musical forms undergo fundamental shifts. Second, the difference that results from these shifts is not primarily of interest at the level of the signified but as the site of specific encounters between socially and culturally determined processes of signification, mimesis, and duplication. What I am interested in, above all, is the racial underpinnings of such mass-mediated practices. Although one might possibly conceive of some generic Africanness or "happy safari" feeling as one of the meanings commonly invested in "The Lion Sleeps Tonight," of greater interest to me here are the racial pressures and social tensions that help to produce and shape the syntax of such covers.

1	2	3	4
C	C	-	-

5	6	7	8
C	C' obbligato I	A	A

9	10	11	12
C	C' obbligato II	A	A'

13	14	15	16
- obbligato II saxophone	- obbligato II saxophone	C	C' obbligato I

17	18	19	20
B obbligato I	A obbligato I	C	C (fade)

FIGURE 3-8. "The Lion Sleeps Tonight," song form.

It is here that the Tokens offer a fascinating clue to the complex interplay of racial fear and fascination occasioned and reflected by "The Lion Sleeps Tonight." "We were embarrassed by it," member Phil Margo recalled the group's reaction to RCA's decision to release the song (Bronson 1985: 102). The remark is revealing. Embarrassed by what? By the inane minstrel lyrics about lions in the jungle and peaceful villages? By Mitch Margo's trite falsetto? Whether the Tokens' embarrassment confined itself to matters of musical taste or was motivated by political awareness is not clear. What *is* clear is that the Tokens took the song for a "folksong" and that they were familiar with Linda's original and also with Pete Seeger's remake. And so, I would suggest, what Phil Margo's embarrassment really was about was a sense of guilt, a tacit admission of the industry's and the group's complicity in the plundering and counterfeiting of black culture.

I do not make this charge lightly. The ownership of cultural capital is a matter of considerable importance to black South Africans, as it is, of course, to African Americans (Meintjes 1990). More significant, what makes certain forms of intercultural "borrowing" so vexing and guilt ridden is not so much the fact of theft posing as some more legitimate form of exchange as it is the way such mass-mediated transactions of cultural capital between Africa and the West are cryptically configured in shifts of musical form and how, at the same time, these shifts gloss over the power imbalances of such transactions.

I use the somewhat undetermined and ambiguous term *transaction* advisedly here. For the "breaks" and "fills" the Tokens use for veiling the deadly monotony of their version are false currency. They are, as Carol J. Clover puts it in a parallel discussion of white appropriations of black dance in film, "the 'memories' that surface in the process of 'forgetting,' as though in a perverse bargain, they must be admitted *in order* to be overridden" (Clover 1995). In the same breath as the drum triplets and the "hop-hop" shouts remember the "folk" origins of "Mbube," they forget them. Thus, regardless of their intended meanings—"tom-toms," "savages," whatever—their function is indeed purely nominal. They pretend to restore in a token act of equal exchange to the original a racial authenticity that they denied to it by counterfeiting it in the first place. This, I believe, is the true reason for the popularity of a song such as "The Lion Sleeps Tonight." It is the inscrutability of these racial encodings, their character as a social hieroglyph, that explains the grip the Tin Pan Alley remake of "Mbube" has on Western audiences.

After this excursion into the music industry's racialization of musical form let me, at long last, return to Spike Lee, the Mint Juleps, and Ladysmith Black Mambazo. Black South African performers have always been keenly aware of the parallels between their own vocal traditions and African American forms of harmony singing, even though the opportunities for such intercultural comparisons may have been few prior to the 1950s, and such staples of African American performance as gospel quartet singing remained altogether unknown in South Africa. But as the recent work of Ladysmith Black Mambazo after *Graceland* demonstrates, the group's interest in black American vocal traditions deepened as they came into contact with black performers in the diaspora, such as the Fairfield Four, Four Eagle Gospel Singers, the Birmingham Sunlights, the Winans, and, last but not least, the Mint Juleps.

As for the last, the recording that issued from their encounter with Ladysmith Black Mambazo in Spike Lee's documentary is characterized by two partly contradictory, partly complementary tendencies. Ladysmith Black Mambazo, for instance, throughout the performance hardly swerves from Linda's original, maintaining the basic simplicity and brittle balance I described earlier between Western four-square regularity and African circularity. The Mint Juleps, by contrast, follow the format firmly fixed by three decades of covering, at best underpinning

Linda's basic structure with somewhat richer harmonies or by propping up—or, rather, watering down—the "African" four-bar cycle to a standard pop song eight-bar phrase.

These Western revisions are further accentuated by the overall imbalance in the entire performance between the two groups and, hence, between echoes of Linda's original and Western cover versions. Thus, although Ladysmith Black Mambazo starts the song, they slip into the background in the middle of the song, only to reemerge fully in the final part of the performance in a way that comes very close to the Linda original.

Yet in spite of all these imbalances, "The Lion Sleeps Tonight" also has something of a recuperative effort. Not only was Lee's project as a whole framed as a nostalgic search for the good old days of doo-wop in Brooklyn, but discernible in the collaborative venture of the Mint Juleps and Ladysmith Black Mambazo is also a clear attempt to arrive at a certain integration, to achieve what Paul Gilroy has called "diasporic intimacy." This endeavor is noticeable at several moments in the performance, but especially when both groups disrupt the binary syntactic structure by first polyphonically juxtaposing the first melodic line and the third—the "hook"—and then launching into a spirited interlocking of different variants of the second melodic line (Figure 3-9).

To wit, this innocent little device leaves intact the Western idea—present in earlier cover versions but also to a lesser degree in the original "Mbube" itself—of highlighting contrasting melodic patterns as a means to achieve narrative progression and lyrical density. But at the

FIGURE 3-9. "The Lion Sleeps Tonight," Mint Juleps and Ladysmith Black Mambazo.

same time the juxtaposition of these melodic patterns is entirely located on a metacommunicative level. The patterns confront not so much different orders of meaning—orders that, as we have seen, are difficult to connect to the hybrid jumbling of musical matter present even in Linda's song—but two profoundly related and yet highly distinct ways of signifying: repetition as a commercial process—represented here by the "hook"—and repetition as practice, as the African mode of interaction required for the demonstration of character. In this way, the overlaying of patterns seeks to draw attention to itself. It is a self-referential move that foregrounds the process of communication itself and the pleasure of endotropic listening that it affords.

Clearly, then, the Mint Juleps and Ladysmith Black Mambazo are not merely invoking tradition, restating an authentic, unproblematic original as a means to consolidate diasporic unity. Rather, they seem to acknowledge the fact that while modern mass cultural reworkings of black traditions are produced, in Gilroy's phrase, "in the long shadow" of black ancestral traditions, they also occur "in the jaws of modern experience"(Gilroy 1993: 101). But above all, it is not a racial signified itself that is being envisaged by these creative labors. It is rather, as Gilroy states, "the rituals of performance that provide prima facie evidence of linkage between black cultures."

In conclusion, let me refer to an idea introduced by the German philosopher of cynical reason, Peter Sloterdijk, in his book on the hyperpolitics of the twentieth century (Sloterdijk 1993). One way of reading the history of political ideas, Sloterdijk writes, is to see in them a series of attempts at resolving a dilemma: the paradox, namely, that the longer we undergo experiences with those of our own kind the more it becomes evident that we do not get along with them. Therefore, Sloterdijk argues, all known forms of politics have consisted of the art of the possible, of the ability to think the widest possible community—primal horde, tribe, nation—and to ensure its survival through the successful manipulation of all-inclusive, collective imaginations and autohypnoses (11–12, 41). But, Sloterdijk cautions, the price man had to pay for achieving this goal is high, too high. In the age of hyperpolitics, everything reaches a point of no return: raw materials without return, species without return, atmospheres without return, and, ultimately, human beings without return. And so, Sloterdijk concludes, in the age of the "last" people, it is time to reconsider smaller forms of association in which man must learn anew the oldest art, that of reproducing man through man (79–81). When all known political forms fall apart, he seems to suggest, when the supraorders of Empire, the nation-state, Eastern bloc, and Western bloc desintegrate, it is time to think about new, more small-scale models for what is humanly possible.

In my essay I have chosen a different line of reasoning. Diasporic performances such as "The Lion Sleeps Tonight" provide eloquent proof of the impossibility of seizing on music as a means to sustain an organic blackness. They support the notion that black ecumenes operate within an impossible logic of sameness and difference. But more than anything else, they demonstrate the crucial role the autohypnoses and fictions of identity and global order, with all their contradictory intermixtures and mirrored affinities, play in formulating the rudiments of a politics of the twenty-first century. Although Sloterdijk's analysis is compelling, I do not think that the answer to the world's relentless drive toward ever vaster, ever more all-embracing forms of association lies in a new paleopolitics, a retreat into the insular, the social uterus. Rather it seems to me that it is in the arts that we can begin to recognize the irrevocable interdependency, complicity, and even contamination of people, technologies, cultural topographies, and musical practices and their potential in a fully globalized world. The question, then, is not what truth may reside in any given musical style—and, hence, what forms of truthful living might possibly be constructed through and out of it—but rather whether the truth about Western music, Ladysmith Black Mambazo, and Michael Jackson, the truth about South Africa and the West, might not turn out to lie elsewhere, in their inescapable relatedness with one another and with all the other musics they are surrounded by. Put another way, while we may well have to take seriously the sort of strategic essentialism implied in musical constructions of modern black political cultures as pure and unified, the more pressing question to me seems to be this: how fictions of black identity, and, for that matter, any diasporic identity may invigorate a different kind of hyperpolitics, a future politics and cultural practice that is perhaps better understood as the art of the impossible.

Notes

[1]For good overviews of African rhythm, see Robert Kauffman (1980).

[2]For a good overview of African performance practice and, therein, a discussion of repetition, see Margaret Thompson Drewal (1991).

[3]On Linda and *mbube,* see Veit Erlmann (1996: 60–69).

[4]The recording is RCA 447-0702.

References

Adorno, Theodor W. 1941. "On Popular Music." *Studies in Philosophy and Social Sciences* 9: 17–48.

Brackett, David. 1995. "James Brown's 'Superbad' and the Double-Voiced Utterance." In *Interpreting Popular Music,* edited by David Brackett, 108–56. Cambridge: Cambridge University Press.

Bronson, Fred. 1985. *The Billboard Book of Number One Hits: The Inside Story Behind the Top of the Charts.* New York: Billboard Publications.

Brown, Matthew. 1994. "Funk Music As Genre: Black Aesthetics, Apocalyptic Thinking and Urban Protest in Post-1965 African–American Pop." *Cultural Studies* 8/3 (1994): 484–508.

Chernoff, John M. 1979. *African Rhythm and African Sensibility: Aesthetics and Social Action in African Musical Idioms.* Chicago: University of Chicago Press.

Clover, Carol J. 1995. "Dancin' in the Rain." *Critical Inquiry* 24: 722–47.

Drewal, Margaret Thompson. 1991. "The State of Research on Performance in Africa." *African Studies Review* 34(3): 1–64.

Dyson, Michael Eric. 1993. *Reflecting Black: African American Cultural Criticism.* Minneapolis: University of Minnesota Press.

Erlmann, Veit. 1996. *Nightsong: Performance, Power and Practice in South Africa.* Chicago: University of Chicago Press.

———. 1999. *Music, Modernity and the Global Imagination: South Africa and the West.* New York: Oxford University Press.

Floyd, Samuel A., Jr. 1995. *The Power of Black Music: Interpreting Its History from Africa to the United States.* New York: Oxford University Press.

Gates, Henry Louis, Jr. 1988. *The Signifying Monkey: A Theory of Afro-American Literary Criticism.* New York: Oxford University Press.

Gilroy, Paul. 1993. *The Black Atlantic: Modernity and Double Consciousness.* Cambridge: Harvard University Press.

Kauffman, Robert. 1980. "African Rhythm: A Reassessment." *Ethnomusicology* 24: 393–415.

Ladysmith Black Mambazo. 1981. *Phansi Emgodini* [sound recording]. Gallo, Mavuthela, BL 321.

Lee, Spike. 1990. *Spike & Co. Do It A Cappella* [sound recording]. Elektra 60953–2.

Lott, Eric. 1995. *Love and Theft: Blackface Minstrelsy and the American Working Class.* New York: Oxford University Press.

Meintjes, Louise. 1990. "Paul Simon's Graceland, South Africa, and the Mediation of Musical Meaning." *Ethnomusicology* 34(1): 37–74.

Middleton, Richard. 1986. "In the Groove, or Blowing Your Mind? The Pleasures of Musical Repetition." In *Popular Culture and Social Relations,* edited by Tony Bennett, Colin Mercer, and Janet Woollacott, 159–75. Milton Keynes, Eng.: Open University Press.

Monson, Ingrid. 1994. "Doubleness and Jazz Improvisation: Irony, Parody, and Ethnomusicology." *Critical Inquiry* 20(2):283–313.

Rose, Tricia. 1994. *Black Noise: Rap Music and Black Culture in Contemporary America.* Hanover, NH: Wesleyan University Press.

Rycroft, David. 1967. "Nguni Vocal Polyphony." *Journal of the International Folk Music Council* 19: 90.

Seeger, Pete. 1992 [1972]. *The Incomplete Folksinger*. Edited by Jo Metcalf Schwartz. Lincoln: University of Nebraska Press.

Shapiro, Nat, and Bruce Pollock, eds. 1985. *Popular Music, 1920–1979: A Revised Cumulation*. Detroit: Gale Research Company.

Sloterdijk, Peter. 1993. *Im selben Boot. Versuch über die Hyperpolitik*. Frankfurt: Suhrkamp.

Snead, James A. 1984. "Repetition As a Figure of Black Culture." In *Black Literature and Literary Theory,* edited by Henry Louis Gates Jr., 59–80. London: Routledge.

Trewhela. Ralph. 1980. *Song Safari*. Johannesburg: Limelight Press.

CHAPTER 4

Jazz on the Global Stage

Jerome Harris

Introduction

Over its approximately eighty years of existence, jazz has achieved a presence in the culture of many lands far from its African American birthplace. Over this same period, the same technical and social developments (sound recording and broadcasting, international commerce) that aided the spread of jazz have given musics from many remote locales a vital presence in the lives of members of the U.S. jazz community.

The ramifications of these cultural currents are insufficiently recognized by many people both within and outside of the jazz world. Examination of the character and extent of this transnational flow reveals a rich global context in which jazz exists. This context has a palpable effect on the working lives of many jazz musicians worldwide, on the art they create, and on audiences' perception of that art. The global stage on which jazz is created and performed also has implications for identity and aesthetic issues that have recently been contested within the jazz community.

My intent here is to present a view of this transnational context in which I, as a jazz musician, find myself; in academic parlance, to "situate" myself and the music I play. I attempt to describe the main structural and dynamic characteristics of this artistic environment as I've observed them during more than twenty years of professional involvement. In addition, I will examine how some prominent issues within the jazz community (issues of cultural identity and artistic direction) look from a vantage point that includes this global context.

A key aspect of this context as I experience it is a complex, often tense interplay between jazz as a mediated "product"—a recorded, broadcast, bought-and-sold commodity with a life quite separate from its place of origin and processes of birth—and jazz as a manifestation of the ongoing intercourse between personal creative expression and one specific, culturally and socially sited tradition of aesthetics and musical practice. While these two aspects of jazz—the mediated and the personal/cultural—have existed throughout the music's history (indeed, they are not even necessarily opposed, since mediation is inherent in all interpersonal phenomena), the multinational nature of today's jazz creators, audiences, and mediators affects both of these aspects in ways that have potential for setting the future course of the music itself.

The Ecology of Jazz

Here I will state a conception of how the fundamental "agents" in the art enterprise formally interrelate, since this conception underlies all of my views on further matters. This particular formulation seems to be congruent with the thoughts of most musicians I have discussed these things with, as well as with people involved with other arts.

Structurally, the world of art consists of the activities of art makers (in the case of music, composers, arrangers and performers), art users (audiences), and various intermediary elements (enablers, conveyers, interpreters, etc.) that collectively I call mediators. I use the term *jazz community* to refer to this system (the term is widely used among members of the jazz realm in the United States).

In this system, communications—in the form of artworks, material support, words and images of emotional and intellectual response—circulate among these entities, with the prime flow being that of the art object as it moves from the art maker through the mediators to the art user. Note, however, that the mediators can act—intentionally or accidentally—as filters, amplifiers, shunts, and so forth, of this flow. Also, these mediators may be individuals, groups, or institutions, with various motivations, degrees of organization, and allegiances. They may even be nonhuman; technologies (such as audio and video recording and broadcasting, and long-distance transportation infrastructures) and social processes (such as education and commerce) play important roles in modulating the flow of art from maker to user.

Since this is not an isolated or closed system, the involvement that any of these three structural entities has with other social realms (cultural, economic, religious, political, etc.) can affect their functioning in the art system. The three entities may exist in different locales in geography or time, with contact made possible through physical media—recordings, books, and the like.

Since, wherever they are situated, engaged contact between any of these entities tends to result in some form and degree of influence, sometimes mutual, the character of this web of dynamic interrelations can be justly described as ecological. I will argue that, in the case of jazz, the ecology is global.

Jazz's Global "Playing Field"

By examining some of the activities central to the creation and mediation of the music, one can gain a clear sense of the multinational, transnational scope of jazz. The activities I will describe are touring, recording, broadcasting, criticism and pedagogy, governmental support, and cross-cultural influences. In doing so, my perspective will be that of a U.S.-based, African American jazz performer, observing how the music has spread outward from its birthplace, for the purpose of assessing the extent to which jazz has "taken root" abroad.

Touring

The global reach of American jazz today is reflected in the travel itineraries of New York–based touring jazz musicians. In addition to the major cultural capitals of Western Europe (London, Paris, Berlin, Rome, Copenhagen, Amsterdam, Vienna, etc.), many small-to-mid-sized cities host annual festivals or concert series that present foreign touring bands (examples include Moers and Cologne, Nancy and Vienne, Willisau and Biel, Florence, Innsbruck, Pori). Even some towns with populations under 150,000 (Schwaz, Saalfelden, Bolzano) and some that Americans do not usually associate with jazz (Warsaw, Istanbul, Ljubljana, Tallinn) present foreign performers on a regular basis in concerts or clubs. Less common European ports of call for American players include several of the former Warsaw Pact countries (the Czech Republic, Macedonia) and Greece.[1]

One European tour promoter I spoke to estimated that, overall, the business of live jazz performance in Europe generates $250–300 million per year (Gluch 1996). While much of this activity involves a community of European musicians whose careers are based entirely in Europe and who seldom, if ever, appear in the United States, most of the New York–based jazz players I know rely on regular performance work in Europe for a substantial portion of their income (the exceptions are those players who have consciously developed alternative income sources, such as teaching or playing in Broadway shows).

The Asian presence of American jazz performers is mostly concentrated in Japan (which also has a self-contained scene similar to Europe's), with Hong Kong and India visited less frequently. A few high-profile players, such as Pat Metheny, have appeared in nations with rising economies such as Malaysia, Singapore, South Korea, Indonesia, and Thailand (Sholemson 1996; Pignato 1996). Australia, despite its level of prosperity and its language kinship with the United States, is not a common stop for mid-level bands owing to its comparatively small population and the expensive airfare.

Africa and (to a lesser degree) South America are not frequented much by mid-level American jazz artists owing to a lack of economic, infrastructural, and audience development necessary to support the commercial enterprise of jazz touring. Exceptions include certain Caribbean nations, Brazil, and the occasional high-profile cultural festival such as 1977's FESTAC in Nigeria (see Apter 1996).

By comparison, the number of foreign-based artists presenting their art on the U.S. jazz scene is quite small. There are many jazz artists from all over the world who move to the United States for a period of time to study or to test the professional waters, but the same challenges that make it difficult for most American jazz artists to book strings of performance dates longer than one or two weeks (long distances between supportive audiences and high travel costs; difficulty getting effective publicity; intense competition for leisure time and funds; heavy corporate marketing of the most popular genres and artists, which crowds out diversity and lessens listener taste for more challenging fare; etc.)

largely preclude all but a handful of foreign performers—those with the strongest international name recognition or with corporate or governmental backing—from touring the United States. Touring in Europe and Japan is both more feasible and more lucrative.

Another indicator of the internationalization of the marketplace for live jazz is the attempt by some presenters to conduct operations in several countries. The European Jazz Festivals Organisation is a consortium of some of Europe's largest summer festivals, covering ten nations (Laipio 1995; International Live Music Conference 1996). The Europe Jazz Network, a nonprofit organization that uses computer-based telecommunications to aid coordination and collaboration between promoters, presenters, and musicians, has members in twelve countries. The Japanese electronics and media firm JVC is prominently involved in sponsoring large jazz festivals in the United States, Europe, and Japan; they work closely with George Wein's Festival Productions Inc. (one of the largest jazz concert promoters in the United States and founder of the Newport Jazz Festival). The New York multiarts venue the Knitting Factory, which has booked European (as well as some North American) tours for several jazz artists, has maintained an office in Amsterdam to help support their promotional activities. One prominent New York jazz club, Sweet Basil, is owned by a Japanese citizen. There have been numerous offers—all declined—made by foreigners interested in partial or full ownership of the famed Village Vanguard club (Browne 1996). And Blue Note, the high-profile New York nightclub, is now the headquarters of Blue Note International, which promotes and manages a network of franchised jazz club-cafe-restaurant-gift shop operations owned by investors. In addition to their New York flagship, they run clubs in Tokyo, Osaka, and Fukuoka, Japan, and new clubs in Seoul, Jakarta, and San Francisco are in the planning stage (Bensusan 1996; Haries 1996).

All of these phenomena are indicative of the increasingly global context that jazz musicians, audiences, promoters, and even club owners now take for granted.

Recording

Regardless of one's feelings or philosophy, the existence and meaning of recordings is something that today's jazz musician must regularly confront. For while the in-person experience of live music performance is the most direct and archetypal, the majority of people in the rich nations of the world (and many who inhabit poorer countries) experience the bulk of their music through reproduced recordings.

The attitude of musicians toward this reality varies. Some jazz musicians enjoy the challenging process of sculpting an "audio object" that will stand up to repeated listenings (Williams 1985: 104–11, 140–48); they sometimes embrace production techniques that separate the recording medium from the real-time (and real-space) experience.[2] Others chafe at the impositions of the studio recording process (sterile acoustics, time limitations, lack of audience presence, magnification of flaws through repeated critical listening, etc.) and find this process less fulfilling and more daunting than the challenge of meeting audiences face-to-face.[3]

The fact that live performance is no longer the dominant mode of musical experience is based on two linked, powerful, worldwide occurrences: the technological development of practical sound recording and reproduction devices (followed by workable electronic broadcasting and receiving equipment and infrastructures) and the embracing of these devices and infrastructures by consumers, corporations, and national governments.

The confluence of these phenomena (in particular, the success of the record player and the radio in the United States) and the emergence of jazz during the first three decades of this century have been noted by many (see Williams 1985: 223–25). Jazz arrived at the right place and time to become (despite its emphasis on dynamic processes such as improvisation, swinging, and its "in-the-field" methods of training practitioners) a part of "the reification of music," as recording technologies brought music into the category of collectible cultural objects to an unprecedented degree (Eisenberg 1987: 13–14).

Nor were the effects of this confluence limited to the United States. In Europe—where earlier black American music styles heard during and immediately following World War I had prepared the ground for the reception of jazz,[4] and where the brass bands of the segregated U.S. Army's black units were influential—the music continued to spread after the war, abetted by its mechanical reproduction.[5] French violinist Stéphane Grappelli's biographer recounts an experience during the early 1920s when, as a young post-Conservatoire journeyman, Grappelli had been playing in a Paris cinema six hours a day:

> As it happened, close by the cinema was a boutique that dealt in all the latest amusements for a nervous, amusing age. "It was a little

shop with all sorts of gadgets. There was one, a machine box—from America, of course—where you could hear some records with something in your ear, for *cinq sous*." That proto-jukebox gave him his first taste of a black band playing at least proto-jazz, and it was a shock. "It was 'Stumbling,' by Mitchell's Jazz Kings. It drove me insane. I was absolutely hypnotized by that kind of music; I used to go every day to listen to the same tune" (Smith 1987: 26).[6]

About three years later, records by Louis Armstrong, Bix Beiderbecke, Joe Venuti, and Eddie Lang were being distributed in France, and Grappelli became enthralled by "real jazz."

The experience of hearing Mitchell's Jazz Kings in Paris in 1921 prompted Russian futurist poet Valentin Parnakh to promote syncopated dance music in Moscow; he organized concerts featuring Russian players who imitated imported protojazz recordings, demonstrations of American dance steps, and readings of his own poetry (Starr 1983: 44–49). Black American bands playing in "straight" (Sam Wooding) and "hot" (Benny Payton, featuring Sidney Bechet) styles began performing in Russia in 1926 (54–66). The new sounds inspired controversy among both the cultural elite and the general public. Among the positive responses was the interest of music theorist Joseph Schillinger, whose compositional system influenced a number of prominent American jazz musicians after he immigrated to the United States in 1928, when the "Cultural Revolution" abruptly halted the expansion of Soviet jazz activity (64–76).[7]

Meanwhile, jazz had entered Germany at the end of World War I and received a boost by the postwar dance craze. Visiting American and British players and bands helped spark interest in the new music; recordings became an additional factor during the 1920s, as gramophones improved in quality and numbers, and domestic and imported records were actively shared and traded among fans—an activity that would gradually be driven underground by the rise of the Third Reich (Kater 1992: 11).

Among the jazz enthusiasts who followed the music in Weimar Germany was a group called the Berlin Melodie-Klub, founded in 1934. One of its "purist" members was Franz Wolf, who fled to New York in 1938 after the anti-Jewish pogrom known as Kristallnacht. In New York he teamed up with Alfred Lion, another Jewish emigré from Berlin who had just founded the Blue Note record label. "Lion and 'Francis Wolfe' later made Blue Note into the pioneer for the emerging bebop style" (Kater 1992: 75–76).

From the late 1960s through the 1980s, non-U.S. jazz record labels performed valued functions for the American jazz community. In periods when some major U.S. companies were neglecting their "backlists," labels such as RCA France and CBS France were making important older works by seminal artists such as Louis Armstrong, Duke Ellington, and Miles Davis available to the public, in well-annotated editions with good sound quality. Columbia's Japanese affiliate CBS/Sony released live recordings by Miles Davis, Weather Report, and Herbie Hancock that furnished insights into their rock- and funk-influenced musical periods. The Japanese licensers of Blue Note, Prestige and Riverside, kept high-quality editions of those catalogs in print with the original cover art and liner notes, including many titles that were out of print in the United States, presaging the later reissue efforts of their American owners. European labels such as BYG-Actuel, ECM, Hat Hut, and Freedom documented significant developments in the exploratory work of artists such as Don Cherry, Dave Holland, Steve Lacy, and Julius Hemphill.

More recently, much music by both established and emerging American artists has been documented by European labels such as Black Saint/Soul Note (Muhal Richard Abrams, Max Roach), Criss Cross (Cedar Walton, Tim Warfield), Enja (Ray Anderson, Marty Ehrlich), JMT (Tim Berne, Steve Coleman), Leo (Joe Maneri, Ned Rothenberg), and SteepleChase (Stanley Cowell, Kenny Drew), as well as Japanese labels such as DIW (Art Ensemble of Chicago, David Murray) and Avant (Bobby Previte, John Zorn).

Because the production and marketing of recordings remains a multinational enterprise, the impact of recordings will continue to hurdle the borders separating segments of the worldwide jazz community.

Broadcasting

In the early 1920s—just before the first recordings of King Oliver's Creole Jazz Band—the first regular radio broadcasts began in the United States. A "radio mania" swept the nation; by 1930 more than six hundred stations were broadcasting to about 40 percent of America's families (Czitrom 1982: 71–79). Other developed countries kept pace with the United States in adopting the new medium. The German broadcast system began in 1923; the forerunner of Japan's NHK began radio operations in 1925; the British Broadcasting Company (BBC) was founded in 1922. Between 1923 and 1928 the BBC expanded their yearly programming from about 1,600 hours to 60,000 hours, for British audiences that grew from one million to fifteen million (Black 1972: 26). "If you had walked down a residential street on a fine Sunday morning in a summer of the 1930s you could have heard, floating through the open windows, the sounds of all the wireless sets; and the sounds that reached your ear would have been of Radio Luxembourg, Radio Normandie, Radio Toulouse, Radio Fécamp and, from Ireland, Radio Athlone" (63).

From the beginning, various types of live and recorded music were part of the fare. Audience interest in dance music was reflected in the programming. The BBC, for example, first broadcast dance-band music in 1923; by 1931, it made up 10 percent of the National Programme and 20 percent of London Regional's air time (Black 1972: 27). While it is hard to say precisely how much of this music—in Europe or elsewhere—was jazz, numerous first-person accounts attest to the importance of jazz broadcasts for publicizing recordings as well as for direct enjoyment of the music (Kater 1992: 12). Today there are numerous commercially available recordings of concert or club performances that began as radio broadcasts; many of these are prized by collectors and musicians for the insights they provide about jazz performance in its native settings.

Differences between European and American audiences in knowledge about jazz are often noted by (and discussed among) players. I would suggest that these differences are due, in part, to the differing ways in which radio evolved on the two continents. While European nations set up systems based on publicly financed, state-operated stations, the commercial model of private broadcasters selling time to advertisers under the aegis of "a weak, administrative type of federal regulation" came to dominate broadcast radio in the United States as early as the late 1920s (Czitrom 1982: 79). In the United States, advertiser preferences and competition among the large number of stations led to a trend toward specificity in defining target audiences—and, consequently, more selectivity in choosing music to reach them. For at least the first thirty years of U.S. commercial radio, there was enough breadth in the makeup of audiences, enough autonomy residing with individual "disk jockeys," and enough adherence to block programming (allocating airtime segments to particular types of music rather than devoting the station completely to a single music category) to provide, within broad genre categories, a measure of variety among the weekly offerings of a single station. Later, as multiple stations began to service the same areas, the desire of owners to differentiate their stations from the competition led to increased specialization in programming.

A marked decrease in variety became apparent around 1970, as the survey-based marketing techniques developed for selling commodities were adopted by the record and radio industries. This soon led to sharply defined station "formats" featuring restricted programming (tightly controlled by "program directors" heavily influenced by marketing-oriented "programming consultants") intended to satisfy advertisers interested in reaching numerically specified "market segments." Joshua Meyrowitz's (1985: 73) description of commercial television's economic structure is fully applicable to commercial radio as well:

> While viewers often think of television programs as "products," themselves as the "consumers," and advertising as the "price" paid to watch the programs, the true nature of the television business is quite different. The products are the viewers who are sold to advertisers. The more viewers a program draws, the more money advertisers are willing to pay to have their message aired. Because of this system, network broadcasters have little interest in designing programs that meet the specialized needs of small segments of the audience.

The adoption of this marketing "technology" has resulted in the demise of commercial jazz radio in America and diminished industry support for other genres of music that lack mass constituencies.[8] There are currently fewer than one hundred radio stations in the United States that program jazz twenty hours or more per week, and the majority of these are college-run or listener-funded stations (Pignato 1996).

In contrast, Europe's systems of state-run radio broadcasting, legally mandated to serve the public interest, are not as closely tied to commercial marketing concepts and techniques. They have maintained block programming, which allows a more "curatorial" approach to music selection. I believe that this approach has helped, over time, to foster a broader knowledge of jazz among members of the music-seeking European public than currently exists in the United States. With the rise of private commercial radio throughout Europe in recent decades, the future may portend more U.S.-style marginalization of jazz, although a recent perusal of the offerings found on state-owned radio in Germany and France suggests that, in contrast to its land of origin, jazz is fairly well represented on the air in Europe.

Criticism and Pedagogy

Turn-of-the-century journalists and critics in Europe responded to jazz as quickly as their American counterparts; their work demonstrates how long the music has been taken seriously abroad. A London magazine, *Melody Maker*, began publishing articles on jazz as early as 1926 (Southern 1983: 385). *Jazz Hot*, the first magazine avowedly dedicated totally to jazz, was founded in Paris by Charles Delaunay on 21 February 1935—only four months later than America's *Down Beat* (Zwerin 1985: 37). Japan's premier jazz periodical, *Swing Journal*, first appeared in 1947. The German magazine *Jazz Podium* has been in existence since 1951 (Boyet 1994b: 36).

Around 1938, the first of a steady stream of American books on jazz were published: *American Jazz Music* by Wilder Hobson and *Jazzman* by Frederic Ramsey and Charles E. Smith (Southern 1983: 385). These were preceded, however, by the 1934 French publication of Hugues Panassié's *Le Jazz Hot*. While the non-English-language works had rather limited impact in the United States (although I do recall Andre Hodier's *Jazz: Its Evolution and Essence* being required reading in my jazz history classes of the 1970s), one possible exception was Ekkehard Jost's *Free Jazz* (1974), published in English as well as German. Its probing, detailed analysis of what was very recent history served to legitimize jazz's avant-garde; its demonstration that this exploratory branch of the music could perhaps be appropriately codified (and, implicitly, learned or taught—as was already the case for swing or bebop) was a controversial catalyst for discussion among American jazz students at the time of its appearance.

The value of any formal study of jazz is, in and of itself, contested within the professional musician community. Still, as jazz has gradually moved from being a vernacular, orally transmitted, segregated-culture music toward more codification, written documentation, and majority-culture acceptance, the role of institutionalized formal study by aspiring players (from within and outside the United States) has grown. Several prominent college-level jazz programs in the United States have had some degree of foreign enrollment for years. The artistic director of the jazz course at London's Royal Academy of Music, Graham Collier, attended Boston's Berklee College of Music in the early 1960s; Sadao

Watanabe, Michael Gibbs, and Dusko Gojkovic were fellow foreign students who went on to international careers. In some cases this enrollment has grown to significant proportions (Collier 1994: 3). The percentage of "international" undergraduate students at Berklee College of Music (the largest of these programs, with more than 2,700 students) has risen over recent years to about 38 percent currently (Economou 1996). The percentage of non-U.S. enrollees at New York's Mannes/ New School jazz program rose from 27 percent in 1990 to 37.8 percent in 1996 (Mueller 1996). New England Conservatory's jazz program has about 15 percent foreign enrollment (Grohman 1996).

There has been growth in the number and influence of conservatory and college-level jazz programs outside the United States as well. The Musik Hochschule in Graz, Austria, has had a jazz department since 1963 (prewar programs included a class at Frankfurt's Hoch'sche Konservatorium (Kater 1992: 17) and a program at the Hans Eisler school in Berlin) (Collier 1994: 3). Programs can also be found at Köln's Musikhochschule, the Hochschule der Kunste in Berlin, the Royal Academy of Music in London, the Royal Conservatory in The Hague, the Conservatoire de Montreux, the Musikhogskolams in Stockholm, Göteborg and Malmö, the Rythmisk Musikkonservatorium in Copenhagen, the Moscow College of Improvised Music, Tokyo's Sensoku College, the Osaka College of Music, and the Koyo Conservatoire in Kobe. Whether one accepts the notion that the conservatory model is effective and appropriate for training jazz musicians, it is no longer absolutely mandatory for those seeking formal jazz training to study in the United States.

Governmental Support

Although the numbers are difficult to document, it is a truism among musicians that one difference between the U.S. and European contexts for jazz that affects musicians and audiences alike is the greater degree of governmental support for the arts in Europe.[9] Booth (1964) and Netzer (1978) mention three factors affecting this difference: the quantity (there is some evidence to bolster the belief—widely held among jazz professionals—that several European governments spend from three to five times more money per capita than the United States to support the arts[10]); stability (which generally does not vary as widely from year to year in affluent European nations as it does in the United States[11] [Booth 1964: 7]); and range of this support (a much wider range of types of venues, from tiny clubs to youth centers to large festivals, are more likely to receive support in Europe than in the United States[12]).

Additionally, Europe provides valuable, though indirect, infrastructural support for jazz touring in the form of an extensive, reliable passenger rail system that offers steeply discounted fare passes to non-Europeans, and the activities of government-owned broadcasters. It is clear that the relatively high cost of traversing the long distances between cities with developed jazz audiences forms a major barrier to touring in the United States; this is largely mitigated in Europe by the government-subsidized rail system. With regard to state-run broadcasting, it is presently quite common for one or two dates on a European tour (or major star–level Japanese tour) to be funded in part by the local state-run radio or television outlet, in exchange for the rights to either a simultaneous or subsequent broadcast of the concert; occasionally these recordings are later pressed and commercially released. Several of these stations host in-house big bands that regularly perform, give workshops, commission new works from noted composers, and feature guest performers, many of whom have been Americans.

Ongoing governmental support of the arts has helped foster sophistication and commitment in European jazz audiences. In my opinion, the effectiveness of such support for jazz in the United States pales in comparison to that in much of Europe.

Cross-Cultural Influences

The final factor that I would like to consider in rounding out this picture of jazz as a global activity is the interest jazz musicians have taken in various nonjazz musics from around the world and how these musics have influenced their work.

Just as modern audio technologies and efficient international commerce and travel have brought jazz to listeners across the world and, especially in Europe and east Asia, inspired the establishment of significant jazz communities, they have also provided listeners with an unprecedented ease of access to the world's other musics. This is quite obviously true for the stable and affluent nations that are well serviced by large commercial record distribution systems. However, the advent of music cassette technology, with its durability, portability, and low purchase and production costs, has made this true to a degree for poorer countries as well (Manuel 1993: 28–29). "Never before have people had such easy access to so much recorded music," and this holds true on a global scale (Wallis and Malm 1984: 281). Many jazz musicians, mediators, and audience members the world over have this access; those who take advantage of it open themselves to influences from a broad and deep musical cornucopia.

The history of jazz supplies precedent for this openness, for jazz has been a syncretic art from the beginning—a genre that evolved its own characteristics "from the fusion of blues and ragtime with brass-band music and syncopated dance music" (Southern 1983: 361). The processes of melding, filtering, juxtaposing, and transmuting that began, for jazz, with Euro- and Afro-American musical materials, practices, concepts, and aesthetics have also been applied, over time, to musics from other periods and lands. Some of these additional influences—musics from North America and the Caribbean,[13] from South America (especially Brazil),[14] from American popular musics of various eras, from musics of the African continent,[15] and from Euro-American tonal fine-art composition[16]—have been thoroughly assimilated and accepted by the jazz mainstream. Others, such as Euro-American atonal composition, Indian classical music, Australian[17] or Asian musics,[18] and European indigenous musics,[19] are not as popular or widely adopted but have still made a notable impact.

These examples—among many others—indicate that the incorporation of influences from nonjazz musics by jazz is quite substantial and is likely to continue to be significant. This engaged interaction of jazz with other musics reflects the era's far-ranging global flow of recordings, travel, and information, and jazz's role as an artistically vital component of this transcultural flow.

Issues of Identity and Aesthetics on the Global Stage

In this final section, I will discuss the implications of jazz's existence as a transnational, transcultural music for two questions that are currently of interest to the U.S. jazz community: Whom does jazz belong to? and What is its appropriate aesthetic?

Jazz as Cultural Emblem

For decades, jazz has been recognized as an important form of cultural production; historically it has had particular significance within the African American society that gave birth to it. In its prenatal milieu (racially segregated nineteenth-century African American life), there was conscious recognition and promotion of the political and spiritual aspects of culture. These aspects included culture as an affirmation of human sensibility in the face of a society that denied the existence of such qualities in blacks; culture as a medium connecting the society's tangled past and anticipated future to its creative present; and culture as a manifestation of the African aesthetic belief that "beauty, especially that created in a collective context, should be an integrated aspect of everyday life, enhancing the survival and development of community" (hooks 1990: 105). Jazz eventually became seen as an exemplar of such characteristics.

A host of specific, detailed meanings associated with jazz and its related source genres have evolved from the functional use of these musics in community life—for instance, as accompaniment to dance, celebration, work, funerals, and other social activities.[20] Throughout the course of its history, the music has accumulated additional connotations and symbolism—some (such as respect for the discipline the craft demands) arising from its core characteristics; some (like disdain for the eccentric night owl musician, envy of his supposed sophistication, or associations with liquor, bordellos, etc.) from more peripheral circumstances surrounding it. While particular meanings such as freedom of expression,[21] intellect,[22] style,[23] and striving[24] have become prominent or muted to varying degrees at different times, the various meanings associated with jazz have, in the aggregate, retained considerable potency—enough, for example, to periodically attract corporate commercial appropriation.[25]

The rapid emergence of jazz as a locus of African American cultural identification can be attributed in part to the emergence of modern media culture, with which it coincided.[26] Ironically, however, the direction of that media culture's development now threatens this relationship. The tendency of modern commerce and electronic media to select and present torrents of "jump-cut," "decontextualized," "low-bandwidth" images, devoid of the subtlety and unruly richness of direct experience, promotes the stripping of jazz and other cultural products of all but the most robust semiotic associations,[27] as do the business marketing techniques that segregate "youth" and "adult" cultural spheres,[28] further weakening identity markers.

Nevertheless, within the black American jazz community, there is a history of concern with the nature and effect of these connotations and of struggle to gain control of this type of mediation. And some of jazz's meanings (especially those judged as "positive"—i.e., those that affirm the realized and potential value of jazz and the culture that spawned it) have been embraced as core elements of self-definition by many African Americans—an identification process that is made more complex by the fact that jazz has, over time, also become part of the self-definition of many *non*–African Americans.

Whom Does Jazz Belong To?

The depth of white Americans' identification with jazz can range from the deeply fundamental to the merely superficial to the grossly exploitative. Most African Americans are all too familiar with so-called identification that is devoid of acknowledgment, respect, and/or honest acceptance of black culture (a lack of "identification *of*" as well as "identification *with*") and that leads to the "constructing [of] African-American culture as though it exists solely to suggest new aesthetic and political directions white folks might move in" (hooks 1990: 21). Add to this indignity the justifiable anger that blacks may feel about their underrepresentation in jazz industry activities such as production, management, and ownership, and it is not surprising that some African Americans have become invested in a definition of jazz (also held by some whites) as a cultural form in which no non–African American can validly participate.[29]

Yet the "problem" of past and present non–African American involvement with jazz persists. Although jazz and its meanings have historically not been as central to the identity of Euro-Americans as to that of Afro-Americans, the degree to which individual white Americans have been "down with" jazz is far from trivial. Among these people are musicians widely acknowledged within the U.S. jazz community to have made historically significant contributions to the music; Bill Evans, Gil Evans, Paul Bley, Charlie Haden, Jim Hall, and Keith Jarrett come to mind in this regard, as well as artists such as Bix Beiderbecke, Benny Goodman, and Lennie Tristano.

Given the multicultural elements that underlie both jazz and the country in which it developed, perhaps this should not be surprising; for many foreign observers, it is not.[30] The image of jazz as exclusively black—hence (along with other cultural forms produced by African Americans) connoting forbidden cultural "otherness" for white America—has never completely matched the reality; this contradiction has caused the semiotic web surrounding jazz to stretch.

The challenge posed to an exclusively black conception of jazz by white involvement can be viewed as an example of the social dislocation that typifies our era. In the past, the fact that the diasporic ethnic culture that gave birth to jazz was unique to the United States (and identified with it, despite the scorn and exclusion aimed at that culture by mainstream America) gave the U.S. jazz community a position of primacy, in some eyes, as the arbiter of jazz legitimacy.[31] Similarly, the identification of jazz with the "blackness" of most of the musicians who created and typified it has sometimes led to essentialist assumptions, such as the notion—formerly widespread in Europe—that all blacks are jazz musicians (Zwerin 1985: 178–79).[32]

Now, however, the prerogatives of ownership are loosening. For a people who have struggled for several hundred years to come to terms with the manifold dimensions of identity—imposed, inherited, and chosen—there is poignancy to be found in this process.

At this historical moment, black people are experiencing a deep collective sense of "loss." Nostalgia for times past is intense, evoked by awareness that feelings of bonding and connection that seemed to hold black people together are swiftly eroding. We are divided. Assimilation rooted in internalized racism further separates us. Neonationalist responses do not provide an answer, as they return us to an unproductive "us against them" dichotomy that no longer realistically addresses how we live as black people in a postmodern world. Many of us do not live in black neighborhoods. Practically all of us work for white people. Most of us are not self-sufficient; we can't grow, build, or fix nothing. Large numbers of us are educated in predominantly white institutions. Interracial relations are more a norm. The "chitlin circuit"—that network of black folks who knew and aided one another—has been long broken. (hooks 1990: 36)

To the above litany one might add the demise of so many of the towering jazz figures of the past; the virtual extinction of commercial jazz radio in the United States; the continuing dearth of blacks involved in the business end of jazz; the widespread involvement of people of various ethnicities and nations in all areas (making, mediating, and using) of the worldwide jazz enterprise; and the advent of many musics competing to fill audience interest in the "novel," the "exotic," the "other" (images that have been attached to jazz in the past). All of these trends underline the "diminished relevance to everyday African-American life" of jazz (Davis 1996b).

Yet the question of who owns not just the music but its connotations is one of continued import for those African Americans who most identify with jazz. And as the trends noted above continue, the pangs of dislocation that they engender could well increase for some in the jazz community, putting more pressure on their narrow definitions of jazz and their exclusivist sense of cultural identity.

What Is the Jazz Aesthetic?

For some years now, a debate over what constitutes a valid jazz aesthetic has raged between two camps within the jazz community.[33] Passionate conflicts over aesthetic values are nothing new in the history of art, and the jazz world is no exception. What is new in this conflict, however, is the role played (though often unacknowledged) by jazz's ongoing evolution into a global art form. Just as with issues of identity and cultural and symbolic meaning, this evolution is the backdrop against which aesthetic issues are being raised—and I believe that both sides of the debate hold attitudes and stances that are in part being adopted and employed (consciously and unconsciously) as conceptual responses to the globalizing forces surrounding jazz cultures.

At first glance, the labels usually given to these two camps ("classic" versus "avant-garde"; "mainstream" versus "alternative"; "traditional" versus "innovative") may seem appropriate. On hearing music from both groups, however, it seems clear that *both* sides can rightly lay claim to embodying aspects of jazz "tradition" and to promoting "innovation" within the style parameters they have chosen. I will therefore describe the two sides of this debate as championing a "canon" versus a "process" approach to jazz.

The canon position (with regard to any art form) extols the art's continuity with past historical practice; consequently, its concern is with the preservation, proper interpretation, and accurate transmission of this practice. It also stresses the art form's rootedness in a specific social context (often tied to a regional, national, class, ethnic, or religious identity and including functional ties, vital or vestigial, to social activities). Taken to an extreme, this position can lead to stasis.

The process position tends to valorize change, risk, surprise, and the development or discovery of fresh varieties of expression and beauty. Often its proponents openly seek inspiration from traditions, disciplines, or eras not their own. Distrustful of excessive codification, they are willing to challenge dogmas and test the limits of widely accepted definitions and truths. Carried to an extreme, this position can lead to chaos.

With regard to jazz, I will define the canon position as one in which jazz is seen as "a music defined by a specific African-American-originated canon and socially constituted guild"[34] and the process position as one that views jazz as "the result of certain African-American-originated processes and aesthetics manifested in music."[35] Of course, pure examples of these positions seldom exist in the real world; with rare exceptions, actual works of art embody aspects of both philosophies to varying degrees. They are thus best understood as idealized points on a continuum that one might use to help understand the complex philosophies, conceptions, and allegiances motivating actual artists.

They also represent very different responses to the increasing globalization of jazz. The canon position may be seen as one of resistance to the homogenizing tendencies of the current media environment, in which powerful corporate filtering through the mass-market mechanisms of selection, distribution and promotion pushes music that is not likely to generate big profits to the edges of the available dissemination channels (Davis 1996c: xiv).[36] In this environment, the defining of a canon functions (ironically, "at a moment when the validity of canons is being questioned elsewhere"[37]) to preserve a place for jazz history amid the commerce-driven wash of the transitory present. Similarly, the current level of attention paid within the New York jazz community to gaining the imprimatur of established mainstream "elders" (higher, I think, than in the late 1970s to the early 1980s) may in part be a response to the perceived "endangered" status of jazz's locale-based cultural production system[38] due to a parallel shrinking of the number and importance of regions and locales generating identifiable jazz styles.[39]

The process camp's response to the increasingly global nature of jazz production, mediation, and use is fundamentally different. Far from actively resisting this trend, the musicians whose central emphasis is on jazz-as-process are empowered and enabled by jazz's global presence and character. This holds true whether those musicians hail from the United States or abroad.

For musicians and audiences in non-American cultures, jazz must almost inevitably be considered a process—first, because members of these communities naturally bring their own musical and cultural backgrounds to bear on the music they make, market, and listen to; and, second, because their distance from the music's home base is such that it is impractical (if not quixotic) to build a local aesthetic on the approval of canonmakers in the United States. People who live halfway around the world cannot rely on getting the approval of an Art Blakey or Miles Davis or Betty Carter or Wynton Marsalis to confirm the validity of what they do; that validity must, of necessity, be confirmed by the players and audiences in their home areas. Thus it is not surprising that members of these communities search for an essence in jazz that is separate from any living relationship with jazz definers in America. Meanwhile, some local and regional jazz scenes are strong enough economically and creatively that even the New York community's acceptance or rejection cannot have much long-lasting impact; rather, they have evolved their own local "guilds" (complete with battles over resources and aesthetic legitimacy).[40] The influence of a traditionally African American jazz aesthetic is still strong, of course; it remains the prime determinant of *how* (by what processes) jazz is constructed. But the *what* of jazz—the set of elements utilized in this process of construction—often includes homegrown content.

A similar phenomenon can be observed among musicians of the "process" school within the United States. Many American jazz players—particularly those who came of age during the 1960s and thereafter, a period in which "youth music" came increasingly to dominate the landscape—"speak" rock, pop, and funk as part of their native musical tongues. For those who do not feel an ideological or aesthetic reason to restrict their influences to those considered "classic" (Ellington, Parker, early-to-middle-period Coltrane, etc.), these musics—and others from further afield—may be employed in building expressive idiolects of subtlety, range, and power. The resulting musics embody and typify not just a "process" approach to jazz, but the process by which jazz will be able to thrive in the broad global environment.

Conclusion

The movement of jazz onto the global stage is a trend that may be judged to hold some dangers. There is, for example, the possibility that jazz may lose benefits that derive from cultural closeness between the makers, mediators, and audience—among them, some easy broad consensus about its aesthetic direction. In the worldwide arena, some audiences may be unfamiliar with the music's expanded pool of influences. It could take longer for these influences to be assimilated and for feedback to circulate from maker to mediator to audience and back. In a way, though, this is part of the price to be paid for the music's success.

Jazz has, throughout its history, held appeal for people from many different societies and from different places within society, including at its margins. It is rooted in—and is a manifestation of—the human ability to redefine marginality as a "location of radical openness and possibility"(hooks 1990: 153). The transnational existence of jazz may, in fact, be evidence that "many other groups now share with black folks a sense of deep alienation, despair, uncertainty, loss of a sense of grounding even if it is not informed by shared circumstance" (hooks 1990: 27). To the extent that this is true, the "shared sensibilities which cross the boundaries of class, gender, race, etc." may represent a threat to those who view jazz as an exclusively African American art form (ibid.).

I am not, however, among them. I believe that the notion of "cultural purity" is largely specious and that such notions generally reflect not reality but a common psychological desire for comforting social boundaries and definitions of self. It seems increasingly apparent that, in all but the most isolated cases, the contributions of members of diverse groups to different parts of cultural systems are at least discernible and sometimes quite significant. The reality and power of phenomena such as sites of origin, temporal precedence, historical prominence, identifiable social units, and the like, does not lessen the concomitant reality of cultural hybridity (which, from a certain perspective, seems less an exception than a rule).

But what of the perceived need for African Americans to defend their cultural turf against incursions and appropriation by society's mainstream? This is a vexed and painful territory for many of us black folks, and I believe it is therefore all the more important to make and hold certain distinctions. Here are mine: I support and applaud efforts to attack racial inequities or injustice in the cultural scene and the music industry (and elsewhere), but I see these efforts as fundamentally distinct from misguided attempts to "hold the line" against non-U.S., non–African American, or non-canonic influences in the music itself. I cherish my right—and the right of others—to love, be influenced by, and try to do justice to *any* music or art, no matter the source. While acknowledging the ever-present political dimensions of art and culture, I experience the aesthetic dimensions as primary. And the aesthetic possibilities for jazz stemming from expanded interaction with the rest of the world's music are valid, meaningful, and exciting to me.

They are, at any rate, inevitable. Looking globally, jazz is already viewed by many folks (black, white, American, other) as being somewhat "whiter"—less exclusively "black" connotatively—than African-diasporic genres from social sectors with perhaps more functionally or economically vital ties to their musics: gospel, say, or gangsta rap, or "Afropop" (not to mention various traditional non-diasporic African musics). Jazz (with its largely white audience worldwide) may, in fact, already be viewed as less exclusively "black" than the blues.[41] Further, it is at least conceivable that, unless present–day dynamics change, the relative amounts of "jazz system" activity in the United States and elsewhere could evolve in such a manner as to eventually give "elsewhere" predominance in most aspects save historical origin.

For some, this is a potential tragedy, but my concern is more with the influence not of global players or audiences but of global corporate mediation. Today, at a moment when more music is more potentially accessible to more people than ever before, most folks are, paradoxically, less aware of any music that does not happen to easily serve a mere commercial interest. For reasons of profit making alone, music that has potentially deep value for many people does not reach its rightful audience.

That, to me, is the real potential tragedy—not that jazz will be owned by too many, but that it will reach too few. For jazz's particular balancings—of knowledge of the old and questing for the new, of individual and group expression, of the head, heart, and body—provide its ability to renew not only itself as an art but to refresh and renew the spirit of players and listeners worldwide, across societal boundaries. As long as this richness (in both what goes into the music and what comes out of it) persists—as long as audiences maintain vital emotional ties to the music and can use it deeply in their lives—its worth will continue to be high. The shape of jazz to come may differ from that which has come before, but if it maintains its vitality, its relevance, its passionate intensity—its (in the widest sense of the word) "soul"—regardless of the ethnicity or nationality of those who love it, jazz in some form is certain to maintain a uniquely prominent position on the global stage.

Notes

[1]Jerome Harris, concert programs, handbills, and tour itineraries, in personal papers. Program listings for European jazz festivals and clubs may be found in magazines such as *Jazz Podium* (Stuttgart: Jazz Podium Verlags GmbH) and *Jazz Jour-*

nal International (London: Jazz Journal Ltd.) and online at *World Wide Jazz Web* (World Wide Web: http://xs4all.nl/~centrale/jazz.html).

[2] Recent examples include the Charlie Haden Quartet West's *Haunted Heart* (1992) and *Always Say Goodbye* (1994), with their interpolations of old recordings by Jo Stafford, Django Reinhardt, Duke Ellington, and others.

[3] During my years as a member of Sonny Rollins's group (1979–81, 1983–94), I repeatedly observed the contrast between his distaste for the studio process and his love of live performance.

[4] "Well before the war, America had begun to export ragtime, a musical style that proclaimed the country's freshness and cultural diversity. . . . [R]agtime combined some of the black heritage of rhythmic sophistication with European form. The resulting mixture of bright tunes and snazzy syncopation entranced the Old World, and ragtime became a bit of a craze, along with the dance that it accompanied, the cakewalk" (Smith 1987: 23). An especially popular band was that of Harlem's 369th Infantry, directed by the celebrated New York bandleader Lt. James Reese Europe (Southern 1983: 349–52).

[5] The first incursion of jazz recordings into Japan occurred at about the same time: "En 1921, Shigeya Kikuki, qui a servi de secrétaire à son père en voyage d'affaires aux Etats-Unis, revient au Japon avec les premiers 78–tours de dixieland" (Boyet 1994a: 16).

[6] Louis Mitchell, drummer, was an alumnus of James Reese Europe's Army band; his Jazz Kings made some of France's first jazz records. "Stumbling" was a tune written by novelty pianist Zez Confrey, composer of "Kitten on the Keys"; according to Bruyninckx (1980) it was recorded ca. September/October 1922 and was issued as Pathé 6572.

[7] "[T]he Soviets announced in 1928 that the importing or playing of American jazz was punishable by a fine of one hundred roubles and six months in jail" (Eisenberg 1987: 25).

[8] "Jazz charts were dropped from *R & R* [trade journal *Radio & Records,* which publishes radio airplay data] several years ago with the demise of commercial jazz radio stations because *R & R*'s mission is centered in commercial broadcasting" (Archer 1996).

[9] My opinions in the area of governmental support have been informed by conversations since 1985 with many local jazz promoters, especially Antonio De Rosa (Ravenna, Italy), Reiner Michalke (Cologne, Germany), Achim Schönwiese (Freiburg, Germany), Peter Schulze (Bremen, Germany), and Kees van Boven (Groningen, Netherlands).

[10] This is notwithstanding the current reductions in general social spending in Europe since the late 1980s. "Anecdotal evidence . . . suggests that the role of public financed support is much larger in continental Europe than in the English-speaking countries" (Netzter 1978: 50). "Both the absence of requisite data and conceptual difficulties preclude the valid comparison of aggregate government funding of the arts in different countries. Apparently, there are no countries in which comprehensive data on public subsidy covering all levels of government are collected in a form that permits international comparisons on a recurring basis, and only in a few countries have efforts been made to assemble such data for a given year. (The United States is *not* an exception to this generalization, despite the celebrated American predilection for collecting statistics on every conceivable subject)" (ibid.).

[11]As Booth (1964: 7) notes, public attitudes about arts funding date from the age of royal patronage. "Tradition has been so firmly established that today there are questions only about amounts or form, not about the existence of the programs themselves." This predictability of future funding allows better advance programming; this is critical for audience development efforts, which require continuity.

[12]The distinction between "commercial" and "nonprofit" presenters is not as rigidly applied in Europe as it is in the United States; even clubs that serve food and alcohol may qualify for support if they can document their valid cultural function (for instance, being managed by a local nonprofit organization of jazz fans). This helps them afford to book foreign touring acts at practical fees and allows them to present a variety of music styles beyond surefire crowd pleasers.

[13]These lines of influence are expressed in the exploration of aboriginal music by drummer Jack DeJohnette, pianist Don Pullen and saxophonist Jim Pepper; in the use of vernacular "roots" musics (country and western by guitarists Bill Frisell and Pat Metheny, funk and R&B by trumpeters Lester Bowie and Miles Davis and bass guitarist Jaco Pastorius, African American gospel and spirituals by pianist Hank Jones and pianist/organist Amina Claudine Myers, and blues by guitarists James "Blood" Ulmer and David Tronzo); in the assimilation of elements from salsa, calypso, and reggae by far too many people to mention; and in the work of strong Caribbean instrumentalists, including Puerto Rican percussionist Giovanni Hidalgo, Trinidadian steel pan player Othello Molineaux, and Cuban pianist Gonzalo Rubalcaba, trumpeter Arturo Sandoval, and drummer Horacio "El Negro" Hernandez. See discography for relevant recordings.

[14]American players have been strongly influenced by the work of Brazilian percussionists Nana Vasconcelos and Airto Moreira, composers Egberto Gismonti and Hermeto Pascoal, and many songwriters, including Antonio Carlos Jobim, Luis Bonfa, Milton Nascimento, and Toninho Horta. South American instrumentalists who are admired include drummer/percussionist Alex Acuña and pianists Edson Gomez (Brazil), Edward Simon (Venezuela), and Danilo Perez (Panama). See discography for relevant recordings.

[15]Examples of the many interactions between jazz and African musics include recordings and live performances with Moroccan Gnawa musicians by saxophonist Ornette Coleman, pianist Randy Weston, and bass guitarist/record producer Bill Laswell (also projects involving New York–based Gnawa musician Hassan Hakmoun); collaborations between various West African drummers (including Mor Thiam and Aiyb Dieng from Senegal and Guinean Abdoulaye Epizo Bangoura) and the World Saxophone Quartet and bassist Mark Helias, among others; rhythmic and textural ideas from West African traditional and popular musics explored by cornetist Graham Haynes, drummer Bobby Previte's Empty Suits, multi-reedman Ned Rothenberg's Double Band, and Danish guitarist Pierre Dørge's New Jungle Orchestra; the work of South African pianists Abdullah Ibrahim (formerly Dollar Brand), Hotep Idris Galeta (formerly Cecil Bernard), and Chris MacGregor, trumpeter Hugh Masekela, and bassist Johnny Dyani. See discography for relevant recordings.

[16]One might cite influences reflected in the work of pianists Anthony Davis, Fred Hersch, Muhal Richard Abrams, and Marilyn Crispell, or John Zorn's "game" pieces. See discography for relevant recordings.

[17]A notable example being explorations of the digeridoo by saxophonist Thomas Chapin and and trombonists Craig Harris and Art Baron.

[18]Interactions between jazz and Asian musics include Tuvan vocalist Sainkho Namchylak's work with Ned Rothenberg and Danish pianist Irene Becker; several Turkish musicians including pianist Aydin Esen, drummer Okay Temiz, and Armenian percussionist Arto Tuncboyacian; an ongoing project combining Austrian saxophonist Wolfgang Puschnig, U.S.-born vocalist Linda Sharrock, and the Korean percussion ensemble SamulNori; influences from India through the playing of guitarist John McLaughlin, drummer Trilok Gurtu, and bansuri flutist and saxophonist Steve Gorn; use of East Asian musics by Japanese pianist Masahiko Sato, saxophonist Kazutoki Umezu, and percussionist Midori Takada. See discography for relevant recordings.

[19]Examples include such indigenous folk musics as those from the Balkans (trumpeter David Douglas, guitarist Brad Schoeppach, saxophonist Matt Darriau, keyboardist Anthony Coleman), Ireland (bassist/bass clarinetist Lindsey Horner), Scandinavia (saxophonist Jan Garbarek), the Caucasus (Azerbaijani pianist Aziza Mustafa-Zadeh); and the Euro-American Jewish genre of klezmer (clarinetist Don Byron, saxophonists John Zorn and Kazutoki Umezu, trumpeter Frank London). See discography for relevant recordings.

[20]Gunther Schuller suggests that the secondary role of rhythmic impetus in ordinary Euro-American "classical" phrasing "is traceable precisely to the fact that it is no longer a socially functioning music (in the primary sense of being related to physical activities), and has therefore developed a broader and necessarily leveled-off approach to rhythmic feeling. In a culture in which music is not used *primarily* in conjunction with work, play, ritual, and recreation, there is no consistent need for a strongly identifiable rhythmic impulse" (Schuller 1968: 8 fn).

[21]This association, manifested musically in improvisation, is especially highlighted in the image of the "heroic" star soloist. It is congruent with the broad iconic concept of American individualistic freedom. In some periods and styles of jazz, the individualistic focus has obscured the role of the group ("sidemen" or community or culture), which forms the necessary context for the individual's expressive freedom.

[22]An association that is often manifested through processes of abstraction but also coupled with physicality: "Bebop's wanton speed and abstraction—its affronts to melody and its cubist approach to harmony and rhythm—still account for a large part of its appeal" (Davis 1996a: 101). The intellectual aspect of jazz serves to validate its "high" art status: "I have no kick against modern jazz / unless they try to play it too darn fast / and change the beauty of the melody / until it sounds just like a symphony / that's why I go for that rock and roll music" (Berry 1957).

[23]Elegance, grace, and pleasure in integrating the many dimensions of real-time creative musical performance are seen as characteristic of jazz. This is often thought to be connected with individual and group expressions of style in other realms (fashion, speech, etc.).

[24]Jazz is symbolic of quests for emotional connection, artistic attainment, and for deserved social status (paralleling the evolution of the image of the music's settings from bordellos to concert halls, and of the music's creators from segregated pariahs to respected citizens).

[25]Recent examples of jazz images in advertising include photographs of black trumpeters in the Parker Duofold pen ad in Deutsche Bahn's *Mobil* no. 3 (May/June 1996) and the Hennessy cognac ad in *Emerge* 8, no. 1 (October 1996): 37; also see John McDonough (1991).

[26]As Angus and Jhally (1989) note: "In contemporary culture the media have

become central to the constitution of social identity. It is not just that media messages have become important forms of influence on individuals. We also identify and construct ourselves as social beings through the mediation of images. This is not simply a case of people being dominated by images, but of people seeking and obtaining pleasure through the experience of the consumption of these images" (quoted in hooks 1990: 5). Thus, jazz became an element in the effort of one of the United States's largest marginalized groups to create and project its own social identity to itself and to the rest of the world—and this during the start of the modern media age.

[27]Even these are largely experienced through the filtering of commercial media. (In the United States, a good example is New York's WQCD-FM, which bills its offerings of safe-as-milk pop-R&B with jazz and Latin sprinklings as "Today's Cool Jazz.") I believe the resultant "fog" of unmoored, lightweight cultural objects makes it harder for people in the developed world to form coherent, deeply satisfying patterns of cultural identification.

[28]I feel that this trend (which has been expanding since the mid-1950s in the developed world and, increasingly, elsewhere) has played an important role in destabilizing many aspects of American culture, including patterns within African American social life (particularly recreation and the socialization of youth) that formerly supported the existence and "handing down" of jazz culture.

[29]This view has its roots in the historic white American model of exclusionary racial identity, but it may also draw strength from the desire of many blacks to disassociate themselves from repugnant actions done in the name of "whiteness."

[30]"When the Swiss psychoanalyst Carl Jung came to this country he observed that white people walked, talked and laughed like Negroes" (Crouch 1996: 171).

[31]The location of the power to define jazz legitimacy may change in the future, if the amount and depth of foreign-based jazz activity continues to grow (in some respects European activity may already rival that of the United States).

[32]This kind of stereotyping still occurs. After playing a concert near Bari, Italy, with tubist Bob Stewart's First Line Band during a 1990 Europe tour, the group was invited to a disco for drinks by the concert's promoter. On discovering that there were black Americans present (and not knowing or caring that we were probably five to fifteen years older than all of the clientele), the DJ sent a wireless microphone over to us and insisted that we rap over the music he was playing. The drummer and I made a good-faith attempt, but it soon became clear that we could not "rock da house."

[33]Accounts of this recent debate include Francis Davis (1996c: x–xvii;); Giddens (1982); Whitehead (1993); Woodward (1994). For a view from the "alternative" side, see Byron (1995).

[34]An example of a leading jazz musician citing many of the musicians whose work implicitly comprises his canon can be found in Stanley Crouch's (1987) interview with Wynton Marsalis. For accounts of processes of evaluation and acceptance within the professional jazz community see Berliner (1994: 36–59).

[35]A detailed summary of these processes and aesthetic values is given in Schuller (1968: 6–62). My own list of "jazz processes" would include: the centrality of improvisation; a focus on developing strong, individual musical styles and statements; a sophisticated and expansive melodic and harmonic and rhythmic palette; a tradition of not just expressing but of commenting on and interacting with the musical materials in real time; and an embrace of fluidity and change.

[36]As potential audiences are presented with the newest work of a tiny group of heavily promoted artists and genres, a thinning and homogenizing of musical inputs tends to occur, both among genres and within categories such as jazz; one of the casualties is audience exposure to the music's recorded history (and aspiring musicians are also audience members). In general, "smaller countries are finding it harder and harder for their own music to compete with international repertoire" (Wallis and Malm 1984: 281). Compared with mainstream pop, jazz is a very "small country" indeed.

[37]This irony persists (and perhaps intensifies) if one views the current efforts at canonizing jazz works and figures as an attempt, by some African American musicians and critics, to exercise a prerogative formerly reserved for white critics and scholars.

[38]For a thorough analysis of the corporate and media mechanisms involved in this process, see Meyrowitz (1985).

[39]The sources of generative and influential elements in jazz's global "ecology of ideas" are now almost always individuals or small networks of like minds, not necessarily based in the same locale.

[40]Examples of such communities include Holland, where Misha Mengelberg, Han Bennink, Willem Breuker, and kindred players have developed a uniquely theatrical approach to jazz; France, where several distinctive styles coexist (including examples of the Romany-influenced sound exemplified by Django Reinhardt, that of conservatory-schooled players such as Louis Sclavis and François Jeanneau, and jazz influenced by the many strong Parisian musicians from Francophone Africa); Russia, where musicians like the Ganelin Trio are using Russian materials with jazz processes; and Japan. For an in-depth examination of the Netherlands scene, see Whitehead (1998).

[41]Ironically, the blues (as a genre, not as a modality of expression within other genres) has been substantially abandoned by much of the record-buying, club-visiting African American audience; see Francis Ward (1996).

References

Angus, Ian, and Sut Jhally, eds. 1989. *Cultural Politics in Contemporary America.* New York: Routledge.

Apter, Andrew. 1996. "The Pan-African Nation: Oil-Money and the Spectacle of Culture in Nigeria." *Public Culture* 8(3): 441.

Archer, Carol. 1996. (NAC Editor, *Radio & Records*). Correspondence with author. Los Angeles, 10 Sept.

Bensusan, Steve. 1996. (Blue Note International). Telephone interview by author. New York, 4 Oct.

Berliner, Paul F. 1994. *Thinking in Jazz: The Infinite Art of Improvisation.* Chicago: University of Chicago Press.

Berry, Chuck. 1957. Lyrics to *Rock and Roll Music.* New York: Arc Music.

Black, Peter. 1972. *The Biggest Aspidistra in the World: A Personal Celebration of Fifty Years of the BBC.* London: British Broadcasting Corporation.

Booth, John E. 1964. *Government Support to the Performing Arts in Western Europe.* New York: Twentieth-Century Fund.

Boyet, Didier. 1994a. "(Jazz) Made in Japan," part 1. *Jazz Magazine,* no. 433 (Jan.): 16.

———. 1994b. "(Jazz) Made in Japan," part 3. *Jazz Magazine,* no. 436 (Apr.): 36.

Browne, James. 1996. (Music director, Sweet Basil jazz club). Interview by author, New York, 30 Sept.

Bruyninckx, Walter. 1980. *Sixty Years of Recorded Jazz, 1917–1977.* Belgium: Walter Bruyninckx, Lange Nieuwstraat.

Byron, Don. 1995. "Statement." Program notes for 1995 Next Wave Festival. Alternative Jazz concert series. Brooklyn: Brooklyn Academy of Music.

Collier, Graham. 1994. "Jazz Education in America." *Jazz Changes* 1 (1: Spring): 3.

Crouch, Stanely. 1987. "Wynton Marsalis: 1987." *Down Beat* 54 (11: Nov.): 16–19.

———. 1996. "Race Is Over." *New York Times Magazine* 146 (50,564: 29 Sept.): 171.

Czitrom, Daniel J. 1982. *Media and the American Mind: From Morse to McLuhan.* Chapel Hill: University of North Carolina Press.

Davis, Francis. 1996a. "Bud's Bubble." *Atlantic Monthly* 277 (1: Jan.): 101.

———. 1996b. "Like Young." *Atlantic Monthly* 278 (1: July 1996): 94.

———. 1996c. *Bebop and Nothingness: Jazz and Pop at the End of the Century.* New York: Schirmer Books.

Economou, Emily Woolf. 1996. (Director of Admissions, Berklee College of Music). Telephone interview by author. Boston, 12 Sept.

Eisenberg, Evan. 1987. *The Recording Angel: Music, Records and Culture from Aristotle to Zappa.* London: Pan Books.

Giddins, Gary. 1982. "Jazz Turns Neoclassical." *Atlantic Monthly* 250 (5: Nov.): 156–60.

Grohman, Bryon. 1996. (Assistant Registrar, New England Conservatory of Music). Telephone interview by author. Boston, 12 Sept.

Gluch, Ralph. 1996. Interview by author. Thun, Switzerland, 13 May.

Haries, Sal. 1996. "Franchise Development: A Letter to Potential Investors" [Web page]. http://interjazz.com/clubs/bluenote/franchis.html. Cited 30 Aug.

hooks, bell. 1990. *Yearning: Race, Gender and Cultural Politics.* Boston: South End.

International Live Music Conference. 1996. "The Axis: Association" [Web page]. http://www.ilmc.com/assoc.html. Cited 19 Sept.

Jost, Ekkehard. 1994. *Free Jazz.* New York: Da Capo. Originally published in 1974.

Kater, Michael H. 1992. *Different Drummers: Jazz in the Culture of Nazi Germany.* New York: Oxford University Press.

Laipio, Matti. (Pori Jazz Festival). 1995. Correspondence with author. Helsinki, 29 Sept.

Manuel, Peter. 1993. *Cassette Culture: Popular Music and Technology in North India.* Chicago: University of Chicago Press, 1993.

McDonough, John. 1991. "Jazz Sells." *Down Beat* 58 (10: Oct.): 34.

Meyrowitz, Joshua. 1985. *No Sense of Place: The Impact of Electronic Media on Social Behavior.* New York: Oxford University Press.

Mueller, Martin. 1996. (Assistant Dean, Mannes Jazz and Contemporary Music Program, New School for Social Research). Telephone interview by author. New York, 12 Sept.

Netzer, Dick. 1978. *The Subsidized Muse: Public Support for the Arts in the United States.* Cambridge: Cambridge University Press.

Pignato, Joe. 1996. (Product Manager, ECM/BMG Classics). Interview by author. New York, 9 Sept.

Schuller, Gunther. 1968. *Early Jazz: Its Roots and Musical Development*. New York: Oxford University Press.

Sholemson, David. 1996. (Vice President/Director of Management, Ted Kurland Associates). Telephone interview by author. Boston, 19 Sept.

Smith, Geoffrey. 1987. *Stéphane Grappelli*. London: Pavilion/Michael Joseph.

Southern, Eileen. 1983. *The Music of Black Americans: A History*. 2nd ed. New York: W. W. Norton.

Starr, S. Frederick. 1983. *Red and Hot: The Fate of Jazz in the Soviet Union, 1917–1980*. New York: Oxford University Press.

Wallis, Roger, and Krister Malm. 1984. *Big Sounds from Small Peoples: The Music Industry in Small Countries*. London: Constable.

Ward, Francis. 1996. "Black & White Blues." *Emerge* 7 (8: June): 50–56.

Whitehead, Kevin. 1993. "It's Jazz, Stupid." *Village Voice* 38 (47: 23 Nov.): special section, 11.

———. 1998. *New Dutch Swing*. New York: Billboard Books.

Williams, Martin. 1985. *Jazz Heritage*. New York: Oxford University Press.

Woodward, Richard B. 1994. "The Jazz Wars: A Tale of Age, Rage, and Hash Brownies." *Village Voice* 39 (32: 9 Aug.): 27–28.

Zwerin, Mike. 1985. *La Tristesse de Saint Louis: Jazz under the Nazis*. New York: Beech Tree Books/William Morrow.

Discography

(Note: Except where indicated, year cited is the year of the recording's copyright.)

Abrams, Muhal Richard. 1995. *Think All, Focus One*. Black Saint 120141-2.

Abrams, Muhal Richard, and Marty Ehrlich. 1996. *The Open Air Meeting*. New World 80512.

Anderson, Ray. 1985. *Old Bottles—New Wine*. Enja ENJ-79628.

———. 1998. *Blues Bred in the Bone*. Enja 5081 2.

Art Ensemble of Chicago with Amabutho. 1991. *Art Ensemble of Soweto: America–South Africa*. DIW/Columbia CK 52954.

Bangoura, Abdoulaye Epizo. 1995. On Mark Helias: *Loopin' the Cool*. Enja ENJ-9049 2.

Baron, Art. 1996. On Glen Velez and Handance: *Rhythm Color Exotica*. Ellipsis Arts CD 4140.

Bennink, Han. 1995. On Clusone Trio: *I Am an Indian*. Gramavision GCD 79505.

Berne, Tim. 1995. *Tim Berne's Bloodcount: Low Life–The Paris Concert*. JMT 697 124 054-2.

Bonfa, Luiz. 1962. *Luiz Bonfa Plays & Sings Bossa Nova*. Verve V/V6-8522.

Bowie, Lester. 1986. *Lester Bowie Brass Fantasy: Avant Pop*. ECM 1326.

Breuker, Willem. 1975. *Willem Breuker Kollektief Live at the Donaueschingen Music Festival 1975*. MPS 529089-2.

———. 1990. *Heibel*. BVHaast CD 9102.

Byron, Don. 1992. *Don Byron Plays the Music of Mickey Katz*. Elektra Nonesuch 79313-2.

———. 1995. *Music for Six Musicians*. Elektra Nonesuch 79354.

Chapin, Thomas. 1990. *Radius*. Muworks 1005.

Cherry, Don. 1969. *"Mu" First Part*. BYG-Actuel 529.301.

Coleman, Anthony. 1995. *Sephardic Tinge*. Tzadik 7102.

Coleman, Ornette. 1977. *Dancing in Your Head*. A&M/Horizon SP722.

Coleman, Steve. 1987. *World Expansion*. JMT 834 410.

Coleman, Steve, Robin Eubanks, Greg Osby, and Cassandara Wilson. 1993. *Flashback on M-base*. JMT 514 010-2.

Cowell, Stanley. 1996. *Mandara Blossoms*. SteepleChase SCCD 31386.

Crispell, Marilyn. 1994. *Stellar Pulsations/Three Composers*. Leo CD LR 194.

Darriau, Matt. 1995. *Paradox Trio*. Knitting Factory Works KFWCD-171.

Davis, Anthony. 1981. *Episteme*. Gramavision GCD 79508.

Davis, Miles. 1956–62. *Facets*. CBS 62 637.

———. 1964. *Miles in Tokyo: Miles Davis Live in Concert*. CBS/Sony SOPL 162.

———. 1970. *A Tribute to Jack Johnson*. Columbia Legacy CK 47036.

———. 1975. *Pangaea*. CBS/Sony SOPZ 96/97.

DeJohnette, Jack. 1992. *Music for the Fifth World*. Manhattan CDP0777 799089 2 9.

Dieng, Aiyb. 1980. On Jon Hassell/Brian Eno: *Fourth World, Vol. 1: Possible Musics*. Editions EG EGS 107.

Dørge, Pierre, and New Jungle Orchestra. 1996. *Music from the Danish Jungle*. Dacapo DCCD 9423.

Douglas, Dave. 1994. *The Tiny Bell Trio*. Songlines SGL 1504-2.

Drew, Kenny. 1986. On Kenny Drew, Niels-Henning Ørsted Pedersen, and Philip Catherine: *In Concert*. SteepleChase SCCD-31106.

Dyani, Johnny. 1979. *Song for Biko*. SteepleChase SCCD 31109.

Ehrlich, Marty. 1995. *New York Child*. Enja ENJ-9025.

Esen, Aydin. 1992. *Anadolu*. Columbia CK 48811.

Frisell, Bill. 1991. *Where in the World*. Elektra Musician 61181-2.

Galeta, Idris Hotep. 1991. On Jackie McLean: *Rites of Passage*. Triloka 188-2.

Garbarek, Jan, and Agnes Buen Garnås. 1989. *Rosensfole*. ECM 1402.

Gismonti, Egberto. 1993. *Música de Sobrevivência*. ECM 1509.

Gomez, Edson. 1995. On Don Byron: *Music for Six Musicians*. Elektra Nonesuch 79354.

Gorn, Steve. 1989. On Glen Velez: *Assyrian Rose*. CMP CD 42.

———. 1995. On Jack DeJohnette: *Dancing with Nature Spirits*. ECM 1558.

Gurtu, Trilok. 1995. *Bad Habits Die Hard*. CMP CD 80.

Haden, Charlie. 1959. On Ornette Coleman: *The Shape of Jazz to Come*. Atlantic SD 1317.

———. 1970. *Liberation Music Orchestra*. Impulse AS-9183.

———. 1992. *Haunted Heart*. Gitanes Jazz/Verve 314 513 078-2.

———. 1994. *Always Say Goodbye*. Gitanes Jazz/Verve 314 521 501-2.

Hakmoun, Hassan, and Adam Rudolph. 1991. *Gift of the Gnawa*. Flying Fish FF 70571.

Hancock, Herbie. 1975. *Flood: Herbie Hancock Live in Japan*. CBS/Sony 4OAP 565-6.

Harris, Craig. 1994. *F-Stops*. Soul Note 121255-2.

Haynes, Graham. 1994. *The Griots Footsteps*. Antilles 314 523 262-2.
Helias, Mark. 1995. *Loopin' the Cool*. Enja ENJ-9049 2.
Hernandez, Horacio "El Negro." 1993. On Edward Simon: *Beauty Within*. Audioquest Music AQ-CD1025.
Hersch, Fred. 1993. *Red Square Blue: Jazz Impressions of Russian Composers*. Angel/EMI 54743.
Hersch, Fred, Michael Moore, and Gerry Hemingway. 1997. *Thirteen Ways*. GM Recordings 3033.
Hidalgo, Giovanni. 1996. *Time Shifter*. TropiJazz RMD-81585.
Horner, Lindsey. 1995. *Mercy Angel*. Upshot 111.
Horta, Toninho. 1993. *Durango Kid*. Big World BW2012.
Ibrahim, Abdullah, and Dollar Brand. 1973. *Good News from Africa*. Enja 2048.
Jeanneau, François. 1977. *Éphémère*. Owl 07.
Jobim, Antonio Carlos. 1963. *The Composer of "Desafinado" Plays*. Verve 843273-2.
Jones, Hank, and Charlie Haden. 1994. *Steal Away: Spirituals, Hymns & Folk Songs*. Verve 527 249-2.
Laswell, Bill (producer). 1990. *Gnawa Music of Marrakesh: Night Spirit Masters*. Axiom 314-510 147-2.
London, Frank. 1992. On the Klezmatics: *Rhythm & Jews*. Flying Fish FF 70591.
London, Frank, and Greg Wall. 1997. *Jews & the Abstract Truth*. Knitting Factory Works KFWCD-192.
Masekela, Hugh. 1973. *Hugh Masekela Introducing Hedzoleh Sounds*. Blue Thumb BTS 62.
McGregor, Chris. 1991. On Chris McGregor and the Castle Lager Big Band: *Jazz—The African Sound*. Teal TELCD 2300.
———. 1994. *Chris McGregor's Brotherhood of Breath*. Repertoire REP 4468-WP.
McLaughlin, John. 1976. *Shakti, with John McLaughlin*. Columbia PC 34162.
Metheny, Pat. 1995. *We Live Here*. Geffen GEFD-24729.
Metheny, Pat, and Charlie Haden. 1997. *Beyond the Missouri Sky (Short Stories)*. Verve 314 537 130-2.
Molineaux, Othello. 1993. *It's About Time*. Big World BW2010.
Moreira, Airto. 1971. *Seeds on the Ground*. Buddah BDS 5085.
Murray, David. 1995. *Fast Life*. DIW/Columbia CK 57 526.
Myers, Amina Claudine. 1987. *Amina*. RCA Novus 3030-2-N.
Namchylak, Sainkho. 1996. On Sainkho Namchylak/Ned Rothenberg: *Amulet*. Leo CD LR 231.
Namchylak, Sainkho, and Irene Becker. 1992–93. *Dancing on the Island*. Olufsen Records DOCD 5147.
Nascimento, Milton. 1975. *Minas*. EMI [Brazil] 830431-2.
Pascoal, Hermeto. 1983. *Lagoa Da Canoa Municipio De Anapiraca*. Melopea Discos CDMSE 5033.
———. 1987. *Só Não Toca Quem Não Quer*. Som Dagente CDSDG 001/87.
Pastorius, Jaco. 1976. *Jaco Pastorius*. Epic PE 33949.
———. 1990. *Live in New York City*. Vol. 1. Big World BW1001.
Pavone, Mario. 1991. *Toulon Days*. New World/Countercurrents 80420-2.
Pepper, Jim. 1987. *Dakota Song*. Enja CD 5043-34.
Perez, Danilo. 1996. *Panamonk*. Impulse IMPD-190.

Previte, Bobby. 1988. *Claude's Late Morning*. Gramavision 18-8811-2.
————. 1993. *Slay the Suitors*. Avant AVAN 036.
Pullen, Don. 1995. *Sacred Common Ground*. Blue Note 7777 32800 2.
Reinhardt, Django. 1996. *Intégrale Django Reinhardt, Vol. 5*. Frémeaux & Associés FA 305.
Rothenberg, Ned. n.d. *The Crux*. Leo CD LR 187.
————. n.d. *Overlays*. Moers Music 02074 CD.
Rubalcaba, Gonzalo. 1993. *Rapsodia*. Blue Note CDP 7243 8 28264 2 2.
Samul Nori. 1995. *Then Comes the White Tiger*. ECM 21499.
Sandoval, Arturo. 1987. *Tumbaito*. Messidor 15974-2.
Sato, Masahiko. 1990. *Select Live under the Sky '90*. CBS/Sony ESCA 5171.
Schoeppach, Brad. 1997. *Brad Shepik and the Commuters*. Songlines SGL 1518-2.
Sclavis, Louis. 1993. *Acoustic Quartet*. ECM 1526.
Simon, Edward. 1993. *Beauty Within*. Audioquest Music AQ-CD1025.
Takada, Midori. 1995. On Ton-Klami: *Paramggod*. Nippon Crown CRCJ 9125.
Temiz, Okay. 1995. *Magnet Dance*. Tip Toe TIP888819 2.
Thiam, Mor. 1996. On World Saxophone Quartet with African Drums: *Four Now*. Justin Time JUST 83-2.
Tronzo, David. 1994. *Roots*. Knitting Factory Works KFWCD-154.
Tuncboyacian, Arto. 1992. On Marc Johnson: *Right Brain Patrol*. JMT 849 153-2.
Ulmer, James "Blood." 1988. On Music Revelation Ensemble: *Music Revelation Ensemble*. DIW DIW-825.
Umezu, Kazutoki. 1994. On Tetsuhiro Daiku: *Okinawa Jintu*. Off Note ON-1.
————. 1994. On Betsuni Nanmo Klezmer: *Omedeto*. Nani Record NCD-01.
Vasconcelos, Nana. 1979. *Saudades*. ECM 1147.
Walton, Cedar. 1989. *Bluesville Time*. Criss Cross Jazz Criss 1017 CD.
Warfield, Tim. 1996. *A Whisper in the Midnight*. Criss Cross Jazz Criss 1122 CD.
Weston, Randy. 1992. *African Sunrise*. Antilles 314 517 177-2.
World Saxophone Quartet with African Drums. 1996. *Four Now*. Justin Time JUST 83-2.
Zadeh, Aziza Mustafa. 1993. *Aziza*. Columbia 53415.
Zorn, John. n.d. *Live at the Knitting Factory*. Knitting Factory Works KFWCD-124.
————. 1994. *Tokyo Operations '94*. Avant AVAN-049.
————. 1994. On Masada: *Alef*. DIW DIW-888.

PART II

Beyond Tradition or Modernity

CHAPTER 5

Women, Music, and the "Mystique" of Hunters in Mali [1]

Lucy Durán

Dunun nègè be sogo faa bali la [2]
(Those who don't hunt are crazy for hunters' music!)

Introduction

In his study of Maninka and Bamana hunters' initiation societies (*don-sotonw*), the Malian scholar Youssouf Tata Cissé quotes a significant line from one hunter's song text: *dunun nègè be sogo faa bali la* (Those who don't hunt are crazy for hunters' music!) (Cissé 1994: 207.[3] Despite the fact that, in Mali, game is now scarce and protected by legislation, the cultural traditions and moral values of hunters' societies continue to be of deep symbolic importance for contemporary Malians. The mere sight of a hunter, dressed in the traditional hunter's cap and tunic of mud-dye cloth, conjures images of Mali's glorious past, going back to the master hunter (*simbon*) Sunjata Keita, the founder of the Mali (Mande) empire in 1235.

As a way of life, hunting is certainly on the wane, but it is still surrounded by a powerful mystique, more so in Mali than anywhere else in the Mande cultural world.[4] One of ways in which hunters continue to be vivid symbols even in the context of popular urban culture is through their music.

137

A huge landlocked country made up of many different peoples, Malians place great store on their musical heritage. Mande hunters' songs have gone far beyond the closed, ritual world in which they are meant to be performed. They circulate on recordings—some published locally, some bootlegged off radio and other sources—listened to by a wide sector of the population. The great hunters' musicians, such as Bala Jimba Diakite and (the late) Seydou Camara, are revered and celebrated by scholars, Malian musicians, and the general public. The loping sounds of hunters' harps, whistles, and iron scrapers, with their punchy rhythms and strong vocal choruses, are cherished by city dwellers who may have had very little real interaction with "the bush."

In Mali's vibrant local music scene, hunters' songs have been an important source of inspiration for Mande musicians since independence (1960). The evocation through hunters' music of a specifically Malian, non-ethnic-based identity has been an important factor in this. In this sense, it contrasts with the dominant musical voice, that of the *jeliw* (sing: *jeli*), the hereditary class of endogamous musicians who have monopolized most forms of professional music in Mali's capital, Bamako. The *jeliw* are found throughout the Mande cultural area including the neighboring countries of Guinea and the Ivory Coast and therefore are not associated with the exclusive identity of any one locus. Their musical styles have been used by other West African countries such as Guinea and Gambia as the main presence in the music of national and regional ensembles. In the particular case of Mali, whose three presidents, Modibo Keita (1960–68), Moussa Traore (1968–91), and Alpha Oumar Konare (1992–) have all been Mande, the state-subsidized Ensemble Instrumental National is composed predominantly of *jeliw*, and the national hymn is adapted from one of the most important pieces in the *jeli*'s repertoire (a song in praise of Sunjata Keita).

Since the early 1970s, when Mali's dance bands were encouraged by President Moussa Traore's government to draw on local traditions in their music, there have been many attempts to recreate hunters' traditions for the dance floor. Certain bands have made a feature of their hunters' styles (e.g., Super Biton de Segou and the Super Djata Band), while others have routinely included one or two songs in their repertoire.[5] In recent years, since the late 1980s, the use of hunters' traditions has if anything become stronger. Mali's best-known male solo artists such as Kassemady Diabate, Abdoulaye Diabate, and Habib Koite have recorded hunters' songs.[6] The singer who has most closely associated himself with a hunter's ethos is Salif Keita, in a deliberate attempt to reflect his own heritage as a noble Keita, son of a hunter. In his filmed concerts and on his album covers of the late 1980s, Keita is invariably seen wearing a hunter's costume, and he also uses the hunters' harp in his music, partly to show that he is not a *jeli*.[7]

Less known, but equally important is the fact that women singers, too, have been increasingly involved in the popularization of hunters' styles. They dress up for television appearances as hunters with rifles slung over their shoulders and use hunters' melodies to sing songs in praise of patrons or about women's issues. This could be considered the most extreme manifestation of "the craze for hunters' music by those who don't hunt," since women are ritually kept away from all aspects of hunting. While hunters' societies are made up of individuals of all ages and from different ethnic and social backgrounds, the only sector of the population who are totally and permanently excluded from *donsoya* are females.[8] Hunters are supposed to abstain from all contact with women prior to the hunt, because of "the ancient suspicion and apprehension held by hunters against women as distracting sexual beings, impending chances of a successful hunt" (Conrad in Austen: 1999). Women do not normally participate in hunters' celebratory events (except as onlookers), much less in their music, except, in certain nonritual circumstances, as the vocal chorus. The song texts of the hunters' musicians exalt ostensibly male values such as bravery and prowess in the hunt, and the rhythms of the hunters' harp and scraped iron percussion rod are perceived in Mande culture as strong, "heavy," and masculine. While hunters' societies are not an "instrument of women's oppression" (unlike, for example, other male initiation societies such as the *komo*), there is simply no role for women to play in them (Camara 1992: 52–53).

In this essay, I look at the portrayal of hunters' styles by women singers over the past decade in Bamako, Mali's capital. I analyze the "how and why" of this phenomenon. The re-creation of hunters' styles is never accorded by Malian audiences the same kind of cultural value that real hunters' music has, and yet, women's hunter-derived styles of music are greatly enjoyed and appreciated by Mande audiences. Here, I focus on the particular contribution of women to the mystique of hunters and what we can learn from this about social dynamics in Mali today.

Mande Gender Ideology and Its Impact on Contemporary Urban Music

The Mande are a widespread group of people living across seven different West African countries, with substantial expatriate communities.

They speak a number of closely related languages and are united by a sense of common heritage, going back to the Mande empire, founded by Sunjata Keita. The heartland of the empire was located in what is today western Mali and eastern Guinea, where Maninka (French: Malinke) is spoken. In this article, the term *Mande* refers primarily to two subgroups of the Mande found in Mali: the Maninka and the Wasulunke (people of Wasulu, a region in southern Mali).[9] These two ethnicities have played important roles in creating local forms of popular music, especially in Bamako, capital of Mali, where the national media and the local music industry are located.

Within the Mande social hierarchy of "nobles" (*horonw*), artisans (*nyamakalaw*), and descendants of slaves (*jonw*), professional music is traditionally the domain of the endogamous artisan group, the *nyamakalaw*, to which the *jeliw* belong. The more prestigious forms of *jeliya* (the art of the *jeli*) such as the reciting of family histories are considered the male domain. Among the *jeliw*, women are the specialized singers for life-cycle ceremonies, and men play instruments and narrate histories and lineages on particular ritual occasions. The greater value placed on male versus female genres of music is a microcosm of male-female status in Mande society at large, though the prominence of female singers in public performance presents some contradictions to this.

The Mande are patrilineal, patriarchal, and patrilocal. In the male-dominant discourse, women are regarded as subservient to men; in its most extreme articulation this is expressed in the phrase "the woman is a slave in marriage," sung frequently by women at weddings and on recordings.[10] Women have little or no say as to who they marry. They are excluded from all forms of traditional power—only males may be leaders of religious institutions, heads of villages and families, or of the *jeliw* associations. The only context in which women are leaders is in the numerous all-female self-help associations (*musutonw*).

Across the spectrum of Mande music, as in the wider social context, there is a strict gendered division of labor. Women are the preferred singers, and men are the instrumentalists. Singing, dancing, and rhythmic clapping are all considered female activities to such an extent that Mande men do not sing at all, except in the case of hunters' musicians and *jeliw*.[11] Male *jeliw* do sing, but ironically, the designation of song as a "female" activity and the importance of wedding music as a "hot-house" for popular urban styles have meant that women have gradually come to dominate in music performance in Mali.

With the growth of urban culture since independence (1960), Mande music has undergone various transformations that have partly been determined by changing contexts. Apart from the years 1970–78, a time when Mali's dance bands enjoyed great popularity and also benefited from state sponsorship, bars and nightclubs have played a relatively minor role in Mali's music scene. Such venues (generally associated with alcohol and prostitution) have been considered outside the boundaries of acceptable performance for women, except for occasional guest appearances. Excluded from nocturnal subculture, women have held the limelight in most other areas of musical activity.

Only since independence have nonhereditary types of musicians challenged the *jeli*'s monopoly on public performance within Mande culture. Since the 1970s, a new form of professional music has emerged in western Mali, called *wassoulou*. It developed in Bamako as a named style in the mid-1970s, and its performers are musicians by choice, calling themselves *kono* (bird). Most of the singers are female, while the men play instruments. This music draws on several regional traditions from Wasulu in southern Mali, a region famous for its hunters. The ensembles almost invariably feature a smaller version of the six-string Wasulunke hunters' harp, called *kamalengoni* (youth harp), which has become the trademark of *wassoulou* music, borrowing directly from hunters' playing techniques and pentatonic melodic styles. Gender issues are of paramount importance in *wassoulou* music, usually expressing the female viewpoint (Durán 1995b).

Since a singer's ability is judged primarily on his or her skill with words, rather than on beauty of voice, great attention is paid to what women singers express through song texts. Since women are the preferred singers, and song is regarded as female, women are the leaders of their ensembles in both contemporary *jeliya* and *wassoulou*. They are the focus of performance, and they receive a larger share of the economic rewards than their male accompanists. The current trend in Mali's national television (ORTM) of "playback," where the lead singer mimes existing recordings, has meant that men are frequently not featured at all in performances.[12] This provides an interesting reversal of the otherwise subservient role of women, and women singers exploit this situation to address women's issues and transgress certain boundaries of proscribed behavior. Thus, music has become one of the most powerful means for women to express themselves, and the use of hunters' idioms serves as a potent background for this.

Most women singers do not, however, see their music as feminist, in the Western sense; they do not see themselves as attempting to occupy the same musical territory as men. On the contrary, while they reference hunters' styles, they transform them both musically and textually. They are extolling the moral values that hunters embody and therefore they are urging society to emulate those values. By their own account, this is an extension of their given role, whereby they encourage men to do brave and difficult tasks. They see their music as an outsider's representation, in which the world of hunters is necessarily metaphorical and symbolic—intrinsically one of mystification. Male popular singers on the other hand could in principle become hunters—if they were able to meet the moral and physical criteria for acceptance into hunters' societies. Therefore, a man who sings hunters' songs but who is not a hunter may be perceived as subverting or mocking their ethical values and ritual power. The more he quotes directly from a hunter's song, for example, by reciting a hunter's tale, the more this criticism may apply. "He only sings these songs because he isn't capable of being a hunter himself" is the sort of comment sometimes directed at male singers.

The story of women, music, and the hunters' mystique is thus an excellent case study for exploring the "relationship between gender, music and social standing or prestige" (Koskoff 1989: 14). What changes and adaptations are women making to hunters' styles, and why? What effect does hunters' music have on their success as musicians? What resistance (if any) have they met? By seeking to answer these questions, this essay hopes to show that gender is of central importance in studying Mande culture and to redress the prevailing view that women in West Africa play marginal roles as professional music makers.

Women, Hunters, and Mande Studies

An understanding of the roles of women singers and the way in which they draw on the prevailing hunters' mystique contributes to a more balanced picture of women as professional musicians in West Africa. Since DjeDje (1985) wrote her overview, new material has emerged to change this picture, particularly in Mali, where women play such a central role in public performance (see Hale 1994; Durán 1995a). Academic research on Mande oral traditions and music has largely ignored this role, focusing instead on the historical epics such as Sunjata, which are recited mainly by male elder *jeliw*. This reflects the dominant discourse on gender hierarchy and the relative value of male versus female genres.

Such discourses tend to underrate or ignore completely the importance of popular song, where women dominate.

Though there now are a number of excellent studies of hunters, these have focused on hunters in their traditional environment (Cashion 1984; Cissé 1988; McNaughton 1988). No mention has been made of their impact on popular culture or of the contribution of female artists to their mystification.

The study of popular Mande music is still in its infancy and has concentrated on aspects of the instrumental traditions of the *jeliw* (e.g., Charry 1992), which explicitly exclude women singers because they are not instrumentalists. The only publication to date on *wassoulou* music, which since the mid-1980s has been one of the most popular styles locally, is by this author (Durán 1995b). In the international music industry, the musicians who have established links with international record labels and concert circuits have mostly been men (Salif Keita, Toumani Diabate, Kassemady Diabate, etc.). Malian male singers such as Salif Keita have achieved considerable fame since the mid-1980s through recordings and concert performances, but here too, there has been an imbalance. The representation of male versus female artists abroad reflects the fact that women dominate the live music scene within Mali, and record for the local cassette industry. If they perform outside Mali, it is mostly to their own expatriate communities at weddings and community celebrations. Prior to 1990 only a few *jelimusow* (female *jeliw*) such as Fanta Damba, Ami Koita, and Tata Bambo Kouyate were known outside the country.

A major breakthrough for female artists occurred when, in 1989, the young *wassoulou* singer Oumou Sangare had her first hit with her cassette *Moussolou* (1991), leading to an international career. Her success drew worldwide attention to the existence of Mali's women singers and to the *wassoulou* style of music, though with some cross-cultural misunderstandings.

As Malian female artists begin to establish international reputations through recordings and concert tours, there has been a tendency by non-Malian writers to paint them all with the same brush and misunderstand the different social spheres they represent. There is some confusion as to who is and is not a *jeli,* and the importance of this distinction within Mali itself. Oumou Sangare, for example, is sometimes erroneously described as a *jeli.* Although she is now well known as a champion of women's rights, her song lyrics are in fact rarely overtly critical or confrontational; her Mande listeners, however, understand the implied criticism through their knowledge of the social context in which she has composed her songs.

Maninka and Wasulunke Hunters' Societies

The hunter king is as much a cliché of African myth as the blacksmith king; he is the immigrant stranger, bringing civilisation and new technologies.

(HERBERT 1993: 165)

The traditional importance of hunters' societies in many African cultures is well known, although with urbanization, deforestation, and many other factors, hunting as a way of life is becoming increasingly obsolete. In Mali, the special respect for hunters arises out of their important historical role, amply documented by Cashion (1984), Cissé (1994), and others, who provide detailed accounts of the rich cultural, symbolic, and spiritual world of Mande hunters (*donsow, donsolu*). The first Mande armies were drawn from hunters' societies, and hunters gave protection and food for the villages. Hunters are thus associated with traditional systems of authority. Their ritual celebrations were, not surprisingly, suppressed by the French colonial administration but have been actively condoned in independent Mali (Cissé 1994: 61 n 41).

On major holidays, such as New Year's Day and Mali's Independence Day (22 September), members of hunters' societies gather for secular festivities in different parts of the country. In Bamako (the capital), where Mali's National Association of Hunters has its headquarters in Ntomikorobougou (underneath the hill where the Presidential Palace is located), the celebrations take place within the army barracks.[13] All day long on the grounds of the barracks, they dance special hunters' dances to the music of the hunters' harps, dressed in their hunters' tunics and firing their locally manufactured muskets into the air. The gunshots echo off the rocky escarpment of the presidential hill (Koulouba) and resound around the city, so that everyone is aware that the hunters are celebrating.[14]

Mande hunters' musicians are also hunters themselves. With their music, they mediate between the hunters and the *nyama* (vital force) of slain animals and the forest spirits (*jinns,* often transformed into animals or human beings). Musical activities happen mainly in the context of initiation ceremonies, preparations for the hunt, celebrations after a successful hunt to counteract the unseen forces (*nyama*) released by the slain animal, and at funeral wakes and commemorative ceremonies for deceased master hunters (*Simbon si*). If a hunter is gravely ill, the musician is called to play music at his bedside (Cissé 1994: 118).

Within their own song texts, hunters' musicians refer to themselves as *kono* (bird) while nonhunters mostly refer to them by the name of "hunter's *jeli*" (*donsojeli*). This is an important distinction, since it has implications in the context of popular music as well. Hunters' musicians are vocational (unlike the Mande *jeliw* [*griots,* hereditary musicians]); their status as musicians is achieved, not ascribed by birthright. The term *kono* draws on the rich symbolism of the bird in Mande culture (metaphor for wisdom and freedom), denoting someone (male or female) who is a musician by choice, with a beautiful voice, and with the kind of insight that a "bird's-eye view" gives, and freedom to comment on society. Birds in Mande culture are also widely associated with esoteric power, as in the hunter's phrase: "Don't you know that *konoya* [the art of the *kono*] demands a little sorcery?" (Cashion 1984, part 2: 136–37). Songbirds (nightingales, etc.) are of course common metaphors for singers in many cultures around the world (see Durán 1995b).[15] *Wassoulou* musicians choose to identify themselves with hunters, and they differentiate themselves from *jeliw,* by using the term *kono* to describe themselves in both their song texts and their discourse.

The role that hunters play as "guardian of the cardinal virtues" of a glorious Mali is well expressed in the words of Mamadou Diatigui Diarra, secretary-general of the National Association of Hunters of Mali, in his comments on the music of one hunters' musician, Sibiri Samake:

> Mali lies at the heart of African history and hunters lie at the heart of Malian history . . . Guardians of the animistic rites, the hunters are by far the oldest traditional organisation spared by the sands of time; neither Islam nor Christianity have succeeded in modifying their character . . . In putting the accent [in his songs] on those [master hunters] who have died, Sibiri wants their courage, generosity, patriotism and integrity to serve as an example to present and future generations. He asks today's youth to act as the guardian of the cardinal virtues of a Mali of warriors, a Mali of hunters, a Mali proud of its historic past. (liner notes to Samake 1991)

Hunters' associations, *donsotonw,* date from before the time of Sunjata Keita (himself a master hunter or *simbon*), and are therefore among the oldest initiation societies among the Mande. The epithet *simbon* is still generally used to describe master hunters, a term also used by *jeliw* to praise members of the Keita lineage, in recognition of the fact that they descend from Sunjata, the greatest of all master hunters. The cultural phenomenon of hunters' societies in Mali is widespread and by no means confined to rural areas. "Membership" is exclusively male but otherwise is open to all ages and ethnicities, including non-Malians. The single most important criterion for membership is character and behavior, and all initiates, even those in the city, must undergo a rigorous period in the bush, in which their endurance, courage, strength, and skill are tested.

While the rituals of hunters are reserved for members of the hunters' societies, the character qualities that the hunter embodies are well known to the general Mande population and much admired. The ability to hunt game is by itself of minor significance in the mystique of hunters. In the words of a hunter's song:

A hunting head-dress and a hunting shirt
do not make a man a hunter.
One is a hunter in everyday life.
(LINER NOTES TO *GUINÉE* 1987: 15)

This reflects the fact that while anyone can hunt animals, only those who have been accepted into the *donsoton* are truly considered hunters in the widest sense of the word. One of the attributes of the hunters' world (*donsoya*) is a strict code of honor. Hunters should be honest and straightforward in all aspects of life. While this is considered an ideal for the Mande in general, it is accepted that few put it into practice; hunters are, however, required to do so, since failure to comply would mean loss of power and status. For example, one way in which hunters differ from nonhunters is in their relationships with women. Hunters are supposed to be highly controlled in their relationships with women and indeed are praised for this quality in hunters' songs: "a woman-lover will not be a hunter until the end of the world."[16] Before the hunt, men are expected to avoid sexual relations. The best young hunters are those who "scorn marriage" (Cashion 1984: 129–30). If polygamous, a hunter must genuinely treat all his wives equally and must not indulge in extramarital relationships. (In villages, women often aspire to have a hunter spouse, whom they contrast with the *dugukamalemba,* the town womanizer.)

Linked with sexual abstention are the qualities of bravery, fearlessness, and stoicism, an important part of the hunters' mystique. Hunters are meant to withstand extreme hardship, such as long periods in the bush without food, water, or rest. Stoicism and fearlessness are traits that are generally valued in Mande culture, but it is hunters who exemplify them.[17] In the words of hunters' songs: "*E né siran mogo do gné a té siranan*" (I fear a person who is fearless), from Samake (1991), bd 2: Djine Musso; "if I see a hunter, I shake with fear" (Cashion 1984: 141–42, line 1126).

Bravery and skill at hunting go hand in hand with esoteric power, a major part of the hunters' mystique—they are healers and "sorcerers" (*somaw*). They understand the medicinal properties of plants and fabricate amulets (*sebenw*). They have power objects called *boliw*. Their songs and dances are charged with *nyama* (vital force), which can backfire on them if not performed in the correct circumstances by the right hunters. The centrality of healing and occult power to the hunters' way of life is expressed frequently in song: "a person cannot be a hunter unless he knows medicine" ("*Mogo te ke dosso ye ni ma furabo*"[18]); "you will not become a hunter if you have no sorcerer's power" (Cashion 1984 part 2: line 1060).

Esoteric power (*somaya*) is probably the single most important factor in the hunter's mystique and is praised by women in their songs, as in Ami Koita's song "Soma" (see below). Visually, this power is manifested in the distinctive hunters' dress, which is believed to protect the hunter against *nyama* and other unseen forces and spirits. A version of the hunters' costume is sometimes worn by musicians, including women singers, indicating a strong psychological identification with or admiration for the hunters' ideology, though not necessarily that the musicians belong to a hunters' society. The best-known example of a musician who chooses to identify himself with hunters in this way, while not actually belonging to a hunters' association, is Salif Keita, whose father, Sina Keita, was the leader of the hunters of Djoliba (his native village), and who on his third album, *Amen,* is pictured wearing a hunter's costume (Keita 1991).[19] The *jelimuso* (female *jeli*) Kandia Kouyate has also drawn on visual imagery of the hunter in her 1995 cassette, *Sa kunu sa* (the title is in praise of hunters), where she is pictured holding a musket (see Figure 5-1).

In everyday discourse in Bamako, one hears many stories about the supernatural abilities of hunters and the mesmeric effect of hunters' music, which is believed to call out the hunters' *jinns*. In a television documentary shown on ORTM (Radio Television Mali) of a hunters' meeting in Wasulu, some twenty musicians play hunters' harps while the chief of the association (*donsotigi*), dressed in full hunters' regalia,

FIGURE 5-1. Kandia Kouyate, *Sa kunu sa.*

appears to draw large quantities of water (which he then drinks and washes his face with) directly out of the camera lens, then finally from the calabash resonator of the harp itself (*Les chasseurs du wassolou et sogoninkoun* 1995).

Koly Keita (1996), an influential television producer with ORTM, comments:

To catch animals in the bush one has to know nature. That's why hunters are also healers. They know many plants, they know many secrets of nature. We who are in "the village" who don't have this ability, we say that they have an occult power. Those who go into the bush know more than those who stay in the village. So when you say *donso* it's always accompanied by an aura of mystique. At the time of the Mali empire, even before Sunjata, even at the time of the Ghana empire, the hunters were the healers and the defenders of the population in war. So when you say *donso,* it's a courageous man. They go into the bush for a whole week, they bear the sting of insects, thirst, hunger, pain, heat, etc. It's endurance. They're a kind of superman.

Koly Keita is the director and producer of many of the "videoclips" of leading Malian musicians, and likes to put hunters' symbolism in his clips, thus playing on the popular mystique. In one of his televised videoclips of *wassoulou* singer Oumou Sangare, for instance, he features a young hunter holding a musket and performing the hunters' dance to Oumou's song "Ko Sira" (1993).

A full discussion of Mande gender ideology is outside the scope of this article,[20] but it is interesting to note here that, ironically, some parallels can be seen between hunters and women. First, women are expected to be faithful to their spouses and highly controlled in their sexuality. Second, women are supposed to exercise physical and emotional restraint and stoicism, as in the proverb *Muso mana munyu i be barika den bange* (If a woman is stoic, she'll give birth to a blessed child).[21] Women are expected to suffer; the tolerance of suffering is a manifestation of womanhood. Hunters too are required to tolerate suffering (as in the greeting between hunters, "you and suffering" [*i ni niani*]). Several women singers whom I talked to suggested that they identified with and admired hunters because, like women, hunters had to endure extremes of endurance and pain. Third, women, like hunters, are widely associated with supernatural powers and have always been so, as is evident from their roles in historical epics of the *jeliw,* such as the story of Sunjata (Conrad 1999). Hunters' musicians particularly celebrate the magical powers of women in their narratives, since "there is no bravery without magic and no magic without bravery" (liner notes to *Guinée* 1992).

In some narratives, hunters' wives have the power to prevent their husbands from being able to kill wild animals, if they feel they have been slighted. The legendary master hunter Famori, for example, in one account by Seydou Camara, had quarreled with his first wife, Nuntenen, as a result of which he was unable to kill a wild beast. He therefore takes her into the bush with him, determined to make her a hunter. "Famori took the long gun . . . put it on the woman's shoulders / and together they entered the bush / for a whole day of walking" (Cashion 1984: 197–98 [lines 1534–37]). In another incident, Famori is turned by a *jinn* into a "lovely big-breasted girl" just as he is about to make love to his youngest wife (288).

Indeed, in most of the well-known hunters' tales such as Famori and Kambili, the hunter succeeds in his battle against the animals and/or *jinns* of the bush only with the help of a wife (Belcher 1995). In Famori, it is Nuntenen, the least-favorite wife, who saves Famori from being killed by the *jinn*, with a single gunshot. She chides him for his cowardice, saying "all your shitty old trousers have been laid upon Nuntenen's head, I am the least-loved wife. Your favorite wives could not do such a thing as this. It was the least-loved wife who had to get her man's hands out of his mess." Whereupon Famori strips off all his clothes and exchanges them for hers, even tying her headscarf and wrap, and they return to the village dressed in each other's clothes (Belcher 1995).

Coulibaly reports that some hunters' musicians refer to hunters as their "husbands," and the hunters too treat the musicians as their "wives," to whom they give gifts, and so forth. For example, the celebrated blind Maninka hunters' musician Bala Jimba Diakite sings: "Here is the resonating-in-my-hands *Janjun* [a well-known hunters' song], the *Janjun* of my real husband!" (Coulibaly 1985: 50; my translation).

In Mande culture, the inability to produce children is almost invariably believed to be the fault of the woman; not so in hunters' culture. Male fertility among hunters is considered low because of the *nyama* (vital force) of the wild animals they kill. In Diakite's narrative, Kanbili ("a hunter without equal") is unable to produce children until he makes sacrifices at the crossroads—the same sacrifices that women do when they are childless. After a few months, his wife conceives, and Kanbili celebrates, saying: "the game eaters had said / that I had become a sterile man. / . . . because of having killed so much game, I became sterile" (Coulibaly 1985: 58). Similarly, Famori also was rendered sterile by his pact with a *jinn*, which only Nuntenen was able to reverse by shooting the crocodile, with a single bullet: "from the moment the gun was fired at Marikon [the crocodile] / the man's [Famori's] penis and testicles had returned" (Cashion 1984: 322 [lines 2485–66]).

Thus hunters' narratives reflect a less bounded, more fluid concept of gender than in the nonhunters' world. They provide models of women who are both good, faithful wives as well as able hunters, hunting on an equal footing with their husbands. They tell of men who become infertile and change into women, growing long hair and breasts. Though always sung by men, such narratives address the consequences of male-dominant gender roles on both men and women, as, for example, in polygamous marriage. Seen in this light, the appropriation of hunters' music by women singers and its use in commenting on gender relations is not such a clear-cut case of reversal of gender ideology as it may first appear.

Hunters' Music

Cissé (1994) provides the most comprehensive study to date of hunters' societies, but does not, however, comment on musical style, and therefore does not distinguish between Maninka and Wasulunke traditions. Very little research has been done specifically on the music of these hunters' groups (see Charry 2000). Although hunters' associations may be multiethnic, the musicians themselves and musical instruments and styles they perform are firmly within the ethnic traditions of the region. Two stylistic areas are important to note here, because they carry into contemporary music. Maninka hunters' music, from the area west of Bamako, is heptatonic and lyrical melodically; this is the style that feeds into *jeliya*. Wasulunke hunters' music is invariably pentatonic and highly rhythmic, imitated in *wassoulou* music.

Both types of hunters' music use a form of harp and the iron scraper as their principal instrumental accompaniment. Both repertoires involve solo, free-rhythm, rapid-fire solo singing, with continuous interjections from the *namunamina* (a person who interjects affirmative words such as *namu, ate* after every song line) and frequent one-line responsorial choruses.

The Wasulunke hunters' harp (*donsongoni,* literally, the "hunters' string instrument") has only six strings, cut from nylon fishing line (formerly twisted leather), arranged in two parallel rows across a raised bridge. The *donsongoni* has a varied repertoire based on sequences of four-beat ostinati called *ngonisen* (literally, "the leg of the string instrument"—the *ngoni*'s riff) and is accompanied by a metal scraper called *karinyan,* consisting of a piece of iron rolled in on itself with serrated edges. The *karinyan* is played with a steady down-up-down motion (echoed in *wassoulou* music) that propels the dance. The most celebrated exponent of the Wasulunke hunters' style was the late Seydou Camara, whose epic recitations were transcribed by Cashion and others and whose recordings show a musician of great virtuosity and charisma. Contemporary performers of repute include Toumani Kone. Most *wassoulou* singers like Oumou Sangare listen repeatedly to the recordings of these performers and emulate their styles.

Around the old Mande heartland, from Joliba to Kela and farther west, the principal ethnicity is Maninka (Malinke). Maninka hunters' musicians play a harp called *simbin* with seven to ten metal strings mounted on a raised bridge. A large metal rattle is attached to the end of the neck, adding an extra percussive effect. The songs are heptatonic and highly melodious. Little has been published on the style of this music, but fortunately there are recordings, in particular those of Bala Jimba Diakite, generally regarded as the finest hunters' musician in the Maninka musical style (Cashion 1984: part 1, 296). A blind musician of the Badugu hunters' association whose music circulates widely in Mali on cassette, his epic narratives have been transcribed by Cissé and Coulibaly among others (Cisse 1994: 139 n 120). His song "Balakonininfi" (The little black bird of the river) has been recorded in several versions by dance bands as well as by Mory Kante, Salif Keita, and most recently by the *jelimuso* Kandia Kouyate (see below). Many of the songs quoted in Cissé's 1994 study of the hunters' societies are attributed to Bala Jimba, whom Cissé acknowledges as a great master, and his songs "touch on the foundations of Mande civilization" (Cisse 1994: 139; my translation). On many occasions I have watched the reactions of Malians when they listen to (often very poor quality) recordings of Bala Jimba. Even just the sound of his *simbin* elicits a strong aesthetic response— with its simple, leisurely paced ostinato, the strings heavily damped, and buzzing effects of rattles, the *simbin* and its melodies evoke a sense of history and nobility. As Salif Keita remarks, "Sunjata Keita himself played the *simbin*" (Durán 1995c).

Despite musical differences between the two regional styles, the core of Wasulunke and Maninka hunters' performance in both cases is a type of epic narrative (*donsomaana*), based on a number of stories that relate the struggle between hunters, wild animals, and bush spirits. Women play important and heroic roles in these stories.[22] The narrative is sung in a free-rhythm, recitational style, punctuated by frequent chorus refrains of one or two lines performed antiphonally by the soloist and his chorus. Occasionally, the wives of the soloist may form part of the chorus; otherwise, it is made up of the soloist's (male) apprentices. The musicians dance and swing their harps from side to side, much the way the hunters swing their rifles as they dance, sometimes in procession, sometimes individually.[23]

Hunters' musicians do not always narrate tales in their songs, especially when they record for cassette. In such cases, they may sing songs that comment on social relations, including male-female relations from the male perspective, as in Harouna Doumbia's "Bi Mousso" (Women of today).[24] Female *wassoulou* singers such as Oumou Sangare sing similar songs, but from the female perspective. Thus "the hunters' traditions which once served to integrate populations across ethnic lines are now being called into play to foreground the modern social pressures expressed across gender lines. This is the new social battleground" (Belcher 1995).

Hunters' Music in a Wider Context

The documentation on hunters' musical traditions elsewhere in West Africa is scattered and relatively scarce and says little about the extent to which they have entered the realm of popular culture. More research is needed, but a cursory review of the literature points to the conclusion that Mali—with its singers like Salif Keita and styles like *wassoulou*—provides the most tangible West African examples of a hunters' aesthetic in popular music. Even within the wider Mande cultural area, it is the popular music of Mali that draws most heavily on hunters' traditions. There seems to be no comparable trend to *wassoulou* music in Guinea, just over the border, despite the existence of the same styles of hunters' music in Guinea's own Wasulu region. Charry (1992: 74) reports a hunters' influence in Guinean modern music, though the Malian guitarist Mamadu Doumbia says: "that's the difference between Malian and Guinean guitarists—that . . . *wassoulou* style, there's no such style in Guinea" (quoted in Prince 1996).

For example, Sekouba "Bambino" Diabate, former lead singer with the country's top dance band, Bembeya Jazz National, explains that his "hunters' songs" are in fact praise songs for patrons who are descended from great hunters. "I praise them," he comments, "more for their sorcery, since they no longer hunt," though he does not quote from actual hunters' tunes. Thus he uses the well-known *jeli* tune "Lamban" to praise a businessman, Kessaly Camara, the son of a great hunter, singing "if his father would get up in the morning and say I'll bring back such and such type of animal, he would" (S. B. Diabate 1997; see also Durán 1997).

In Gambia and Senegal, where hunters' associations have virtually disappeared, hunters' music appears to have made no impact on contemporary music (cf. Charry 1999: 74). Looking at the Mandinka *kora* repertoire, hunter-derived pieces like "Janjon" and "Duga" are sometimes played, but "Kulanjan" (see below) is conspicuously absent (Knight 1973). There is little trace of a hunters' mystique in their popular culture. It is notable that in the Mandinka style of music, women play a marginal role. In Gambia, Senegal, and Guinea Bissau, it could be argued that the *nyancho* (warrior prince) takes the place of the hunter as the heroic personality in contemporary Mandinka society; hence, the popularity of songs like "Kelefa" and "Cheddo"—epic historical songs about warfare, with few female characters.

Elsewhere in West Africa, in places where hunters' associations historically have been important, their music nevertheless remains separate from popular culture. For example, Yoruba hunters' songs (*ìjálá*), described by Euba as "one of the best known" of Yoruba song forms accompanied on *dùndún* drum ensembles, seem to have made little impact on Yoruba popular music styles like *jùjú* (Euba 1990: 406).[25] The same is true for Ghana, despite the fact that it has strong hunters' traditions—for example, among the northern Ewe (Agawu 1995: 94–96).[26] Writing in the early 1960s, the Ghanaian scholar Nketia (1963) refers to Akan, Ga, Adangme, and Ewe hunters' associations but concludes that "as the popularity of hunting as a means of livelihood dwindles, the ritual of hunters becomes less and less important and the music associated with it ceases to be practised in the given area" (18–21). Of course, other factors are also involved, such as the colonial experience in those countries, the role of the church, and the development of (predominantly male) interethnic popular styles like Highlife, which has no references to hunters' music.

Nevertheless, the role of hunters in West Africa seems every so often to renew itself, suggesting a more dynamic situation than described by Nketia. For example, in Sierra Leone hunters have reasserted themselves in the present context of political crisis.[27] In Sierra Leone, hunters in full costume are often depicted in wall paintings. There have also been reports of hunters acting as an unofficial police force in Abidjan, to control local crime. Their ancient traditions and connections with esoteric power, apparently anachronistic, emerge as a stabilizing influence. In a newspaper report, a British journalist (Elroy 1996) gives a vivid description of these hunters—one that could well apply to the Mande *donso*:

> In their colourful tunics and cloth caps, adorned with talismans, shells and mirrors, primitive rifles and machetes slung over their shoulders, Kamajor hunters may appear more akin to Robin Hood's merry men than to a feared and respected fighting force. Yet since the outbreak of civil war in Sierra Leone five years ago these traditional hunters have transformed themselves into a formidable civil defense force. They claim to have magical powers which have been more successful against the rebels of the Revolutionary United Front than the military tactics of the army.

Diabolical Strings: The Re-creation of Hunters' Styles in Wassoulou Music

As a social phenomenon, *wassoulou* music occupies an interesting space between global and local, popular and traditional. Professional *wassoulou* groups or singers sometimes perform at weddings (for example, for people of Wasulu origin in Bamako), in which case they sing songs of advice to the bride, from the *jagawara* repertoire. The main contexts for performance, however, are the concert hall (though these are far from formal, seated occasions), the recording studio (mainly locally produced cassettes), and the local media. For example, on Mali television's main weekly music program, *Top Etoiles,* which presents the ten most popular artists of the week, around one-third of the artists featured are *wassoulou*. At concerts organized in Bamako's main venues such as the Palais de la Culture, where it is customary to have up to ten acts or more, *wassoulou* artists are regularly included. Those who listen to and enjoy *wassoulou* come from diverse social, economic, and ethnic backgrounds, and the music makes no financial demands on them—that is, they are not expected to reward the musicians with gifts, as is the case with the *jeliw*. The main musical frame of reference is local to southern Mali, but a few artists (e.g., Jah Youssoufou, Askia Modibo) use reggae rhythms. Strong dance rhythms are an important part of the appeal of *wassoulou*.

Though *wassoulou* has developed as a professional genre primarily in Bamako since the mid-1980s, its performers, invariably of Wasulu origin, evoke a sense of continuity with rural life in the urban context. The people of Wasulu are Mande speaking but trace their ancestry to a Fula migration to the region many centuries ago. Their Fula background is shown in their four most common family names (Diallo, Diakite, Sidibe, and Sangare). Wasulunke identity is thus one of mixed ethnicity, and some *wassoulou* groups deliberately emphasize this in their instrumentation—for example, in the use of the one-string fiddle (*soku*) and a flute (*fle*), which are typically considered Fula.

Wasulu is a thickly wooded and relatively remote region, known in Mali for its hunters and blacksmiths (*numuw*) (indeed, some hunters' musicians as well as *wassoulou* singers are of the blacksmith lineage).[28] Although there are *jeliw* in Wasulu, they play a relatively limited musical role in comparison with vocational musicians who call themselves *konow* (birds). The term *kono* applies to both singers and instrumentalists in all contexts of music performance in Wasulu, including hunters' music (see above). This is one of the important symbolic features of Wasulunke traditions that carries over into the urban context. In their own discourse, *wassoulou* musicians emphasize that they are *konow*, to distinguish their role and status from those of the *jeliw*.

The origins of *wassoulou* are mainly in Wasulunke performance traditions: *sogoninkun* (a nonritual acrobatic dance performed by two or more men in masquerade, with women singers), and *jagwa*, also known as *jagawara*, songs performed by unmarried youth at informal parties for the bride the night before she leaves her village to go to her husband's home. Included in the *jagawara* is a type of music known as *kamalengoni nyenaje* (literally, "young boys' harp entertainment," a youth version of the hunters' harp), which imitates the sounds of hunters' music. Of these three, the last named gives *wassoulou* its most characteristic sound—that of the harp—and its youth ethos.

Music in Wasulu is highly participatory. The most frequent type of musical ensemble is a group of three or four drummers (two or three *jembe* [goblet-shaped drums] of different sizes and one *dunun,* a cylindrical drum played with a crooked stick) who interlock in polyrhythm, usually with spectacular virtuosity. They accompany one or more solo female singers who engage in a kind of dialogue with the dancers—the singer performs a few lines of song, the dancers (predominantly female, except for masked dancers, who are invariably male) respond with gestures and movement. The crowd participates with responsorial choruses and hand clapping.

Among the growing community of migrant workers from Wasulu in Bamako in the decade following independence, performances of *sogo-*

ninkun and *jagawara* were common, and in this environment certain female singers established a name for themselves—for example, Kagbe Sidibe, occasionally recording for national radio. At this stage, however, the only instrumentation they used was the drum ensemble, djembe, and *dunun* described above. Such music was not yet known as *wassoulou*. It was only when musicians began adding the youth harp, *kamalengoni* (as well as electric guitars) to the drum ensemble that this music began to be so designated. This type of ensemble was developed quite specifically by female singers in the mid- to late 1970s, and its essential ingredient is the *kamalengoni*.

The story of this instrument is interesting and highly relevant, since it is one of the main aural hooks into the hunters' tradition. It was created by young boys in Wasulu and is always played by males (in accordance with the general division of musical labor in Mande), but women have been most responsible for popularizing it. According to oral testimony, the *kamalengoni* dates from the 1950s. It developed in some isolation in remote villages of Wasulu, and yet, it mirrors the ways in which popular music has developed around the world as a youth culture confronting the values of an older generation. In the 1950s, boys who were too young to be hunters would imitate hunters' songs for their own amusement. To simulate the sound of the hunters' harp, they played a six-string pluriarc called *ndan or kamalendan* (youth *ndan*).[29] This instrument consists of six individual sticks or pieces of cane, each with its own string. The sticks are mounted in a half calabash, facing downward with the round part facing the player.

Most of today's *kamalengoni* players attribute the origin of the instrument to one particular *ndan* player from Badani (near Kalana in southwest Mali) called Allata Brulaye Sidibe.[30] In 1996, in the only interview Allata Brulaye ever gave (some months before his death in February 1997), he explained how the idea came to him:

> I used to play *ndan* from the age of ten, but the *ndan* had wire strings and a small voice. One day a *marabout* told me to turn around the calabash resonator as God did not like it facing downwards. So I made a harp like the hunters' harp, only smaller, for kids, but I used the same way of playing as the *ndan*. The hunters' harp is for the elders. It's only for the *marafatigi* [those who own the hunters' rifle]. With the youth harp, there are no limits on who can hear it and what we can play on it. Here in Wasulu, everything is *donsoya* [the art of hunters]. When you hear *kamalengoni,* it

doesn't have the power of *donsoya,* but it has the sounds of *don-soya.* If you can play the *kamalengoni,* it means you can play *don-songoni.*

A farmer and hunter (though not a formal member of a *donsoton*), Sidibe traveled widely in Wasulu in his teens, playing the *kamalengoni* and teaching others to play. The jittery rhythms on Allata Brulaye's imitation hunters' harp were instantly popular among the youth. "This was our own dance music. We didn't listen to records or the radio. Young boys and girls would meet in the evenings outside the village and dance to this music until the early hours of the morning, they made up their own dances—like hunters' dances. Some people called it 'bordello' music because they were shocked that we were using hunters' sounds for boys and girls together" (B. Sidibe 1996 [Allata's brother]).

The village elders forbade the instrument, calling it *samakoro* (flea), a pejorative term stemming from the idea that young people were compelled by its rhythms to dance furiously, as if they were itchy from flea bites (Durán 1995b). But the music had caught on in the region and became an essential part of all festivities. Though it has now lost most of its shock value (some elders in Wasulu nevertheless do still call it bordello music), it continues to be an important part of musical life in Wasulu villages today. The "corrupting" and seductive aura of the *kamalengoni* is part of the mythology of *wassoulou.*

The *kamalengoni* is strung exactly like the hunter's harp (*don-songoni*) with two parallel rows of three strings across a wide, raised bridge, in a pentatonic scale. (Since the early 1990s, a few players have been adding an extra pair of bass strings to make a total of eight strings.) The tuning is a fourth higher, however, and players say that its sound is "strings" while the *donsongoni* is "skin" (i.e., bass). Each tune is based on a short two-part ostinato melody called *ngonisen* (a term that translates literally as "the string instrument's leg," meaning the *ngoni* riff or basic tune). The riffs of both hunters' and youth harps arise naturally out of the layout of the strings (left-hand row: EAD, right-hand row: DGC), since they tend to be played alternating right and left hands. Different strings can serve as the "fundamental" or starting note (see Durán 1995b).

Most *kamalengoni* players claim that they adapt hunters' styles without quoting directly from them and that their instrument is "powerless," unlike the "sacred" *donsongoni.* Nevertheless, there are interesting parallels in the way that both types of musician personify the harp strings.

For example, hunters' musicians refer to the harp strings as "diabolical" (liner notes, *Guineé* 1987),[31] asking them to calm down or boasting of their power.[32] Similarly, the *kamalengoni* players sing lines to their strings, such as "cool down, you're running away. Be careful of the strings! The strings are angry, I ask them to be patient,"[33] chiding the strings for getting out of control, as if they had a life of their own. This personification is echoed when female *wassoulou* singers sing phrases such as *juru i nin su!* (Good evening, strings/melody).

Allata Brulaye was the first to record on the *kamalengoni*, accompanying his niece, Coumba Sidibe, from Koninko.[34] While he may have been responsible for "inventing" the instrument, it was Coumba Sidibe (known as Coumba Saba—three Coumbas) who began adapting specific hunters' songs for the *kamalengoni* and who took the music to the capital. Coumba started out as a *sogoninkun* (masquerade) singer (her father, Diara Sidibe, was a famous *sogoninkun* dancer) but gradually became attracted to hunters' music as a source for her own singing.

> The *sogoninkun* only uses *jembe* [drum], I thought maybe it wouldn't please everyone. So I had the idea of using the hunters' harp with *jembe*. Hunters' music, that's only for hunters. Allata Brulaye and I, we were the first to turn this music into a *nyenaje* [entertainment] thing, music for young people's pleasure. My older brother [Brulaye] and I got together and said, "Let's try to change the hunters' harp a little so that the youth can dance to it." We called it *kamalengoni* . . . but the elders were against it. They couldn't understand why we should bring this culture to many people; for them it was something reserved for hunters' societies . . . When we started doing this, the hunters rose up and protested everywhere. They felt it was unacceptable to have hunters' music played for public amusement. So Brulaye and I, we brought them kola nuts, chickens, even goats and local alcohol [as sacrifices] to ask their pardon. We told the elder hunters we promised not to touch the secrets of their ancestors. But any village that didn't have a *kamalengoni nyenaje*, that village was not a nice place to be. (C. Sidibe 1996)

Several contemporary performers of *wassoulou* have stated that Wasulunke musicians could not develop musically prior to the fall of Mali's first president, Modibo Keita, as they "were not free to sing what they like" under Keita's regime, given that the spirit of *wassoulou* is freedom of expression, an alternative to the praise songs of the *jeliw* (B. Diallo 1994). They attribute the emergence of *wassoulou* music to Coumba Sidibe's re-creation of hunters' styles in the mid-1970s. Coumba, the first Wasulunke singer to join the Ensemble Instrumental National (EIN), the state-subsidized ensemble of traditional Malian instruments, was assigned the task of developing a repertoire for the EIN that gave a flavor of the Wasulu region. In 1977 the EIN recorded (with Coumba as lead singer) the song "Diya ye banna" (The pleasure is over), which comes from the *jagawara* prewedding repertoire (Ensemble Instrumental 1977). Its success turned Coumba Sidibe into one of Bamako's most popular singers, on a par with the most sought after *jelimusow* of the period (such as Fanta Damba), paving the way for other female *wassoulou* artists.

Though Coumba Sidibe's early recordings drew on her own background as a *sogoninkun* and *jagawara* singer, it was after she left the EIN in late 1977 to take up a solo career that she began to work on the idea of using hunters' songs, with Allata Brulaye.[35] As a woman, she says, she felt obliged to adapt them with "caution and respect":

> There are some *ngonisenw* [harp riffs], normally they shouldn't be played just for fun, you know. Some melodies, one shouldn't sing them except for hunters. Some words, they too shouldn't be sung for just anyone. Some pieces are reserved just for a great hunter, like someone who's killed a lion. That piece in his honor, you can't just go singing it for someone who's killed a goat in town. There are others that can only be played for the funeral of a great person in the village. Like *Ntanan,* in the old days it couldn't be played for all men, let alone for any woman . . . some of these songs, they can kill you. *Ntanan,* that's from the hunters' repertoire. It can be played on the *kamalengoni,* some do, but not me, I know what the word means . . . [If you sing a song like *Ntanan* and put love lyrics to it], it could even cost you your life. Yes! . . . because some songs oblige you to do things you can't do . . . a singer comes and sings for me, that pushes me to kill a lion . . . there are even people who will be dancing in the nightclub [to my music], and they'll understand." (C. Sidibe 1996).

Such views on the consequences of transgressing boundaries between music for "play" (for mixed audiences) and ritual (for male audiences only) is echoed in other Mande art forms, such as the carving of masks (Brett-Smith 1994: 155).

The *ntanan* (also known as *ntanaani, ndanani*: meaning "little *ntanan*") is one of several songs performed at funerals for great hunters. On such occasions, only great hunters may dance. *Ntanan* refers to an ensemble of three drums called *donso tanan* ("hunters' bells") to mark the opening of the last stage of mourning ceremonies (Cissé 1994, caption to photo between pp. 128–29). "Only those who have slain any of these animals [lion, hyena, leopard, or buffalo] may dance these songs [e.g., the *ntanan*]. If a hunter who has no right to dance these songs should get up and dance when they are played, he would break the rules of the association and risk illness or death brought about by hunters obviously having fetishes powerful enough to slay such animals. Only the foolhardy or demented would bring this upon himself" (Cashion 1984, part 1: 220–21). Interestingly, both Coumba Sidibe and another *wassoulou* female singer, Sali Sidibe, have recorded versions of these songs, in which they make no direct reference to hunters other than the powerful image of the *ntanan* itself.

Coumba Sidibe dedicates her song "Hee, ndanani" to Malians who are distant from their roots in one way or another (geographically or symbolically, by abandoning their cultural values). Themes that deal with the issue of migration are common in *wassoulou*—there are large immigrant Wasulunke communities outside the region (Coumba herself has spent several long periods out of Mali, in Abidjan, Paris, and most recently the United States, where she was from 1995–1999). With the constant refrain "hey little hunters' bell," she reminds her Malian listeners that this is a special song, only for those who are worthy of it—and capable of appreciating its message.

Hee, ndanani
wulani ka jan
The place is far away
i man ndanani kan me
Don't you hear the sound of the hunters' little bell?
ni be do furuni la, ne ko, furuni ko ye jigiya ye,
If you enter into a marriage, it's because you can get trust from it
jigiya kuma banna duniya la
Words you can trust are finished in today's world
ni be do kanuni la, ne ko, kanu ko ye jigiya ye,
If you love someone, love is trust
jigiya banna duniya la
Trust is finished in the world
Bamako julaba yoro ka jan ne la

The traders of Bamako, the place is far away
Yanfolila sila, sila ka jan ne Coumba la,
The road to Yanfolila is far for me, Coumba
Wasulunka denw yoro ka jan ne la
People of Wasulu, the place is far away
Abijan wula, wula ka jan ne la
Abidjan is far away
Maliden nyumaw yoro kan jan ne Coumba la
People of Mali, the place is far away
Ayi, aw ma ndanani kan me
Don't you hear the sound of the hunters' little bell?
Ayi, jagakodeli man nyin de
Ah, indeed, it is hard to be fond of someone [because of
    separation]
wulani ka jan
The place is far away
Bamako Mamu Diallo yoro ka jan ne la,
Mamu Diallo of Bamako, the place is far away [here she names
    several other people who are her personal friends]
Ko wula mana janya ne la
If they are far away from me
senekelalu yoro ka jan ne la
Farmers, the place is far away
monikelaw yoro ka jan Coumba la
Fishermen, the place is far away
ani bagangenalaw yoro ka jan ne la
Cattle herders, the place is far away
Malibaw jeuni fiw aw ma kuma kan me wa
Young girls of Mali, don't you hear the sound [of the music]
Ayi, ko jagako deli man nyin
Ah, indeed, it is hard to be fond of someone
Nga ko ni mana ke nyumakela ye i ka ke a donbaga ye
If you're going to do something good, do it for someone who will
    acknowledge/appreciate it,
hali ni i mana ke i ka ngaraya kuma fo la, i ka fo a donbaga ye
Even if you're going to sing with mastery, do it for those who will
    understand
hali ni kera ngara ye, i ka ngaraya kuma kera fuyi ye i bulu
Otherwise your mastery is in vain
Hee ndanani, nyebaw don foli ngoni kan bora
This song is for the leaders, the song for the leaders is sounding

Hee ndanani, doninkelaw don foli ngoni kan bora
This song is for those who possess knowledge, their song is
    sounding
Hee ndanani, cekun don foli ngoni kan bora
This song is for the leaders, their song is sounding . . .

(C. SIDIBE 1998)

This song, like many hunters' songs, has a driving ternary rhythm and
is based on the major pentatonic scale CDEGAC. As usual, Coumba
Sidibe's backing group is composed of two solo guitars and one bass
electric guitar, a *kamalengoni, jembe* drums, and a drum machine. Thus,
the sounds of hunters' music are framed within those of a modern
Malian band.

Another well-known *wassoulou* singer, Sali Sidibe (who was with the
EIN from 1980 to 1985), also recorded a song entitled "Ntanan" on her
debut cassette (S. Sidibe 1989) (though with its minor pentatonic scale
and duple rhythm, it bears little musical relation to Coumba Sidibe's
"Hee, ndanani"). At the time this cassette made a considerable impact in
Mali because of its use of an acoustic ensemble of traditional instruments (as opposed to the electric guitar and keyboards sound of Kagbe
Sidibe, Coumba Sidibe, and others). The instruments are *kamalengoni,* a
pentatonic *balafon,* the *bolon* (bass harp with four strings), an orchestral
flute, and a *soku* (one-string fiddle). During the late 1980s, which were
the last years of President Moussa Traoré's military regime (1968–91),
the country was facing serious political and economic problems. Sali
uses the symbolism of the *ntanan* to rally a sense of hope for "Maliba"—great Mali, as in the middle section of her song:

To see a person and to know him is not the same
Real trousers and undercloth are not the same
Good evening, great Mali, good evening to the hope of the nation,
    good evening to the hope of the Muslims
The diginitaries of Wasulu say hello
Today is a day of prayer
Today is a day of travel to Mali
If you don't get anything, you will at least learn something
All those who believe in God are in the hands of their mother
Individuals have no power, the country does
A good woman in marriage, her child will never be useless
There are few people left in whom one can trust, few of God's
    people

People who worship the Koran are few now
I am singing in great Mali
What can I do? The person whose roots are from Wasulu will
    speak a little
What did the *ntanan* tell me about life?
The *ntanan* gave us a cow, what do you think that cow is called,
    Malians?
The cow is called "one day," a day in the future
No matter how far away the day away is, this is nothing in God's
    terms.

                                                                (S. SIDIBE 1989)

Throughout the 1980s, both Sali Sidibe and Coumba Sidibe performed regularly for state occasions. In several cases, they used hunters'
songs as a backdrop for praising individual politicians, though their
praises, in the spirit of *wassoulou,* often contained implied criticism. It
was precisely this "barbed praise" that both brought them into occasional conflict with the authorities and also won them public admiration.
For example, Sali Sidibe performed regularly in Bamako for the armed
forces; her second cassette was entitled *Armée malienne.* "I dedicated it
to Mali's army because every year I have played for army bases, for all
their fetes, also for the presidential palace. They gave me a piece of land
[across the river from Bamako]. I was their star . . . when other presidents visited, they'd invite me to play." Sali often performed with her
acoustic ensemble in the same army barracks at Ntomikorobougou
where hunters' musicians played on national holidays. When Mme.
Therese, wife of the late president of the Ivory Coast, Houphouet
Boigny, visited Mali, the government arranged a reception for her with
two well-known *jelimusow*: Hawa Drame and Tata Bambo Kouyate, as
well as the Ballet National Malien. Sali was invited to perform just with
a *kamalengoni,* and her music was so well received by Mme. Therese
that she dedicated her next cassette to her (interview, 1996).[36]
    One of her songs, "Nya ka nyagami" (If things get messed up),
recorded in 1990 (the year before Traoré's downfall), got her into
trouble with Traoré's government when she praised a minister for inter-
cepting a shipment of gold out of the country.[37] "I was inspired by . . .
the Minister of Finance, Zoumana Sacko, I don't know him, I had only
heard of him. He stopped the gold of Mali from leaving the country, I
admired him for this. So at a reception in front of ten ministers, I sang
this song: 'If gold disappears, . . . Malians must guard their heritage, it's

for them. Everyone must love their country.' The minister of defence didn't like this song, not at all, it brought me real problems. He said, 'How could you sing this, what does it mean?' I had such problems I had to go to Djibril Diallo [Deputy Prime Minister]."

"Nya ka nyagami"

If Malian affairs get messed up, it's up to Malians to sort it out.
If Malian gold is lost, it's the Malians who lost it
Malian money that went missing, it's thanks to the press that Mali
    became aware of it
The war that started [in the north of the country], the disastrous
    war that started, the people will sort it out
If things get messed up with the law, it's the Malians who will
    fix it
If things get messed up with the law, it's the political parties who
    will fix it
If things get messed up, RTM [Mali Television and Radio] will
    fix it
If Mali's music gets messed up, it's the artists who will fix it,
Here, in Mali!

                                                    (S. SIDIBE 1992)

Shortly after recording this song, Sali was invited by *Badenya,* an association of Malians in France, to perform for them. This tour meant she was out of the country at the time of the coup d'état that deposed Traoré (March 1991). "After the coup I came back from France and sang "Nya ka nyagami" for the new government, and everyone liked it . . . Those who don't like truth, they don't like this piece, because it's criticizing them. Every time something happens in Mali, it's sure to be played. It speaks to everyone—family, government, men and women."

At around the same time, between the late 1980s and the early 1990s, a younger generation of *wassoulou* singers (both male and female) began to record. A number of male "stars" of *wassoulou,* such as the *kamalengoni* player Yoro Diallo and his brother Samba and so-called wass-reggae artists Jah Yousoufou and Askia Modibo, emerged. The best-known *wassoulou* singer of the new generation, both within the country and internationally, is Oumou Sangare (born 1969). Unlike most *wassoulou* artists, she was born and has spent most of her life in Bamako. Her link with the Wasulu region is only through her mother, who was born in Medina Diassa (and is also a singer). Her father is from Guinea, and since ethnicity is inherited through the father, some do not see her as true Wasulunke. Oumou's music has two overall characteristics: it is heavily evocative of hunters' music, and it addresses mainly women. Indeed, Oumou herself claims that almost all her songs are "for" women—that is, she sings about issues that concern women, from the female point of view. She bases most of her compositions directly on the *kamalengoni nyenaje* repertoire of prewedding songs of advice to the bride. Her style is determined by the *kamalengoni* and the *karinyan* metal scraper, which are constant throughout her music, as are her hunter-style responsorial vocal choruses.

Oumou states that she uses the *kamalengoni* because of its youth ethos: "If you want to bring about social change, you need to address the youth. You can't make the elders change their ways" (Sangare 1997). Her most frequent theme is the subjugation of women in marriage: the favoritism of one wife over another in a polygamous marriage ("Tiebaw," Sangare 1996); the subjugation of women by husbands and their families ("Worotan," ibid.); the financial aspect of marriage whereby parents "sell" their daughters ("Bi Furu," Sangare 1993). She also sings of the pressure on women to have children, and how it is the mother, not the father, who cares for the child ("Denw," Sangare 1996), and how women can and do contribute to the *faso baara*— working for the country ("Moussolou," Sangare 1991). She also celebrates female sensuality in her most famous song, "Diaraby nene" (ibid.).[38]

Among her few songs on "men's issues" is "Wula bara diagna," a song that she describes as "a song about migration and separation." In this song, she sings the refrain:

Nostalgia is hard for me
The place is far away for me
Don't you hear the sound of the *ndanani*?
Your beloved is greeting you.

(Sangare 1991)

Although the pace and style of this song is slower, "Wula bara diagna" and Coumba Sidibe's "Hee, ndanani" are in fact different arrangements of the same song. It is a common practice for Mande singers to change titles of songs and arrange parts of the song or compose new lyrics in order to make them "their own" compositions.[39]

When Oumou quotes specifically from hunters' songs, she does so to achieve a particular effect. For example, at public performances, she frequently performs a hunter's song as her final piece. One of her favorite songs is "Mogo te dia be ye" (you can't please everyone), based on a recording by the hunters' musician Toumani Kone (1996), which she performs just with *kamalengoni* and *karinyan*.[40] This, she says, is her way of acknowledging her debt to the hunters' tradition. She plays on this effect by telling her *kamalengoni* player to do a "real" hunters' style, to play it like a *donsongoni yere yere* (authentic hunters' harp). On one of her ORTM video clips, she performs a song, with hunters dancing next to her, firing their muskets in the air: the song, "Sa juna man nyi" (Early death is bad), laments the death of great hunters, saying, "If I were God, hunters wouldn't die" (*ka se ke nye Alla di, donso te sa*). On her third compact disc, *Worotan*, she sings two hunters' songs, accompanied only on *kamalengoni* and *bolon* harp: "Kunfeko" and "Sabou."

To summarize, it is important to remember that female *wassoulou* singers do not narrate hunters' tales in their songs, whereas some male *wassoulou* singers do (this is in keeping with the Malian view that men are the custodians of oral narratives). The principal way in which *wassoulou* female singers re-create a sense of the hunters' repertoire is through choruses, musical style, and textual symbolism. Instrumentation is also an important factor, and there has been an increasing trend toward a more acoustic sound over the past decade.

"Snake-Eating-Snake": Hunters' Imagery in the Art of the *Jelimuso*

Certain aspects of the performance art of Mande *jeliw,* the social group of endogamous musicians, are well documented, particularly their instrumental traditions (Knight 1973; Charry 1992) and their oral epic narratives (Conrad 1995; Austen 1999). However, as these areas of musical expertise are both firmly within the male domain, the art of the female *jeliw,* the *jelimusow* (sing: *jelimuso*), has received little scholarly attention. *Jeliya* is not connected as directly and overtly with hunters' music as is *wassoulou;* nevertheless, over the past decade, some of the most prominent *jelimusow* have deliberately cultivated a certain hunters' mystique in their own music, for special effect.

Like *wassoulou,* contemporary *jeliya* stands in-between the global and local. On the one hand, it is more tied than *wassoulou* to a specific ritual function (mostly weddings), even in the urban context. Audiences are expected to respond to *jeliw* in certain ritual ways, marked by the giving of money or other gifts (cloth, gold, jewelry, etc.), which is not the case with *wassoulou* singers. The textual and musical parameters of *jeliya* are also more clearly defined than those of *wassoulou:* certain formulas must be respected. Nevertheless, *jeliya* has over the past decade been increasingly influenced by global dance music, especially the Congo/Zaire guitar and drumkit sound. Young *jelimusow,* and their predominantly female audiences, perform dance styles derived from Congo/Zaire dance trends such as *Pesa-pesa*.

The musical role of the *jelimuso* is exclusively that of singer, accompanied by an all-male ensemble of the typical instruments of the *jeli* (electric guitar, *ngoni, balafon, kora,* etc). Their contemporary repertoire is generally described as *donkiliw* (songs), as opposed to *tariku* (spoken genealogies and histories) and *maanaw* (narratives) that are performed by men, though women are involved as chorus singers. Just as female *wassoulou* singers do not narrate hunters' tales in their songs, so the *jelimuso*'s verbal arts revolve around proverbs, praises, and fragments of stories, rather than narrative. The main contexts for the *jelimuso*'s solo performance are wedding and child-naming ceremonies (*sumuw*), and the repertoire that they perform on such occasions forms the basis for their radio, television, and cassette recordings, as well as concert appearances. Most recently, the dance-band scene has been somewhat revitalized in Bamako by a growing economy under the third republic. Some bands, such as the Rail Band and Zani Diabate's Super Djata, are now including *jelimusow* in their lineup, as chorus and even solo singers.

Drawing on a relatively circumscribed but constantly evolving repertoire of standard pieces that traditionally were dedicated to Mande kings and warriors, the *jelimusow* arrange these melodies with new choruses and new texts, in honor of their "patrons" (*jatigiw*). Among these melodies are a small number of songs that are connected with Maninka hunters. The first kings were hunters, so their *jelimusow* sang hunters' songs for them: as in Johnson's version of Son-jara: "The Kuyate matriarch took up the iron rasp. She sang a hunter's song for Nare Maghan Konate" (Johnson 1986/1992: 65).

The music of the *jeliw* is usually regarded as a bounded tradition, occupying a very different domain from that of hunters' music. Yet, both scholars and musicians generally acknowledge that the origins of the *jeli*'s verbal skills and musical instruments are most probably in hunters' traditions. Comparing the hunters' songs listed by Cissé (1991), Thoyer

Rozat (1978), Cashion (1984), and Bird (1972a, b), only a few titles, especially "Janjon," "Duga," and "Kulanjan," are common to both hunters and *jeliw*.

Of these, "Janjon" and "Duga" have become incorporated into the main *jeliw* repertoire and do not retain direct links with the world of hunters, though they are considered "serious" and "heavy" pieces that should be performed only by senior *jeliw*, for the same kinds of reasons that Coumba Sidibe cites (above): if performed in the wrong contexts or without the proper respect, it is believed that this could have serious consequences for the singer. "Janjon," a song that the *jeliw* originally dedicated to the thirteenth-century blacksmith warrior Fakoli Doumbia, derives from a funeral song and dance for great hunters. It is also sometimes performed at funerals of renowned *jeliw*.[41] "Duga" (The vulture) is widely performed by *jeliw* and has arguably lost its immediate associations with the world of hunters, except in the broadest sense, through the vulture, which is both symbol of bravery in battle and of hunters (see below). "Kulanjan," on the other hand, retains direct musical and textual links with hunters' songs. Indeed, *jeliw* acknowledge its relationship to hunters' music by calling it *donso-foli-Kulanjan* (hunters'-music-*Kulanjan*).[42]

Whether or not the *jelimuso* will choose to perform one of these songs for a particular patron is partly determined by the status of the singer and partly by the patron's family background. Thus, if singing for a Keita (for example, at a wedding party), the *jelimuso* will probably choose one of the melodies from the Sunjata repertoire. However, not all modern-day patrons have such connections with great Mande kings or warriors; indeed, some are non-Mande. In such cases, the *jelimuso* may choose any melody she considers appropriate. The choice of melody is an important part of the *jelimuso*'s performance strategy. This is where hunters' songs come into play.

When the *jelimuso* sings hunters' melodies or references hunters' texts, it is usually in someone's honor, comparing that person to the moral values and skills of a hunter. However, the *jelimuso* also quotes from hunters' songs to enhance her own status. The ability to perform hunters' songs is one way of showing that she is a *ngara* (master musician) or at least of *ngara* lineage. *Ngaraya*, a crucial concept in the evaluation of *jeliya*, is connected with fearlessness and esoteric power—just as *donsoya* is; in fact, great hunters are described as both *donso ngana* (master hunter in action) and *donso ngara* (master hunter in the art of hunting). Two of the most successful and best-known *jelimusow* of the past decade, Kandia Kouyate (born Kita, 1958) and Ami Koita (born

Bamako, 1951, though her parents were from Badugu Djoliba) state that they quote from the hunters' repertoire as their duty to keep alive Mali's great heritage. They state that they deliberately choose hunters' songs and/or melodies sparingly; too much of a hunters' style would undermine its power on the listener. For example, when they record a "cassette locale" (i.e., an individualized recording specially commissioned; not for general release), they may include just one hunter-derived tune, while the rest are based on standards from the *jeli*'s repertoire.

Kandia Kouyate, who comes from a *ngara* lineage, is regarded as one of the most powerful and also more traditional of the contemporary "star" *jelimusow*. For example, in her instrumentation, she does not use a drum machine, instead using *tama* (variable pitch) and *dunun* (cylindrical) drums; instead of an electric bass she uses a *bolon* (bass four-string harp, formerly played to accompany kings into war), and she makes minimal reference to global styles except in the use of electric guitar (played, however, like a *ngoni, lute*). Her cassette, *Sa kunu sa* (Kouyate 1995) pictures her on the insert carrying a rifle (in one edition of the cassette, she is sitting on a buffalo), as a reflection of the title song, which is dedicated to hunters (see below). She remarks that "at every concert, I must pay tribute to hunters. We all owe respect to hunters, they are our history" (K. Kouyate 1997).

Kandia Kouyate emphasizes the prestige of this repertoire, the importance of learning it in the correct manner, with due respect, from elder musicians in their families. She contrasts this with the way that the younger generation of *jelimusow,* those who are sometimes termed *jelidisquette,* debase the tradition by not learning it in the proper manner (Kouyate 1997; Koita 1996).

Another "star" *jelimuso,* Ami Koita, makes a similar point, though she represents a different and more modern (and controversial) approach to *jeliya.* Her performance style has been a major influence on young *jelimusow.* She comes from one of the most celebrated *jeliw* families, that of Wa Kamissoko (her maternal uncle) from Kirina, considered one of the most knowledgeable *jeliw* of Mande history (Cissé 1988, 1991). Unusually, she composes some original melodies, claiming that "sixty percent of my songs are my own compositions; the rest are traditional—I rescue them and renew them. That is my role" (A. Koita 1996). Her use of various nontraditional instrumentations and styles—even a Cuban-sounding dance piece, with synthesized flute and violin "a la charanga"—has been heavily criticized by some Malians, who particularly targeted her for her cassette recording, *La Sublime* (1994), in which she was accompanied by the Congo/Zairean band Orchestra Afrisa in 1990.[43]

After this "fracas" (as a result of which she withdrew the cassette from the local market), Ami Koita recorded an "answer" to her public, significantly entitled *Le Defi* (Defiance).[44] This included a song she composed herself "in hunters' style": its 6/8 rhythm imitates the ternary rhythms of Maninka hunters' music, and above all, it glorifies the esoteric skills of hunters as *somaw* (sorcerers/healers). Women cannot be *somaw,* but if they are from a *soma* lineage, they too are attributed with esoteric powers. In this song, Ami Koita traces her own ancestry back to the world of healers and hunters.

Soman
Chorus:
Yiri-o yiri-o so yiriyala le, sa dogolen be kogo la[45]
Tree oh tree, going under the tree, it's the hidden snake that grows
    big
ce denw man nyin de
The children of brave men are dangerous
yiri-o yiri-o so yiriyala le, soma kolon te
"   "   "   There is no such thing as a useless
    sorcerer/healer
soma wo man nyin de
The *soma* is dangerous
N'i bi fa di somama, soma b'i ko
If you give your father to a *soma,* he'll be after you too
n'i bi ba di somama, soma b'i ko
If you give your mother to a *soma,* he'll be after you too
soma denke folo ye soma do di
The *soma*'s first child is also a *soma*
Hali soma musoni folo ye somaya la
Even the *soma*'s first wife is involved in sorcery
hali soma kuna fugula ye soma do di
Even the *soma*'s hat is a *soma*
hali soma kanda juru ke somaya la
Even the *soma*'s neck scarf is involved in sorcery
soma ye mogo faga mbee ka n suma,
The *soma* killed a person [i.e., has the power to kill], let us all
    cool down [be careful],
ce denw man nyin de
The children of the brave are dangerous
Improvised solo (teremeli):
Ah, mogolu, ah mogolu, mogolu, Mandenka

Ah people, people of Mande
Mande tonya te banna de
There is no end to the truths of Mande
Mande nganalu, ndarila
You the able of Mande, I believe in you
Mande be lombo lamba
The Mande are swishing from side to side
ko fulemba la ji
Like water in the calabash
Mande be lombo lamba
The Mande are swishing from side to side
i ko dagabaro ji
Like water in a big jar
Mande tonya te banna la la-wo
Mande truth is unending
Mande tonya te ban fen ti
Nothing can put an end to the truth of Mande
Ah, tintina nin Kabadina, sadugu ni basidugu
[Mande praise names], the protective snake of the village, the
    protective fetish of the village
maniyatigi bobo donso
The python-owning silent hunter
minogoro munyu jula mb'i wele la
You who withstand thirst, I am calling you
kongoro jula mb'i wele la wo,
You who withstand hunger, I am calling you
suba sogoma, ah ngana mb'i n'aw ye
You who get up first thing in the morning
fajiridala ah ngana, mb'i aw ye
You who rise with the 5:00 A.M. prayer
dugutala gengen ah ngana mbe aw ye
You who get up with the cock's crow, I am talking to you
Ah, m be jigui Segou
I am going down to Segou [i.e., to talk about Segou's sorcerers]
Sido Diarra anin balazan do
(praise name for Segou)
balanzan banaani
Four thousand *balanzan* trees
balanzan keme naani
Four hundred *balanzan* trees

balanzan naani, ka tugu ni balanzan kokuruni kelen
Four *balanzan* trees, and then one crooked *balanzan*
Segou nganalu, a ye wuli
You the able of Segou, rise up
Ah, nganalu, Kita nganalu,
Ah the able, the able of Kita
anin Kayes nganalu
And the able of Kayes
doolu sara, jama fana be balu tun
Some have died, many are still living
Ah nganalu m be n'aw ye de
Ah the able, I am talking of you
M be jigui Koulikoro
I am going down to Koulikoro
Koulikoro nganalu
The able of Koulikoro
Kenedugu ngalalu
The able of Kenedugu
Santoro nin Karantela la wo, aw ye wuli
You of San and of Karantela, rise up[46]
Ni nko soma,
If I say "*soma*"
n te nyina Fakoli ko
I won't forget Fakoli [Doumbia, Sunjata's general]
Fakoli kumba Fakoli daba wo, jamajan Koli
Big-headed Fakoli, big-mouthed Fakoli.
Kele-mina Fakoli
Warring Fakoli
baya-bila Fakoli
Fakoli of the royal family (Bila) of Baya
balimabila Fakoli-o Fakoli kumba
Fakoli of the royal family Bila
Fakoli bi na lun min na ka bo Macca
The day that Fakoli came from Mecca
Korote foro ko keme saba anin saba
He came with 303 sacks of *korote* [esoteric poison]
ni be naana Fakoli bulula la wo
All this came with Fakoli
Fakoli ko nin bee mankan de
Fakoli has no equals

Kamisoko Bila, Bagayoko Bila
Kamisoko Bila, Bagayoko Bila
Sakiliba ye Sora ye
Sakiliba [= female of Sissoko] is Sora
Camara ye Sora ye
Camara is Sora
Sora Maghan Fakoli, kiliya Musa nin nooya Musa
Sora, king Fakoli, jealous Musa and able Musa
Ah Kamisoko muso be barika kuma doni
The Kamisoko woman is speaking words blessed with *barika*
Yiri-o yiri-o so yiriyala le, sadugulen be kogo la
ce denw man nyin de.

(KOITA 1995)

This text is dense in its references to esoteric power and Mande history, in typical *jelimuso* fashion. It quotes from well-known proverbs, such as "the Mande swish from side to side like water in a calabash, but will not spill," a proverb that refers to the tenacity of the Mande people at the time of Sunjata. It calls on the people of different Mande regions (Segou, Kita, etc.) to uphold the character of hunters who withstand hunger, thirst, and fatigue. They are "silent" because they are stoic; they are python owners as symbols of power. Finally she refers to the sorcerer/warrior Fakoli Doumbia (one of Sunjata's generals), who brought occult power objects back from Mecca.[47] At the end of the song, Koita establishes her own place within the world of hunters, sorcerers, and Mande history—on her mother's side, she is a Kamissoko, descended from the ancient Mande Bula lineage.[48] This song can be interpreted in various ways; perhaps Ami Koita is herself the *soma/donso,* who withstands, with lips sealed, the pain of public censure, and yet who continues to sing with *barika,* as her birthright.

In addition, the *jelimuso* may use imagery associated with hunters within the context of another nonhunters' song, as in Ami Koita's "Bambougoudji." Though it commemorates the reign of Bambugu Nce Diarra, an eighteenth-century king of Segou, Ami Koita recorded it on a cassette dedicated to one of her renowned patrons, Sambayal "Concorde" Gaye. Without mentioning Gaye by name, she uses references to the great Segou king and to the bravery of hunters, formerly also the king's soldiers, as indirect praise for him, as in the following lines:

Ni ye kala ta Banbuguci mana mogoya kala ta
If you take up the [archer's] bow, if Banbuguci takes up the bow

i be ne samba mogo joli la
And you bring me blood [i.e., Banbuguci's enemy's blood]
ne b'a ke nye ku ji ye
I will make it the water for washing my face
ni ye kala ta Banbuguci mana mogoya kala ta
If you take up the [archer's] bow, if Banbuguci takes up the bow
i be ne samba mogo nugu la
You bring me entrails
ne b'a ke ce-sirila ye
I will use them as a string to tie my trousers.

(KOITA 1993)

Similar imagery occurs in hunters' songs:

He gave me huge intestines for I had no sleeping cloth,
He gave me some blood for face-washing water,
He gave me small intestines as the belt for my waist.[49]

The quoting of such lines within nonhunters' songs is one way in which contemporary *jelimusow* attempt to reclaim a strong sense of history: *Alu ma ye, folo folo ko le tile be se an ma* (Don't you see, the old days will come back to us).[50]

The metaphors of certain birds, some real, some mythical (*duga* [vulture], *kulanjan* [long-crested hawk-eagle],[51] *wentere* [the night bird who never closes its eyes], *balakono* [river sandpiper], *nyama tutu* [the "coq de pagode"]) provide the titles of important songs, relating to key hunters' myths. These birds feature in both *jeliw* and *wassoulou* repertoires—for example, *Wentere* by the Kita singer Adama Diabate (in which she praises the Kita *ngaraw*—Kita's master musicians, such as her own father, Kele Monson Diabate; the tune is Jawura).

Unlike *wassoulou* singers, the *jelimusow* do not use the hunters' harp in their ensembles. However, the ostinati melodies of the ten-string Maninka harp (*simbin*) may be copied on guitars. In Kandia Kouyate's "Sa kunu sa," she bases the accompaniment on a *simbin* line as played by the hunter's musician Bala Jimba Diakite in his "Balakononinfi" (Diakite n.d.). Under the busy, richly textured, *bajourou* (wedding style) arrangement (electric guitar, *ngoni* [lute], *kora, dunun,* and *tama* drums), the evocation of the *simbin* runs throughout and is reinforced with the vocal chorus:

Balakononinfi, duga bee ni yororo
Little black bird of the river, all vultures have their place
Balakononinfin de, donsolu be ni yororo
Little black bird of the river, all hunters have their place
duga te bin nemu la
The vulture does not lick grass.

This chorus, first made famous by Bala Jimba Diakite, and later recorded in popular versions by Mory Kante with the Rail Band and by Salif Keita, has powerful symbolism. "The vulture is the symbol of the master hunter, for he is never empty-clawed or empty-beaked, never without a kill. From his vantage point high in the sky or at the top of a tree, he sees all and knows all. He nurtures himself on game he has killed. He is believed to be long-lived and it is said that he stays young by having many offspring" (Cashion 1984, part 1: 245). The phrase *vulture does not eat grass* expresses metaphorically the idea that hunters are not agriculturalists.

The bulk of Kandia Kouyate's song text is improvised praise, in the vigorous recitational style of the *jeliw* known as *teremeli.* Her praise is densely metaphorical, with a string of epithets for great hunters, such as "snake-swallowing snake," "arrow-holding snake men," "sleep-resisting hunters," "*soma* [sorcerer] hunters." She also sings other choruses from Bala Jimba's song:

Mankan ye mankan ye mun koson,
Noise, noise, for what?
mankan ye sogolu ko, wulala
Noise behind the meat in the bush.

The "noise" is the sound of gunpowder. With such phrases Kandia commemorates great hunters who have recently passed away, and also Bala Jimba himself, whom she describes repeatedly in her song as a *donso-ngara* (master hunter's musician). *Sa kunu sa* was well received by Malian audiences, especially by traditionalists and critics of modern *jeliya.* Young *jeliw* admire the song for its "heavy words, full of meaning," and undoubtedly it greatly enhanced Kandia Kouyate's reputation.

As already stated, "Sa kunu sa" and its parent tune, "Balakononinfi," tie in with the song "Kulanjan." According to some musicians, most notably the late Sidiki Diabate, whom many considered the leading authority on the "genealogies" of Mande melodies, "Kulanjan" is the "parent" of an important "family" of *jeli* songs: including "Sunjata Fasa," "Jawura" (from Kita), and even "Tutu Jara." "This song comes from no other piece. On the contrary, all pieces like "Sunjata" and "Tutu Jara" come from it. The same arms that were used to catch game were used to fight wars. All our ancestors were hunters. The great hunters who do extraordinary things, who make the noise of glory, this song is dedicated to them: they who take refuge from the rain underneath the elephant."[52]

The *kulanjan* is a hunting bird of the river: the long-crested hawk-eagle (Cissé 1994). (In Bailleul's Bambara-French dictionary, it is erroneously translated as pelican.) As a symbol of hunting, *kulanjan* is not specific to the Maninka hunters. It is mentioned by Seydou Camara, for example, when he sings: "eh kulanjan, fishing bird of the hunters, don't you hear the drum?" (Cashion 1984, part 2: 114). The *jelimusow* who are reputed to be "traditionalists," perform versions of "Kulanjan," usually as praise for an individual who is described in their songs as a *donso* (hunter).[53] Cissé remarks that the *jeli*'s version of this song is "in general richer than that as sung by the hunters' singer" (Cisse 1994: 353). Thus, "Kulanjan" is one song in particular that the *jelimusow* can use to tap into the mystique of the hunters' world and bring it into the wider musical vocabulary of contemporary *jeliya*.

Conclusion

The mystification of hunters in contemporary Mali stems from the glorification of Maliba, Mali's great historical past, in the context of an increasingly urban and globalized Mande society. Far from being ruthless killers of animals as a sport (as in the Western concept of hunting), Mali's hunters are respectful of all forms of animal life and its *nyama* (vital force). Many of their rituals are intended to harness the power of this force. The representations by women singers of hunters' music are symbolic of social dynamics in contemporary Malian society. Occupying the center stage of popular performance, star female performers represent a contradiction in the gender ideology and are criticized for transgressing the moral code of behavior assigned to women and for debasing the tradition. Playing on the mystique of hunters, they use references from hunters' music to overcome some of these criticisms and enhance their status. Hunters' melodies and choruses trigger a strong associative response from the listener. They are the musical equivalent of a "memory-text" (Mudimbe 1991).

The link between women, music, and the mystique of hunters, unique to Mali, is a strong thread running through the fabric of Malian popular music over the past decade and represents a "back to roots" trend, going back to the very foundations of Mande society. This is music that is primarily intended for local audiences who can interpret, to varying degrees, the dense metaphorical and musical references. But as Malian women singers such as Oumou Sangare increasingly extend their audiences beyond Mali and Mande peoples, only certain aspects of their music are understood. At the most basic level, the mere presence of a lead woman singer is in itself a potent symbol, placing *wassoulou* and *jeliya* in the arena of a "new social movement"—"locally based and territorially defined," they play out local rivalries and speak to local politics but derive their strength from working "*through* rather than *outside* of existing structures" (Lipsitz 1994: 33–34). The symbolism of hunters' music provides a strong vehicle for women to "'turn the guns around' . . . and put them to other uses" (Lipsitz: 1994: 35). It is the cultural world, not the guns, of hunters that provides a springboard for women to transcend ethnic and even gender boundaries, a springboard from which they can claim their place within Mali's great historical past and renegotiate their own social status.

Notes

[1]This essay is an expanded version of a paper presented at the African Studies Association, 38th annual meeting, San Francisco, 1996. Panel: "Renewal in Mande Music." I conducted research on *wassoulou* music in Bamako, and Europe (the last while on tour with Oumou Sangare) primarily between 1995–97. My research on the *jelimuso* and *jeliya* in Mali has been ongoing since 1986 with annual fieldtrips to Mali and additional work with Malian musicians in Europe (Durán 1994, 1995a, b, c, 1996, 1997, 1999a, b). I have not, however, conducted any firsthand research on hunters' music and have relied primarily on the studies of Cashion (1984), Cisse (1964, 1994), Coulibaly (1985), Bird (1972a, b), and Thoyer (1978, 1995) as source material.

[2]From a recitation of the saga of *Boli Nyanan*.

[3]Cissé's translation is: "oui! Les non-chasseurs raffolent du rythme des chasseurs!"

[4]The term *Mande* (rather than *Manding*) is used here in accordance with current scholarly Anglophone usage (for example, by MANSA, the Mande Studies Association). The Mande are a widespread group of people found in a number of West African countries speaking closely related languages and tracing their ancestry to the Mande empire (1235–1469). In this essay I am referring principally to two ethnic groups of western Mali, the Maninka and the Wasulunke, who for a variety of histor-

ical and political reasons have tended to dominate music performance in the urban context.

[5]For example, the Rail Band (1975/1990) recorded "Balakononinfi" with Mory Kante.

[6]See "Guede" (K. Diabate 1975/1995) and "Kulanjan" (K. Diabate 1999); "Namawou" (A. Diabate 1995); Koite 1999/1998.

[7]In an interview about his album *Folon* Salif Keita (1996) said:

> For me hunters' music is very important, it tells a story, praising great hunters, and when you understand them it's as if you're in the cinema, whether Maninka or Wasulunke, I love that. It's very rich. I feel more at home with hunters' music than with *jeliya,* because in *jeliya,* there are lots of words which you have to know what they mean. With a single word you can make a whole book. You can use this same word many times, it's the same word but not the same meaning. Not even all the *jelis* can understand them. So you can see that these are words invented long long ago. They're encyclopedic, key words. Me too I use them, they've become a habit. Sometimes I mix *jeliya* with the hunters' music and enjoy myself!

[8]Thoyer (1995: 15), however, states that women are now allowed into the hunters' associations in Bamako.

[9]Throughout this essay, to avoid confusion, I distinguish between Wasulu, the geographical region, and *wassoulou,* the style of music (though in fact they are the same word). The first is in accordance with modern orthography, the second (French orthography) reflects common usage in the local Malian music industry. For a fuller discussion of *wassoulou* music, see Durán (1995b).

[10]The idea that the "woman is a slave," especially in marriage, is a frequent theme of women's songs in both *jeliya* and *wassoulou* (Durán 1999a, Chapter 2).

[11]For example, the Malian anthropologist Sory Camara, in his important study of the Maninka *jeliw,* states categorically that "in Maninka country, males do not sing at all, except for the griots" (Camara 1992: 124; my translation).

[12]This occurs in the weekly program *Top Etoiles.*

[13]According to one report, the association (which has under its aegis all the local rural hunters' associations) is composed of "90,000 members and 90,000 guns— more than the entire *Malian* army" (Ploquin 1991; my translation). Its members include many expatriates.

[14]During 1997 a teacher at the American International School in Bamako was interested in inviting a group of hunters to the school; however, when the hunters insisted that they would fire their guns in the air, the school board refused to have them (personal communication).

[15]While some *jeliw* occasionally call themselves *kono,* it is used to signal extreme talent or beauty of voice, not artisan status.

[16]Quoted in Cashion (1984, part 2: 128). Another example, in praise of a deceased hunter from Kanalan, called Kiyama, says: "Kiyama the Red was not a witch doctor / but neither was he a simple human. O listener / searching for this man / I have wandered a long way . . . / looking for Kiyama the Red / who never lay with a woman" (liner notes, *Guinée* 1987).

[17]I had an experience of these character traits when, during a trip to Wasulu, my car broke down on a dirt road in an area far from the nearest town. Sitting by the

baking road for many hours while we waited for some form of help, with nothing but hot water to drink, even my host from Wasulu began to despair. Toward the late afternoon a figure appeared from the bush, a young hunter in his 20s wearing a blackened hunter's shirt and carrying nothing but a rifle. He greeted us as if it were quite normal to find us there, asking no questions; but when we explained our situation, he vanished. Not long afterward he returned with mangoes and cool water, which he gave us; and then, hardly allowing us even to thank him, he headed back into the bush.

[18]Liner notes, Samake (1991: 5–6). Not surprisingly, there is some tension between the dominant religion, Islam, and the popular admiration for the hunters' occult powers. "The hunters' songs . . . do not necessarily denigrate Islam but they go to great effort to show that the knowledge to be gained from Islam is inferior to their own" (Bird 1972a: 281).

[19]See also Salif Keita (1990). For more discussion of Salif's self-portrayal as a hunter, see Cherif Keita (1996).

[20]There is still very little published on the subject of Mande gender ideology. See Grosz-Ngate (1989); Hoffman (1994); also Durán (1999a). Brett-Smith's study of creativity in Bamana sculpture suggests that male creativity is linked with the appropriation of female fertility and is believed to result in impotence (Brett-Smith 1994).

[21]For example, sung by Kandia Kouyate in her song "Ballasama," on the audio cassette Amary Daou (1983).

[22]As in Kambili (Bird 1972a: 282).

[23]As filmed in Djoliba with Salif Keita, featuring the music of Bala Jimba Diakite, see Salif Keita (1990).

[24]*Chasseur* (n.d.). The song tells the story of a king with two wives—a favorite but childless wife and an unliked wife with twelve children.

[25]However, Euba (1990) also reports that *ijála* artists, who traditionally sing praise songs to the deity Ogun, "are increasingly being invited to perform for the entertainment of non-hunters and in this context it is customary for them to charge" (408). Waterman (1990) reports only one case of a commercially recorded version of *ijála* (Yoruba hunters' chants).

[26]Agawu observes that "one of the best known of 'serious' Northern Ewe dances is *Àdèvú*, a form of 'bravery' dance. *Àdèvú* is a hunters' dance that may be seen in practically every town or village in which there are organized groups of hunters." Agawu reports that these dances enact the hunt and teach the audiences about hunt culture. Both men and women participate in this dance-drama, women also carrying a hunting weapon.

[27]It would be interesting to discover whether the popularity of these Kamajor hunters has given rise to new styles of music based on their traditions.

[28]For example, the female singer Nahawa Doumbia, and Seydou Camara, mentioned above. Cashion (1984, part 1: 297) says that hunters' musicians "who are also blacksmiths and who have knowledge of the hunters' fetishes as well are considered the most powerful and respected."

[29]The Mande pluriarc *ndan* has been reported in passing by Roderic Knight (1973) and Eric Charry (1992).

[30]The information presented here is based on interviews with a wide range of musicians, including leading *wassoulou* performers in Bamako; with people in three Wasulu villages: Badani, Daoula, and Medina Diassa; and with Mali television pre-

senters and producers. It supersedes research presented in a previous essay (Durán 1995b), especially because at that time I had not yet interviewed Allata Brulaye Sidibe, who died in February 1997, in his late 50s.

[31]Unfortunately, the text is in French only. See also Cashion (1984, part 2: second story, lines 657–62). Seydou Camara calls out several times "change the tune" (*juru yelema*), even though he is the only player.

[32]For example, Seydou Camara's line *i te n ke donso di, jurufo bara n ni laban* (make me a hunter, the string player wants to take my soul) (Cashion 1984, part 2: first story, line 505).

[33]These lines are from two of Allata Brulaye's songs (A. B. Sidibe 1983): "Mousso keleyato" (The jealous woman) and "Yayoroba" (The beautiful woman).

[34]The first recordings of *kamalengoni* were by Brulaye for Radio Mali and date from 1977. In 1983 Allata Brulaye recorded his only long-play album, entitled *Specialiste de kamalengoni* (A. B. Sidibi 1983). Claiming that he was never paid for this recording, Allata Brulaye refused ever to record again, though shortly before his death (late Feb. 1997) he spent some time in Bamako at the house of Oumou Sangare and recorded with her (unpublished recordings by Ousmane Haidara).

[35]Sidibe's work can be heard on C. Sidibe (1990, 1994, 1998).

[36]Coumba Sidibe had also composed a song for Boigny and his wife called "Mougoukan" (The sound of gunpowder); for a translation of this song, see Durán 1995b.

[37]See also S. Sidibe 1995.

[38]This song, which is Oumou Sangare's "fetish" piece, is an adaptation of a *jagawara* song, sung by young girls for the bride before she goes to her husband's home.

[39]This is becoming increasingly the trend as women who have achieved "star" status are believed to be making a great deal of money out of their songs. Oumou Sangare, for example, tells how a woman came to her house from a remote village in Wasulu, claiming to have composed the song "Bi Furu" and demanding compensation.

[40]The title, as listed on the cassette insert, is "Mokotaidia Baignai" (*Mogo te dia bee ye*).

[41]For example, it was sung at the funeral of the kora player Sidiki Diabate, in Bamako, Oct. 1996.

[42]For example, this is how the kora player Batrou Sekou Kouyate (former accompanist to the *jelimuso* Fanta Damba) calls "Kulanjan."

[43]"Defa Wane," from her cassette *Mory Djo* (Koita 1992).

[44]This was first released on cassette, recorded in Abidjan, rereleased on compact disc (Koita 1995).

[45]This is one of several proverbs quoted in her song. See similar proverbs quoted in Kone (1995). The reference to the tree is because many *somaw* work with wood as power objects.

[46]Reference to Youssouf Traoré, who was minister under Moussa Traoré and is now a deputy in the National Assembly.

[47]See Moraes Farias (1989) for further discussion of this legend.

[48]Cissé remarks that the Kamissoko of Krina declare that "they are authentic Boula and their ancestors were great hunters" (Cissé 1994: 353; my translation).

[49]Seydou Camara quoted in Cashion (1984, part 2, Famori: 132).

[50]From Ami Koita's version of *Kaira* from her CD *Songs of Praise* (1993).
[51]Not marabout stork, as sometimes listed.
[52]Written correspondence, Sidiki Diabate, May 1995.
[53]An example can be found on D. Koita (1995).

References

Agawu, V. Kofi. 1995. *African Rhythm: A Northern Ewe Perspective*. New York: Cambridge University Press.

Austen, Ralph, ed. 1999. *In Search of Sunjata: The Mande Epic As History, Literature and Performance*. Bloomington: Indiana University Press.

Belcher, Stephen. 1995. "Cross-Dressing and Other Switches." Paper presented at the 38th annual conference of the African Studies Association, Orlando, FL.

Bird, Charles. 1972a. "Heroic Songs of the Mande Hunters." In *African Folklore,* edited by Richard M. Dorson, 275–93. Bloomington: Indiana University Press.

———. 1972b. "Bambara Oral Prose and Verse Narratives Collected by Charles Bird." In *African Folklore,* edited by Richard M. Dorson, 441–77. Bloomington: Indiana University Press.

Brett-Smith, Sarah C. 1994. *The Making of Bamana Sculpture: Creativity and Gender*. Cambridge: Cambridge University Press.

Camara, Sory. 1992. *Gens de la Parole: Essai sur la Condition et le Rôle des Griots dans la Société Malinke*. 2nd ed. Paris: Karthala. Originally published in 1975.

Cashion, Gerald A. 1984. "Hunters of the Mande: A Behavioral Code and Worldview Derived from the Study of Their Folklore." Ph.D. diss., Indiana University.

Charry, Eric. 1992. "Musical Thought, History and Practice among the Mande of West Africa." Ph.D.diss., Princeton University.

———. 2000. *Mande Music: Traditional and Modern Music of the Maninka and Mandinka of West Africa*. Chicago: University of Chicago Press.

Cissé, Youssouf Tata. 1964. "Notes sur les Sociétés de Chasseurs Malinke." *Journal de la Société des Africanistes* 34(2): 175–226.

———. 1994. *La Confrérie des Chasseurs Malinké et Bambara: Mythes, Rites et Récits Initiatiques*. Paris: Nouvelles du Sud/Arsan.

Cissé, Youssouf, and Wa Kamissoko. 1988. *La Grande Geste du Mali: Des Origines a la Fondation de l'Empire*. Bamako: Karthala-Arsan.

———. 1991. *Soundjata: la Gloire du Mali. La Grande Geste du Mali, vol. 2*. Paris: Karthala-Arsan.

Conrad, David. 1999. "Mooning Armies." In *In Search of Sunjata: The Mande Epic As History, Literature and Performance,* edited by Ralph Austen. Bloomington: Indiana University Press.

Conrad, David, and Barbara Frank. 1995. *Status and Identity in West Africa: Nyamakalaw of Mande*. Bloomington: Indiana University Press.

Coulibaly, Dosseh Joseph. 1985. *Récit des chasseurs du Mali—Dingo Kanbili: Une Épopée des Chasseurs Malinké de Bala Jinba Jakite*. Paris: Conseil International de la Langue Française.

Diabate, Sekou "Bambino." 1997. Interview by author, London.

Diallo, Boubacar. 1994. Interview by author, London.

Diallo, Mamadu. 1988. *Essai sur la Musique Traditionnelle au Mali*. France: ACCT.

DjeDje, Jacqueline Cogdell. 1985. "Women and Music in Sudanic Africa." In *More than Drumming—Essays on African and Afro-Latin Music and Musicians*, edited by Irene Jackson, 67–89. Washington, DC: Howard University.

Durán, Lucy. 1994. "Music Created by God: The Manding Jalis of Mali, Guinea and Senegambia." In *World Music: The Rough Guide*, edited by Richard Trillo and Simon Broughton, 243–60. London: Rough Guides.

————. 1995a. "Jelimusow: The Superwomen of Malian Music." In *Power, Marginality and African Oral Literature*, edited by Liz Gunner and Graham Furniss, 197–210. Cambridge: Cambridge University Press.

————. 1995b. "Birds of Wasulu: Freedom of Expression and Expressions of Freedom in the Popular Music of Southern Mali." *British Journal of Ethnomusicology* 4: 101–34.

————. 1995c. "Monsieur l'ambassadeur (Salif Keita)." *Folk Roots* 149: 42–47.

————. 1996. "Fanned, Fetished and Female: On the Road with Wassoulou Superstar Oumou Sangare." *Folk Roots* 154: 40–45.

————. 1997. "Guinean Gold—In Praise of Sekouba 'Bambino." *Folk Roots* 168: 41–45

————. 1999a: "Stars and Songbirds: Mande Female Singers in Urban Music, Mali 1980–99." Ph.D. diss., London University.

————. 1999b. *Kandia Kouyate: Kita kan*. STCD 1088; liner notes.

————. 1999c. "Flying in Kita . . . Lucy Duran Profiles the Awesome Kandia Kouyate." *Folk Roots* 189: 20–25.

Elroy, Claudia. 1996. "Magic Soldiers of Sierra Leone." *The Guardian,* 26 October: 15.

Euba, Akin. 1990. *Yoruba Drumming: The Dundun Tradition.*

Grosz-Ngate, Maria. 1989. "Hidden Meanings: Explorations into a Bamanan Construction of Gender." *Ethnology* 28: 167–83.

Hale, Thomas A. 1994. "Griottes: Female Voices from West Africa." *Research in African Literatures* 25(3): 71–91.

Herbert, Eugenia W. 1993. *Iron, Gender, and Power: Rituals of Transformation in African Societies*. Bloomington: Indiana University Press.

Hoffman, Barbara. 1994. "Mande Gender Ideology in Proverbs." Paper presented at the 37th annual conference of the African Studies Association, Toronto.

Johnson, John William. 1986/1992. *The Epic of Son-jara—A West African Tradition. Text by Fa-Digi Sisoko*. Bloomington: Indiana University Press.

Keita, Cheick M. Cherif. 1996. "Donso or Hunters' Music: a Matrix of Salif Keita's Artistic Identity." Paper presented at the 39th annual conference of the African Studies Association, San Francisco.

Keita, Koly. 1996. Interview by author, Bamako, April.

Knight, Roderic C. 1973. "Mandinka Jaliya: Professional Music of the Gambia." Ph.D. diss., University of California at Los Angeles.

Koita, Ami. 1996. Inteview by author, Bamako, Apr.

Kone Kassim. 1995. *Mande Zana ni Ntalen wa ni ko, Bamanakan ni Angilekan na*. West Newbury, MA: Mother Tongue Editions.

Koskoff, Ellen, ed. 1989. *Women and Music in Cross-Cultural Perspective*. Chicago: University of Illinois Press.

Kouyate, Batourou Sekov. 1986. Interview by author, Avignon, France.

Kouyate, Kandia. 1997. Interview by author, Bamako, Feb.

Lipsitz, George. 1994. *Dangerous Crossroads: Popular Music, Postmodernism and the Poetics of Place*. London: Verso.

McNaughton, Patrick R. 1988. *The Mande Blacksmiths: Knowledge, Power, and Art in West Africa*. Bloomington: Indiana University Press.

Moraes Farias, P. F. de. 1989. "Pilgrimages to 'Pagan' Mecca in Mandenka Stories of Origin Reported from Mali and Guinea-Conakry." In *Discourse and Its Disguises: The Interpretation of African Oral Texts,* edited by Karin Barber and P. F. de Moraes Farias, 152–70. Birmingham, Eng.: Centre of West African Studies.

Mudimbe, V. Y. 1991. *Parables and Fables: Exegesis, Textuality, and Politics in Central Africa*. Madison: University of Wisconsin Press.

Nketia, J. H. Kwabena. 1963. *African Music in Ghana*. Chicago: Northwestern University Press.

Ploquin, Frederic. 1991. "Sebenikoro: le Serpent Nymphe de Kala ne Pardonne pas." *Trad Mag,* 1991, 8–9.

Prince, Rob. 1996. "Mali Rising: Rob Prince Hears What Ex–Salif Keita Guitarist Mamadou Doumbia Is Doing in Japan." *Folk Roots* 162: 37–39.

Sidibe, Allata Brulaye. 1996. Interview by author, Badani, Apr.

Sidibe, Burahima. 1996. Interview by author, Badani, Apr.

Sidibe, Coumba. 1996. Interview by Banning Eyre, New York.

Thoyer-Rozat, Annik. 1978. *Chants des Chasseurs du Mali par Mamadu Jara*. Paris: n.p.

———. 1995. *Récits Épiques des Chasseurs Bamanan du Mali de Mamadu Jara*. Paris: L'Harmattan.

Waterman, Christopher. 1990. *Juju: A Social History and Ethnography of an African Popular Music*. Chicago: University of Chicago Press.

Discography (compact discs unless otherwise stated)

Chasseur Harauna Doumbia & Bougouni. n.d. Alpha Sako ASF 323.

Diabate, Abdoulaye. 1995. *Djiriyo*. Sterns STCD 1066.

Diabate, Kassemady. 1990. *Kela Tradition*. Sterns STCD 1034.

Diabate, Kassemady, and National Badema. 1975/1995. "Guede," on *Musiques du Mali: Banzoumana*. Syllart 38901.2.

Diabate, Kassemady, with Taj Mahal and Toumani Diabate. 1999. *Kulanjan*. Hannibal HNCD 1444.

Diakite, Dieneba. n.d. *Dieneba Diakite*. Mali Stars CD 38108-2.

Diallo, Yoro. *Yoro Diallo dit "Tiekorobani,"* vol. 1. [audio cassette] Samassa SAM 0182924.

Ensemble Instrumental National du Mali. 1977. *Ensemble Instrumental National du Mali "Diya ye Banna."* [LP] Syllart 38758-1.

Guinée—Récits et Épopées. 1992. Ocora HM 83.

Guinée: Les Peuls du Wassolon—La danse des chasseurs. 1987. Ocora CD HM83.

Keita, Salif. 1990. *Destiny of a Noble Outcast*. [video cassette] BBC/Island Visual Arts.

————. 1991. *Amen*. Mango 9910.

————. 1995. *Folon . . . the Past*. Mango CIDM 1108/524 149-2.

Koita, Ami. c. 1992. *Mory Djo*. [audio cassette] EMI 120590-4.

————. 1993. *Songs of Praise*. Sterns STCD 1039.

————. 1994. *La Sublime*. [audio cassette] Camara Productions CK7 083.

————. 1995. *Carthage*. Esperance CDS 6840.

Koita, Diaba. c. 1995. *Khassonké*. [audio cassette] Bolibana BP 91.

Koite, Habib, and Bamada. 1999/1998. *Maya*. Putumayo PUTU 146-2.

Kone, Toumani. c. 1996. *Toumani Koné, vol. 2*. [audio cassette] Super Sound SS33.

Kouyate, Kandia. 1983. *Amary Daou présente Kandia Kouyaté*. [LP] Amary Daou AD001.

————. 1995. *Sa Kunu sa*. [audio cassette] Camara Productions CK7 094.

————. 1999. *Kita Kan*. Sterns STCD 1088.

Les Chasseurs du Wassolou et Sogoninkoun—1995. [video cassette] Africa Audio Visuel AAV 004.

Rail Band, with Mory Kante. c. 1975/1990. *Rail Band: Mory Kante*. [audio cassette] SYL 8378.

Samake, Sibiri. 1991. *Mali: Musique des Chasseurs de Sébénikoro*. Cobalt 92523.

Sangare, Oumou. 1991. *Moussolou*. World Circuit WCD 021.

————. 1993. *Ko Sira*. World Circuit WCD 036.

————. 1996. *Worotan*. World Circuit WCD 045.

————.1997. *Oumou Sangare and Women's Rights in Mali*. [Television documentary broadcast on ABC's *Foreign Correspondent* in May 1997. Unpublished. Researcher: Lucy Durán; interviews with Oumou Sangare and others.]

Sidibe, Allata Brulaye. 1983. *Allata Brulaye Sidibe: Spécialiste de Kamalengoni*. [LP] MAILPS 1024.

Sidibe, Bintou. c. 1993. *Bintou Sidibe*. [audio cassette] Super Sound ENC SS 37.

Sidibe, Coumba. 1990. *Coumba Sidibe. Mali*. Stars CD 38111-2.

————. 1994. *Sanghan*. Camara Productions CD FDB032.

————. 1998. *Janjonba*. [audio cassette] Camara Productions CK7.

Sidibe, Sali. 1989. *Sali Sidibe*. [audio cassette] Syllart SYL 8362.

————. 1992. *La Perle noir du Wassoulou*. [audio cassette] Camara Productions CK7 044.

————. 1995. *Wassoulou Foli*. Sterns STCD 1047.

CHAPTER 6

Mamaya: Renewal and Tradition in Maninnka Music of Kankan, Guinea (1935–45)

Lansiné Kaba and Eric Charry

Among the Mandekan-speaking groups of western Africa, including the Mandinka of the Senegambia region, Bamana and Xasonka of Mali, and Maninnka of Guinea, certain locales have earned a widespread reputation for the creativity, ingenuity, and expertise of their musical artists. Specialists in the *koni* (lute) and *dundun* (bass drum) from Xaso (northwestern Mali), *ngoni* (large lute) from Segou (Mali), *kora* (harp) from The Gambia, and *jembe* from Kouroussa (Upper Guinea) are treasured far and wide for their local traditions. The capital cities Conakry and Bamako have attracted musicians from all over to their renowned national ballets, ensembles, and guitar and brass-based orchestras that launched the international careers of singers Sory Kandia Kouyate, Aboubacar Demba Camara, Mory Kante, and Salif Keita, guitarists Sekou "Bembeya" Dioubaté and Manfila Kante, and drummer Mamady Keita. Upper Guinea has proven to be an especially rich musical area. The region of Siguiri has produced the core of the original *Les Ballets Africains* in the 1950s, the first dance troupe of its kind: founder Fodeba Keita, lead dancer Fanta Kamissoko, and lead drummer Ladji Camara grew up there; musical director Facelli Kante lived there as well as in Kankan and Kissidougou at different times. South of Siguiri, guitar and *bala* (xylophone) players enhanced the reputation of Kankan and Kissi-dougou in the decades preceding independence.

The regional and colonial-era metropolis Kankan has since the 1930s enjoyed a reputation for being the birthplace of a musical movement that has touched all corners of the Mande diaspora. Known as *Mamaya,* this movement represents the innovations of Maninnka youth working within the confines of their centuries-old cultural traditions. The musical composition *Mamaya* has attained the status of a modern classic, rivaled in reputation only by the old pieces that have been around for centuries. Malian and Guinean singers and bands still routinely include *Mamaya* in their repertories or compose new songs based on its music. Not only have the words, melodies, and harmonies of *Mamaya* become widely known and appreciated, but the time and place that it represents is fondly remembered as yet one more instance of a local flowering of a broadly influential Mande expressive culture.

In the aftermath of the late nineteenth-century wars of the *almami* Samory Touré followed by French colonial rule in 1898, Kankan, the former capital of the kingdom of Bateh, emerged as the major cultural and political center in Upper Guinea (Kaba 1973). The city became known for its entrepreneurial and erudite Muslim culture with a rich musical life to match. Renowned mystics and other religious leaders who held court there attracted students and prominent followers from near and afar in West Africa. When the generations born in the late 1910s and early 1920s reached adulthood in the late 1930s, they celebrated their artistic tastes and lifestyle in *Mamaya,* one of the most innovative and influential musical movements in the Maninnka world.

Played on xylophones (*bala; balafo* means "to play the *bala"*) with a female chorus, and occasionally a bass drum (*dundun*) or Western drum set, *Mamaya* was an exquisite and joyful music and dance event—or *ambiance,* as it is called in West African French—in which both young men and women participated, dressed in their finest clothes. *Mamaya* was created by a renowned Kankan composer and *bala* player, Sidi Djéli Dioubaté, for his children's enjoyment. Although it was primarily centered around Sidi Djéli's family, and more specifically associated with his sons Sidi Karammò, Sidi Mamadi, and Sidi Moussa (and later Djanka Amò), whose *bala* trio was recorded in 1949 and in 1952, *Mamaya* involved musicians from other Kankan musical lineages, including the Kouyaté, Diawara, and Kanté families.

The actual piece of music called *Mamaya,* as distinguished from the whole event of the same name, holds a special place in the repertory of Maninnka musicians due to its unique character. An extended *bala* and

N'i ma saya
If you are not dead, [your should know that:]

saya te jon too la
Death leaves no one behind.

Juwa ma sinin lon na
A simpleton does not know tomorrow.

n na ronin Djidaba Conde moyi la
My stepmother Djidaba Conde has [truly] given birth.

Tolon te sebe saa la
Playing does not prevent seriousness.

Djemory lanin Commissariat.
Djemory is resting in the Commissariat.

(fenti mako)
(The hope of the owner of possessions.)

wariti mako
The hope of the wealthy person.

saninti mako le
The hope of the owner of gold.

Jon ke kurubati wo
That owner of a large group of slaves.

La ila ilan (Ra)suru lahi.
There is no God but Allah, [and Mohammed] is the messenger.

kana n mida moo kan ne la
Do not hold me according to the voice of others.

i kana n mida moo kan ne la wo
Do not hold me according to the voice of others.

Karamo Kaba
Karamo Kaba.

i kana n mida moo kan ne la wo
Do not hold me according to the voice of others.

N fa wo fama den.
That father of mine, a prince.

Mamaya wo jeli mina jeliti la
[In] Mamaya, hold the jeli according to the standing of his patron.

Mamaya jeli koron ne jeliya tinya la
[In] Mamaya, the bad jeli is the one who spoils the art of the jeli.

Mamaya wo fina mina finati la
[In] Mamaya, hold the fina according to the standing of his patron.

Mamaya fina koron ne finaya tinya la
[In] Mamaya, the bad fina is the one who spoils the art of the fina.

Mamaya wo n ne ma lawuli nin ma
Mamaya, I did not intend for this.

Manden jeli la Saralon taa
The Manden jeli going to Sierra Leone,

N ma lawuli nin ma
I did not intend for this.

N ne wa mooken so
I will go to the town of the beautiful people.

Mamaya wo, Mamaya wo
Mamaya o, Mamaya o.

Hina ye dari le do
Compassion lies in acquaintanceship.

N fa kun fe ko
My father, it is a matter for the unaware.

Sandiya na nin biriwi le di
The age group Sandiya has brought excitement.

Sandiya mansa.
The leader of Sandiya.

Mari Kera le, Mari Kera le, Mari kera le
Mari Kera, Mari Kera, Mari Kera,

(wo safi la i na moyi la denke la.)
[you are truly the son of your mother.]

FIGURE 6-1. *Mamaya* lyrics from the 1949 recording made by Arthur S. Alberts. From the Archives of Traditional Music at Indiana University, Accession no. 68-214-F, ATL 3566, band 1. Maninnka transcription and English translation by Lansiné Kaba with Eric Charry. The text in parentheses appears only on the 1995 version sung by Nakande Dioubaté.

FIGURE 6-2. The melody to *Mamaya*, as sung by Nakande Dioubaté. From Mamady Keita (*Mogobalu*, 1995). Transposed to a tonic of C. Dioubaté sings at an approximate tonic of A (a minor third below); the 1949 vocalists sing at an approximate tonic of F# (a tritone below), and jump up an octave whenever the range moves below G on the transcription. *(continues on facing page)*

vocal composition, the core of *Mamaya* is a long section of lyrics sung to a melody with few repetitions and many twists and turns. It is one of the most through-composed melodies in the repertory of *jelis* (called *griots* by the French), the Maninnka hereditary professional musical and verbal artists widely associated with Maninnka musical culture (see Figures 6-1 and 6-2). Several *bala*-based musical accompaniments can be played before and after this extended song. *Mamaya* performances usually involved verse after verse of choral singing, set to other melodies and punctuated by *bala* solos, praising the young Kankan notables of the day. The sum total of a *Mamaya* performance reflects a large-scale compositional design not often found in traditional music from West Africa.

The word *Mamaya* has no clear meaning in the Maninnka language. It implies, however, a sense of collective excitement, joy, and refined pageantry cultivated in a prosperous urban environment. It also conjures up images of serious artistry in music and dance of a colonial era in which local African culture was celebrated with finesse and pride. A popular youth music firmly grounded in Kankan's traditions, *Mamaya* expressed the musical preferences of the younger generations as well as the cosmopolitan culture for which that city was known in the first half of the twentieth century. An inquiry into the cultural and historical background of *Mamaya* can provide insight into how Africans, specifically Maninnka of Upper Guinea, have confronted and integrated diverse influences into their own unique cultural expressions in the mid-twentieth century, with continued strong reverberations through several generations into the next century.

The Social Background of Mamaya

Kankan is located in the Upper Niger River valley region in Upper Guinea (*Haute-Guinée*) and was part of the "Grand Mandén" or the Mali empire established by Sunjata Keita in the thirteenth century. Upper Guinea formerly consisted of local chiefdoms, such as Hamana, Toron, and Sankaran. Bateh emerged as a Muslim theocracy in the seventeenth century long after the decline of imperial Mali (Figure 6-3). Before the beginning of French rule in the late nineteenth century, the Bateh Muslim theocracy had for centuries been ruled by settlers of Soninke (Sarakolleh) origin from the Sahel region in present-day northern Mali, particularly those from the Kaba lineage (Humblot 1921). Throughout the Maninnka world in West Africa, these Muslim settlers are known as *Maninnka-Mori* (Muslim literate Maninnka).

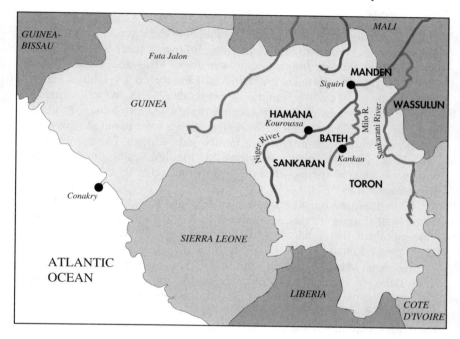

FIGURE 6-3. Chiefdoms in precolonial Upper Guinea.

The growth of Kankan before the nineteenth century can be traced to its position at the crossroads of the main regional trade routes and to the policies of its rulers. Alfa Kabiné Kaba (ca. 1730–1800) made it *Nabaya,* that is, "the city that welcomed every one." Alfa Mahmud Kaba (ruled 1835–74), who welcomed the would-be famous Islamic reformer al-Hajj Umar Tal to Kankan in 1837, also contributed to its precolonial prominence by conquering parts of neighboring Toron and Wassulun and by promoting security on the trade routes. This process increased further when Karammò Mory Kaba allied with the emerging warlord (*kele-tigi*) Samory Touré in the late 1870s. Together they waged a series of wars against regional foes before turning on one another in a feud that led to the siege and defeat of Kankan in 1881. Samory's stunning victory over Kankan, which resulted in his gaining the Muslim title of Commander of the Faithful (*almami* in Maninnka), and his defiant resistance against the French (documented in great detail by Person [1968]) attracted musicians and singers to his entourage.

After capturing Kankan from Samory in 1891, Colonel Archinard built a garrison with a large staff, establishing the town as the political headquarters of Upper Guinea. In 1896, following this process of integration, the French authorities detached the Milo and Upper Niger Rivers region from Soudan (modern Mali) and joined it to Guinea. After the ultimate defeat of Samory in September 1898, which signaled the definitive onset of French colonization of Upper Guinea, Kankan emerged as the metropolis of the region, with a large population of new settlers, including Samory's own family and veterans. The completion of the Conakry–Kankan railroad in 1914 significantly elevated its regional status as the terminus of an elaborate network of interregional communication.

Colonial rule implied economic change, and Kankan benefited from the establishment of branches of major European trading companies that monopolized the distribution of goods throughout West Africa. The coming of Levantine and Greek businessmen intensified commercial activities in the city and its hinterland. The market-based economy introduced by the colonial administration to facilitate both the payment of taxes and the incorporation of local economies into the capitalist system gradually produced a new class of people recognizable by their activities and lifestyles, an affluent local bourgeoisie in Jean Suret-Canale's (1970) words, avid for music and dance performances. Not surprisingly, music making in Kankan would gel in the late 1930s to reflect this new social atmosphere.

The growth and vibrancy of musical culture in Kankan also stemmed from the Maninnka social system, which divided the society into three large estates, one of which, the *nyamakala,* was assigned the crafts and the musical arts on a hereditary and endogamous basis (Camara 1976). Accordingly, such artisans as the blacksmiths (*numu*), cobblers (*garanke*), and musicians and praise singers (*jeli*) were by birth dependent on noble lineages (*horon*). Prominent noble lineages, including Kaba, Touré, Diané, and Chérif, served as patrons (*jatii*) to the Kouyaté, Kanté, Diawara, and Dioubaté (Diabaté in Malian spelling) *jeli* lineages.

Musical life in Kankan reflected local politics. The life of the community centered around three major leaders, Alfa Amadou Kaba, Cheikh Muhammad Chérif, and Karammò Talibi Kaba (Kaba 1997). Their consensus (or lack thereof) not only determined the political climate but also influenced certain aspects of music making, as evidenced by the multiple compositions made in their honor. They wielded power and influence because of their positions, their charisma, and their grounding in the essence of Kankan's cultural and religious identity.

Alfa Amadou Kaba, the chief (*kanda*) of the district of Kankan, headed the princely family of Djinn-Kono, in the quarter of Timbo, which ruled the theocracy of Kankan-Bateh until the French conquest. From the year of his appointment in 1936 to the suppression of traditional authority by Sékou Touré in 1957, he performed the role of royal patron to several important *jelis,* including Kani Fodé Kouyaté, the head *jeli* of Kankan (*konkoba*), and the well-known Sidi Djéli Dioubaté.

Cheikh Muhammad Chérif, often referred to as *Le grand Chérif* (Karammò Sékouba), figured among the greatest Islamic mystics in West Africa during the first part of the twentieth century. Born into a famed family of scholars in 1874 (his father was Samory's main adviser), he was celebrated in various musical compositions by the composers of *Mamaya* as well as by other musicians. His reputation as a holy man attracted disciples and admirers from all of West Africa, including Kwame N'Krumah, the first leader of independent Ghana; Fily Dabo Cissoko, the first elected representative (*député*) to the French National Assembly from Soudan (Mali); and Ouezzin Coulibaly, *député* from Upper Volta (Burkina Faso). The death of Cheikh Muhammad Chérif in September 1955 was mourned throughout West Africa by Muslims and non-Muslims alike.

Karammò Talibi Kaba had been the leader of Kabada, the largest quarter of Kankan, since 1928. His own clan, Manfinnah or Kefinnah, often competed with Timbo for leadership of the theocracy, and he was known as one of the richest and most erudite men in the region. Unlike Alfa Amadou Kaba, he maintained strong and loyal relations with the Grand Chérif. (Gilbert Rouget [and Schwarz 1969: 48] initially confused Karammò Talibi Kaba with the Grand Chérif, and later [1999: 6] partially corrected it—Kaba was not his *secrétaire,* but rather his friend and confidant.) In 1955 he was appointed Native Mayor (*Maire indigène*) of Kankan. By the time Rouget visited Kankan in December 1952, *Mamaya* had gone out of fashion, but Karammò Talibi's influence on the *jeli* community remained undisputed. His entourage of musicians included the imposing Boundjala Madi Koyita, the legendary *soron* (harp) player Mamadi Dioubaté, and the vocalist Condé Kouyaté, whose voice greatly impressed Rouget (Rouget and Schwarz 1970). By his expertise in Arabic and Maninnka-kan (the Maninnka language), Karammò Talibi had an enduring influence on the cultural and musical scene. When he died in July 1962, Kankan and its *jelis* lost one of their main sources of inspiration.

Also contributing to the cultural life of the city were other important members of the Kankan oligarchy who made valuable gifts to the *jeli* and other *nyamakala* (artisans). Perhaps al-Hajj N'Faly Kaba was the most distinguished of this group of patrons. His generosity is exalted in the extraordinary *bala* and vocal performance on Rouget's recordings from 1952 (1999). These affluent businessmen (known as *dyula* or *juula*) acquired their wealth in the long-distance trade of gold, grains, cola nuts, diamonds, and other commodities and performed a pivotal role in the economy as intermediaries between the big trading companies and the rural markets.

A bustling trade linked Kankan and neighboring cities in French West Africa and English-speaking territories. Local traders would generally venture into Sierra Leone and Liberia (jointly referred to as *Dji kòma*, "beyond the river") to seek different goods. Commerce with the English territories, however, involved some risk because it affected the monopoly held by the French importers. Despite a prohibitive customs rate levied on items entering Guinea through Freetown or Monrovia, the Maninnka-Mori consumers of Kankan greatly valued British-manufactured items and fabrics. An exquisite and lustrous damask material known as *bazin*, from which the tailors made beautiful caftans or large sleeveless gowns (called *boubou*) for men, and camisoles for women, came from Sierra Leone. Kankan turned into a "city of *bazin*" during the holidays. Moreover, the trade of firearms, which used to be a highly lucrative part of the long-distance trade, was legal in Liberia, unlike in the French territories. Therefore, trade with *Dji kòma* appealed to brave young men from Kankan who were interested in earning large profits, despite the vigilant border patrol by the *gendarmes* and customs officers.

The lyrics to *Mamaya* preserve some of the exploits of these daring young traders, and versions true to the original preserve their now obscure names: Djémory, son of Djidaba Condé; Karammò Kaba, a nephew of Karammò Talibi; Mari Kéra, a *bon vivant* who would be enlisted in the army; and others who extensively traveled in search of wealth (see Figure 6-1). Extended versions of *Mamaya* mention other personalities such as the renowned ivory carver Bandian Sidimé, a charismatic member of the *san diya* age group of Timbo who died in mysterious circumstances; Hawa Sadan Mori, a brother of al-Hajj N'Faly; and Madina Sidiki and his brother, Sarata Mory Kaba, of Timbo. As for Djémory Kouyaté, he impressed many by his elegant stature, excellent manners, and eagerness to excel beyond his ascribed *nyamakala* status. The line "Djémory is resting at the police station" (*Djémory lanin commissariat*) refers to his arrest for carrying forbidden goods and not paying dues on his merchandise. Both Djémory and his mother Djidaba Condé, known as "stepmother" to members of his age group, were praised with the simple line: "Our stepmother Djidaba Condé has [truly] given birth" (*N'na rònin Djidaba Condé moyi la*).

A key to understanding the importance of *Mamaya* during its time, as well as its ongoing status, is appreciating the significance of age groups among the Maninnka. Known as *sèdè* among the Maninnka of Kankan (or *kare* farther north in Mali), age groups effectively define and bind generations together. In Kankan there are five *sèdè* and each has a name: *dan diya* ("End's happiness"; perhaps an allusion to the dictum that there is an end to everything), *san diya* ("Year's happiness"), *hara makònon* ("Expecting good tidings"), *du diya* ("Town's happiness"), and *jamana diya* ("Country's happiness"). *Sèdè* are initially based on the groupings of children born during the same epoch, and membership lasts a life-time. Males and females are grouped together under the same *sèdè* name, but they each have their own group leaders. Every three or four years, new initiates enter into the next rotation of *sèdè,* so that every fif-teen or twenty years the *sèdè* names cycle around. The *sèdè* known as *san diya* groups together those born in the early 1920s. They were the first performers of *Mamaya.*

The time of the *san diya* generation born in the early 1920s was cru-cial in colonial Kankan. By that time, European culture and values had filtered into the urban environment through travels, schooling, and contact with some members of the white community. Africans, however, did not adopt all of the European cultural symbols they had observed. Rather, they reshaped those elements of European culture they had found attractive to fit their own lifestyles. The young men of the *san diya* and other age groups admired such European musical instruments as the guitar and drum set, and such dances of the day as the tango, waltz, rumba, and bolero. They were eager to live their own lives, as every gen-eration desires. But, rigid cultural mores and constraints prevented Kankan youth from introducing European-dance styles based on physi-cal contact between male and female dancers into their beloved home-town. For Kankan, although a modern metropolis, was home to Cheikh Muhammad Chérif and other religious leaders who made it an abode of Maninnka rigorism and a city of strict adherence to Islamic codes of behavior. Early testimony is provided by the French traveler René Cail-lié (1968: I, 269), who sojourned in Kankan in 1823: "Music and danc-ing are forbidden among the Musulmans [Muslims], and consequently their amusements are far from equalling in frolic and gaiety those which prevail among the pagans."

The strength of Islam in any particular region has had a significant impact on the survival of certain musical traditions. Kankan is known not so much for *jembe* drumming, but for its xylophone (*bala*) playing traditions, which found ready patronage among the devout Muslim aristocracy. Neighboring Kouroussa, on the other hand, is not known for its *bala* traditions, but for its *jembe* drumming and is the wellspring of the most widespread *jembe* rhythm in Guinea and Mali, *Dundunba* (Dance of strong men). Although dancing was permitted in Kankan with certain restrictions, it was genteel in style and did not take on the sometimes frenetic and violent nature of *jembe*-based rhythms such as *Dundunba*. For *jembe* drummers and *bala* players, pedigrees from Kouroussa and Kankan, respectively, were and still are highly valued.

The generational problems of the *san diya* and *dan diya* youth of the 1930s and 1940s found a creative solution in *Mamaya*. They had to initiate an open theatrical forum to conform with their generational attitudes and preferences that would also be compatible with the culture of Kankan. A new artistic form had to be invented, composed, rehearsed, and performed in public. *Mamaya* expressed this harmony between the imperatives of renewal and respect for tradition.

Mamaya Performance

The primary composers of *Mamaya* are thought to come from an extraordinarily gifted family of xylophone players headed by Sidi Djéli Dioubaté. Three of his sons constituted a trio that was the premiere exponent of *Mamaya*: Sidi Mamadi (born ca. 1922), Sidi Karammò, and Sidi Moussa. They were recorded in Kankan by Arthur S. Alberts in 1949 and by Gilbert Rouget in 1952. Another son, Djanka Amò, replaced Sidi Mamadi when he left Kankan.

The elder Sidi Djéli Dioubaté had a reputation for musical genius, a concept closely related to its etymological relationship to a genie or *jinn*, a creature invisible to ordinary humans, according to Islamic mythology. Mysterious intervention by a *jinn* is a common theme in the discovery of musical instruments and the composition of new musical works in West Africa. For instance, the elderly xylophone master Bala Doumbouya, who comes from Norassoba (located northwest of Kankan) and teaches at the National Conservatory in Dakar, readily cites Sidi Djéli Dioubaté as the creator of *Mamaya* and attributes his abilities to a mysterious creature, a *jinn* called *komo kuduni*. Every evening Sidi Djéli would go into the bush (in a feared area located near the present airport) where a *jinn,* it was believed, would teach him a new piece of music. Sidi Djéli's musical abilities were so impressive that they were attributed to a supernatural force, a notion consistent with the history of the *bala,* which goes back to Sunjata Keita's foe, Sumanguru Kante, a sorcerer with extraordinary magical powers credited by widespread Maninnka oral traditions as the first *bala tii* (*bala* owner).

In addition to the family of Sidi Djéli, there was a healthy network of *jelis* based in Kankan (often related through intermarriage) that contributed to a vibrant musical culture. Soronfò-Mamadi Dioubaté was a renowned player of the *soron,* an Upper Guinea variant of the more familiar twenty-one-string Senegambian Mandinka harp known as *kora.* Diarraba Kanté (born ca. 1922), a lead *bala* player in the National Instrumental Ensemble in Conakry after independence, came from a distinguished family of musicians. Kanté's relatives included guitarist Facelli Kante (born ca. 1922 in Siguiri), who teamed up with Fodeba Keita in the creation of *Les Ballets Africains* in the late 1940s and 1950s; the three famed Manfila Kantés (all singers and guitarists); and the great singer Nyamakoron Kanté, wife of Sidi Mamadi Dioubaté and mother of Oumou Dioubaté, one of Guinea's great singers of the 1990s. (Oumou Dioubaté [n.d.] has recorded an homage to her grandfather Sidi Djéli, called *Sididou,* citing her extended family members.) As for the Kouyaté lineage, Konkoba Kouyaté and his wife, N'na Kankou Djéli, had a daughter, Nakandé Kouyaté, who sang as a youngster on the 1949 recordings made by Alberts and often teamed with Sidi Karammò in his public performances.

A typical *Mamaya* performance involved three *balas,* a chorus of female singers standing behind them, and sometimes a *dundun* (bass drum) or jazz drum set player. Youth organized the performances to begin in the mid-afternoon. Groups of the same age set (*sèdè*) would compete for the most elaborate and successful performance, and two *Mamaya* performances were often held the same day in Kabada and Timbo, the two largest sections of Kankan. The male members of the *sèdè* would wear white or azure damask caftans or *boubous* (robes), white socks, and open-backed shoes (*babouches*). They danced in front of the musicians *à la ronde* holding a staff or handkerchief in their hands. As the dancers would turn to face the musicians, their names would be sung. The length of the *Mamaya* core and extended lyrics, unusual in African musical traditions, derived from the need to recognize each dancer, his or her family, and specific quality. This implies that *Mamaya* belonged to the Maninnka tradition of praise song, but performed in a new style and a new context.

Although there are probably private recordings circulating in Guinea, the only currently known recording of *Mamaya* in its original context was made by the American Arthur S. Alberts in 1949. Only one of the twelve *bala* pieces he recorded in Kankan has been released so far (Alberts 1998). In 1952, Gilbert Rouget made recordings of the same *bala* group in Kankan, the trio of Sidi Djéli Dioubaté's sons, and issued two pieces, but not *Mamaya*. Rouget's landmark article on *bala* tuning was primarily based on his research with the same Dioubaté trio in Kankan.

Mamaya in the Repertory of the *Jeli*

In order to appreciate more fully what *Mamaya* is, it would be helpful to sort out what it is not from the standpoint of musical repertory. There are four major spheres of professional music making among the Maninnka: music for hunters (or *donso dònkili*), music of the *jeli* (or *jeliya*), drumming (*jembe* or *dundun fòli*), and modern urban music by orchestras (*musique moderne*). *Mamaya* is not related to hunters' music but rather falls squarely into the category of *jeliya* or the art of the *jeli*. It also touches the boundaries of the modern music of the orchestras as well as dance drumming. Unlike the music of the orchestras, though, *Mamaya* is firmly rooted in an indigenous instrumental tradition, that of the *bala*. Guitars, brass instruments, or other *jeli* instruments were not used in its original context, although the composition was probably transferred onto the guitar early on. Unlike dance drumming, *Mamaya* does not use *jembe* drums but instead sometimes a *dundun* or some kind of jazz drum set.

Jeliya differs in social function from *jembe* drumming in part because it celebrates single persons and their lineage rather than groups of contemporaries. For instance, the *jembe* rhythm known as *Soli* is played for groups of children about to undergo circumcision, regardless of their parents' social status, and *Dundun*ba is a group dance to be executed by athletic young men who enjoy exhibiting their strength. *Mamaya*, which may lack some of the physical features of these dances, integrates the excitement of drumming and dancing with the melodic and harmonic sophistication of the *jeli*. Within this context, the xylophone appears as the most suitable instrument to create this festive mood. It is a percussion instrument and melody instrument in one; it is fully compatible with drums and also with the intimate string instruments of the *jeli*.

The closest historical model for *Mamaya* is probably the piece *Lamban,* which, like *Mamaya,* is distinguished from the rest of the *jeli*'s repertory in two ways. First, both *Lamban* and *Mamaya* have a specific dance associated with them. This occurs with very few other *jeli* musical compositions, notably *Janjon,* which originated in the hunters' repertory. With some exceptions, traditional *jeliya* is for listening, not dancing. Second, neither *Lamban* nor *Mamaya* are dedicated to a particular patron or event of political significance, another rare occurrence in the *jeli*'s repertory. *Lamban*'s uniqueness lies in its origin as a music created by *jelis* for their own entertainment, and it is primarily danced by female *jelis* (*jelimusolu*). *Mamaya,* on the other hand, was danced by youth of all social backgrounds, and the songs celebrate a variety of local young men. By and large, *Mamaya* reinforced the cohesion of the age group, functioning as the music and performance of a Maninnka association (*ton*).

Mamaya may also have provided the inspiration for later popular musical movements among the Maninnka in the capital cities of Conakry, Bamako, Abidjan, and Dakar. The falling in and out of fashion of musical styles in Kankan since the heyday of *Mamaya* is similar in manner and concept to changing popular music styles elsewhere in the world and illustrates the trends toward innovation and retraditionalization in Maninnka society. For example, in 1956 an association of *jelis* with more than eighty members came into existence in Bamako under the name *jeli ton* (*jeli* association). In 1963 it became the *Association des artistes du Mali, l'Ambiance,* with more than three hundred members (Meillassoux 1968: 107–12). Performances at *Ambiance* events featured an orchestra including a *kora* (twenty-one-string harp), *bala, jeli dundun, taman* (squeeze drum), and electric guitars. By the late 1960s, an event called *Apollo,* featuring electric guitars, *jeli* instruments, and a sound system, was widespread in Bamako and Kankan. The notes accompanying the Kankan-based Horoya Band's (1971) recording of the piece *Apollo* (associated with the event) refer to it as "the current rage in dance in Guinea" (*Apollo est en ce moment la grande fureur à danser en Guinée*). In the 1970s a more intimate style of music, known as *Bajourou,* became a dominant genre in Malian Maninnka music. Rooted in string instruments fronted by a vocal soloist, *Bajourou* shunned the brass instruments and drums of the orchestras, opting instead for guitars occasionally mixed with a *kora* or *koni* (lute).

Like the *Ambiances* and *Apollos* of the 1960s, *Mamaya* belongs to a long line of musical events associated with youth of a particular time.

Undoubtedly, it is the earliest surviving popular music style of Maninnka music that can be documented. Can *Mamaya* provide a window into the possibly age-old phenomenon of the changing of the musical guard associated with successive generations? Or was it a modern development in Maninnka music uniquely linked to Kankan's social context in the 1930s and 1940s, especially its age groups (*sèdè*) in general, and *san diya* in particular? These questions strike to the core of the traditional versus modern dichotomy, and there is no easy answer.

Mamaya, a modern innovative music in its day, has now been elevated to the rank of a classic composition and has acquired a special position in Maninnka traditional music. Although it is not in the same category as such historical pieces as "Sunjata," "Tutu Jara" (dedicated to a Bamana king), "Taara" (dedicated to al-Hajj Umar Tal), or "Kémé Burama" (sung for Samory Toure and the commander of his armed forces, his younger brother Ibrahima), it is nevertheless revered as reflecting past glory days. For the present-day Maninnka younger generations, it symbolizes the music and culture of their fathers' and grandfathers' generations.

The phenomenon of *Mamaya* also raises an important issue of stylistic innovation associated with particular age groups. For example, many of the major personalities responsible for the innovations of modern music in Guinea and Mali in the 1970s were born at the end of World War II: Sekou "Bembeya" Dioubaté (1944), Manfila Kante (1946), and Salif Keita (1949). Facelli Kanté, the original *Les Ballets Africains* guitarist, who was one of the first to transfer the *bala* repertory onto the guitar and arrange it for an ensemble, was born around 1922. Not coincidentally, he belonged to the same age group as *Mamaya* virtuoso Sidi Mamadi Dioubaté and fellow Siguiri native Fodéba Keita (1921), founder of *Les Ballets Africains*. Studies of modern music in Africa will need to take account of not only the intersecting forces of the ethnic, social, and national origins of the players but also their age groups and the times in which they lived.

Conclusion

A comparison of the core section of the lyrics of *Mamaya* between the 1949 recording of the Dioubaté brothers (Alberts 1949) and a recording made forty-six years later by Nakandé Dioubaté (Keita 1995), a daughter of Sidi Mamadi, reveals a remarkable continuity in the tradition, no doubt because of the younger Dioubaté's bloodlines. The lyrics as well as the melody are virtually identical. (L. Kaba is of the opinion that the singer from 1995 is Nakandé Kouyaté, a contemporary of the Dioubate brothers, rather than one of their daughters.) Versions by Ami Koita (1993) and Nainy Diabate (1998) from Mali, on the other hand, substitute some names of local interest and hence lack great authenticity. The relative merits of one or another version, and whether or not Malian singers have reshaped or corrupted the lyrics as well as the original sense of the song and its associated ambiance (as critics from Kankan have argued), may partially depend on which side of the border one's allegiances lie.

Transformation of the tradition has also included the use of instruments other than *balas* for *Mamaya* recordings. (See El Hadj Djeli Sory Kouyaté [1992] for *bala* recordings and Djeli Moussa Diawara [1988] for a recording using *bala,* guitar, and *kora.*) Recall that a typical *bala* ensemble consists of at least three instruments. Two *bala* players each play an accompaniment pattern that is complete in and of itself. Often they are in a polyrhythmic relationship with each other that builds up a dense musical texture. The third *bala* player leads the ensemble, weaving in and out of the melodies sung by the female chorus, accompaniment patterns that complement those of the other *bala* players, and solo cascading melodic lines during breaks. The sight and sound of three or more *bala* virtuosos playing at full force is truly powerful. Modern renditions of *Mamaya* often add other instruments, such as guitars, electric bass, keyboards, and brass, while reducing the role of the *bala.* Once again, whether this is a renewal or a corruption depends on one's vantage point and the creativity of the artist.

One recent version of *Mamaya,* by Baba Djan Kaba (1992), a singer-composer from Kankan, is particularly noteworthy. Kaba's arrangement transforms the rich three-*bala* ensemble into a powerful orchestra of 1990s Guinea that moves past the Cuban-influenced, brass-dominated orchestras of the immediate postindependence period of the 1960s and 1970s. The ensemble includes one *bala,* one *kora,* three electric guitars, a *jembe,* electric bass, synthesizer, drum machine, and female chorus singing in two-part harmony. Although Kaba does not sing the classic lines that form the nucleus of the original, his rendition is grounded in the tradition just the same. Kaba evokes the Kankan of both today, with its many "men-about-town," and of his parents, with references to Karammò Sékouba, Karammò Talibi, and the Kankan cemetery *M'Bemba-kodon,* where only the great are laid to rest (Figure 6-4). The

N'i wara mbemba kodon
banankoro da la

Anna Muhammed rasul Allah

When you go to the cemetery where
only the great are laid to rest, in
banankoro [a quarter in Kankan
Mohammed is the apostle of Allah

chorus: Kankankanu, an ye salaatu kewolo ye
     People of Kankan, let us pray for these men.

Karamo Sekouba ani Karamo Talibe
olu tere Kankan de.
Olu bee ka dugawu ke Kankan ye,
Kankan de.

Karamo Sekouba and Karamo Talibe,
they indeed lived in Kankan.
They all blessed Kankan, yes Kankan.

FIGURE 6-4. Verses from *Kankan* by Baba Djan Kaba (from Baba Djan Kaba: 1992).

chorus closes by responding with the name of the late Bandian Sidimé, a *Mamaya* hero of the *san diya* age group. By citing and praising the Kankan notables of the era, a sign of respect for tradition, Baba Djan has reinforced the authenticity of his version, much to the delight of his compatriots.

That Baba Djan comes from the aristocratic Kaba lineage, rather than from the ranks of the Dioubaté or Kante *jelis* as would normally be expected, is one more sign of an African, a Guinean, indeed a Maninnka-Mori reinterpretation of past traditions. *Mamaya* continues to inspire Maninnka musicians and charm not only Maninnka audiences, but also lovers of African music abroad. It remains a symbol of musical innovation within the *jeli*'s tradition, the opening up of that tradition, and of a Maninnka genius for creative renewal in musical expression.

Note on the Orthography

Maninnka ("person or thing from Mandin"; the loss of the *d* is a dialect variant) refers to those in Guinea who claim origins in the homeland located on both sides of the Upper Guinea–southern Mali border, known in various dialects as Mande, Manden, Manding, or Mandin. More common spellings are Mandinka (from the Senegambia region) and Maninka (from Guinea and Mali), who are called Malinké by the French. French spellings of personal names have been used here, but phonetic spelling for Maninnka terms has been used (a grave accent indicates a short vowel sound).

Acknowledgments

This article is a synthesis of two distinct papers read by Lansiné Kaba and Eric Charry on the panel "Renewal in Mande Music" at the 1996 annual meeting of the African Studies Association in San Francisco.

References

Caillié, Réné. 1968. *Travels through Central Africa to Timbuctoo.* 2 vols. London: Frank Cass. Originally published in English and French in 1830.

Camara, Sory. 1976. *Gens de la parole: Essai sur la condition et le rôle des griots dans la société malinké.* Paris: Mouton. New edition, 1992, Paris: ACCT/ Karthala/ SAEC.

Charry, Eric. 2000. *Mande Music.* Traditional and Modern Music of the Maninka and Mandinka of Western Africa. Chicago: University of Chicago Press.

Humblot, P. 1921. "Kankan, métropole de la Guinée." *Revue Coloniale* 129–40, 153–61.

Kaba, Lansiné. 1973. "Islam, Society and Politics in Precolonial Baté (Guinea)." *Bulletin de l'Institut Fondamental d'Afrique Noire,* B, 35(2): 323–44.

―――. 1997. "Cheikh Mouhammad Chérif de Kankan, le devoir d'obéissance et la colonisation, 1923–55." In *Le Temps des marabouts: Itinéraires et stratégies Islamiques en Afrique Occidentale, 1880–1960,* edited by David Robinson and Jean-Louis Triaud, 277–97. Paris: Karthala.

Meillassoux, Claude. 1968. *Urbanization of an African Community: Voluntary Associations in Bamako.* Seattle: University of Washington Press.

Person, Yves. 1968. *Samori, une révolution Dyula.* Dakar: Institut Fondamental d'Afrique Noire.

Rouget, Gilbert, and Jean Schwarz. 1969. "Sur les xylophones equiheptaphoniques des malinké." *Revue de Musicologie* 55(1): 47–77.

―――. 1970. "Transcrire ou décrire: Chants soudanais et chant fuégien." In *Échanges et Communications: Mélanges offerts à Claude Lévi-Strauss à l'occasion de on 60ème anniversaire,* edited by Jean Pouillon and Pierre Maranda, vol. 1, 677–706. The Hague: Mouton.

Suret-Canale, Jean. 1970. *La République de Guinée.* Paris: Editions Sociales.

Discography

Alberts, Arthur S. 1949. *Field Recordings from Guinea and Mali.* Archives of Traditional Music, Indiana University. Accession no. 68-214-F, ATL 3564-3567, 3574-3577.

―――. 1954. *The Field Recordings of African Coast Rhythms: Tribal and Folk Music of West Africa.* Riverside RLP 4001.

―――. 1998. T*he Arthur S. Alberts Collection: More Tribal, Folk, and Café Music of West Africa.* Rykodisc RCD 10401.

Diabate, Nainy. 1998. *Nafa.* Stern's Africa STCD 1083.

Diawara, Djeli Moussa (aka Jawara, Jali Musa). 1988. *Soubindoor.* Mango CCD9832.

Dioubaté, Oumou. n.d. *Femmes d'Afrique.* Africando DK-041; Melodie 38147-2.

Horoya Band. 1971. *Apollo.* Syliphone SYL 535.

Kaba, Baba Djan. 1992. *Kankan.* Sonodisc 5510.

Keita, Mamady. 1995. *Mogobalu.* Fonti Musicali FMD 205.

Koita, Ami. 1992. *Mamaya.* Melodie 38120-2.

―――. 1993. *Songs of Praise.* Reissue of 1992 and earlier material. Stern's STCD 1039.

Kouyaté, (El Hadj) Djeli Sory. 1992. *Guinée: Anthologie du balafon mandingue,* vols. 2 and 3. Buda 92534-2 and 92535-2.

Rouget, Gilbert. 1954a. *Musique d'Afrique Occidentale: Musique des Malinké, Musique des Baoulé.* Contrepoint MC-20045. Also issued as Counterpoint CPT-529, Esoteric ES-529 (1956), Vogue LDM-30116. Reissued in 1993 on CD along with other material on Laserlight Digital 12179.

―――. 1954b. *Dahomey: Musique du Roi. Guinée: Musique Malinké.* Contrepoint MC-20146. Malinke music also issued on Vogue LDM 30113 (1972).

―――. 1972. *Musique Malinké.* Recorded in 1952. Contains selections from 1954b and others recorded at the same time but unreleased on 33 rpm LP. Vogue LDM 30113.

―――. 1999. *Guineé: Musique des Malinke/Guinea: Music of the Mandinka.* Le Chant du Monde/Harmonia Mundi, CNR 2741112. Reissue of all Guinean material from 1954a, 1954b, and 1972 with expanded notes.

CHAPTER 7

Concepts of Neo-African Music as Manifested in the Yoruba Folk Opera

Akin Euba

In the course of the twentieth century, many new types of music developed in Africa, and these coexist with the traditional types of African music. In most cases, the new types bear imprints of traditional music, to a greater or lesser degree. There are some new types in which the essential stylistic resources are derived from traditional music; the connection between these new types and their traditional prototypes are obvious. Average Africans have no difficulty in identifying themselves with such new types. In other cases, the relationship with traditional music is obscure, and I refer in this instance to music composed by Africans whose training has been in Western music. Although such composers usually incorporate elements of African culture into their works, these elements tend to be lost because they are presented in a stylistic context that is overwhelmingly Western. It is difficult for average Africans to relate to the works of such composers, and the question therefore arises about the relevance of these works to the African society.

In African traditional culture, the relevance of music, or to put it another way, the function of music in society has always been an important factor and is, consequently, one that is also desirable in modern culture. We cannot, then, lightly dismiss the question of the relevance of modern African music to contemporary African society.

In making this point, it should be acknowledged that the various types of music practiced in Africa (even those modeled on Western art music) have their different patrons and that there are various levels of relevance. Moreover, African musicians operate not only within Africa but also increasingly on the international scene. It stands to reason, therefore, that all types of music practiced by Africans, whether highly or marginally relevant within the African continent, are valid in the context of an expanding African heritage in music, in regard to Africa's international relations, and in terms of Africa's contribution to the world of music at large.

In this essay, I will attempt to show that the Yoruba folk opera is one of those neo-African types of music that derive their essential style from traditional culture. The folk opera is firmly rooted in Yoruba traditional culture and is a natural evolution from traditional sources. The folk opera is, in effect, a modern interpretation of Yoruba traditional performing arts. For these reasons, it is a viable concept of neo-African music and a good model for modern African composers who seek to develop neo-African idioms that are highly relevant to contemporary African societies.

Historical Background of the Folk Opera

Music theater has always been an important aspect of the cultural life of the Yoruba. Traditional ceremonies of the Yoruba are almost invariably performed with music and, in these contexts, music is often associated with other arts. Yoruba music theater, as originally conceived, formed part of ritual observances.

Between 1610 and 1650, a new type of Yoruba music theater emerged that was nonritualistic and was designed for entertainment. The new type was based on the dramatic roots of the Yoruba ritual masquerade, *egúngún,* and developed under the patronage of Aláàfin Ogbolu, King of Ọ̀yọ́. The new music theater was at first restricted to the royal court at Ọ̀yọ́ but eventually moved out of the palace to become the *alárìnjò* (traveling) theater (Adédèjí 1981: 221–24). Today, *alárìnjò* masquerades (also known as *egúngún apidán,* "masquerades that present magical displays," are a common feature of Yoruba life.

The *alárìnjò* theater "provided a structural and methodological paradigm" for the Yoruba folk opera and other types of modern Yoruba popular traveling theater (Jeyifo 1984: 39).

Two centuries elapsed between the beginning of the *alárìnjò* theater and another significant set of events in the history of the Yoruba folk opera. From about the 1860s, concerts and other forms of Western-derived entertainment were mounted in Lagos by members of a new African elite, comprising returnees (former slaves and their descendants) from Sierra Leone, Brazil, and Cuba. The principal forms of entertainment were the "variety concert and operatic drama"; these two forms survived well into the 1940s and "indirectly influenced the development of an integral performance idiom by the (modern Yoruba) Travelling Theatre troupes" (Jeyifo 1984: 41).

The producers and performers of the nineteenth-century Western-derived entertainment at Lagos were well familiar with the variety shows of the English music hall of that period, and it was these variety shows that provided the "form, content and inspiration" for the Lagos productions. The programs of these productions were built around typical music hall fare, such as "comic songs, romantic songs, dramatic sketches excerpted from longer plays, comic monologues and duologues" and so forth (Jeyifo 1984: 42).

The Christian missions, also, were engaged in theatrical productions during the latter half of the nineteenth century, and "the school rooms of the Church missions served as the major venues for the theatrical productions of the various clubs and organizations." More significantly, "it was . . . the interest of the Christian missions in drama which generated the crucial issues which the theatrical activities of the period bequeathed to future developments in Nigerian theater and drama" (Jeyifo 1984: 42).

It is not surprising that the Western-derived forms of entertainment cultivated by the members of the new elite did not find favor in all quarters of Lagos society. Some members of the church, including African priests, advocated the indigenization of theatrical entertainment by drawing on indigenous cultural and artistic resources, such as dance and drumming. Concurrent with this development, there were voices within the church proposing the Africanization of the liturgy. In view of this, "the indigenist movement in the theater drew moral and ideological support from the Independent African Church movement" (Jeyifo 1984: 44).

The first attempts to create a neo-African theater, consisting of a blending of Western theatrical forms with local content, took place in the 1880s, the major centers being Lagos, Abẹ̀òkúta, and Ìbàdàn (Jeyifo 1984: 45).

One of the models for contemporary Yoruba theater was a play, *King Elejigbo,* which was written by D. A. Olóyèdé in 1903 and was the "first recorded modern Yoruba play" (Jeyifo 1984: 47) Olóyèdé's work may also have been one of the very first examples of the folk opera.

By the early 1940s, "the form and characteristic themes of the Yoruba Operatic Theatre had been clearly established." The main practitioners were in Lagos, but there were others also in Abẹ̀òkúta and Ìbàdàn. These early pioneers include A. K. Ajíṣafẹ́, Ajíbọ́lá Láyẹni, E. A. Dáwódù, A. B. David, and G. T. Onímọlẹ̀ (Jeyifo 1984: 50).

Traditional Basis of the Folk Opera

I would like in this section to discuss the relationship between Yoruba traditional culture and the folk opera.

As already suggested, music and other arts are frequently integrated in the context of Yoruba traditional ceremonies. An important ceremony would often feature music, dance, poetry, and mime, as well as costume and other visual arts.

Yoruba traditional dance is composed of motifs that depict events from everyday life. In essence, Yoruba dance is dance-drama and, to the extent that dance relies on music, traditional music too may be described as dramatic.

Poetry in Yoruba culture is typically performed in the context of music and, indeed, the arts of poetry and music in Yoruba tradition are synonymous (Euba 1975b).

The Yoruba practice the art of talking with musical instruments and much of their poetry is performed through this medium. The use of musical instruments to talk, in other words, the act of a drummer who employs his instrument as a speech surrogate, to say things that could well be said by mouth, is to my mind one that has dramatic connotations.

When we consider the various contexts within which Yoruba traditional music is customarily realized (the ritualistic and the multiartistic contexts), we can reasonably conclude that Yoruba traditional music is music theater.

The Yoruba folk opera, too, is a multiartistic event, combining music, dance, drama, poetry, costume, and other arts its seeds existed in traditional cultural practice. One of the major differences between the folk opera and traditional music theater is that the combined arts in the opera are presented for their own sake, whereas in traditional culture, the arts are embellishments of ceremony, ceremony being the prime object of attention.

Is the Yoruba Folk Opera Related to European Opera?

The statement that I made earlier, that the Yoruba opera derives its essential style from Yoruba traditional culture, should not be understood to mean that there has been no foreign influence at work in the development of the folk opera. The transposition of Yoruba performing arts from their traditional contexts to the modern theater reflects various degrees of European influence. To begin with, a performance in which there is no audience participation is more typical of the European than of Yoruba culture. In Yoruba traditional society, there is always room for spectators to join professional performers, either by singing refrains or by dancing. In the performance of operas, however, there is a clearer line of demarcation between audience and actors than exists in traditional culture; in the folk opera, audience participation is restricted to applause and to audible comments on what is happening on the stage.

This separation of performers from their audience is, I believe, an aspect of European influence.

Another element of European influence comes from the European theater of the spoken word. The plays of Shakespeare were for many years standard material for literary studies in Nigerian schools, and Nigerians who have been to school are familiar with the European concept of spoken drama. Either directly or indirectly, this concept has played a role in the transposition of Yoruba performing arts to the modern stage.

There is, however, no evidence that the European opera has been the model for the development of the Yoruba folk opera. Although performances of European opera and operetta are sometimes staged in Nigeria, such performances are infrequent, and the composers of folk opera have little or no exposure to them. It is more likely that these composers have seen films of American musical comedies and have received a generalized impression of Western musical theater through this medium.

There is no doubt, then, that the main conceptual basis of the folk opera is to be found in traditional music, dance, and drama and that the

influence of Europe lies more in the general technique of theatrical production than in opera. This view is shared by Jeyifo (1984: 19) who
writes: Although "many aspects of western stagecraft have been incorporated by Travelling Theatre troupes, the performance conventions
remain ineluctably non-western."

Stylistic Influence of the Church

It would be wrong to conclude that traces of European music are totally
absent from the Yoruba folk opera. An analysis of the opera reveals the
coexistence of two distinct styles: the traditional style and the church
style. The latter refers to the neo-African type of music that is characteristic of the Yoruba church, particularly the Africanized church.

A brief history of the development of Yoruba church music will show
how this idiom found its way into the folk opera.

The first Christian missions were established in Yorubaland in the
1840s and, to begin with, the missionaries provided music for worship
by translating European hymn texts into Yoruba. In church, Yoruba
words were sung to European tunes, a procedure that was stylistically
unsuitable. Yoruba is a tone language and, in Yoruba culture, the intona-
tions of words determine the contours of song melodies. The practice of
singing precomposed tunes to Yoruba words inevitably results in the
distortion of the meanings of words.

In due course, Yoruba church musicians began to compose original
hymns that were more consistent with the tone-tune principle of Yoruba
culture. The hymns produced by the Yoruba composers, although faithful to this principle, could not entirely avoid elements of European
music that had become lodged in the creative minds of the composers. I
refer, for example, to European modality, the European concept of equal
temperament, and the use of European instruments.

The neo-African Yoruba hymns, therefore, are a synthesis of Yoruba
and European musical elements (Euba, 1992).

By the second and third decades of the twentieth century, the church
was beginning to have a strong religious and cultural impact among the
Yoruba. Yoruba Christians became very familiar with European hymns
and later with the neo-African hymns composed by indigenous musicians. The Christians were forbidden from participating in traditional
ceremonies (which the missionaries considered "pagan") and were
therefore dissociated from one of the mainstreams of traditional music.

The contact of Christians with indigenous music was, therefore, limited to the neo-African hymns that they sang in the church.

Many of the composers of folk opera were active Christians at one time or another and were conversant with neo-African church music.

The development of folk opera had other stylistic connections with the church. The indigenous composers of Yoruba church music first wrote hymns to be performed by the choir and congregation. Later, they also produced more ambitious works, such as anthems and cantatas, to be performed by the choir alone on special Sundays. In the Africanized churches, the music performed on special Sundays provided opportunities for theatrical display. During the harvest festival, for example, the various church societies were called one by one to the altar to make offerings. The procession to and from the altar by members of each society was usually accompanied by singing, drumming, and dancing.

The first concrete attempts at the idiom of the folk opera probably consisted of compositions by local choirmasters, in which scenes from the Scriptures were dramatized.

According to Jeyifo (1984: 59–60), "the form of stage enactment (which was referred to as) 'Native Air Operas' and 'sacred cantatas' represented an intermediate phase in the evolution of stage performances in modern Nigeria." The form was "developed under the auspices of the nativist Christian sects which became the principal proprietors of dramatic productions in the thirties and forties; it was considered artistically appropriate to the simple didactic moralities constructed from Bible stories which formed the exclusive dramatic material of these 'Native Air Operas.' "

The folk opera, then, was born within the precincts of the church, and it is not surprising that its composers should have borrowed some of the opera's stylistic resources from the church.

The Creators of the Folk Opera

The typical composer of the folk opera has had little or no formal training in music (that is, in the European sense) but received a sound modern type of school education, followed in some cases by training in a profession, which is not necessarily in the performing arts. His general education would have familiarized him with the elements of modern theater.

The typical composer is highly knowledgeable about Yoruba traditional culture and about modern Nigerian society. It is usual for a composer to lead his own performing company and to have members of his family as core personnel in the company. This way, he is able to ensure stability and loyalty within the company. The typical composer is also the librettist, principal actor, artistic director, and producer, and very often, one of his wives plays the female lead.

In the creation of a new opera, the composer provides the theme and sketches out the basic details of the plot. These are then developed through the improvisation and collaboration of other members of the troupe. The constituent parts (dialogue, songs, dances, poetry, instrumental music) of the finished product are a result of collective creativity (Jeyifo 1984: 95–99).

As with other types of traveling theater, folk opera troupes are constantly on the road, operating a strenuous itinerary that takes them to various parts of Nigeria and often to parts of West Africa. The economic circumstances of these troupes are seldom easy and, according to Jeyifo (1984: 55), "groups like Oyin Adéjọbí's, Kọ́lá Ògúnmọ́lá's and Dúró Ládípọ̀'s initially regularly doubled as either 'highlife' or 'jùjú' musical bands," in order to be commercially viable.

The best-known composers in the genre of the folk opera are Hubert Ògúndè, Kọ́lá Ògúnmọ́lá, and Dúró Ládípọ̀.

Ògúndè was born in 1916 and first worked as a teacher before joining the Nigeria Police Force (Clark 1981: 295). He was also a church organist and composer (Jeyifo 1984: 36).

Ògúndè produced his first opera in 1944 and, in 1946, launched the Ògúndè Theatre, "the first contemporary professional company in Nigeria" (Clark 1981: 295–96). Ògúndè's operatic career lasted little more than a decade; according to Clark (1979: 33) his theater was, by about 1957, no longer operatic in character.

Ògúndè is generally regarded as the father of modern Yoruba theater and for several decades ran a highly successful theatrical organization, in both artistic and financial terms. Through his business organizations, Ògúndè produced and distributed LP records of songs from his plays and also made films.

Kọ́lá Ògúnmọ́lá also started professional life as a teacher and created his first company in this capacity. Members of this company included fellow teachers, school children, traders, and seamstresses, all of whom were Christians (Beier 1954: 33). As Jeyifo (1984: 40) points out, performers and audiences for the Yoruba Travelling Theatre were at that time (that is, around 1954) "predominantly drawn from the lay congregations of the various Christian denominations."

Dúró Ládípọ̀ was born in Ọ̀ṣogbo on 18 December 1931, the son of an Anglican catechist. As a child, he was keenly interested in Yoruba culture and customs, and he closely followed the activities of the various cults and observed traditional festivals. Ládípọ̀ worked as a teacher in Iléṣà and Kaduna before settling down at Ọ̀ṣogbo in 1959. While teaching at the UNA School in Kaduna, he founded a dramatic society and produced his own interpretation of Shakespeare's *As You Like It*. After returning to Ọ̀ṣogbo, Ládípọ̀ composed an Easter Cantata in which he made use of talking drums, the first time these drums had ever been introduced into All Saints Church, Ọ̀ṣogbo, where the cantata was premiered. The church disapproved of this innovation and thus forced Ládípọ̀ to seek a secular setting for his compositions. In December 1961 he presented a Christmas cantata at the Mbari Club in Ìbàdàn and later created his own club, Mbárí-Mbáyọ̀, at Ọ̀ṣogbo. As a result of his wide knowledge of traditional culture, Ládípọ̀ made dexterous use of traditional musical instruments, chants, and dance steps. Before his death on 11 March 1978, he had produced at least twenty full-length operas (Ògúnbíyì 1981: 334–39).

The Operas

The original terminology for the folk opera was "native air opera," and it is not clear when the new name "folk opera" was adopted. There is no doubt, however, that the two terms refer to the same type of work.

Although music and dance almost invariably feature (to a greater or lesser degree) in all plays written in the Yoruba language, not all of such plays are described as folk opera. By current usage among knowledgeable Yoruba, the term *play* and the term *folk opera* denote separate types of drama, even though both share a great deal in common. The existence of a distinction is implicit in Jeyifo's (1984: 11) comment that "the term [*opera*] was only loosely applicable to one phase of the development of the performance idiom of the Travelling Theatre when the dialogue was entirely sung and the text was conceived as a form of 'libretto.' "

This comment introduces the element of the sung dialogue as a possible criterion in our definition of the folk opera, and it would appear that, at the initial stage, works referred to as native air operas had dialogues that were entirely sung. Jeyifo (1984: 60) provides a more detailed description of the original conception of the native air opera:

In this form of theatrical enactment, the dialogue was entirely sung to an invariable, monotonous rhythmic base of rhumba rhythms on which a melodic line adapted from Christian hymns was grafted. Stage movement was rigidly stylised and consisted mainly of a subdued shuffle executed in alternating leftward and rightward motions within a frontal linear formation along the breadth of the platform stage. The aesthetic appeal of the form lay primarily with the auditory effect of the composition and rendition of the sung dialogue.

Our contemporary understanding of the term *folk opera* accommodates works in which the dialogue is not entirely sung and, if operas and nonoperas use music and dance, how do we distinguish between the two? There is no doubt that there is some confusion between the spoken play and the opera. According to Jeyifo (1984: 11), "the term 'opera' used to be universally applied to the form of the Travelling Theatre performance."

It would appear that, even before the emergence of the native air opera, the proponents of an indigenous Yoruba theater had already devised a theatrical form in which traditional song, dance, and drumming were fused with dramatic dialogue. It is obvious that it was the appearance of the sung dialogue that prompted the term *native air opera*. At the time that Ògúndè became active in the theater, he worked within the idiom of the native air opera, but when he and other composers found this form "too restrictive and inadequate for their secular themes and the tastes of their far-flung audiences, they returned to the earlier theatrical mode of fusing traditional song, dance and drumming with dramatic dialogue" (Jeyifo 1984: 60).

It seems clear, therefore, how the term *opera* came to be applied to all types of plays with music and dance, whether or not their dialogue was sung. In other words, the term seems to have persisted even when the composers had changed from the native air opera back to the earlier mode. But this brings us no closer to an answer to the question posed above. At what point does a work cease to be a spoken play and become an opera?

Current terminology allows us, I think, to dispense with the entirely sung dialogue as a crucial element in the definition of the folk opera; otherwise practically all of the works recognized today as folk operas would be ruled out. To my mind, the necessary criteria for a definition are (1) the extent to which music is an integral part of the drama, (2) whether or not such music occurs in the context of the story or as a result of the composer's personal and individual imagination, and (3) whether or not texts set to music might ordinarily (in real life) be spoken.

With regard to the first criterion, a dramatic work in which music is present all the way through (in instrumental form) but has all texts spoken and no singing whatsoever would obviously not qualify as an opera. It seems therefore that the idea of singing rather than speaking texts is important, but not in the sense that all texts must be sung. A work may then qualify as a folk opera if more weight is given to sung texts than to spoken texts.

Regarding the second criterion, there are plays in which music and dance feature, because there are situations in the plays that are replicas of real-life situations that would ordinarily require music (for example, a wedding). Such situational or contextual usages of music should not necessarily qualify a work to be in the category of a folk opera.

The third criterion refers to dialogue and other texts that, in real-life situations, would not be sung. In the conventional folk opera, many (but not all) texts that are normally spoken in real life are set to music.

The description of the native air opera given above calls to mind one of the features by which grand opera (in which all text is sung) is distinguished from light opera (in which dialogue is spoken and other texts are sung) in the pre-twentieth-century idioms of European music theater. Although the composers of native air opera have had little or no exposure to European grand opera, it is just possible that they were advised by members of the neo-African elite who had lived in Europe and were familiar with the style of European grand opera.

Jeyifo (1984: 99–109) identifies four categories of themes for the dramas of the traveling theater, and these are equally useful in classifying the themes of folk operas. The catagories are (1) biblical, (2) historical, (3) legendary/mythological/folkloristic, and (4) social (that is, dealing with contemporary society).

The early operas dealt with religious themes, such as *The Garden of Eden* by Ògúndè, *Joseph and His Brethren* by Ògúnmọ́lá, and *King Solomon,* also by Ògúndè. In the second category, we have *Ọba Kò So, Ọba Mọ́rọ̀,* and *Mọ́remí,* all by Dúró Ládípọ̀. Jeyifo (1984: 104) mentions Ògúnmọ́lá's *Èṣù Ọ̀dàrà* and Ládípọ̀'s *Alajobi* as examples of plays in the third category, but I am not familiar with these works and can only surmise that they are folk operas. Works in the fourth category include *Strike and Hunger* and *Bread and Bullet,* both by Ògúndè and Ògúnmọ́lá's *Ìfẹ́ Owó* (Love of money).

There are other works that may best be described as morality operas—for example, Ládípọ̀'s *Èdá,* which, according to Ogúnbíyì (1981: 342), "was inspired by Ulli Beier's adaptation and translation of Hugo von Hofmansthal's late fifteenth-century version of *Everyman.*

In succeeding sections of this essay, I would like to discuss three works that are characteristic of the tradition of folk opera: Ògúnmọ́lá's *Palmwine Drinkard,* Ládípọ̀'s *Ọba Kò So,* and Wálé Ògúnyẹmí's *Ọbalúayé.*

The *Palmwine Drinkard*

In categorizing Yoruba folk operas, the form used in the native air opera (in which all text was sung) may be described as the old form, while that of operas in which some of the text is sung and some spoken may be referred to as the new form. Ògúnmọ́lá's *Palmwine Drinkard* is in the new form. The opera is based on a well-known novel of the same name by Amos Tutùọlá (1953). In the novel Tutùọlá made use of Yoruba folk stories that, as a child, he heard from his grandmother.

Palmwine Drinkard was composed under a Rockefeller Foundation grant that allowed Ògúnmọ́lá and his company to work for six months on attachment to the School of Drama (now Department of Theatre Arts) at the University of Ibadan. The first performance took place at the Arts Theatre of the University in April 1963 (Axworthy 1968: 1).

The story of *Palmwine Drinkard* is about a man, Làánkẹ́, whose life revolves around the drinking of palmwine (the most popular alcoholic beverage among traditional Yoruba). In the opening scene, Làánkẹ́ hosts a palmwine party, surrounded by fellow "drinkards." When the supply of palmwine is exhausted, his guests threaten to leave and Làánkẹ́ quickly summons his palmwine tapper, bidding him to climb the palm tree and replenish the supply. While climbing up the tree, the tapper falls to the ground and dies. Since no one else can provide Làánkẹ́ with good enough palmwine, he decides to travel to the land of dead people, in order to bring back the tapper.

On his way to the land of the dead, Làánkẹ́ "encounters wondrous beings and still more wondrous trials of wit and strength (Jeyifo 1984: 104). In the end, these encounters turn out to have been a dream and, when he awakens from sleep, Làánkẹ́ is reunited with his tapper and his drinking friends.

The musical idiom of *Palmwine Drinkard* is mainly in the neo-

African church style: occurrences of the traditional idiom are infrequent. As far as I can deduce from the recording of the work, the instrumental ensemble consists of one *agogo* (iron bell), about three single-headed membranophones of the *àkúbà* family (neo-Yoruba drums that are derived from the traditional single-headed fixed-pitch membranophone and the Latin American conga), and an *ìyáàlù* (double-headed hourglass tension drum). This combination of percussion instruments is typical of the Africanist churches of Yorubaland.

Figure 7-1 is an excerpt from the opening song of *Palmwine Drinkard,* in which Làánkẹ́ and his guests eulogize palmwine. The song is characteristic of the neo-African church style and so also is the instrumental accompaniment (Figure 7-2) that goes with it. This accompaniment occurs often in *Palmwine Drinkard* and, on one occasion, in Làánkẹ́'s encounter with a Europeanized god and his wife (Ògúnmọ́lá 1968: 34),[1] it is modified to fit a 4/4 meter (Figure 7-3).

In Figures 7-2 and 7-3, the second and third drums are almost cer-

FIGURE 7-1. From the opening song of *Palmwine Drinkard.*

Played repeatedly. Drums I-III are pitched high to low. Talking drum plays varied patterns.

FIGURE 7-2. Instrumental accompaniment to the opening song of *Palmwine Drinkard*.

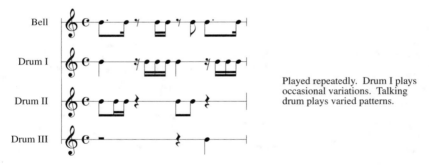

Played repeatedly. Drum I plays occasional variations. Talking drum plays varied patterns.

FIGURE 7-3. Metric modification of figure 7-2.

tainly played by the same person, and the notes written for the third drum appear to me to be damped tones (that is, played with a hollowed hand).

At the death of the tapper, Làánkẹ́ and his friends sing a funeral song (Ògúnmọ́la 1968: 14), which to my mind is one of the finest examples of song writing in the neo-African style. The concluding part of the song is shown in Figure 7-4. Beginning from the third measure of the excerpt, the instrumental accompaniment (hitherto unobtrusive) is accentuated, and the talking drum becomes more rhythmically busy. This

È - fù - fù lè - lè kó gbé ẹ dọ - run ó dì - gbó - ṣe

Sǔn   re   o,   Sǔn   re   o,

Sǔn   re   o   Sǔn   re   o

KỌ́ - lọ́ - run kọ́ ṣọ́ pà - dé   o, Sǔn   re   o,

È - fù - fù lè - lè kó gbé ẹ dọ́ - run ó dì - gbó ṣe

FIGURE 7-4. Funeral song from *Palmwine Drinkard.*

effect is appropriate for the climax of the funeral song and the exit of the mourners.

While being predominantly neo-African in its idiom, *Palmwine Drinkard* features some interesting usages of the traditional idiom, one of which occurs in the market scene. One of the food sellers at the market is a beautiful young lady, Bísí, who, although very much sought after, declines all offers of marriage. Then comes along a handsome young man (who, unknown to Bísí, is a spirit in human form),[2] and Bísí falls instantly in love and decides to follow him. The young man sings a leader-and-chorus song, warning Bísí against such folly, but Bísí is totally charmed by his looks and will not listen. The market scene in *Palmwine Drinkard* is based on a familiar folk story of the Yoruba, and

FIGURE 7-5.   Spirit-Man's song from *Palmwine Drinkard*.

the song that Ògúnmọ́lá assigns to the spirit man (Figure 7-5) is part of the original story.

Another instance of the use of the traditional idiom occurs in the scene *Iwin Òru,* "Night Spirits" (Ògúnmọ́lá 1968: 24). Here, the spirits deliver a eulogy to their king, Olúugbó, using the free rhythm, unaccompanied form of Yoruba chanting. This is followed by a song with instrumental accompaniment, whose general style is derived from Èkìtì traditional music. The single-headed-fixed pitch *àkúbà* drums in Ògúnmọ́lá's ensemble adapt very well to the Èkìtì idiom.

Other instances of the use of the Yoruba traditional chant mode occur in the scene entitled *Ọba Ìkà,* "The Cruel King." The eulogy of Àwòrò, the priest, and the *ìpolówó* (advertisement of merchandise) of the Oníṣòwò Àrùn (seller of diseases) (Ògúnmọ́lá 1968: 74, 76) both use the traditional chant mode.

Ọba Kò So

The story of *Ọba Kò So* deals with episodes from the life of Ṣàngó, a fifteenth-century king of Ọ̀yọ́, who after death became one of the principal Yoruba divinities, the dreaded god of thunder and lightning.

In his lifetime, Ṣàngó ruled over one of the most powerful kingdoms of Yoruba. He encouraged his warrior chiefs to ravage and subjugate other Yoruba kingdoms. Inevitably, two of these warrior chiefs, Tìmì and Gbọ̀ọ́nkáà, became so unruly that Ṣàngó could no longer control them. Ṣàngó sent Tìmì to Ẹdẹ, ostensibly as a toll collector, but hoping in reality that the notorious Ìjèṣà warriors would deal with him. Tìmì, however, prospered at Ẹdẹ and was made king. When Ṣàngó heard this, he was dissatisfied and therefore sent Gbọ̀ọ́nkáà to Ẹdẹ in order to fight Tìmì. He expected that, in such a fight, one of them would surely be eliminated. In the fight at Ẹdẹ, Gbọ̀ọ́nkáà overpowered Tìmì and brought him to Ọ̀yọ́ alive. Ṣàngó thus found himself in the same position as before, with two troublesome warrior chiefs back in town. After some further thought, Ṣàngó decided that the fight should be repeated at Ọ̀yọ́ for the people to see. Gbọ̀ọ́nkáà became suspicious of Ṣàngó's motives and went to seek the help of the *àjẹ́* (the powerful mothers who commute between the natural and supernatural worlds). At the second fight, fortified by medicinal charms that he obtained from the *àjẹ́*, Gbọ̀ọ́nkáà easily disposed of Tìmì and then pursued Ṣàngó, forcing the king to abdicate and to commit suicide. Ṣàngó's few remaining friends at Ọ̀yọ́, unable to accept the shameful news of the king's suicide, sought ways by which they could disprove the news. Ṣàngó suddenly spoke to them through thunderclaps and, for his supporters, this was conclusive proof that *ọba kò so* (the king did not hang).

Dúró Ládípọ̀'s *Ọba Kò So* is an opera in the old form. Almost all of the text is sung, the exceptions being (a) short phrases or interjectory statements, and (b) two sections of extended speech. The following are examples of short phrases that are spoken:

(1) *Ṣàngó:*   Ẹ ṣeun   Thank you (Ládípọ̀ 1968: 67)

(2) *Gbọ̀ọ́nkáà:* Èmi   Me? (ibid. 14–15)

(3) *Tìmì:*   Pé bóo? Jáá lọ jàre   How? Let's go please (ibid. 14–15)

(4) *Ṣàngó:*   È é ti rí   Why? (ibid. 24–25)

(5) *Tìmì:*   Ẹ ẹ́ jèrè   May you prosper (ibid. 36–37)

(6) *Gbòọ́nkáà:*   *Ọkùnrin, ọkùnrin*   I am a man for sure
              lẹ̀ ń ké sí   (ibid. 44–45)
(7) *Gbòọ́nkáà:*   *Bẹ́ẹ̀ni Kábíyèsí baba*   Yes, Your Majesty,
                                    father (ibid. 62–63)

The two sections of extended speech are (a) the part of Àgbà Ẹ̀dẹ̀ Kan (Ládípọ̀ 1968: 36–38) and (b) the part of Olófòfó, beginning *Ọládoyè, n á yó n má mọ̀?/* Ọládoyè, how can I have a full stomach and do not know? (ibid. 42–43).

The historical context of *Ọba Kò So* enables Ládípọ̀ to make copious use of the traditional idiom of Yoruba music. Ṣàngó is still worshipped today among the Yoruba, and his devotees continue to preserve artistic traditions (in poetry, song, dance, and other paraphernalia) that have for centuries been associated with Ṣàngó. A composer treating the life of Ṣàngó, then, has a wealth of material from which to draw, and Ládípọ̀ makes good use of the existing repertoires of the various art forms cultivated by Ṣàngó devotees in real life.

As far as I can tell from a recording, the ensemble of *Ọba Kò So* comprises *bàtá* (conically shaped, fixed-pitch membranophones that, when Ṣàngó was alive, were part of his regalia and are today the instruments favored by Ṣàngó devotees) and *dùndún* (hourglass tension drums, and possibly one or two of the *àkúbà* type). A solo flute is used in one section, for special effect. The overwhelming presence of the traditional idiom, which the story of *Ọba Kò So* suggests, does not, however, mean that the neo-African church style is absent. On the contrary, *Ọba Kò So* is a good example of an opera in which the two idioms are juxtaposed.

The opening scene, in which the Ìwàrèfà (Eunuch, one of the king's servants) and the Olorì (the king's wives) chant and sing the *oríkì* (praise poetry) of Ṣàngó, is in the traditional idiom. Much of the textual material is a direct quotation from traditional sources, as, for example, the following passage, which is one of the best-known texts associated with Ṣàngó rituals:

Àfẹni tí kọgílá kọ lù	Only one whom a devil strikes
Àfẹni Èṣù ń ṣe	Only one whom Èṣù tricks
Ló lè kọ l'Èṣù	Could attack Èṣù
Ló lè kọ lu Ṣàngó	Could attack Ṣàngó
Àfẹni tí Ṣàngó ó pa	Only one whom Ṣàngó will kill
	(Ládípọ̀ 1968: 2–3)[3]

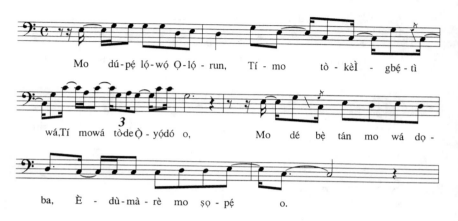

FIGURE 7-6. Ṣàngó's song from *Ọba Kò So.*

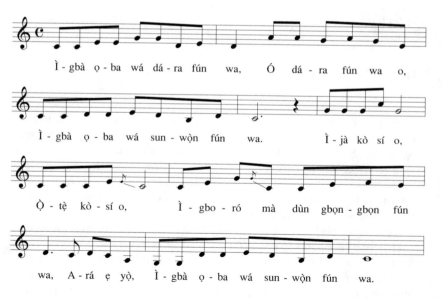

FIGURE 7-7. Chorus from the opening scene of *Ọba Kò So.*

FIGURE 7-8. Chant of the townspeople from *Ọba Kò So.*

Ṣàngó makes his first appearance in the course of the rendition of praise poetry by the Ìwàrèfà and the Olorì and immediately after their rendition, Ṣàngó sings a song (Figure 7-6) that is in the neo-African church style. The chorus (Figure 7-7) that follows the solo song is even more obviously based on the neo-African church style. Its vocal and instrumental idiom is an almost exact replica of the musical style of the Cherubim and Seraphim Church (Euba 1971: 99).

Broadly speaking, it is the nature of the text that determines the musical idiom of a given section of *Ọba Kò So*. Whenever the text is derived from or modeled on traditional poetry, the melodic idiom employed is also traditional. When the text is nontraditional (that is, written in a modern form of Yoruba), then the musical idiom is that of neo-African church music (Euba 1971: 101).

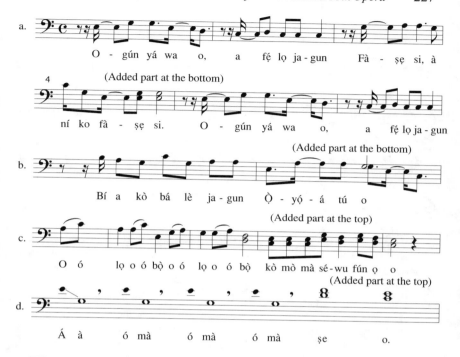

FIGURE 7-9. Examples of European-derived multi-part technique from Ọba Kò So.

The choral style of *Ọba Kò So* is predominantly unisonal, and this conforms with the Ọ̀yọ́ tradition of choral music. There are sporadic occurrences of multipart singing, some of which are based on eastern Yoruba traditional practice, while others reflect European influence. (The eastern Yoruba have a tradition of multipart singing, while the Ọ̀yọ́ Yoruba do not.)

In view of the fact that the story of *Ọba Kò So* is centered in Ọ̀yọ́, Ládípọ̀'s employment of the traditional idiom (in textual, vocal, and instrumental terms) is based on Ọ̀yọ́ practice. The use of eastern Yoruba multipart choral technique cited above belongs in an unusual section in which a non-Ọ̀yọ́ (specifically Èkìtì) idiom is interposed. From a dramatic point of view, this is an important section, and the change of idiom helps to highlight it. The section of Èkìtì style begins with the

FIGURE 7-10. Ọya's lament from *Ọba Kò So.*

reply of the *àjẹ́* to Gbọ̀ọ́nkáà's plea for help and terminates with the choral chant of *Ará Ọ̀yọ́* / Ọ̀yọ́ Townspeople, in which they warn Ṣàngó of impending doom (Ládípọ̀ 1968: 76–80). Excerpts from the chant of the townspeople are shown in Figure 7-8, and these illustrate the characteristic use of heterophony in Èkìtì choral music.

In Figure 7-9 we have a different kind of multipart technique, which is derived from Europe, by way of the church and *jùjú* music.

At the death of Ṣàngó, his favorite wife, Ọya, sings a moving lament that (like the funeral song performed for the palmwine tapper in Ògúnmọ́lá's *Palmwine Drinkard*) is a fine example of the use of the neo-African church style. An excerpt from Ọya's lament is shown in Figure 7-10. Much of the text of this lament consists of *oríkì* praise poetry, but it is nevertheless well fitted into a neo-African church style.

In the Yoruba folk opera, musical dramatization is achieved principally through the singing; the orchestra, as has been noted by Beier (1954: 33) merely provides "background rhythm." There are exceptions in *Ọba Kò So* where instruments are employed to heighten the drama. For example, shouts of *Kábíyèsí* (Your Majesty) are punctuated by drum rolls, the sound of thunder is depicted by drumming, the *ìyáàlù* talking drum is sometimes used to play speech patterns simultaneously rendered by voices, and talking instruments are on two occasions employed in alternation with speaking voices. When Tìmì arrives at Ẹdẹ, he chants a poetic text, pausing after each phrase for the talking drum to repeat the phrase. When Gbọ̀ọ́nkáà also arrives at Ẹdẹ he chants a poem, whose lines are similarly repeated by a talking flute.

Ọbalúayé

I would like next to discuss a folk opera in whose production I was personally involved.[4] After working on an earlier essay on the folk opera (Euba 1971), the idea occurred to me that I should write a folk opera. I therefore approached Wálé Ògúnyẹmí, who is not only a very good user of the Yoruba language but who had also authored several successful plays in English. My aim was that Ògúnyẹmí should write a libretto for me to set to music.

This was a departure from customary practice, since composers of the folk opera usually write their own libretti.

When Ògúnyẹmí delivered the libretto, I was surprised that it was already a completed work that needed no further composition. Without writing a single note of music, Ògúnyẹmí indicated the general plan of the music in terms clear enough for one familiar with the Yoruba tradition. This was done by various means, including giving the text required to be sung by voices or played on the talking drum, identifying a specific combination of instruments for a given passage, and providing a tape recording of his own singing of some of the songs required.

What remained for me, then, was to realize the musical details from the indications supplied by the author; the role of musical director (rather than composer), which I thereafter assumed, was one that I found no less exciting. There are one or two instances in which I included music not specified by the author, but otherwise the resultant production that we premiered at the 4th Ifẹ̀ Festival of Arts in 1971 originated from Ògúnyẹmí's literary and musical conception. In bringing the music of *Ọbalúayé* to life, I had at my disposal a large ensemble including such fine instrumentalists as Làísì Àyánṣọlá, Àyàntúnjí Àmọ̀ó, Múráínà Oyèlámí, Adégbóyè Onígbìndé, and Akin Akínyanjú, whose "collective creativity" was consistent with the normal practice of folk opera companies.

Peggy Harper choreographed the premiere of *Ọbalúayé,* while Georgina Beier designed the sets and costumes. I will now discuss the opera under various subheadings.

Outline of the Story

Ọbalúayé portrays one of the dilemmas faced by Yoruba in modern times. The Baálẹ̀ (principal chief) of a Yoruba town has rejected the traditional òrìṣà (divinities) in favor of Christianity. This causes a general decline of òrìṣà worship in the town, since the Baálẹ̀'s patronage is an essential factor in the people's attitude to the òrìṣà.

Ọbalúayé (otherwise known as Ṣọ̀npọ̀nná, god of small pox) is angered by this state of affairs and summons fellow divinities in order to inflict punishment on the town. The punishment takes the form of a small-pox epidemic that quickly spreads round the town, affecting even people vaccinated against an infection. The Baálẹ̀ catches the disease and dies. His coutiers solicit the help of Adífálà, priest of Ifá (the Yoruba god of divination), who performs a ritual and succeeds in bringing the Baálẹ̀ back to life. The brief encounter with death and the circumstances of his resurrection convince the Baálẹ̀ that he must not neglect the traditional divinities, even if he would embrace Christianity. He vows from thenceforth to keep the necessary traditional observances that would ensure the welfare of his people. The Baálè then accompanies his people to a ritual offering at the shrine of Ọbalúayé.

The Music

The text of *Ọbalúayé* is partly sung and partly spoken, and the work may therefore be categorized as a folk opera in the new form. The classical style of Yoruba traditional music is dominant, but the church style makes brief appearances, notably on the two occasions when the Baálè sings.[5]

The orchestra consists mainly of Yoruba traditional instruments, although a non-Yoruba instrument (the Igbo slit drum) is also employed. *Sámbà* (rectangular frame drums), *àkúbà,* and an ordinary school bell, which are characteristic instruments of the Yoruba Cherubim and Seraphim Church, are used in Scene I to accompany the hymnlike song of the Baálè.

The core of the accompaniment is provided by two instrumental groups (the *dùndún* and the *bàtá*), each of which exists in Yoruba culture as a complete ensemble in its own right. *Dùndún* ensembles are composed of varying numbers and combinations of double-headed hourglass tension drums of different sizes (played with curved sticks) together with one *gúdúgúdú* (a small kettle drum played with two leather sticks). One of the tension drums (designated as *ìyáàlù*) customarily leads the ensemble and plays speech texts.

The *bàtá* are conically shaped double-headed drums of different sizes and have fixed pitches. There are usually four drums in a *bàtá* ensemble. The largest drum (*ìyáàlù*) and the next in size (*omele abo*) are each played with a flat leather striker on the small head combined with the hand on the large head. The two smallest drums (*kúdi* and *omele akọ*) are tied together and played by the same person, holding a flat leather striker in each hand. The *ìyáàlù* plays speech phrases, assisted by the *omele abo.* In addition to the instruments already mentioned, the *Ọbalúayé* orchestra also includes single-headed, fixed-pitch, nonportative traditional drums (sometimes described in Yoruba as *ìgbìn*) as well as several externally struck bells of different sizes and pitches.

Most of the instrumental accompaniment consists of appropriate musical patterns taken from the existing repertoire of Yoruba traditional music. There is a section of "effects music" (in Scene III) in which the musicians are directed to play freely and without metric coordination. The "effects" are heightened by the addition of toy flutes (short lengths of pawpaw stems, sealed off at one end) to the instruments of the main orchestra.

Prologue: The Court of Ọbalúayé

The sounds of *bàtá* drums introduce the entry of Ọbalúayé, with the leading drum declaiming the praise poetry of the god. In his opening speech, Ọbalúayé condemns the new ways of the world, which have caused the neglect of the *òrìṣà*. He summons fellow divinities so that together they can punish the people of the world: Èṣù (the trickster god of fate), Ògún (god of war and iron implements), Ṣàngó (god of thunder and lightning), Ọ̀ṣun (goddess of the river), Ọ̀sányìn (god of medicinal herbs), Ọ̀rúnmìlà (god of divination), and Egúngún (who is not a god but is the ancestral spirit).

When Èṣù enters, the drums change to *dùndún,* with the *ìyáàlù* playing the praise poetry of Èṣù. At Ògún's entry, he chants *ìjálá,* a type of praise poetry cultivated by Yoruba hunters, devotees of Ògún. After chanting for a while, Ògún introduces a song for general singing and dancing.

This music is interrupted by the reentry of *bàtá* drums, announcing the arrival of Ṣàngó; the leading drum plays the praise poetry of Ṣàngó. At the end of Ṣàngó's music, Ọbalúayé summons Ọ̀ṣun by singing a song for her, together with the chorus (Figure 7-11), accompanied by *dùndún* drums. Next to appear is Ọ̀sányìn, who marks his entry by leading the chorus in a song, accompanied by *bàtá* drums. Ọ̀rúnmìlà follows, singing a song (Figure 7-12) accompanied by *dùndún* drums and taken up by the chorus.

Suddenly, the *dùndún* drums change to a vigorous tempo, signifying the arrival of Egúngún, who chants a text invoking success for the impending acts of the divine assembly. Immediately afterward, Ọbalúayé takes over the proceedings, calling forth in extremely powerful words the venom of the divinities. The drums work up to a climax (in which *dùndún* and *bàtá* are combined) and then pause for a moment, while Ọbalúayé casts the *ṣònpọ̀nná* (smallpox) over the world, commanding an unimpeded passage for it, with the other divinities shouting *àṣẹ* (May it come to pass as willed). The scene ends with Ọbalúayé initiating a song for general singing and dancing.

Scene One: The Court of the Baálẹ̀

The first scene opens with the Baálẹ̀ being attended by his wives and his servant, Ìwọ̀fà. He is suffering from an as yet unidentified illness. The Ìwọ̀fà questions the Baálẹ̀ and recognizes the symptoms of smallpox.

Jọ̀-wọ́ bá mi ṣé o, O - o-re Yè-yé Ọ̀-sun Jọ̀-wọ́ bá mi ṣé o, O - o-re Yè-yé Ọ̀-ṣun. A

dín - dí ì dí, A dì - dì - n - dì Ọ̀-ṣun ṣèn - gẹ̀ - ṣẹ́ O - ló - ò - yà i - yùno.

Jọ̀-wọ́ bá mi ṣé o, O - o-re Yè-yé Ọ̀-ṣun. Jọ̀-wọ́ bá mi ṣé o, O - o-re Yè-yé Ọ̀-ṣun. Mo

gbé gbá à - kún, Mo rìn - rìn o - yè Mo rìn sàà - sàà mo tún kan yùn ló - nào.

Jọ̀-wọ́ bá mi ṣé o, O - o-re Yè - yé Ọ̀-ṣun. Jọ̀-wọ́ bá mi ṣé o, O - o-re Yè-yé Ọ̀-ṣun.

FIGURE 7-11. Ọbálúayé summons Ọṣun.

Ẹ má sọ̀ kò lù gbín o, Ẹ má tà gbín ló - fà Ẹ má sọ̀ kò lù gbín o, Ẹ má

tà gbín ló fà, Ẹ - ní bá tà gbín ló fà, Á ká - wọ́ lé - rí sun - kún.

FIGURE 7-12. Ọ̀rúnmìlà's song in *Ọbalúayé*.

The Baálè, who had recently been vaccinated, dismisses the idea of smallpox. The Ìwòfà expresses doubt about the efficacy of vaccination against the wrath of Qbalúayé and promptly offers to go to the *babaláwo* (Diviner of Ifá) to secure a ritual antidote. The Baálè regards this as an impertinence. How could he, a Christian, invite a *babaláwo* to his palace? To reinforce the point, the Baálè sings a song (accompanied by *samba, akuba,* and school bell) in the neo-African church style (Figure 7-13), in which he cautions his courtiers against compromising their Christian beliefs. The song accelerates as it is taken up by the chorus, but is soon interrupted by sounds of drumming coming from outside the palace, with the talking drum playing a characteristic praise text used for royalty:

> *Èrù Qba ni mo bà, Qba tó*   It is the king that I fear, O
> venerable king.

This drumming is followed by the arrival of the townspeople, led by Babalóòṣà (the chief priest of Qbalúayé), who have come to express concern about the outbreak of smallpox in the town. There is a lengthy argument in which the people admonish the Baálè for neglecting the traditions and bringing the purge of Qbalúayé on the town. The only solution, they advise, is for the Baálè to lead the town in a ceremony of pacification to the *òrìṣà*. The Baálè refuses to have anything to do with the *òrìṣà* and instead offers the people money with which to perform

FIGURE 7-13. The Baálè's song in *Qbalúayé*.

whatever ceremonies they think fit. This is unacceptable to the people and, in the end, the Baálè̩ at least agrees to follow them to the graveyard to see the extent of damage being done by Ọbalúayé.

Scene Two: Graveyard

The Baálè̩ and Babalóòṣà arrive at the graveyard to see a burial in progress, that of the latest victim of Ọbalúayé. The wife of the dead man throws earth on the grave and then chants a funeral dirge, an impassioned eulogy in the style of traditional poetry. After the dirge, one of the mourners starts a song (Figure 7-14) for leader and chorus, with instrumental accompaniment, and the burial party departs. The instrumental accompaniment (Figure 7-15) is one of the instances in which I incorporated musical material not specified by the author.

Scene Three: The Death of the Baálè̩

It is night and the Baálè̩ is asleep in his room. His sleep is soon disturbed by the appearance of ghosts, who speak to him and condemn him to

FIGURE 7-14. Funeral song in *Ọbalúayé*.

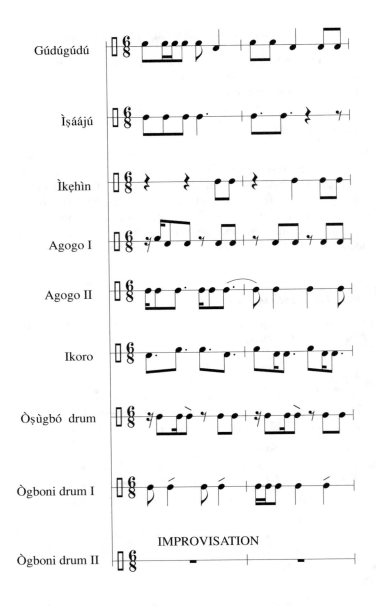

Gúdúgúdú

Ìṣáájú

Ìkẹhìn

Agogo I

Agogo II

Ikoro

Òṣùgbó drum

Ògboni drum I

IMPROVISATION

Ògboni drum II

╲ = lowered pitch obtained by playing with hollowed hand

╱ = raised pitch obtained by pressing the drum head

FIGURE 7-15. Instrumental accompaniment to the funeral song in *Ọbalúayé*.

Ọ-ba-à mi dú-ró   Má fi mí sí-lẹ̀ lọ,   Má fi mí sá-yé lọ,

Sí à-jù-lé ọ̀-run,   Ì-gbà a-yéń-yí,   Áá yí sí re-re fún wa,

Ká   dú-ró   ja-yé,   Ká   rí   re   o   o   ríì   mi.

FIGURE 7-16. Song of the Baálẹ's wives in Ọbalúayé.

death for wronging the *òrìṣà*. The Baálẹ̀ screams for his wives and
Ìwọ̀fà. The latter, realizing that the end is near, goes to summon Adífálá.
The wives sing an agitated song (Figure 7-16),[6] pleading for the Baálẹ's
life. The Baálẹ̀ himself sings the beginning of the Lord's Prayer (consisting of Yoruba words fitted to a European hymn tune) and then falls
dead. The Ìwọ̀fà returns with Adífálá (the Ifá priest), who chants an appropriate *odù* (Ifá divination poem) to the accompaniment of the *àjà* (an
iron bell with clapper), in order to ascertain the cause of death. He then
confirms that the Baálẹ̀s life has been taken because of his "contempt"
for the *òrìṣà*. Since Ọ̀rúnmìlà (the god of divination) has invested
Adífálá with the secret of life and death, the priest resolves to awaken
the Baálẹ̀. He chants an incantation, invoking the help of Ọ̀rúnmìlà and
of *ẹ̀yin ìyáà mi* ("you my mothers," referring to the *àjẹ́*, the powerful
mothers who commute between the natural and supernatural worlds).
After this, Adífálá calls the Baálẹ̀ three times. At the third calling, the
king answers, and the *dùndún* drums sound the kingly motif, *èrù ọba ni
mo bà, ọba tó* (which was cited above).

Scene Four: Offering of Pacification to Ọbalúayé

Babalóòṣà and other devotees, together with the Baálẹ̀ and his courtiers,
approach the shrine of Ọbalúayé, singing a song in his praise. The song

is performed three times unaccompanied, with a pause after each rendition, during which the people dance to the accompaniment of *bàtá* drums. Next, the Babalóòṣà proceeds to say the praise poetry of Ọbalúayé, accompanying himself with the *ṣ́ẹ́ẹ́rẹ́* (an internally rattling gourd idiophone), prior to the traditional throwing of cola nuts to determine whether the plea of the people has been accepted by Ọbalúayé. The saying of praise poetry followed by the throwing of cola nuts occurs three times, but the Babalóòṣà fails at all attempts to secure a positive configuration for the cola nuts. In desperation, he sends for Adífálà. When Adífálà arrives, he performs the appropriate *odù* and then prescribes offerings (two goats for Ifá, two snails for *òrìṣà*, two bitter nuts for Ṣàngó, a dog for Ògún) and other ceremonies that would ensure the benevolence of the divinities. Then follows an intense sequence of chanting, singing, drumming, and dancing, culminating in the Ìwọ̀fà's entering into a trance state. Thereafter, the Ìwọ̀fà begins to speak with the voice of Ọbalúayé, assuring the people that their offerings have been accepted and that the small-pox epidemic will now cease. The scene ends in general merriment, with Adífálà and the Ìwọ̀fà, accompanied by the traditional ensemble of Ifá bells, initiating songs for the people.

Conclusion

African composers trained in the Western tradition of art music face problems of identity. They are unable to disregard the Western idioms that formed the basis of their training and yet they must seek to maintain contact with their indigenous cultural roots, particularly if they choose to live and work in Africa. African composers have the dual role of addressing the international community while at the same time communicating with audiences at home. It is not always possible to perform this dual role by using one single idiom of music, and it is probably desirable that composers develop alternative idioms for different audiences.

In African traditional culture, music is not conceived in "absolute" terms but is typically realized in the context of other arts and of social events. It would seem, therefore, that modern composers who seek to communicate with average Africans should take account of the traditional contextual usages of music. Music theater and dance theater are more likely to appeal to average Africans than symphonies and string quartets!

Nonetheless, modern African composers cannot afford to ignore the symphonic idiom, because there are some African listeners who prefer sounds of European strings to those of African drums. Though few in number, such Africans are highly influential, and their patronage cannot be regarded as dispensable.

For those composers who seek to communicate with average Africans, the Yoruba folk opera provides a useful model. First, the folk opera represents a successful transposition of music and other performing arts from their traditional contexts into the modern threater. Second, it provides a bridge between views of music as something in which one participates (as occurs in African traditional culture) and something that one contemplates (as is characteristic of "absolute" music). Third, the folk opera communicates easily with the average Yoruba.

It would appear, however, that there is currently a decline in the cultivation of the Yoruba folk opera. According to Jeyifo (1984: 21), "the 'opera proper,' in which dialogue and dramatic interaction are predominantly conveyed by vocal music to the accompaniment of an instrumental orchestra, is (today) a minority tradition."

As I remarked earlier, Ogúndè moved away from operatic composition during the 1950s and, since the deaths of Ládípò and Ògúnmólá, there has not been any composer of comparable stature working in the field of folk opera.

It is possible that economic factors are responsible for the decline of the folk opera. In order to make their efforts financially viable, traveling theater troupes need to cater for the tastes of the mass audience and cannot afford to have opera as standard fare in their repertoires.

For composers who do not expect to make a living from operatic writing and whose objectives are artistic rather than commercial, the folk opera provides concepts of neo-African music that are too compelling to be ignored.

Notes

[1] References to Ògúnmólá apply to the libretto only.

[2] Night markets are common in Yoruba towns, and it is believed that some of the shoppers that one meets in such markets are spirits in human form.

[3] References to Ládípò apply to the libretto only.

[4] The discussion that follows was extracted from my notes (Euba 1975a) for the LP record of Wálé Ògúnyęmí's *Qbalúayé*.

[5] Hereafter, my description of *Qbalúayé* refers to the prescribed work as contained in Ògúnyęmí's script which was subsequently published (Ògúnyęmí 1972),

and to the specific realization of the prescribed work as it exists in the LP recording
(Ògúnyẹmí 1974).
⁶The musical transcriptions of Figures 7-1–7-16 were made by the author of this
essay. For the English translations of the texts of the songs illustrated in the examples, readers are referred to *The Palmwine Drinkard* (Ògúnmọ́lá 1968), *Ọba Kò So*
(Ládípọ̀ 1968), and *Ọbalúayé* (Ògúnyẹmí 1972).

References

This list includes works cited in the essay as well as other relevant
studies.

Adédèjì, J. A. 1973a. "The Church and the Emergence of the Nigerian Theatre,
     1866–1914." *Journal of the Historical Society of Nigeria* 6(4).
————. 1973b. "Trends in the Content and Form of the Opening Glee in Yoruba
     Drama." *Research in African Literatures* 4(1).
————. 1981. "Alárìnjò: The Traditional Yoruba Travelling Theatre." In *Drama and
     Theatre in Nigeria: A Critical Source Book,* edited by Yẹmí Ògúnbíyì. Lagos:
     Nigeria Magazine.
Adélùgbà, Dàpọ̀. 1969. "Virtuosity and Sophistication in Nigerian Theatrical Art: A
     Case Study of Kọ́lá Ògúnmọ́lá." *Nigerian Opinion* 5(1/2).
Axworthy, G. J. 1968. "The Stage Version of the *Palmwine Drinkard.*" In *The
     Palmwine Drinkard,* by Kọ́lá Ògúnmọ́lá. Occasional Publications 12. Ibadan:
     Institute of African Studies, University of Ibadan.
Banham, Martin. 1968. "Nigerian Dramatists and the Traditional Theatre." *Insight*
     20.
Beier, Ulli. 1954. "Yoruba Folk Operas." *Journal of the African Music Society* 1(1).
————. 1981. "E. K. Ògúnmọ́lá: A Personal Memoir." In *Drama and Theatre in
     Nigeria: A Critical Source Book,* edited by Yẹmi Ògúnbíyì. Lagos: Nigeria Magazine.
Clark, Ẹbùn. 1979. *Hubert Ògúndè: The Making of Nigerian Theatre.* Oxford:
     Oxford University Press, in association with University Press Limited.
————. 1981. "Ògúndè Theatre: The Rise of Contemporary Professional Theatre in
     Nigeria, 1946–72." In *Drama and Theatre in Nigeria: A Critical Source Book,*
     edited by Yẹmí Ògúnbíyì. Lagos: Nigeria Magazine.
Euba, Akin. 1971. "New Idioms of Music-Drama among the Yoruba: An Introductory Study." In *1970 Yearbook of the International Folk Music Council,* edited by
     Alexander L. Ringer. Urbana-Champaign University of Illinois.
————. 1975a. *Ọbalúayé: A Yoruba Music-Drama by Wálé Ògúnyẹmí.* Companion
     booklet to the LP record ARC 1101. Lagos: Associated Recording Company.
————. 1975b. "The Interrelation of Music and Poetry in Yoruba Tradition." In
     Yoruba Oral Tradition, edited by Wandé Abímbọ́lá. Ilé-Ifẹ̀: Department of
     African Languages and Literatures, University of Ifẹ̀.
————. 1992. "Yoruba Music in the Church: The Development of a Neo-African
     Art among the Yoruba of Nigeria." In *African Musicology: Current Trends, Vol-*

ume 2. A Festschrift Presented to J. H. Kwabena Nketia, edited by Jacqueline C. Dje Dje. Atlanta, GA: Crossroads Press.

Graham-White, A. 1974. "Yoruba Opera: Developing a New Drama for the Nigerian People." *Theatre Quarterly* 14.

Jeyifo, Bíódún. 1984. *The Yoruba Popular Travelling Theatre of Nigeria.* Lagos: Nigeria Magazine.

Ládípò, Dúró. 1968. *Qba Kò So.* Transcribed and translated by R. G. Armstrong, Robert L. Àwùjoolá, and Val Qláyemí. Occasional Publication 10. Ibadan: Institute of African Studies, University of Ibadan.

Ògúnbíyì, Yemí. 1981. "The Popular Theatre: A Tribute to Dúró Ládípò." In *Drama and Theatre in Nigeria: A Critical Source Book,* edited by Yemí Ògúnbíyì. Lagos: Nigeria Magazine.

Ògúnmólá, Kólá. 1968. *The Palmwine Drinkard.* Transcribed and translated by R. G. Armstrong, Robert L. Àwùjoolá, and Val Qláyemí. Occasional Publication 12. Ibadan: Institute of African Studies, University of Ibadan.

Ògúnyemí, Wálé. 1972. *Qbalúayé.* Ibadan: Institute of African Studies, University of Ibadan.

Tutùolá, Amos. 1953. *The Palmwine Drinkard and His Dead Tapster in the Dead's Town.* New York: Grove Press.

Discography

Ládípò, Dúró. 1971a. *Èdá.* Dúró Ládípò and His National Theatre. [two 12" LPs] Nigerian Cultural Records NCR 5-6.

———. 1971b. *Qba Kò So.* Dúró Ládípò and His National Theatre. [two 12" LPs] Nigerian Cultural Records NCR 1-2.

———. 1975. *Qba Kò So.* Dúró Ládípò and his National Theatre. [two 12" LPs] Kaleidophone KS 2201.

Ògúnmólá, Kólá. 1968. *The Palmwine Drinkard.* Ògúnmólá Theatre. [three 12" LPs] Nigerian Cultural Records NRC 10-12.

Ògúnyemí, Wálé. 1974. *Qbalúayé.* University of Ifè Theatre. [one 12" LP] Associated Recording Company ARC 1101.

CHAPTER 8

They Just Need Money: Goods and Gods, Power and Truth in a West African Village

Steven Cornelius

Introduction

In Kopeyia, a small Keta District Ewe village in southeast Ghana, meaning and the concept of social truth itself is increasingly defined not just through time, place, and circumstance, but by an ever more comprehensive and intricate interweaving of West African and Western ideology and economy. This holds especially true as both modernization and Western education increasingly leave their physical and cultural imprint on daily village life.

While Nettl (1985) has effectively illustrated the broad variety of means by which high Western culture impacts on traditional musics, in this essay I attempt to demonstrate that—at least in one West African village—it has been the reconstitution and repackaging of traditional music itself that has been, both consciously and unconsciously, largely responsible for that village's ever widening relationship with the West. As a frame and focus for my argument I ground my discussion around an incident of *juju*[1] that occurred in Kopeyia in January 1993.

The possibility that *juju* (or, for that matter, witchcraft) may account

243

for individual misfortune continues to be a widely held concept among the Anlo Ewe. Most allegations, however, take place at the level of innuendo only; individuals are rarely publicly accused, and insinuations are generally made only within the relative privacy of family or trusted friends. This essay investigates an exception to the norm, a publicly oriented *juju* incident. Accusations that *juju* had been committed and the denouement of those accusations were carried out before an entire village in a large-scale theatrical event that involved music, dance, and numerous occurrences of spirit possession trance.

In this essay—following a brief introduction to the Ewe in general and to my teacher and major informant, Godwin Agbeli, in particular—I describe the *juju* event as I witnessed it. Next, I present Agbeli's interpretation of that event. In subsequent sections, by bringing into play Western methodological concepts of iconicity and reflexivity (Watson 1991), I investigate (1) the social nature of *juju,* (2) the continuing impact that the West has had on Kopeyia's social system, and (3) the factors that mediate the potential fissures between traditional and modernized village society.

The Ewe

The Ewe people number approximately one million and today are found throughout southeastern Ghana, southern Togo, and southwestern Benin. Although details are lost in unrecorded history, accounts suggest that the Ewe's origin might be traced to the southern Sudan, from which they migrated to Yoruba country. By the sixteenth century they had again migrated, this time to their present-day location (Kludze 1973: 4; Locke 1992: 11). The Ghanaian Ewe are divided into three groups (Kludze 1973). The Northern Ewe are found between Lake Volta and the Togo border as far north as Hohoe (Gbi) and southward to Adaklu-Ahunda. While actually a large number of groups and chiefdoms, the Northern Ewe are united by mutually intelligible language dialects, similar living habits, and social and political organization.

To the south in the Volta Region are found the Tongu and Anlo Ewe. The western border of the Tongu Ewe roughly follows the Volta River. There is no central traditional political structure uniting the Tongu Ewe; each town is its own political unit. The Tongu, however, are united by language and custom.

East of the Tongu are the Anlo, who reside in the Keta District of the

Volta Region. Stretching northward from the Gulf of Guinea to Northern Ewe country, the Anlo may be identified by their relatively centralized political system and dialect (which is generally considered to be "Standard Ewe"). While each Anlo village has a chief (although there is often little authority attached to the post), there is a paramount chief to whom all the other chiefs owe allegiance.

In regard to their music, the Ewe are perhaps the most studied peoples in sub-Saharan Africa. Both the social and sonic mechanics of music making have been discussed by Western and Ewe writers, including studies in the 1950s by Gadzekpo (1952), Cudjoe (1953), and Jones (1954, 1959), and more recent works by Koetting (1970), Ladzekpo and Pantaleoni (1970), Ladzekpo (1971), Pantaleoni (1972), Chernoff (1979), Locke (1982, 1987, 1992), Agawu (1995), and others. Further, through the efforts of Godwin Agbeli, Abraham Adzinyah, Freeman Donkor, Alfred and Kobla Ladzepko, Gideon Midawo Alorwoyie, and other artists, all of whom have taught within postsecondary institutions in the United States, the Ewe tradition is presently the best represented of all sub-Saharan musics within the academy.

Godwin Agbeli

Kopeyia is the home of Ewe master drummer, dancer, and choreographer Godwin Agbeli, who claims to have inherited his talent with the spirit of his paternal great-grandfather, Adedi (Locke 1992: 10). Agbeli has made a career of teaching and promoting traditional Ewe (and Ghanaian) music. His teaching credentials include residencies at New York University, Brooklyn College, Tufts University, and North Texas University, to name just a few. In Ghana he has served as senior drum and dance coach for the National Folkloric Company of the Arts Council of Ghana and has served as chairman of the Regional Dance Association of Greater Accra since 1979.

In his home village of Kopeyia he is responsible for starting and heading the Dagbe Cultural Institute, an organization that he established in 1993 to provide housing and rehearsal space for foreigners wishing to study traditional Ghanaian music. Over the past three years, since the completion of the buildings that house the institute, Agbeli has had a semisteady stream of foreigners coming to work and study in the village. While most visitors to Kopeyia have come alone or in pairs, in the summers of 1993 and 1995 Dr. Steven Friedson brought groups of students from North Texas University, and in the summers of 1994 and 1996 I brought students from Bowling Green State University. These groups were in residency for periods of three to six weeks.

The Field Site: Kopeyia

The village of Kopeyia is in the southeast section of the Keta District. The closest city is Aflao, which is situated on the Togo border approximately ten miles to the east of Kopeyia. A smaller town, Denu, which is situated on the ocean four miles southeast of Kopeyia, provides the closest market.

While Aflao and Denu are in near proximity, few of the modern conveniences found there extend to Kopeyia. With the exception of Agbeli's clan, which lives in a compound of cement-block houses with tin roofs, the villagers live in traditionally constructed buildings of dried mud and thatched roofs. Similarly, with the exception of Agbeli, who has also purchased a generator, which (when there is kerosene) serves his family compound and the Dagbe Cultural Institute, there is no electrical service for the village.[2]

There is no running water for anyone in the village. Nevertheless, even here, the Agbeli compound has an advantage, for it is able to use a number of large cisterns to collect rain water from tin roofs. Until the final set of cisterns was dug in 1995–96, during the height of the dry season, water for all villagers had to be carried in from up to four miles away.

On the surface, a traditional lifestyle seems the norm within the village, but outside impact can be seen in virtually every area of life. The local markets and field laborers follow traditional Ewe work cycles of four or five days, but the elementary school is based on the European seven-day week. Ewe is the first language of all villagers, and while many adults (especially the women) do not speak English, children must speak English in the grammar school. Virtually all music making in the village is traditional Ewe with the exception of the Ghanaian national anthem (and an occasional performance of "The Star Spangled Banner" for the American visitors), which is sung before classes begin at the grammar school.

There is very little cash in the village. Some villagers who are able to find work (or have friends who work) in Denu, Aflao, or even the capital city of Accra, listen to popular music styles on portable cassette recorders that they have purchased. One enterprising young weaver has earned enough money selling *kente* cloth to Western students studying with Agbeli that he was able to purchase a portable shortwave radio.

While there are some Christians in the surrounding area, and references to Allah are occasionally heard in song texts, traditional religious beliefs dominate. Within Kopeyia there are important cults dedicated to various deities, including Kunde, Koku, and the lightning god, Yeve. All three of these religions involve complex pantheons in which some of the deities incarnate within their practitioners through the vehicle of possession trance. Undoubtedly there are additional cults in the area with which I have not had contact.

In short, with the exception of Agbeli's compound and the Dagbe Institute, Kopeyia would be a model of traditional Ewe lifestyles. Of course, because of Agbeli, it is not. The grammar school exists in large part because of the efforts of Robert Levin, an American student of Agbeli's who was sufficiently impacted by his own African experience that he took it upon himself to raise the necessary funds to construct the buildings and maintain the school's infrastructure.[3]

While the extent of Levin's financial contribution has been much greater than Agbeli's other foreign students, his interest in supporting the village is typical. Agbeli's students regularly donate both materials and cash. Moreover, monies trickle throughout the local economy every time foreigners come to the village to study. While almost all of the cash influx (generated by providing room, board, and lessons) goes directly to Agbeli, the foreign students inevitably distribute additional monies and goods throughout the village with purchases of food, drink, and *kente* cloth, or through gifts.

An Incidence of Witchcraft

This section consists of a straightforward description of one particular *juju* event. The description is generally derived from my perspective of the event as it occurred; I attempt no explicit interpretation.[4] The activities that I describe, however, ranged over an area too large for a single person to have witnessed. Therefore, at the end of this section I attempt to fill in details of important activities that I did not personally observe. These details were supplied after the event by various male villagers, and while I believe they provide a generally accurate description of what occurred, as shall be discussed later in this essay, the perspectives and general nature of the details supplied are both indexical and reflexive of when they were supplied. Further, while I accept those details supplied by my informants as generally true, they provide only part of the truth. Crapanzano (1986: 75–76) cautions of the "ethnographer's authoritative constructions," when he notes that "Zeus understood when Hermes [and by analogy, the ethnographer] promised to tell no lies but did not promise to tell the whole truth." I would expand Crapanzano's warning to include all the participants in this event, for they too had a stake in authoritative construction and reconstruction.

At approximately 9:30 A.M. on 28 December 1992, while standing in an open-air shelter outside but attached to the Agbeli compound, I was preparing for the first of my two daily music lessons with Agbeli when three men emerged from the palm trees along the village periphery. They were clothed in raffia skirts (rather than the Western clothing that has become normal village attire), naked from the waist up, and their hair was matted with dried mud. They sang and danced as they came, and at least two of the three were apparently in, or modeling, trance.

Although ignoring my presence, they walked through the area where I was playing and made their way into the Agbeli compound. As they did so, the three or four villagers working in the small mill nearby noticed them, stopped their work, and evidently curious as to what was going on, approached the compound's perimeter. Groups of children were forming as well, and they too, while taking care to keep distance between themselves and the three men, stared in from the periphery.

A few minutes later, Agbeli arrived, coming down the same path that the three men had just traveled. He told me to put away the drums and follow. Although the morning study was canceled, the events that were going to unfold would be extremely interesting, "better than a lesson," he said.

Following Agbeli's instructions, I put away my instruments, retrieved a video camera and tape recorder, and entered the compound, where I encountered Agbeli's 25-year-old son Ruben. Ruben affirmed that the three men were in a state of possession trance. They were Kokushio, he said—that is, members of a religious cult devoted to the god Koku.

The Kokushio announced that they had come to deliver an important message that would be revealed only within the confines of the Agbeli compound. A short time later, after waiting for the courtyard to fill with some one hundred people, the Kokushio divulged that Agbeli was the victim of *juju* and that they, as emissaries of Koku, had come to eliminate the danger.

Speaking loudly in a voice audible to all, one of the Kokushio stated that an individual from the village had buried evil *juju* on Agbeli's land. For a small benefaction, these men were willing to find, extract, and neutralize the *juju*. The spokesman requested a cash payment of twenty thousand *cedis* (about twenty-eight dollars at the time), two white chickens (although he stated that a white goat would be more appropriate), and two bottles of *akpetisie,* the locally distilled alcohol.

Agbeli listened to the details, then, without giving an answer, left the compound. He returned about fifteen minutes later, and shortly thereafter, his uncle, the man he had gone off in search of, arrived. The two sat on a bench placed along the side of the building in which Agbeli was living. There, although in full view of all, they spoke quietly and privately for a few minutes. Next they stood up, walked to the center of the compound, and poured libations onto the ground. Once again the men seated themselves. There, they alternated between private conversation and long periods of quiet during which they watched the various activities of the cult.

During this time the Kokushio sang—sometimes accompanied by drummers who had gradually assembled in the courtyard—and engaged in short bursts of dance. They held discussions among themselves and with the onlookers. In order to demonstrate the reality of their trance and the power of the gods who kept them from harm, two of the men engaged in acts of potential self-mutilation in which they would slash themselves with glass or metal or strike themselves with rocks.

On at least four occasions the Kokushio grabbed individuals assembled in the courtyard and either picked them up or threw them to the ground and held them there. The two victims put to the ground were themselves members of the cult and were not allowed up until they too had been overcome by trance. The other two victims, who were merely held (one upside down), were not cult members. Both appeared embarrassed to have been singled out. One accepted his predicament with good humor; the other (Agbeli's brother) did not, and it briefly appeared that a fist fight might ensue.

Eventually, Agbeli said that he would consider allowing the Kokushio to hunt for the *juju*. Thus began the negotiation of terms under which the Kokushio would proceed. After a lengthy discussion, it was decided that the *juju* would be removed for ten thousand *cedis,* one chicken, and two bottles of liquor.

The Kokushio now began to mobilize for their attack on the *juju*. They left the compound, briefly visited the site where construction of the first of the Dagbe Cultural Institute's buildings was taking place, then returned to the Agbeli family compound. Next the Kokushio brought out, and placed on the ground in the middle of the courtyard, a fetish symbolizing the cult's warrior deity, Ogu. Ruben informed me that the fetish was a knife, which was wrapped in cloth saturated and frequently renourished with palm oil. Ogu was there to protect and empower.[5]

Shortly afterward, the search for the *juju* began in earnest. As the Kokushio (with the villagers following close behind) returned to the construction site, Ruben, who was sobered by the serious nature of the allegations, stated that his father appeared troubled. Ruben maintained that the attack made no sense; his father was loved by the villagers, and no one would wish him harm.

When the Kokushio returned to the construction site, a large number of bricks laid out on the ground had to be moved, for it had been divined that some of the *juju* was buried underneath. After some twenty-five minutes of moving bricks (notably, a job undertaken not by the Kokushio but mostly by village children and young adults), the Kokushio began to dig in a variety of places. As the labor progressed, the Kokushio occasionally sang songs, burst into dance movements, consulted the Ogu fetish, and pressed their ears to the ground as if listening for clues.

After a number of false starts, a small packet wrapped in cloth was discovered in one of the holes. Following a short struggle—to the onlooker the *juju* seemed to resist extraction—the packet was pulled from the ground. For many of those watching, this was a defining moment. Unearthing the packet seemed not only to prove the *juju* real but confirmed the Kokushio's power to engage it.

Having supposedly demonstrated their honesty as well as their efficacy, the Kokushio approached Agbeli and stated that they should receive greater compensation for their efforts. Agbeli responded that he was satisfied with their progress and wanted them to continue. A deal had been struck, however. He refused to renegotiate.

The *juju* packet was placed in a container and guarded by an elder. While some villagers crowded in to see it, others watched the Kokushio as they took up the search for a second item. Similar in appearance to the first, this was discovered some thirty minutes later along a line of trees that marked the Agbeli property boundary. The second packet was immediately stored with the first.

Shortly afterward, the Kokushio identified the presence of a third and final *juju* item. Said to be the most powerful of all, the Kokushio warned of the danger involved and strived to keep now hundreds of curious onlookers at a distance. The packet, they said, was buried inside the frame and approximately two yards from the main entrance of the half-constructed Dagbe Institute building. As the bundle was dug up, one of the youngest Kokushio came in contact with it; he immediately dropped to the ground unconscious.

In the ensuing chaos, leaders of the cult had the newest object placed with the other two. There, all three objects were kept hidden and guarded to ensure that no one else could be adversely affected. The Kokushio then picked up their unconscious associate and carried him back into the Agbeli compound. Using a variety of techniques involving music, the application of herbs and water, and the burning of black powder, the Kokushio worked to revive the young man. He showed some ability to move his limbs after approximately thirty minutes and was able to stand (and dance, although fitfully) some fifteen minutes later.

Because it demonstrates the powerfully contagious quality of the Kokushio trances, one final occurrence is worth noting. As the young man—who through all of this, evidently remained in trance—struggled to maintain his equilibrium, he fell backward against a female member of the cult who was busy cleaning the ground of items used in his revival. As he fell against her, the god's energy overwhelmed the woman. She was mounted by the spirit and fell into a powerful trance herself.

A few minutes later, the Kokushio withdrew from the courtyard. Activity within the compound quickly returned to its usual level of quiet activity.

Before proceeding, it is necessary to backtrack slightly in order to trace the fate of the *juju* packets. Although the packets had been removed from the earth and safely stored, the Kokushio were insistent that the bundles' efficacy for harm remained intact. They argued that just as the Kokushio had been responsible for discovering and unearthing the packets, so should they be entrusted with their final disposal. This would entail burning the packets under the proper ritual conditions as soon as possible.

Agbeli objected and stated that he intended to keep the packets. He argued that the evil had been perpetrated against him, and he had paid the gods a fair price for the removal of the *juju* from his land. After substantial contention, the opposing parties, both obligated to follow the general sense of the contract that had been publicly negotiated before the search began, acknowledged that the bundles were now Agbeli's to do with as he pleased. The leaders of the cult agreed to turn over the packets but only after a brief rite was performed to neutralize the *juju*'s power.

Agbeli would not reveal what he planned to do with the bundles but left open the possibility that he might seek revenge. He stated that he was considering taking the bundles to the powerful *juju* priests of Togo in order to discover who had perpetrated the deed. Then, pursuant to the priests' advice, and supported by their assistance, Agbeli would consider retribution.

Shortly after the withdrawal of the Kokushio, Agbeli met with a number of the village men on the shaded veranda that extends from one of his compound buildings into the public space of the village. There, while hosting his guests with gin, he told them "what really happened."

Agbeli's Perspective

I interviewed Agbeli shortly after the meeting on the veranda. We discussed the event again two weeks later as I was preparing to leave Ghana, and again seven months later in the United States as we screened the video footage that I had shot. Agbeli also read and made small corrections to a late draft of this paper.

According to Agbeli, he was not the victim of *juju*. The entire event was simply an elaborately staged attempt to secure money. He stated that he did not believe anyone in the village would commit *juju* against him and supported his position with an extensive rationale.

Agbeli (personal communication, December 1992) pointed out that in the past his wealth alone might have provided sufficient cause to be victimized by *juju* or witchcraft in Kopeyia: "In the olden days, [for] our village here, if you are [living] in Accra and you come to the village and you put up a block building and you put a roofing sheet on it, you won't sleep in it. You will die. You will die. They will kill you. Because, they are here . . . [and] . . . you come into the village for just a few days. You come in to disgrace them." Agbeli went on to state that in general, this would no longer happen.[6] Further, he stated that *juju* would not be used against him because he had disgraced no one, and his success had been good for everyone; he had been generous and shared his good fortune with the village.

Agbeli next discussed the nature of Ewe trance. It is his belief that Ewe possession trance lasts for a couple of minutes only. After that, the gods have communicated everything necessary and release their host.

The Kokushio's drums had been heard in the period around dawn, and when they first approached Agbeli at approximately 9:00 A.M., they claimed to have been in trance since that time. That, contended Agbeli, was not possible. Agbeli says the Kokushio feigned trance in order to complicate their ruse and add authority to their case.

Agbeli stated that while *juju* was once a powerful force, it no longer works in Kopeyia. Only the eldest men still know how to do it, but after witnessing the harm it was causing, they stopped the practice and have refused to teach the younger generation. Further, although a villager could potentially obtain *juju* from one of the neighboring areas, this particular *juju* could not have been real; no negative effects had been detected. Neither he nor any of his employees had been afflicted with bad fortune or ill health.

As further proof that the *juju* was not real, Agbeli stated that the *juju* was found too quickly. Had the packets contained true *juju*, it may have taken many hours, but probably days, to find them. Agbeli described powerful *juju* as if it were an animate object and stated that even if the searchers had been digging in the correct location, true *juju* would have been able to move away of its own accord. In order to contain it, the Kokushio would have required the utilization of a much more powerful counter magic than that which they exercised: "Black powder, they will be throwing it around, [over] the whole land. They will go around the whole land before they will be able to find it. And those things, they will run very fast. They will run very fast. As soon as you put the hole here, it is gone far away. So it is not an easy thing like they did today. What they did today is too easy. And they know, they know themselves" (ibid.).

The *juju* was not real. Agbeli stated that when he went to consult with his uncle, his own skepticism was confirmed. Nevertheless, his uncle believed the event was not serendipitous, and evidently, the gods were indeed requiring something of his nephew. Agbeli agreed, noting that even if the *juju* was not real, a man's personal relationship to the gods is. One must act accordingly. Agbeli was instructed to accept the event as a request from the gods that he make some small sacrifices. Despite the fact that the Kokushio were lying, Agbeli stated that their actions served as a vehicle through which a higher truth and set of obligations was passing. Ultimately, Agbeli framed the entire event thus: "If the gods need something from you it will pass through so many ways. You can be in the house and the blind man will come and say, 'Give me money. If you don't give me money I won't go.' I should find money to give to that man to find [my own personal] blessing"[7] (ibid.).

Agbeli had one final measure of evidence to support his contention that the *juju* was false. While the search for the first of the packets took place, one of the Kokushio—who was observing rather than taking active part in the event—told him that the *juju* was not real. In fact, this man said he knew just where to dig, for he had helped his colleagues bury the objects some months earlier.

According to Agbeli, the Kokushio staged the event simply because they needed money. Agbeli wanted to be sure that I understood (or perhaps, believed) this and repeated the phrase fifteen times during our first interview. He embellished his statements by noting that there was very little employment in the area, and, owing to the current drought, many villagers were struggling with the difficulties of day-to-day subsistence. In casual discussions that took place later, Agbeli took pleasure in noting that the Kokushio women, evidently with the money they had received from him, had been seen heading for the Denu market the following morning.[8]

Interpretation

With the addition of Agbeli's perspective the event becomes less opaque, but a firm analytic foundation for understanding remains elusive. The fundamental question concerns truth. Is there a single truth to be told, or are there multiple competing truths available? Graham Watson (1991: 89) has argued that "the native, as much as the ethnographer, is in the business of constituting meaning," and in the following pages I will argue that meaning (and at least for practical purposes, social truth itself) was not only context dependent but continuously reformulated both during and after the event described above. To do this I will employ Watson's definitions of indexicality and reflexivity. Watson (1991: 75) states that "indexicality refers to the context dependency of meaning; reflexivity, to the way in which accounts and the settings they describe elaborate and modify each other in a back-and-forth process."

I have seen the specter of *juju* (and even witchcraft) invoked on numerous occasions during my four residencies in Kopeyia, and it seems apparent that (despite Agbeli's statement to the contrary) *juju* remains a social reality in the village. Bouts of ill luck, sickness, and sudden death are often accompanied by innuendos that *juju* has been employed. Clearly, *juju* continues to be an effective means to reflexively respond to seemingly unexplainable situations.

Indeed, for the village at large, the event described in this paper appears to have been a relatively convincing display. I have been assured by male villagers that virtually all the women and children who witnessed the events of that afternoon believed the *juju* to be real. While they will not admit it now, it seems likely that—at least until Agbeli intervened with his own interpretation—the majority of the men believed this as well.

Such was the case for the men with whom I spoke. During the event, Edward Tekpah—who was both a friend of Agbeli's and an employee at the American-funded elementary school—told me that not only did he fear for Agbeli, but he was distressed that anyone would intentionally attempt to inflict harm on someone whose achievements had been so beneficial to the village. Tekpah was also troubled that the event occurred when an American was in residence. He feared that if such negative activities were to continue, Americans would no longer want to come to Kopeyia.

In the end, the men who did not believe consisted of two select groups; the Kokushio, who (apparently) were invested in making an essentially theatrical event appear dangerously real, and those in Agbeli's camp who (once presented with Agbeli's explanation of the "true" situation) were invested in making a potentially real event appear theatrical.

Curiously, as with the individuals discussed in the preceding paragraph, both the Kokushio and Agbeli perspectives were informed by traditional belief systems. The Kokushio used the possibility of witchcraft to substantiate a complex staged event. Agbeli and his uncle used their traditional beliefs to interpret and defuse it.

It appears, however, that during the event itself, and clearly after its conclusion, changing context and evolving interaction caused a general reflexive reevaluation of what had transpired. Quite simply, meaning changed as people's perception of the truth changed.

Like a master politician, Agbeli successfully used the meeting on the veranda to put forth his spin on the events that had taken place. In the morning, Ruben Agbeli, Edward Tekpah, and others had told me that the *juju* was both real and dangerous. By evening they stated that they had known all along that the *juju* was a hoax. This general reinterpretation was evidently shared by many of the village men.

What if the attack had been construed to be real? When Agbeli threatened to go to Togo, he also articulated his ability to withstand a genuine assault. After all, to make that trip and pay the *juju* priests, one might need a considerable sum of money. This would not present a problem for Agbeli, but it would for most villagers.

These facts highlight a curious situation. Since Agbeli is certainly the wealthiest individual who still chooses to live in Kopeyia, he is a logical and potentially lucrative choice on whom to feign or even induce an authentic attack of *juju*. Yet, because he is wealthy, he is—or so he would have his potential foes believe—the only person who can access authentic power easily. Therefore, if one is going to genuinely attack him, one had better do it both carefully and powerfully.

In the final reckoning the Kokushio's attempt generally failed. Ultimately, Agbeli controlled the village interpretation of what had happened and retained possession of the bundles. Rather than being the victim, he was able to reframe the event to his advantage. In the future, if the Kokushio bother him, he can raise the possibility of going to Togo and exacting punishment.

The Veil of Ritual

If Agbeli's interpretation is correct and the Kokushio created their artifice simply to get money, why did they bother with *juju*? After all, Agbeli had helped many of the villagers. It is possible that had they asked, they would have been given something. Yet, they did not.

Robin Horton (1979: 244) has noted that in tribal societies, ritual works to allow individuals to "play several different roles with the same partners in the same setting." The event in Kopeyia seems to provide a case in point. For the Kokushio the exhibition may have had three main thrusts: to increase the likelihood of financial success, to save face for those men who did not wish to have to ask for money, and, finally, to exploit an opportunity to raise their own social status in relation to one of the most powerful men in the village.

Even though the event failed to achieve credibility in the eyes of Agbeli and his closest circle, the reputations of Kokushio members were shielded in that their actions were cast within the higher authority of the gods themselves. Because they were supposedly in trance, it was the possessing spirits, not the individuals, who were responsible for their actions. If, on the one hand, the trance-induced actions taking place that morning were believed to be true, the prestige of the cult and its individual members could potentially rise. On the other hand, if those actions were seen as fallacious, prestige would fall.[9]

Agbeli also made use of the gods by framing his actions in terms of fulfilling the metaphysical requirements outlined by his uncle. Agbeli said he was neither fooled nor intimidated by the *juju*, the Kokushio, or even Koku. Rather, Agbeli acted in response to the possibility that his own gods were requiring something. For Agbeli, it was the act of giving, not the specifics of this particular situation, that was important.

Ultimately, the ritualization of the event by both parties seems to have provided a double safety valve. While the Kokushio and Agbeli stood to gain or lose material wealth and social stature, both had leveraged their positions by having framed their actions in terms of divine authority.

The Social Nature of *Juju*

One finds interesting parallels between Ewe *juju* and Evans-Pritchard's (1937: 100) description of witchcraft among the Azande. Evans-Pritchard established that Azande witch attacks are "motivated by hatred, envy, jealousy, and greed" and that an individual will be hated if he becomes rich or rises in social position. Agbeli identified similar motivations for witchcraft in Kopeyia.

Similarly, Evans-Pritchard wrote that witches are marginalized in Zande society, where they "tend to be those whose behavior is least in accordance with social demands" (112). So too with the Kokushio, who as a group engage in behavior that goes contrary to the social norm. Informants stated that not only are these people not to be trusted, but they also "like dirt and all sorts of nasty things."

Evans-Pritchard found that a jealous person will not only "seek to avoid suspicion by curbing his jealousy," but that he must be doubly careful because the person of whom he is jealous may be a witch himself (117). *Juju* in Kopeyia seems to play out in similar fashion.

In one of our discussions Agbeli told me that he was going to tell the village at large, not just those men close to his circle, that *juju* no longer works in Kopeyia. Yet, he had said nothing when I left Africa three weeks later, nor had he said anything when I returned to Kopeyia in May 1994. The fact is, even though *juju* has negative consequences, it remains part of a larger traditional culture that Agbeli does not want to undermine.

Hallen and Sodipo (1986: 96) have noted that, in part, African witch-craft may be regarded as an "index of certain social stress points." Regardless of its phenomenological efficacy, witchcraft, or even the threat of witchcraft, not only helps to reveal and potentially mediate social fractures but assists in upholding social standards. In Kopeyia, where there are no locks on doors and no one to watch fields at night, the threat of powerful *juju* will keep thieves at bay. Here *juju* acts as a silent watchman by protecting the innocent. This is *juju*'s positive side and represents a level of jurisdiction that the men of Kopeyia are in no hurry to surrender. On the other hand, "real" attacks of *juju* motivated by greed or jealousy, and "false" attacks such as the one described in this essay, represent *juju*'s negative side. This is the *juju* that the elders have tried to eliminate and the *juju* that embarrasses the younger modernized men.

Undoubtedly the social and religious principals that support *juju* will come under greater stress as Kopeyia continues to move closer to the modern world. Working in Oceania, LiPuma (1994) noted that modernization in Maring society has led to arguments about both sorcery's legitimacy and very existence. Further, he found that for the Maring "modernity is simultaneously conducive to an increase in sorcery, insofar as it creates new forms of violence and inequality that people must deal with and explain, and antithetical to its perpetuation, insofar as modernity endorses those forms of knowledge and power (such as positive science and Western religions) that have little tolerance or use for it" (147).

For Agbeli, it is his success in the Western world that separates him economically from his peers in Kopeyia and thereby makes him a candidate for *juju* attacks. These same resources, along with considerable political savvy, also help him to dispel such attacks.

The Old and the New

The social forces attending urbanization, Westernization, and modernization continue to have significant impact on traditional musics throughout the world. As Koetting (1979–80), Waterman (1990), and others have observed within West African society, when social institutions change, the music that served those institutions will be readapted or perhaps even abandoned. In Kopeyia, traditional Ewe music genres support specific traditional Ewe lifestyles, and, vice versa, those lifestyles support specific music associations. There is every reason to believe that in a general sense this relationship will continue and that the future of traditional music will remain married to social development.

Yet Agbeli's work in Kopeyia represents a curious twist on the forces of change, for he has made his career teaching traditional music outside of its traditional context, and he has now brought that paradigm to his home village. Agbeli's instruction of traditional music may presage a new era for Kopeyia in which music performance embraces both the older traditions and a newer folklorization of Ewe music that embodies ideals and mythologies of performance relevant to the West but not necessarily relevant to the peoples who created and have sustained that music.

For many of Agbeli's foreign students—perhaps because they are so strongly enculturated into the notion that aesthetic value resides within the composition itself, that is, in what Floyd (1995: 146) identifies as the "perfect performance and intense enjoyment of 'great works' "—it has been the music and dance, not the manner in which those sounds and movements support social institutions, that has drawn them to African music.

The residents of Kopeyia seem to be digesting this fact. They say that they are proud of their music tradition and that so many Westerners come to study in their village. Children, teenagers, and adults all have their music and dance ensembles, but these ensembles now also function in a folkloric manner, and for a moderate fee, perform for foreign visitors. Today, traditional performances that are internally generated by social imperatives exist side by side with performances produced for outsiders.

Where did the Kokushio's performance reside? The dawn drumming, for the Kokushio alone, was evidently traditional in terms of its satisfying an internally driven social imperative. Perhaps the trances generated during this time were real as well. The later performance for Agbeli and the village at large was evidently artifice, yet if its development was internally generated, I would continue to argue that it was socially traditional.

Was the public performance internally generated? I questioned Agbeli about why the Kokushio chose the time they did to stage the event. Was the fact that a family from New Zealand and I were staying with Agbeli a factor? Agbeli stated that it was not. The event had nothing to do with us; the Kokushio simply needed money at that particular time.

Perhaps this is true, but I am not convinced. Other villagers were clearly aware and concerned that we were in the village to witness the event. Perhaps the Kokushio somehow hoped to use our presence as leverage. The chances are good that Agbeli, who also has a home in Accra, would not have been in the village if not for his foreign students.

These points are for speculation only; I raise them to highlight the ways in which the West has been interwoven into daily life in Kopeyia.

Curiously, and contrary to the villagers' fears, *juju* and other such cultural artifacts are not only what many Westerners hope to experience in Kopeyia but also what Agbeli has a stake in supporting. He promotes Kopeyia rather than Accra to his students, confirming their hopes for an "authentic" experience by telling them that in Kopeyia they can experience life as it is traditionally lived within the village setting.

While Merriam (1964) and others once maintained that the ideal fieldworker should strive to be an invisible set of eyes and ears involved in the documentation and decoding of sonic constructs and cultural and behavioral processes, a later generation (Gourlay 1978) has criticized this approach and argued persuasively that field research involves a reflexive paradigm in which the field and field researcher impact on each other.

The majority of Agbeli's students who have come to Kopeyia are musicians, not ethnomusicologists, and they have not attempted to avoid cultural impact or to document and analyze that impact. But every foreign visitor, whatever his or her motivation for coming, has impacted Kopeyia and helped to mold the symbiotic relationships developing between it and the West. What is so fascinating about the Kopeyia situation is that while contemporary ethnomusicologists would seek to acknowledge that impact, Agbeli, perhaps in part because of his stake in maintaining tradition, does not.

Conclusion

In closing, I would like to return to the notions of indexicality and reflexivity discussed earlier. I have attempted to reveal and interpret the different meanings that individuals attached to the events that occurred in Kopeyia. For the villagers witnessing the event, as new issues came to light, the reflexive shifts in the interpretation of what had transpired represented an enormous change. For the actual players within this theater of illusion, the *juju* victim emerged triumphantly as a model for correct social behavior, stability, and justice. The Kokushio, however, were reframed as impotent and self-serving.

The event also revealed the competing layers of ancient and modern that coexist within Kopeyia's social institutions. The very nature and role of *juju* in a modernizing and Westernizing society came into question, as did the ideas of how Kopeyia's social institutions must function if the village is to continue to provide an authentic and simultaneously inviting home for foreign students.

Perhaps by now most of the ramifications of that afternoon have been played out. Yet, the West intruded one last time before all was said and done. While the village as a whole has no electricity, Agbeli owns both a television and a videocassette recorder, both of which are powered by his electric generator.

Agbeli requested and was given a copy of the videotape that I shot. When I presented the tape, he stated that if the Kokushio attempted to trouble him again, he would show the footage to the villagers. Two years after the event (although he says it was done more in fun than retaliation), Agbeli issued an open invitation for Kopeyia residents to come to the Dagbe Cultural Institute's performance hall in order to view the tape. The Kokushio did not attend.[10]

Notes

[1]While outsiders might tend to classify *juju* as witchcraft, the two categories are discrete to the villagers of Kopeyia. The potencies associated with *juju* may be used for a variety of reasons such as accumulating wealth, attracting a mate, or improving health. In its destructive aspect, *juju* may be used to invoke revenge and other matters of a more negative nature. *Juju* is generally "farmed out." An individual wanting to make use of it will go to some sort of traditional priest or doctor for assistance. Witchcraft is more directly applied. Witches are seen as being particularly dangerous and tend to have specific offensive weapons (bullets or poisons) physically implanted and available for use within their bodies. These efficacious materials, when unleashed, are believed to have devastating effects on their victims.

[2]This may change in the relatively near future. Power lines extend to within a few miles of Kopeyia from both directions along the highway on which the village is situated.

[3]A number of adolescents in Kopeyia have T-shirts celebrating the school's construction. On one side is a picture of Levin, below which are the words *Long live Robert Levin.* The other side of the shirt displays a similar monument to Agbeli.

[4]I realize of course that it is not that simple. Even as the event unfolded, the particular events I chose to observe and what I gleaned from my observations was informed and colored not only by my own developing insights but also those of the specific villagers with whom I spoke.

[5]A warrior deity symbolized by iron, Agbeli later identified Ogu as the same entity worshipped as Ogún by the Yoruba in Nigeria and their descendants in the New World.

[6]Perhaps this is in part because many villagers now have family working in Accra. The time may have come in which it is more prudent to work with, rather

than against, villagers who extend their world to include the cities and the lifestyles that accompany urban life.

[7]While this statement embodies Agbeli's moral rationale for giving money, his pragmatic rationale was equally convincing. He stated that should he refuse to give them money, "They won't go. They won't just feel bad and go. They will stay to collect the money. If not, by now they would have been in the house, playing the drum and dancing."

[8]Once the money was divided up, the total take was probably less than one thousand *cedis* per cult member (approximately $1.40). Even in Kopeyia that was hardly a windfall. While Agbeli supposedly benefited by gaining the favor of the gods for his gift, materially, the Kokushio gained little.

[9]Socially, there seems to be plenty of room on the upside for this marginalized cult. While non-Kokushio admit that Koku is indeed a god, for many villagers at least, that does not justify his worship. While supposedly powerful, the spirit is also widely regarded as malevolent. The Kokushio, say nonmembers, are not to be trusted because they model their god in daily actions: they use poor hygiene, steal (a supposed requirement for admission into the cult), and lie.

[10]Godwin Agbeli died in March 1998 after a brief battle with pancreatic cancer. An estimated five thousand people, including colleagues from the United States, attended the funeral. On returning to Kopeyia in May of that year, I spoke with a number of villagers who attributed his death not to cancer but to *juju*.

References

Agawu, Kofi. 1995. *African Rhythm: A Northern Ewe Perspective.* New York: Cambridge University Press.

Agbeli, Godwin. 1992. Personal communication. 28 Dec. 1992.

Chernoff, John Miller. 1979. *African Rhythm and African Sensibility.* Chicago: University of Chicago Press.

Crapanzano, Vincent. 1986. "Hermes' Dilemma: The Masking of Subversion in Ethnographic Description." In *Writing Culture: The Poetics and Politics of Ethnography,* edited by James Clifford and George E. Marcus. Berkeley: University of California Press.

Cudjoe, S. D. 1953. "The Techniques of Ewe Drumming and the Social Importance of Music in Africa." *Phylon* 14: 280–91.

Evans-Pritchard, E. E. 1937. *Witchcraft, Oracles and Magic among the Azande.* Oxford: Oxford University Press.

Floyd, Samuel A. 1995. *The Power of Black Music.* New York: Oxford University Press.

Gadzekpo, B. Sindezi. 1952. "Making Music in Eweland." *West African Review* 23: 817–21.

Gourlay, K. A. 1978. "Towards a Reassessment of the Ethnomusicologist's Role in Research." *Ethnomusicology* 22(1): 1–35.

Hallen, Barry, and J. O. Sodipo. 1986. *Knowledge, Belief and Witchcraft: Analytic Experiments in African Philosophy.* London: Ethnographica.

Jones, A. M. 1954. "African Rhythm." *Africa* 24: 26–47.

————. 1959. *Studies in African Music*. 2 vols. London: Oxford University Press.
Kludze, A. K. P. 1973. *Restatement of African Law: 6. Ghana: Ewe Law of Property*. The Restatement of African Law Series. London: Sweet & Maxwell.
Koetting, James T. 1970. "Analysis and Notation of West African Drum Ensemble Music." *Selected Reports in Ethnomusicology* 1(3): 115–46.
————. 1979–80. "The Organization and Functioning of Migrant Kasena Flute and Drum Ensembles in Nima/Accra." *African Urban Studies* 6 (Winter): 17.
Ladzekpo, Kobla. 1971. "The Social Mechanics of Good Music: A Description of Dance Clubs among the Anlo Ewe-Speaking People of Ghana." *African Music* 1: 6–22.
Ladzekpo, Kobla S., and Hewitt Pantaleoni. 1970. "Takada Drumming." *African Music* 4(4): 6–21.
LiPuma, Edward. 1994. "Sorcery and Evidence of Change in Maring Justice." *Ethnology* 33(2): 147–63.
Locke, David. 1982. "Principles of Off-Beat Timing and Cross-Rhythm in Southern Ewe Dance Drumming." *Ethnomusicology* 26(2): 217–46.
————. 1987. *Drum Gahu*. Crown Point, IN: White Cliffs Media.
————. 1992. *Kpegisu: An Ewe War Drum*. Tempe, AZ: White Cliffs Media.
Merriam, Alan P. 1964. *The Anthropology of Music*. Evanston, IL: Northwestern University Press.
Nettl, Bruno. 1985. *The Western Impact on World Music: Change, Adaptation, and Survival*. New York: Schirmer.
Pantaleoni, Hewitt. 1972. "Toward Understanding the Play of Atsimevu in Atsia." *African Music* 5(2): 64–84.
Waterman, Christopher Alan. 1990. *Juju: A Social History and Ethnography of an African Popular Music*. Chicago: University of Chicago Press.
Watson, Graham. 1991. "Rewriting Culture." In *Recapturing Anthropology: Working in the Present,* edited by Richard G. Fox, 73–92. Santa Fe, NM: School of American Research Press.

PART III

Contradictory Moments

CHAPTER 9

Militarism in Haitian Music[1]

Gage Averill and Yuen-Ming David Yih

In 1995 President Jean-Bertrand Aristide formally disbanded the Haitian armed forces, marking the end of two centuries during which the army exercised extraordinary sway over government, labor, land use, the legal system, and the economy. In this essay, we suggest that the complex relationship between the Haitian people and their army—or, more exactly, between the people and militarism—stretches back to the colonial era and to the independence struggle, and that it has left an indelible mark on expressive cultural forms and practices, most notably in music. This approach may strike some as counterintuitive: researchers of African diasporan societies are perhaps more accustomed to viewing colonial and postcolonial armies in the role of repressive agents or adversaries of peoples of African descent. While we do not deny the importance of military repression, we argue that the experience of militarism for many peoples of the African diaspora has been more complex and textured and that it plays a more serious role in structuring African diasporic consciousness than is commonly attributed to it.[2]

Many contemporary expressive traditions in Haiti reveal a residue of military contexts, roles, terminologies, social interactions, imagery, paraphernalia, musical instruments, and musical styles, adding up to a pervasive trace of militarism in Haitian social and cultural life. We believe this legacy is attributable to: (1) the military backgrounds of many first-generation slaves, especially maroons (escaped slaves) and those who formed African "national" organizations; (2) the slaves' experience of—and involvement in—colonial militarism; (3) the protracted military struggle for independence; (4) a deeply ingrained commitment to struggle against oppressive national and imperialist authority; and (5) the postcolonial dominance of the Haitian army. To pursue this idea, we will examine a number of Haitian musical performance complexes to reveal the role played by military symbols, practices, and ideology. Although African militarism left a clear mark on Haitian culture—in the proliferation of Ogou deities long associated with iron and warfare among the Fon and Yoruba peoples, for example—many of the symbolic manifestations of military influence draw on the Franco-Haitian military tradition, which was absorbed deeply (and early on) into an array of folk and popular expressive forms.

Because its population is nearly exclusively of African origin and because of its early, successful war of independence, Haiti occupies a distinctive niche within the African diaspora. Nevertheless, we are convinced that our findings concerning the military influence on social organization and expressive culture are germane to a wide swath of African diasporic life and may be especially significant for discussions of secret societies, maroon communities, mutual aid societies, work brigades, carnivalesque processionals, and formerly clandestine Afro-Caribbean religious ceremonies.

A Brief History of Militarism in Haiti

John Thornton has argued that "African aristocratic and military culture helped to fire rebellion and provide leadership" (1992: 280). African slaves traded to European slave traders were often drawn from among combatants captured by their opponents in battle, and the slave trade contributed directly to the escalation of warfare in West Africa. Fon military societies are still active in parts of Benin, and their friendly rivalries are enacted through the use of proverb (*asafó*) flags.[3]

As a result, we assume that a significant portion of African slaves transported to the Americas were steeped in military traditions of their own, and this assumption is borne out by patterns that developed in the colonies. Ten years after Columbus first landed in the Americas, Spanish authorities were already concerned about runaway slaves in Hispaniola[4] who had joined forces with Indian rulers during the Taino rebellion against the Spanish in 1519–32 (Thornton 1992: 285). Wolof slaves in Hispaniola, familiar with West African forms of equestrian warfare, successfully defended their rebellion against Spanish cavalry charges in 1522 and trained their own cavalry to raid Spanish plantations during the 1540s (294). Some of the "nation" organizations on the plantations—which were encouraged by some slave holders because they took care of a number of important social functions, such as burial, mutual aid, holiday celebrations, substitute kinship, and so forth—constituted themselves along militaristic lines, electing military hierarchies and assuming some of the juridicial and punitory functions of African secret societies. All of this confirms early and continuous African militarism in the colony.

From the beginnings of the French colony of Saint Domingue, slaves were called on to serve, and serve in, the colonial armed forces, and after whites began fleeing the colony in the late eighteenth century, the French became increasingly reliant on a black military. Additionally, free people of color served in a series of voluntary or compulsory militias (including the *Chasseurs-Royaux,* who fought alongside the Americans against the British at the siege of Savannah during the American Revolutionary War) (Hall 1971: 114–17). In one of the great ironies of European colonial history, it was the French colonial armed forces in Saint Domingue that became the backbone of the anticolonial struggle. This is an extremely complicated chapter in Haitian history, but a brief outline of the events should help to explain how a colonial military metamorphosed into a revolutionary one.

Following the French Revolution of 1789, resistance among Saint Domingue's slaves escalated, and a rebellion broke out in August 1791, forcing most of the colony's European settlers to flee. The black general Toussaint L'Ouverture was appointed governor to restore order. In 1801, L'Ouverture assumed the title of governor for life and declared Saint Domingue an "autonomous" colony, which provoked Napoleon Bonaparte to order an invasion. Captured by the French at a negotiating session, L'Ouverture was taken prisoner and died two years later in a French prison. Most of his forces then aligned themselves with General Jean-Jacques Dessalines, who continued the war against Napoleon's army. Former slaves, free people of color, and maroons all participated in this war for independence and for an end to slavery. Dessalines defeated the French at the Battle of Vertiers, near Cap Haïtien, on 18 November 1803 and declared the colony an independent black republic, the Republic of Haiti, on 1 January 1804. The pride that Haitians have typically taken in the army and the army's historic reputation as the guarantor of national sovereignty descends from this defeat of the French and the founding of the Haitian state.

In the postindependence period, the Haitian army remained the most powerful organization in the country. Dessalines's Constitution of 1805 organized the country into local and regional divisions administered by the army. Rural *Commandants de la Place* and *Chefs de Section* were given the power to rule in their domains with little outside interference, and they were charged with enforcing a colonial-style plantation system (collectivized peasant agriculture) deemed essential to maintain the new nation's export base and food self-sufficiency. Trouillot characterizes the agricultural system as being organized along lines of *"caporalisme militaire"* (Prussian-style militarism) (1990: 43), and Dupuy refers to the "militarization of labor relations" (1989: 88).

After the assassination of Jean-Jacques Dessalines in 1806, Haiti effectively split in two. The northern part was ruled by General Henry Christophe (who later declared the territory a monarchy and himself its king), while the southern section remained a republic under General Alexandre Pétion. Pétion enacted limited land reform measures, resulting in the subdivision and distribution of former plantations (some of which went as spoils to former and current military officers) and allowed extensive squatting on unclaimed land. Thus the south made a decisive break with the system of militarized agriculture, institutionalizing a system of subsistence agriculture on small landholdings supplemented by the production of cash crops. Under the rule of Henry Christophe, the north continued with nationalized plantations, but here, too, peasants squatted on distant and more mountainous terrain to escape the militarized neoplantation system. Pétion's successor, Jean-Pierre Boyer, who unified the country after Christophe's death, and who then took over the eastern, Spanish-speaking portion of the island, implemented Pétion-style land reform throughout the entire territory.

Haiti's independence received a chilly reception from European and American powers. As late as 1814, Napoleon was still scheming for the return of Haiti to French control, complete with the restoration of slavery. The threat of French, British, or American control of neighboring Santo Domingo, long a forgotten backwater of the Spanish empire in the New World, was cited by Haitian leaders as justification for their invasion of the Spanish-speaking eastern portion of the island, which Haiti ruled from 1822 until 1844. In 1825 France imposed an enormous debt on Haiti as a precondition for recognition and state-to-state relations. The United States did not recognize Haiti until 1862, and the first Latin American state to do so was Brazil in 1865. To the leaders of the new nation, independence must have seemed very precarious indeed; thus the maintenance of Haitian military strength in the nineteenth century can be viewed in part as a response to these perceived threats to the nation. With a European audience in mind, Henry Christophe declared: "At my voice, Hayti will be transformed into a vast camp of soldiers" (Nicholls 1985: 171). By 1842, "on a per capita basis, Haiti's standing army was more than twice the size of Britain's as well as of most other major European powers" (Heinl and Heinl 1978: 191).

In the seventy-two-year period from the fall of Haitian president Boyer in 1843 to the U.S. occupation in 1915, Haiti was "wracked by at least 102 civil wars, revolutions, insurrections, revolts, coups, and *attentats*" (Ibid.: 404). One scholar offered this bleak assessment of nineteenth-century Haiti: "This country is without doubt one of the rare examples of a society that has never known any condition but that of war" (Laroche 1978: 122).[5] By the early twentieth century, foreign speculators were financing Haitian revolutions for investment purposes (Allen 1930: 328–29). The period of the nineteenth century through the early twentieth century was known as "the era of generals," and "anyone [including civilians] could be promoted by the president to the rank of general as a form of compensation" (Laguerre 1993: 23, 42). Not until 1913 did Haiti get its first civilian president, Michel Oreste. Throughout Haiti's history, the military has been the paramount institution and key to state power, its authority asserted over every corner of the country. The military's role in the colonial regime, the Haitian Revolution, the postindependence government, and the struggle for economic and political power has kept the army in the foreground of Haitian consciousness.[6]

Militarism in Haitian Expressive Culture

The centrality of the military in Haitian politics and consciousness had powerful repercussions for Haitian expressive culture, especially because cultural institutions were shaped in the image of military models. In his seminal article, "Folklore du militarisme," Emmanuel C. Paul

(1954) drew attention to the effects of militarism on peasant work societies in Haiti: "despite their diversity, these organizations possess a military structure, a military discipline, and a military hierarchy; moreover, their rituals draw on a political etiquette that reminds us of the military governments of former years. Among the names for these groups we have noticed a whole military terminology: Escort, Squad, Battalion, etc. The honorific titles . . . correspond to military grades and are used for the prestige they confer" (26).[7] In the following sections, we will follow this line of investigation into the effects of militarism on culture with special attention to how music interacted with these social and historical processes (Figure 9-1).

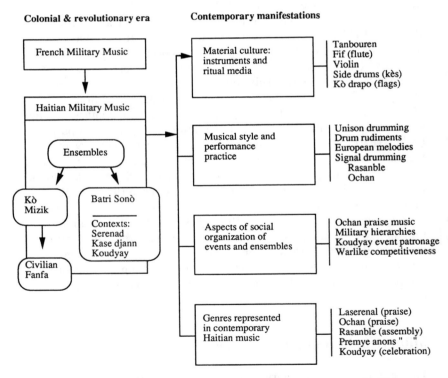

FIGURE 9-1. This diagram traces the historical influence of the French military tradition on Haitian expressive culture. Contemporary manifestations of this influence are grouped under four headings (briefly: "material culture," "musical style," "social organization," and "genres").

Music was central to the military endeavor in the eighteenth century. Most important, it was crucial to the communication of commands amid the din of the battlefield. The French drum major (like his counterparts in neighboring European countries) communicated commands to the musicians visually by the motion and positioning of his staff (*baton*). A 1754 manual of French military regulations states that "soldiers will cease marching every time the beating of the drum stops" (Kastner 1973: 396). Since any error could have catastrophic consequences, the signals had to be standardized, memorized, and carefully rehearsed. They were therefore codified and issued in manuals that appeared inter-mittently during the period, providing a precise record of French signal music. One such manual, the *Ordonnance des Tambours et Fifres de la Garde Imperiale,* lists six types of drum strokes, including flams (*fla*) and three- and five-stroke rolls (*rat*). These strokes, indicated in notation by a letter above a note head, were in use by 1705. In Mel-chior's 1831 *Batteries et Sonneries de l'Infanterie Française,* every note is garnished with a symbol (3, 19, 24 of the notation). Thus, flams, drags, rolls, and other strokes that comprise the "rudiments" of Western drumming and precise unison playing were central features of French military drumming.

While it is not clear that African military musics survived substan-tially intact in Saint Domingue, it is likely that the slaves easily syn-cretized the functions of European military signal music with those of comparable traditions in Sub-Saharan Africa, where the use of musical signals was widespread. Central African military signal music was described in the late fifteenth century by Duarte Lopes, who wrote, "The movements of the combat are regulated . . . by different ways of beating the drum and sounding the trumpet" (Forbath 1977: 97).[8]

A number of references in the historical literature speak to the concern with which revolutionary-era combatants approached the topic of mili-tary music. For example, Toussaint L'Ouverture once spoke of a defeated opponent as being "with neither drum nor trumpet" (James 1963: 159). A French soldier recounted the role that music seemed to play in the rebel-lious Haitian army: "They advanced singing . . . Their song was a song of brave men, and it went as follows, 'To the attack, grenadier / Who gets killed, that's his affair' " (Lemmonier-Delafosse in James 1963: 368).

Each military division—chasseurs (light infantrymen), grenadiers, artillery, sharpshooters, and palace guard—was assigned a *corps de mu-sique* (military music corps). There was a total of sixteen such corps in Port-au-Prince alone and many more in the provincial towns (Dumervé

1968: 32–33, 281). Also called *fanfa* (fanfares), these corps used a wide variety of wind and percussion instruments and provided a training ground for musicians—wind instrumentalists in particular. The repertoires of colonial regimental bands included excerpts from popular operas of the day as well as social dance music, and the bands were accustomed to performing not only in military contexts but in concerts and for society balls (Fouchard 1988: 94, 104–5).

In addition to the *corps de musique,* the Haitian army maintained fife, drum, and bugle corps called *batteries sonores.* Dumervé has described the repertoire of these groups as comprising three types of composition (differentiated by context): *koudyay, kase djann,* and *serenad. Koudyay,* from the French *coup de jaille* (meaning a joyous and spontaneous bursting forth) was used for large public ceremonies, such as the consecration of Dessalines as emperor in 1804 and the four-hundred-drum *koudyay* of the first anniversary of independence in 1805. The term has been generalized and now covers any spontaneous or sponsored street gathering (often used for a show of political support) with a carnivalesque atmosphere.[9] The second type of composition for the *batteries sonores,* the *kase djann* (from *casser la diane,* "to break the dawn"), served as a reveille. The third form, *serenad* (French: *la sérénade*), was performed in honor of respected leaders and distinguished persons. It was typical of those so honored to respond with gifts of food, drink, and money (Dumervé 1968: 290–93). This type of honorific and remunerative complex is preserved in the widespread practice of *ochan,* performed in a variety of contexts. Laroche (1978: 209–10) describes this practice in the context of a *koudyay*:

> This hommage in words and music is encountered in the *koudyay* which can be considered to be an *ochan* danced and sung by a whole crowd which, circulating through the streets of a city, wishes to celebrate the visit of an important person (the head of state, for example), celebrate the nomination of a favorite to a key post, or simply manifest its joy on the occasion of an important event . . . A *koudjay* is inconceivable without the crowd having the feted one's house as the turning point of their route. According to the traditional scenario, then, the man of the hour expresses his thanks to the crowd that sings his praises by giving a speech from his balcony. He also has the refinement to manifest his satisfaction in a more concrete manner, by certain gifts, in currency or in kind, which he has distributed to all his celebrants or at least to the musicians considered the spokespeople for the group.[10]

Militarism and Vodou

Vodou played a significant role in the resistance to and eventual over-throw of French domination. The slave uprising of 1791 is believed to have been launched at a Vodou ceremony in a secluded woods known as Bwa Kayiman (Caiman Woods). At this ceremony, the slave leader Boukman Jetty is reputed to have used a machete to sacrifice a pig to the African gods. Those who drank the blood of the pig swore themselves to war against the colonists.[11] Although this ceremony is given prominence in most histories of the revolution, it was only one of many crossovers of African religious belief into the political arena. An early chronicler of the French Caribbean, Moreau de Saint-Méry, wrote of a leader from the south of Haiti called Dom Pedro who had been implicated in subversive plots and who inspired his followers with daring and "superstition" (Courlander 1960: 129). Immortalized as the Vodou deity Jean Pétro, Dom Pedro is considered the founder of Petwo, the branch of Vodou considered more militaristic, fiery, and violent than its counterpart, Rada. Petwo and Rada constitute the two principal rites of Vodou.[12] Anthropologist Michel Laguerre (1980: 114) notes that the congregation he studied in the Bel-Aire neighborhood of Port-au-Prince celebrates the Bwa Kayiman ceremony every year on 14 August with a sacrifice of a pig to the Petwo spirits. André Pierre, a Haitian painter and priest, distinguished between the "civilian" Rada and the "military" Petwo (Thompson 1984: 165). Robert Farris Thompson has used descriptions such as "ritualized aggression," "spiritualized militancy," and "salvation through extremity and intimidation" in reference to Petwo (180–81). Petwo ceremonies are characterized by the prominent use of fire, gun-powder, alcohol, whips, and whistles—ritual media associated with "hotness," warfare, and rebellion. To most practitioners or *sevitè*-s of Vodou, Petwo balances the "coolness" of Rada.

    Consonant with their military origins, many of the Petwo *lwa*-s have military associations and titles.[13] Sobo dresses as an army general and Bosou is a fierce bull deity, but the most warlike are the avatars of Ogou, especially Ogou Feray, Ogou Badagri, and Ogou Balendjo. Originally called Gun and of Fon and Yoruba origin, Ogou (wherever he emerges in the African diaspora) is considered a deity of warfare and iron, sacred to blacksmiths, hunters, and warriors. When he possesses his devotees in ceremonies, Ogou typically wears red (or red and blue), carries a machete, and drinks rum.[14] Ogou is syncretized with the Catholic Saint James (Saint Jacques in French), who is pictured in some chromolitho-graphs riding a white horse and brandishing a flaming sword, an image that took root during the *reconquista* of the Iberian Peninsula (Cosentino 1995: 246). His icongraphy, represented in symbols (*vèvè-s*) traced on ceremonial floors and on banners (*drapo-s*) carried and displayed in Vodou temples, includes a knife and two flags. Studying Haitian *drapo,* art historian Patrick Polk has argued that they "are deliberately patterned after military flags used in Africa and Haiti during the colonial and post-colonial eras" (Polk 1995: 331).

As with the *drapo,* some military influences in Haitian music are of Sub-Saharan African origin. African slaves brought with them many warlike dances and songs on militaristic themes. For example, the Ibo nation, which had a reputation for resisting slavery, is honored in Vodou ceremonies with a dance meant to evoke military combativeness. The Nago dance performed in Vodou ceremonies (especially for Ogou) is also considered a war dance, and it is included in the repertoires of most Haitian folkloric dance troupes. Saint Domingue was also home to a version of the dance called *kalenda* (*calinda*), a widespread form of Caribbean stick fighting brought from West Africa and performed to music. According to Harold Courlander (1960: 131–32), the *kalenda,* also known as *mousondi,* is associated with the Kongo nation, and its lyrics, like those from many Vodou songs, dwell on militaristic themes. Words to a *mousondi* song illustrate:

Mousondi n a fè lagè, eya,	Mousondi (a Kongo nation)
eya, eya	will make war
Nou se nanchon lagè	We are a warrior nation
Ou pa tande kanon-m tire?[15]	Can't you hear my cannon fire?

But true to its syncretic nature, Vodou has also adapted many elements of Franco-Haitian military culture. One of the most striking emerges early in ceremonies of most Rada rites and features machete-wielding officiants called *laplas* (from *Commandant de la Place,* the name for a commander in charge of a town or city) and flag bearers—called *pòt drapo-s* (flag carriers) or, collectively, *kò drapo* (flag corps). Fleurant (1996: 167), among others, has described this ritual sequence:

At a certain point in a ritual, the society's flags are brought out . . . [The *laplas*], flanked by the two *potdrapo* or flag bearers, dances ritually before each *oungan/manbo* [priest/priestess] in attendance. The *oungan, ason* [sacred rattle] in hand, mirrors the movements of the trio in the prescribed ritual manner. After saluting the four cardinal points, the moment ends with the flag bearers kneeling while they are presenting the flags to the *oungan* who kisses the tops of each flag, symbolizing his support of the congregation.

The *laplas* often makes vigorous, even dangerous, slicing motions with the machete and sudden, rapid shifts of direction akin to a battlefield reenactment.

The ceremonial discourse of Vodou is rich in military allusion. Healing ceremonies may be called "expeditions," with certain classes of deities invoked first so as to act as a vanguard (Fleurant 1996: 163). Certain Vodou deities may be thought of as traveling together as a military *èskò* or *èskwad* (escort or squad). Vodou song texts, especially those addressed to the more militant *lwa*-s, may be replete with military imagery and themes, as in the following:

Ogou-o, gè, gè	Ogou-o, war, war
Kanno tire	Cannon fired
Nou pa pran yo	We didn't get hurt (ibid.: 158)

Fleurant notes that the Ogou song above is sung to a *nago cho* (hot Nago) rhythm, which we have previously identified as linked to Ogou and to a militaristic ambience. The theme of the song echoes the revolutionary-era belief that devotees of the *lwa*-s would not be harmed by cannons and bullets. Other songs to Ogou explore the role of flags, talk about the need for vigilance, discuss weapons, and in general explore themes of battle and war. The following text is addressed to Ogou Feray (Saint Jacques Majeur) and praises the strength and discipline of his army:

Alantran sen jak	To the coming of [the army of] Saint Jacques!
Map rive avè yo	I am arriving with them
E tèt-an-mwen nan lanmè	And my head is in the sea
Latye-mwen nan letan	While my tail is in the pond
Alantran sen jak	To the coming of [the army of] Saint Jacques!
Map rive avè yo	I am arriving with them[16]

Many Vodou songs evidence an outlook characterized by conflict, mistrust, and adversarial relations with the outside world, an outlook fostered by centuries of intermittent religious persecution and unrelenting political and economic oppression of Haiti's peasants (Yih 1995: 66–118, 473–96).

At Souvenance, a famous Vodou center near Gonaïves, the approximately thirty-six deities recognized in ceremonies are classified into two groups, called *chasè* and *grennadye. Chasseurs* and *grenadiers* (the French terms from which the Creole words were derived) were two categories into which French soldiers were classified during the *ancien régime.* The terms survived both the French and Haitian Revolutions and were used in Dessalines's army as well as in Napoleon's. An antique *asotò* drum from the town of Cabaret depicts two grenadiers dressed in uniforms of the First Empire (Roumain 1943: 65). In the Souvenance ceremonies, the leaders of the two *ekip, kan,* or *batayon* (teams, camps, or battalions) are called *chèf chasè* and *chèf grennadye.* The dance steps and drum rhythms associated with each camp are also identified as either *chasè* or *grennadye* (Yih 1995: 273–94). In rituals, the *chasè* deities are greeted first, followed by the *grennadye.* The two groups maintain a kind of friendly rivalry, competing to see whose ceremonies will be the most splendid.

Ochan and Rasanble

By the middle of the eighteenth century and at least through 1831, *aux champs* was a command in the French military signal music repertoire meaning "Forward march!" (literally, "To the fields!") (Kastner 1973: 395). As the command to begin marching—the sonic boundary between stasis and mobility—*aux champs* (Creole: *ochan*) epitomized the solemn splendor and grave significance of an army on the move. We speculate that it came to symbolize the power of military rulers and generals. Thus, *ochan* became, like *serenad,* a genre appropriate to honoring the rich and mighty.

The practice of *ochan* reflects a cultural disposition toward power in Haiti whereby less powerful individuals unite to honor those more powerful in order to stake a claim to the redistributive largesse of the patron. The dispossessed seek a *moun-pa* (literally, a person for them)—someone with connections who can intercede for them. The sponsor or patron of a musical group trades tangible gifts, along with the promise of protection and connections, for support of the masses. The *ochan* demonstrates the size and power of the mass, evoking both opportunity and danger for the patron: if a patron rejects an entreaty from a group, the loyalty of the masses may shift to a rival leader. This type of exchange characterizes much Haitian economic and political activity.

During the 1990 presidential campaign, Yih observed a number of candidates who appeared at the week-long *banda* ceremony at the Desronville temple of the late Hérard Simon, president of Zantray, an organization formed to promote Vodou. Although Zantray favored a former president, Leslie Manigat, for his past support of Vodou, each candidate was accorded an *ochan* on arrival.[17] In Vodou ceremonial contexts, *ochan* may be performed not only for dignitaries, visiting priests and priestesses, and special guests, but for the spirits as well. This reveals the nature of the patron/client relationship between spirits (*lwa*-s) and members of the Vodou religion (*sèvitè*-s). The centrality of exchange and the need for a *moun pa* extends to the spirit world.

Another form of French signal drumming preserved in Haitian ritual is *l'assemblée* (assembly call), called *rasanble* in Haiti. A French military ordinance from 1754–56 states: "To muster a troop, or to make it close ranks once it is assembled, have the drums issue the call" (Kastner 1973: 395).[18] Unlike *ochan,* which changed its message while preserving its musical style, *rasanble* retains both the style and the function of the military signal music. Southern Kongo societies play *rasanble* to call on members to gather together. *Konbit* work societies use a rhythm called *rapèl* to summon members to work.[19] The name probably stems from the *l'appel* and *rappel* signals of the French military. In the south, similar brigades are sometimes called *eskwad* or squads, making the military metaphor even more explicit.

Ochan and *rasanble* drumming is strongly suggestive of European military signal style. In contrast to the interlocking, polyphonic style of most Vodou drumming, *ochan* and *rasanble* are essentially in heterophonic rhythmic unison, with each player free to elaborate somewhat on the same underlying rhythm. They also draw on other features of European drumming, as exemplified by the rudiments, including flams, ruffs, and rolls. Other beats used in Vodou show this influence too: *sagwe* in Cap Haïtien (like *ochan,* a salutation), the last section of the *salitasyon* of Port-au-Prince, and *premye anons* in Cavaillon.

During the colonial period, large numbers of people from the Congo River Basin were brought to Saint Domingue as slaves, and Kongo societies arose in many parts of the country, especially in the southern peninsula. In Dalva Jèfò, a Kongo society near the town of Bois Laborde,[20] instrumentalists carry the title of *majò* (major)—a drummer is *majò tanbou,* a flutist *majò flit.* Southern Kongo societies perform both for recreational dances and for Vodou ceremonies. When Dalva Jèfò is hired to animate a ceremony, the *majò-s tanbou* play *rasanble* to assemble the members before departure to the compound (*lakou*) where they are to perform. Upon their arrival at the gate, they play it again to call forth the owner of the *lakou.* The owner is then greeted with an *ochan* and the society enters the compound. Thereafter, *rasanble* is played only to regroup the musicians after a pause in the proceedings. As it is strictly signal drumming, there is no singing with this beat. Notice the unison playing style and use of flams and ruffs in the following example (Figure 9-2).

Dalva Jèfò has three *ochan* drumbeats in its repertoire: *ochan, ochan militè* (military *ochan*), and *ochan Fòs Ame Dayiti* (*ochan* of the Haitian

*flams, similarly throughout

FIGURE 9-2. *Rasanble.* Played by the group Dalva Jèfò in Bois Laborde on two drums (*legede* and *tanbou Rada*). This piece demonstrates the importance of flams and the heterophonic unison approach. Two types of strokes are articulated on the *legede* drum, a low open stroke and a muted press tone. Recorded by Yih; transcription by Yih, notation by Averill (true of all transcriptions unless otherwise noted).

armed forces). Unlike *rasanble,* the *ochan* beat accompanies singing. Below are two examples of *ochan* songs. The *ochan* for Dessalines is an excellent example of the nationalistic fervor that underlies and inspires much militarism. The second *ochan* discusses the redistributive nature of the *ochan* event; if the person in authority has money or food, the group assumes that some will be shared. There is also a certain self-deprecatory tone to this *ochan* that is consistent with the goal of flattering a figure in authority. During the performance of *ochan* by this group, an official holds the society's flag while dancing around the person being saluted. The flag then becomes the repository for the requested donation.

Desalin mouri kite peyi-a se pou nou	Dessalines died leaving Haiti for us
Ou ap sonje byen depi lontan	Remember well from long ago
Pou aprann de Desalin	To learn about Dessalines
Avèk zanm-yo a lamen	With our weapons in our hands
Oriyo nanpwen lafwa (×2)	Once there was no hope (×2)
N ap mache ewa a libète o	Now we're working for liberty
Se pèp-la ki resèvwa	The people are ready
Pou antre de Desalin	For the entrance of Dessalines
Ou ap salye a libetè	You're saluting freedom
Mesyedam gad on ochan	Ladies and gentlemen, look at the *ochan*
M frape pou ou la	I'm playing for you here
Se pa anyen se pou otorite	There's nothing to it — it's for authority
Si genyen genyen	If there's something to be had
Genyen-an pou nou tout	We'll all have something
Si nanpwen nanpwen	If there's nothing to be had
Nanpwen-an pou nou tout, Majèst o	There's nothing for any of us, Majèst oh[21]
Se pa anyen m ap chante	There's nothing to this singing
Se bonswa m ap di ou bonswa	I'm wishing you a good evening

(last two lines repeat)

The transcriptions of these two *ochan* examples (see Figures 9-3 and 9-4) exemplify the European melodic and harmonic influences on *ochan*

FIGURE 9-3. "Desalin Mouri Kite Peyi-a Se Pou Nou" (see Figure 9-2). An *ochan* recorded by Yih near Les Cayes in lessons with Josile Brinal, Dieupuissant Jèdi, and Wilfrid Clergé, and with members of the Forestal and Cadesty families. The strongly triadic feeling of the melody is established in the opening measure on the tonic chord.

style. Although there is no harmony line sung, the melody implies a harmonic progression.

Kò Mizik Mennwat

Another institution with roots in colonial and postcolonial culture is the *kò mizik mennwat,* a small ensemble tradition active in the southern peninsula. Deriving their name from the military *corps de musique* and from the French court dance, the *menuet,* these ensembles have as their primary venue the *bal lwa* or ball for the spirits. Their repertoire has two distinct parts: one is European derived, the other is African. The first portion of the repertoire reads like a history of elite European social dances (in close to the order of their rise to popularity in Paris): *mennwat,*

FIGURE 9-4. "Mesyedam Gad On Ochan" (see Figure 9-3).

contredanse, quadrille, polka, valse, *à la visite,* and *les lanciers.* Like layers of geological time visible in exposed rock, the repertoire shows a process of accretion, one dance at a time, from the colonial period to the 1850s.

The musicians of the group Premye Nimewo (First Number),[22] a *kò mizik mennwat* based in the rural area of Macombe, open *bal lwa*-s with the performance of *premye anons* (first notice), announcing to participants that the dancing will begin shortly (Figure 9-5).[23] The *premye anons* is made up of three to five brief sections (each about a minute long) linked by drum rolls. In its military style (unison playing, rudiments, rolls) and in its structure, it resembles certain *ochan* and *rasanble* beats, which are similarly strung together in short sections linked by rolls. In fact, the first section is identical to the *rasanble* of the Kongo group Dalva Jèfò (see above). Taken together, the sections of *premye*

FIGURE 9-5. Members of the ensemble Gwoup Premye Nimewo featuring two *tanbouren* frame drums, fiddle, and flute. Photo credit: Chantal Regnault. Used by permission.

anons constitute a kind of catalog of military-derived beats. These beats may be rearranged or some may be omitted in a given performance. They may be used to end performances of other genres such as *mennwat* or *kadri* (Figure 9-6).

Another item in the repertoire of the *kò mizik mennwat* is an important honorific piece for the *lwa*-s, called *laserenal*. Although it is not significant in terms of its length and is played only in opening rituals of the ceremony—and not for dancing—musicians insist that *laserenal* is the piece for which they are engaged and that it is the piece that secures remuneration from their patrons. It appears to derive both name and function from the *serenad* of the *batteries sonores*. In one appearance by Premye Nimewo at a *bal lwa,* the group played *laserenal* at a tree near a spring, at the spring itself, at a tree near the gateway to the compound, and before the altar in the home. In each case, a set of three *laserenal* pieces was required.

The four musicians of this *kò mizik mennwat* are a fiddler, two drummers playing frame drums called *tanbouren*-s, and a dance caller who also plays an iron hoe blade called *fè*. Some groups use a fife or accor-

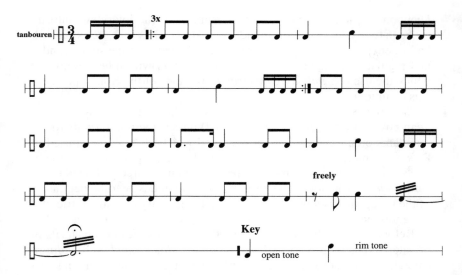

FIGURE 9-6. A section from a performance of Premye Anons, as played by Romère Thes, leader of the *mennwat* group, Premye Nimewo. This example demonstrates the use of the five-stroke roll (four sixteenth notes in one measure landing on a downbeat in the next measure). Noteheads below the line denote an open, ringing tone, and those above the line represent higher-pitched rim tones.

dion instead of a violin. *Tanbouren*-s resemble the tambourines used in the French military, called *tambours de Basque,* which appear in a nineteenth-century manual of French military music (Kastner 1973: Plate XIX).[24] Both instruments are frame drums with metal tighteners and flat, circular jingles attached to the frame of the drum. This allows us to assert some probable etymologies. The name *Basque* survives in the Creole verb *baske* (which refers to the act of playing the accompanimental *tanbouren*) and in the noun *bas* (which refers to a frame drum common in Carnival and *rara* bands).

Rara and Carnival Bands

In her research on Haitian *rara,* Elizabeth McAlister (1995) interviewed a gentleman named Papa Dieubon (reputed to be more than one hundred years old) about a *rara* band he had directed some forty years earlier.

Dieubon seemed confused about the subject of the interview until he broke in to say, "Oh, you mean the *army!*" (127). His *rara,* he explained, had a general as well as a colonel to direct the group in the streets, and it had regularly engaged in militaristic encounters with other groups, in which the use of *zanm kongo* (spiritual weapons of the Kongo peoples) was commonplace.

Rara bands use military titles (along with those of royalty and republican government). The *kolonèl* (colonel) directs the group on its route, maintains order, and employs a whip and whistle (ritual media used in Petwo ceremonies). The drum majors, called *majò jonk,* are elaborately dressed in sequined costumes and perform with a sacred, baptized baton called a *jonk.* The *pòt drapo,* or flag bearer, marches near the beginning of the group and may use the flag—as in the military—to signal friendly or aggressive intentions to other bands the group encounters.

Before *rara* bands go on the road, they hold a series of rehearsals in private; in *rara* terminology, they are said to *balanse an plas.* To *balanse* (literally, to rock or sway) can mean to "heat up" the ceremony in spiritual terms, and it can mean to get an automobile or a large group such as a battalion going. Later in the *rara* season, which coincides with Lent, the bands will hold *egzèsis* (the same term that is applied to military maneuvers), marching through the streets but still not with their *majò jonk* in full regalia. Among the instruments in a *rara* band is a local version of a European military side drum (similar to a snare drum) called a *kès* (French: *caisse*).

The militaristic elements in *rara* come into play during intense local competitions among the various *rara* bands. The *kolonèl* may resort to using *zanm kongo* (Kongo arms), including various powders and charms (*makandal*-s, *wanga*-s), in order to "crush" other bands. *Rara* bands circumambulate territory that they consider their own, stopping at the houses of important patrons to perform *ochan. Ochan* is typically played while the *majò jonk* executes figures with the *jonk* or while he passes it around the head of the dignitary. This gesture is called *zèklè* (lightning) or *twa limyè* (three lights). The *kolonèl* may also pass his whip around the head of the person honored or around the cross on tombstones of ancestors venerated at the cemetery. Some scholars have suggested that the baton twirling of the *majò jonk* descends from Sub-Saharan African practices and may have influenced North American parade choreography (personal communication, Robert Farris Thompson; see also McAlister 1995: 79–81). McAlister further suggests that, "It is likely that American baton twirling, in fact, derives from the Rara festival, and was carried to the United States by Haitian refugees of the independence war of 1804" (79). Abrahams and Szwed call baton twirling a "black cultural innovation" (1983: 1). While there may have been a great deal of intercultural syncretization of baton traditions, and while the tradition may have been significantly elaborated by African American exponents, we maintain that the baton twirling of the *majò jonk* (as well as that in North American parades) is in a direct line with the European military "drum major" tradition, transplanted to both Haiti and Nouvelle Orlèans. The stick or baton of the drum major was used to indicate to the musicians which command signal they were to drum (Kastner 1973: 396, 399). Baton twirlers in North American parades are still called drum majors (and majorettes), and the rank of the baton manipulator is consistently that of major. It is unclear to us presently which if any specific gestures of the *majò jonk* grow out of the signals of the French military drum major.

Living recipients of *ochan*-s are approached for donations with the band's flags, with a basket held by the *renn kòbe* (basket queen), or with some other receptacle for anticipated contributions. The sponsor of a *rara* band is generally a person of some local reputation and relative wealth, who, by sponsoring a cultural group, boosts his or her status and popularity, receives *ochan,* and may take a cut of the group's receipts as repayment.

During Carnival in Port-au-Prince, local pedestrian carnival bands (*bann apye,* or bands-on-foot) and commercial dance bands (*mini-djaz*) that play on flatbed trucks in the carnival parade depend for their remuneration on the mayor's office and central government. Thus one finds *ochan* performed in front of the City Hall, in front of the National Palace, and on the carnival staging grounds on the Champ de Mars, near the National Palace. Many commercial carnival recordings by *mini-djaz* keep the *ochan* section at the opening of their carnival songs (*méringues de carnaval*). We have included a transcription of a carnival *ochan* played by a *rara*-style band outside of the City Hall. Note the strong implication of a harmonic progression, the arpeggiated chord figures, and the alternation between 3/4 and 4/4 meter (Figure 9-7).

Carnival *bann apye* share some of the military nomenclature of *bann rara.* Carnival and *rara* bands move through space in competition with rival bands, they engage in rehearsals, and require a military-like coordination of large groups of people; in this way they are very much like armies. And one should recall that *koudyay,* the delirious ambience of Carnival, is derived historically from the practice of military victory celebrations.

FIGURE 9-7. An *ochan* played by Zepi Band before the mayor's office at Carnival. The trumpet (notated here) was accompanied by *tanbouren, bas,* and Kongo drums along with sticks and rattles. Recorded and transcribed by Averill.

Conclusion

Many of the slaves brought to the colony of Saint Domingue were well acquainted with military strategies, tactics, and organization by virtue of the persistent warfare in parts of West and Central Africa during the period of the middle passage. Some of the resistance to slavery and colonization in the Western Hemisphere arose in maroon communities that were organized as African kingships or as military dictatorships, and militaristic secret societies (along African "national" or ethnic lines) appear to have also been active in the struggle against France. To free the colony of Saint Domingue, however, Haitians reclaimed the French colonial army and made it the instrument of nationhood. Evolving into a paramount institution of the new nation, it left its symbolic and organizational mark on forms of peasant social organization and cultural expression. Haitian peasants defended the critical spaces of economic and social autonomy won by previous generations through employing models of military discipline and militancy. As a result, Haitian peasant history reveals a continued spirit of resistance, generically called *mawonaj* (escape from slavery). Traces of African and colonial militarism in contemporary expressive culture reveal the residue of struggles against slavery, colonialism, and marginalization, and the covert self-organization of African slave society in the Americas.

We have described how militarism has coexisted with—and reinforced—a system of patronage whereby people organize hierarchically to partake in sponsorship of those more powerful than they. We intend for this insight to balance the emphasis that some researchers place on egalitarian and utopian principles in Vodou and peasant social organization.[25] While there are many democratic and egalitarian ideals and practices in Vodou and traditional Haitian peasant culture, peasant life is nonetheless impacted by class and status differentials, unequal access to resources, hierarchies, and subtle forms of patronage and protection.

Military musical organizations have influenced popular culture in two ways: they have served as performers and disseminators of music with a distinct military character and function (e.g., signal music) and as popularizers of music not military in origin but generally of European provenance (including European social dance music). Militarism is audible in *ochan* and *laserenal* praise music and in *rasanble* and *premye anons* calls to assembly, which demonstrate a stylistic relationship to French military signal drumming: unison playing, European instrumentation, drum rudiments, and diatonic melodies that imply European harmonic progressions. In a country where much of the traditional music draws on African aesthetics and performance practices, the preservation of a European-derived repertory and performance practice within genres that refer to power and hierarchy is an intriguing legacy of colonization and a window into the contradictions of the postcolonial experience.

Notes

[1]Versions of this essay were delivered at 1994 meetings of the Society for Ethnomusicology (Milwaukee), the International Association for the Study of Popular Music (Havana), and the Haitian Studies Association (Boston). We would like to thank the many people who provided advice, criticism, and logistical assistance, including Carrol Coates, Julian Gerstin, Roberta Singer, Elizabeth McAlister, Karen Davis, Vincent Hu, Gerdes Fleurant, Giovanna Perot-Averill, and Thomas Turino. We would also like to thank our volume editor, Ingrid Monson, for her help and encouragement.

[2]The cultural effects of militarism have seldom been thoroughly investigated, but a number of works have touched on it at least cursorily. The seminal work in this respect for Haiti is a brief article by Haitian folklorist Emmanuel C. Paul (1954),

"Folklore du militarisme," which outlined the impact of militarism on Vodou, Carnival, and peasant work societies in Haiti. His research is the most influential predecessor of our own work on this subject. More recently, the history of the Haitian military was the subject of Michel S. Laguerre's book, *The Military and Society in Haiti* (1993). Although he does not address cultural issues per se, Laguerre characterizes epochs of Haitian history by analyzing the variable balance of power among the military, civil society, and civil government, and he succedes in demonstrating that a focus on the military is critical "if we are to understand and explain the functioning of Third World societies" (1). Patrick Polk's (1995) article on Haitian ritual flags, "Sacred Banners and the Divine Cavalry Charge," forms a striking parallel with this article. Among other relevant findings, Polk convincingly demonstrates that the regimental colors on the *étendards* (square flags) of Napoleonic demibrigades served as the models for the background patterns on Vodou *drapo* (338). Finally, we should mention a rather idiosyncratic but intriguing book, *Keeping Together in Time: Dance and Drill in Human History,* by William H. NcNeil (1995), which makes a case for a long, intertwined coevolution of military drill, esprit de corps, ritual, and music/dance.

[3]Karen Davis (personal communication).

[4]Before European colonization, indigenous Arawak peoples referred to their island home as Aiti (mountainous land). The name Hispaniola derives from the Spanish La Isla Española and became the commonly used name for the island during the period of Spanish colonization. After the western third of the island was ceded to France in the Treaty of Ryswick (1697), the French colony was named Saint Domingue, while the Spanish colony was commonly referred to as Santo Domingo.

[5]"Ce pays est sans doute l'un des rares examples de communauté nationale à n'avoir jamais connu d'autre état que celui de la guerre." All translations from French and Creole by the authors, except where previously translated. Haiti is a diglossic society; Haitian Creole is the language of daily use for 99 percent of Haitians, but until 1987, French was the country's only official language. Since we make frequent reference to French as well as Haitian culture in this work, italicized terms are sometimes Creole, sometimes French.

[6]The relationship of Haitians to their military involves many contradictions: most are proud of the army's revolutionary tradition, but they have resented and often resisted the army as an instrument of centralized control and domination of the nation by the Port-au-Prince elite. Generals are parodied in popular carnival masques and in songs, yet several Vodou deities are understood to be generals in the spiritual realm.

[7]"[C]es organisations à travers leur diversité ont une structure militaire, une discipline militaire, une hiérarchie militaire encore que les fonctions empruntent des étiquettes politiques, ce qui nous rappelle nos gouvernements militaires d'autrefois. Parmi les noms de ces groupements, nous avons relevé toute une terminologie militaire: Escorte, Escouade, Bataillon, etc. Les titres . . . honorifiques, correspondent à des grades militaires. Et on y tient pour le prestige social qu'ils donnent."

[8]On signal drumming in Africa, see Nketia (1971).

[9]Averill has discussed the political functions of *koudyay* and *ochan* in carnival and in Haitian popular music in general (1994: 217–45; 1997: chapter 1).

[10]"Cet hommage en musique et en paroles se retrouve dans le *koudjay* qui peut être considéré comme un rochan [*sic*] dansé et chanté par toute une foule qui, en cir-

culant dans les rues d'une ville, veut célébrer la visite d'un personnage important (le chef de l'Etat, par example), fêter la nomination à un poste-clé d'une personnalité bien considérée ou tout simplement manifester sa joie à l'occasion d'un événement important . . . Un *koudjay* ne se conçoit d'ailleurs pas sans que le défilé n'ait la maison du célebré pour point tournant de son parcours. Alors, selon une mise en scène, pourrait-on dire, traditionnelle, à la foule qui l'acclame et chante ses mérites, l'homme du jour exprime ses remerciments en faisant un discours du haut de son balcon. Il a aussi le bon goût de manifester d'une manière plus concrète sa satisfaction par quelques largesses, en nature ou en espèces, qu'il pourra faire remettre à tous ses célébrants ou du moins aux musiciens considérés comme les porte-parole du groupe."

[11]This legend is deeply ingrained in the Haitian historical consciousness, but details of the ceremony—and even whether it happened at all—are subject to dispute. The same skepticism prevails in discussions of the role of Don Pedro in inspiring the Petwo rite of Vodou. Whatever the role of Don Pedro, the rite absorbed many of the practices of a healing cult that was popular in Kongo called Lemba. Petwo is apparently still called Lemba-Petwo in some rural areas of Haiti. The prominence of Kongo beliefs and practices in Petwo leads many scholars and even practitioners to refer to Petwo rites as Petwo-Kongo.

[12]The relationship between these two rites is variable in Haiti. Many congregations practice only one or the other. Some congregations practice both but at different times and even in different temples, keeping them ritually discrete. The distinctive drums, rhythmic sequences, song cycles, costuming, and beliefs of these two rites are detailed in most of the major works on Haitian Vodou. Musicologist Gerdès Fleurant (1996) has completed an analysis of the Rada rite and is at work on a companion book on Petwo-Kongo.

[13]Many terms are used for Vodou deities in Haiti. Among them are: *lwa, mistè* (mystery), *zany* (angel), and *envizib* (invisible ones).

[14]Leslie G. Desmangles (1992: 172) notes that Ogun became "identified with the heroes of the revolution, the symbolic embodiers of Vodouisants' national ideal, the bringers of a higher order which was to be a perfected Haiti . . . Thus Ogou Feray has inspired Haitians to resist political and religious suppression many times in their history. His persona reflects Vodou's ability to re-create the past, for in every ceremony in his honor, Vodouisants relive the political and religious traditions of their national past—a symbolic reenactment of the Haitian revolution."

[15]We have modified the Creole spelling to conform to contemporary usage.

[16]This song is included in Laguerre (1980: 177). We have adjusted the Creole spelling to conform to contemporary usage, and we have departed slightly from Laguerre's translation. The image suggested by the riddlelike formula: "my head is in the sea while my tail is in the pond" is of something vast—an army stretching out over great expanse. For translation, Laguerre suggests: "I am a soldier in the army of St. Jacques / His battalion starts on the seashore and reaches the lakeshore / I am a member of this big army," which he interprets as: "St. James is praised as a person of order; he knows how to keep his army together" (ibid.).

[17]This was the election won by Father Jean-Bertrand Aristide. Aristide announced his candidacy rather late and did not attend the *banda* ceremony in question. Although he was a Catholic priest of the Saliesian order at the time of his election, Aristide nevertheless demonstrated his respect for Vodou by wearing a Vodou

vèvè design on his priest's robes and by holding gatherings after his election with Vodou priests.

[18]"Pour rassembler une troupe, ou pour lui faire serrer les rangs lorsqu'elle est rassemblée, on fera appeler les tambours."

[19]See the chapter in Courlander entitled "Land and Work" (1960: 111–21).

[20]This group is now defunct, a casualty of rural migration to the capital.

[21]Majèst is a proper name. It is a common practice in Haitian traditional music for singers to directly address persons present or to otherwise interpolate their own comments in the course of singing a song.

[22]Premye Nimewo can be heard on the recording *Angels in the Mirror: Vodou Music of Haiti* (1997, Ellipsis Arts), coproduced by Holly Nicolas, Yuen-Ming David Yih, and Elizabeth McAlister. Two performances by Premye Nimewo are included: a *mennwat* dance and a Kongo society song. A *laserenal* by the same group is included on *Rhythms of Rapture: Sacred Musics of Haitian Vodou* (1995, Smithsonian/Folkways), produced by Elizabeth McAlister with notes by Elizabeth McAlister, Gage Averill, Yuen-Ming David Yih, Gerdès Fleurant, and others.

[23]At early twentieth-century balls in Les Cayes, *l'annonce* was a brief piece of music indicating which dance would come next. It also gave dancers time to get into formation (personal communication, Marcel Lubin, 1991. Yih interviewed Lubin, a retired lawyer born in 1894, about the elite society balls that he attended in Cayes as a young man).

[24]*Tanbouren* players often use a friction technique called *wonfle* (snore); the tip of the thumb traces a figure eight on the drum head, yielding a continuous groaning sound. This represents a likely creolization: the addition of a West African percussive technique to a French military drum.

[25]See, for example, Fleurant's characterization of Vodou as "non-classist, non-racist and non-sexist . . . hospitable and humanistic" (1995: 9).

References

Abrahams, Roger D., and John F. Szwed. 1983. *After Africa.* New Haven, CT: Yale University Press.

Allen, J. H. 1930. "An Inside View of the Revolution in Haiti." *Current History* 32(2): 325–29.

Averill, Gage. 1994. "*Anraje to Angaje*: Carnival Politics and Music in Haiti." *Ethnomusicology* 38(2): 217–47.

———. 1997. *A Day for the Hunter, a Day for the Prey: Popular Music and Power in Haiti.* Chicago: University of Chicago Press.

Averill, Gage, and Verna Gillis. 1991. Liner notes to *Caribbean Revels: Rara in Haiti, Gaga in the Dominican Republic.* Smithsonian Folkways SF 40402.

Cosentino, Donald J. 1995. "It's All for You Sen Jak!" In *The Sacred Arts of Haitian Vodou,* edited by Donald J. Cosentino. Los Angeles: UCLA Fowler Museum of Cultural History.

Courlander, Harold. 1939. *Haiti Singing.* New York: Cooper Square Publishers.

———. 1960. *The Drum and the Hoe: Life and Lore of the Haitian People.* Berkeley: University of California Press.

Desmangles, Leslie G. 1992. *The Faces of the Gods: Vodou and Roman Catholicism in Haiti.* Chapel Hill: University of North Carolina Press.

Dumervé, Constantin. 1968. *Histoire de la Musique en Haïti.* Port-au-Prince: Imprimerie des Antilles.

Dupuy, Alex. 1989. *Haiti in the World Economy: Class, Race, and Underdevelopment since 1700.* Boulder, CO: Westview Press.

Fleurant, Gerdès. 1996. *Dancing Spirits: Rhythms and Rituals of Haitian Vodun, The Rada Rite.* Westport, CT: Greenwood Press.

Forbath, Peter. 1977. *The River Congo: Discovery, Exploration, and Exploitation of the World's Most Dramatic River.* Boston: Houghton Mifflin.

Fouchard, Jean. 1988. *Plaisirs de Saint-Domingue: Notes sur la vie sociale, littéraire et artistique.* Port-au-Prince: Editions Henri Deschamps.

Hall, Gwendolyn M. 1971. *Social Control in Slave Plantation Societies: A Comparison of St. Domingue and Cuba.* Baltimore: John Hopkins Press.

Heinl, Robert D., Jr., and Nancy G. Heinl. 1978. *Written in Blood: The Story of the Haitian People 1492–1971.* Boston: Houghton Mifflin.

James, C. L. R. 1963. *The Black Jacobins: Toussaint L'Ouverture and the San Domingo Revolution.* New York: Vintage. (Originally published 1938.)

Kastner, Georges. 1973. *Manuel général de musique militaire à l'usage des Armées Françaises.* Geneva: Minkoff reprint. (Originally published 1848.)

Laguerre, Michel. 1980. *Voodoo Heritage.* Beverly Hills, CA: Sage.

———. 1993. *The Military and Society in Haiti.* Knoxville: University of Tennessee Press.

Laroche, Maximilien. 1978. *L'image comme écho: Essais sur la littérature et la culture haïtienne.* Montreal: Les Editions Nouvelles Optiques.

McAlister, Elizabeth. 1995. " 'Men Moun Yo/Here Are the People': Rara Festivals and Transnational Popular Culture in Haiti and New York City." Ph.D. diss., Yale University.

McNeil, William H. 1995. *Keeping Together in Time: Dance and Drill in Human History.* Cambridge: Harvard University Press.

Nicholls, David. 1985. *Haiti in Caribbean Context: Ethnicity, Economy and Revolt.* New York: St. Martin's Press.

Nketia, J. H. K. 1971. "Surrogate Languages of Africa." *Current Trends in Linguistics* 7: 699–732.

Paul, Emmanuel C. 1954. "Folklore du militarisme." *Optique* 6: 24–27.

Polk, Patrick. 1995. "Sacred Banners and the Divine Cavalry Charge." In *The Sacred Arts of Haitian Vodou,* edited by Donald J. Cosentino, 325–47. Los Angeles: UCLA Fowler Museum of Cultural History.

Roumain, Jacques. 1943. *Le sacrifice de tambour-assoto(r).* Port-au-Prince: Imprimerie de l'Etat.

Thompson, Robert Farris. 1984. *Flash of the Spirit: African and Afro-American Art and Philosophy.* New York: Vintage.

Thornton, John. 1992. *Africa and Africans in the Making of the Atlantic World, 1400–1680.* New York: Cambridge University Press.

Trouillot, Michel-Rolph. 1990. *Haiti, State against Nation: The Origins and Legacy of Duvalierism.* New York: Monthly Review Press.

Yih, Yuen-Ming David. 1995. "Music and Dance of Haitian Vodou: Diversity and Unity in Regional Repertoires." Ph.D. diss., Wesleyan University.

CHAPTER 10

Musical Revivals and Social Movements in Contemporary Martinique: Ideology, Identity, Ambivalence

Julian Gerstin

In 1993–95 I lived in Martinique, researching and participating in various genres of music: the drum/dance *bèlè,* Carnival marching bands, jazz combos, Guadeloupean drumming, the martial art/dance *danmyé,* resort hotel re-presentations of *bèlè* and *danmyé,* Afro-Cuban *batá* and rumba, the old popular dance-band styles biguine and mazurka, the newer dance style zouk, and Christmas party songs known as *chanté Nöel.* I observed, without pursuing in depth, many other genres: symphonic music, Trinidadian steel pan, Catholic masses, the reggae-based popular music *ragga,* the Haitian popular dance *konpas,* North American rap, soul, jazz, and gospel, the old quadrille styles *haute taille* and *réjane,* the music of hand-pushed merry-go-rounds or *chouval bois.* And there were other styles, including blendings and permutations of those listed here: jazz and *bèlè, gwoka* and *chouval bois* and zouk, zouk and *ragga* and rap, mazurka and zouk and quadrille. At the same time, I found myself surrounded by a political and literary discourse comprising several competing ideologies, more intense in some contexts than others, sometimes spotlit by the mass media and sometimes not, and linked—but with much crosscutting and with exceptions to every rule—

295

to social groups identifiable by race, age, class, gender, and location. As one might expect, many Martinicans perceived correlations between genres of music and political ideologies. As one might also expect, these correlations were contested. Not everyone saw the same connections or agreed on their meaning.

Certain discontinuities particularly intrigued me. Despite highly political discourse about some genres of music in some contexts, such discourse seemed entirely lacking in others—including some contexts in which such discourse might be expected. For example, virtually no one in publicly visible political or media positions invoked indigenous Martinican musical genres (either traditional or popular) as representations of nationality or ethnicity. Such links are made on virtually every other Caribbean island. Musicians in a number of genres did make such links and attempted to popularize them, but were ignored. I saw this lack of interest as evidence of another type of discontinuity: a lack of coalition between various realms of oppositional discourse and action. What kept highly motivated, like-minded people working in different yet related realms apart from one another? Why was music *not* used more generally as a representation of national or ethnic identity?

Questions like these led me to look closely at two musical genres: *bèlè*, a traditional rural dance/drum style that had been revitalized during the 1980s and 1990s by politically motivated, young, urban performers; and Carnival, also revitalized during the 1980s and 1990s by young, urban performers but with scarcely any political intent. In what follows, I sketch the history of contemporary Martinican ideological discourses, describe their relevance (or lack of relevance) to performers of *bèlè* and Carnival, and suggest how the discontinuities between realms of Martinican oppositional cultural production have been shaped by the island's neocolonial history. The larger theoretical context of this essay is the study of social movements and resistance, particularly the *limits* on social movements and resistance. What circumscribes the possibilities for political mobilization in Martinique?

The extensive sociological literature on "new social movements" (NSMs) is perhaps unfamiliar to many ethnomusicologists (excepting those engaged mainly in popular music studies, such as Eyerman and Jamison [1998], Garofalo [1992], and Pratt [1990]). NSMs have been characterized as arising in the context of postindustrial society (Touraine 1985) in which power is less and less consolidated in the hands of fixed nation-states. Political groups no longer follow class, racial, or ethnic divisions but instead represent a myriad of shifting, interwoven alliances (Laclau and Mouffe 1985). They seek to pluralize existing society rather than revolutionize or dominate it (ibid.); that is, their struggle is a "self-limiting radicalism" (J. Cohen 1985: 664). Their struggle frequently unfolds through de Certeau's everyday "tactics" rather than as a Gramscian battle for hegemony. It thus often takes place outside the political domain, narrowly conceived. NSMs involve interest groups that are not political parties, that seek social changes rather than electoral power. They seek cultural as well as political change; not only political self-determination but also control over identities and their symbolic expression (Melucci 1985).

The NSM literature, which I am only skimming here, seems to offer ethnomusicologists a fruitful approach to what Abner Cohen has termed "the issue of the relation between art and politics," which "is part of the broader question of the relation between culture and power relationships, the central theoretical concern of social anthropology" (1980: 83). (At least, it is *one* of the central concerns of anthropology, and of ethnomusicology as well.) NSM theory highlights the flexible and "relational" (Grenier and Guilbault 1990) construction of social groups. It handles particularly well the subtle interplay of expressive culture, identity, and politics, which is in itself often a key part of the construction of groups. Since the early 1980s, ethnomusicologists and performance theorists have made increasingly strong claims for the constitutive power and "real world" effects of performance (MacAloon 1984; Seeger 1987; Waterman 1990). Good material on this theme may be found in the NSM literature.

In addition, NSM theory, especially its North American "resource mobilization" school, provides detailed analyses of the organization and dynamics of social movements (see Klandermans et al. 1988 and the assessment of this school in J. Cohen 1985). I have drawn on resource mobilization theory, for example, in describing the internal organization of Martinican movements and their ability, or lack of ability, to mobilize popular support.

NSM theory turns also on the question of resistance versus co-optation. The mainstream of NSM theory, as sketched above, finds NSMs an effective (if not the only effective) form of resistance in contemporary global society. Critics of this mainstream tend to feel that real political change involves money, power, and the public sphere, and that the frequent focus of NSMs on culture and identity is "soft" and ineffective. They point out that identity politics leads to balkanization, as small groups concentrate on legitimizing themselves. They claim that the emphasis in NSMs on cultural expression makes them "safe" for elites and the middle classes. (In Martinique, Marxist critics have said much the same thing about the island's literary/intellectual movements; see Blérald 1981 on *négritude*'s "culturalization" of politics.) In its late twentieth-century, First World form, the focus on private self-determination and expression shades into radical-chic consumerism ("buy this product and save the rainforest"). Thus, critics conclude, post-modern capitalism recoups any subversive impetus an NSM may have had (Epstein 1990: 46–47; Kauffman 1990: 78).

In researching Martinican cultural movements, I found it difficult to side with either the NSM mainstream theorists or their critics, impossible to characterize Martinican NSMs as either "political" or "identitary," "oppositional" or "co-opted." In their ambiguity, these movements invoke the highly qualified "everyday resistance" and "hidden texts" to which anthropologists and ethnomusicologists have paid increased attention in recent years (de Certeau 1984; Scott 1990). The studies of qualified resistance by de Certeau, Scott, and their followers often involve situations where overt protest would be dangerous. In contrast, the French state is relatively tolerant of dissent. Nonetheless, Martinican feelings about their situation are both strong and mixed, and the expression of those feelings is ambiguous.

Martinique is an island where outside money controls a moribund economy, where many people depend on French welfare (*assistance*), where people still feel racially oppressed by those on whom they depend, where they feel their own cultural identity slipping away, where dissatisfaction is pervasive. At the same time, the island's standard of living is the highest in the Caribbean in terms of basic services, infrastructure, health care, and the massive presence of imported consumer goods. Thus Martinicans worry about their political and economic *dépendance* even as they fear that greater independence would drop them into the stark poverty of other Caribbean islands ("*haitianisation*"). When discussing the seemingly limited extent of opposition on their island, conservative speakers laugh that French largesse makes life too easy. Radicals state the same sentiment in tones of lament, as, for example, the writer Edouard Glissant, describing Martinicans as a "communit[y] condemned as such to painless oblivion" (1989: 2).

All this strongly reminded me of similar discourse in my own country. During the years in which I lived in Martinique (1993–95), the United States saw a revival of conservative power and an attack on two pillars of the "safety net" established by the federal government under the New Deal and the Great Society, and through the struggles of the civil rights movement: welfare and affirmative action. The conservative argument rested on a variation of the Protestant ethic: government intervention makes people dependent; giving it up will be good for them. This pseudoexplanation perfectly illustrates the power of hegemony to define "reality." It locates the cause of a social phenomenon, poverty, in the effect that phenomenon produces on individuals—or rather, the purported effect: dependency (see Frasier and Gordon 1994 for a dissection of the ideology of "dependency").

But the dependency explanation is true for neither the United States nor Martinique. Dependence on state assistance may make it more difficult for Martinicans to mobilize than would otherwise be the case, but it does not explain the underlying causes of poverty, and it does not explain the structural limitations that have hampered Martinican oppositional social movements—which are rather obvious once one starts looking for them. I begin, then, with a sketch of Martinique's modern history and a survey of the political/cultural ideologies that history has both engendered and circumscribed.

Contemporary Martinican Ideologies

For observers of contemporary Martinique, a pervasive but ambivalent expression of political themes should come as no surprise. Much of the rest of the Caribbean became independent after World War II, but Martinique, then a colony of France, opted in 1946 to incorporate as a full-fledged part of the republic. It became a *département*, the French equivalent (more or less) of a state in the United States. There were several reasons for this. Ideologically, *départmentalisation* flowed logically from France's longtime political/economic/cultural policy of *assimilisation*, itself an outgrowth of the *mission civilizatrice*. The light-skinned *mulâtre* members of the middle class and the professions, a group that had always looked to France as a source of rights and benefits, saw departmentalization as a further step along this road. Departmentalization was popular among the black masses as well, as full citizenship promised equality and an end to racism. In this immediate postwar period, with Martinique newly liberated from a wartime Vichy regime, enthusiasm for the republic ran high. Also during the postwar years, the already well-known poet Aimé Césaire emerged as Martinique's leading politician. A dynamic speaker, Césaire mobilized popular sentiment in favor of departmentalization. Elected mayor of the island's capital, Fort-de-France, and *député* to the *Assemblée National* in 1946, Césaire held both those powerful positions until resigning his role as *député* in 1993; as of this writing (1998) he remains Fort-de-France's mayor.

Martinique's acceptance into the republic did not result in an end to inequality and racism. Civil unrest and militancy marked the period from the late 1950s through the mid-1970s; unions and numerous small, militant *indépendantiste* political parties faced harsh repression from French police forces. Césaire played a difficult mediating role, fighting for economic and social rights in the *Assemblée National* while attempting to curb unrest and to establish various social programs at home. His goal, repeated in numerous speeches, was "autonomy," not "independence." In his fight for civil rights, Césaire revitalized the rhetoric of *négritude,* the literary movement he had helped found in the 1930s. *Négritude* provided a vision of human rights and black pride, a radical vision that Césaire held up to both Martinicans and metropolitan French. On the cultural front, Césaire promoted an arts movement during the late 1960s, the *retour aux sources* (return to roots), which, like *négritude,* looked to Africa for inspiration (although it looked also to the black pride movement in the United States). In the 1970s Césaire institutionalized this movement by founding a series of cultural centers in Fort-de-France, collectively known as SERMAC, which attracted dynamic artists in virtually every field through the 1980s.

Césaire and his party, the Parti Progressif Martiniquais (PPM), gradually won a modest amount of economic and political self-determination for the island, largely in the form of budgetary and administrative control. Such control accrued mainly to the PPM, which as of the mid-1990s still dominated the island's political scene (or at least that of Fort-de-France, the only population center of magnitude), although there were signs this might be changing (Burton 1995a: 16–18). The PPM's centrality has also been due to the drastic decline of Martinique's primary agricultural sector after World War II. As the unemployment rate soared (30 percent and higher since the war), employment has increased only in the tertiary sector (services, tourism, clerical, administration). By the 1960s, the PPM-dominated administration had become the island's largest employer, a position it still retains.

In 1981 France elected a socialist government under François Mitterand. Suddenly the PPM found itself allied with the state, and took advantage of Mitterand's *décentralisation* laws, enacted in 1982 and giving increased autonomy to France's various regional governments, to further entrench its position as the island's political center (Constant 1989, 1993; Hintjens 1994; Réno 1994a, b). Tellingly, after Mitterand's election Césaire called for a "moratorium" on debate about autonomy and independence.

The departmental era, particularly since the 1970s, has also seen a shift in the island's economy to a welfare-fueled consumerism. The old colonial families (the *bèkè*) had held onto their land and capital after abolition (1848). They weathered the decline of the sugarcane-based plantation economy after the development of the European beet sugar industry in the late 1800s, but after World War II, increasingly allying themselves with metropolitan French capital, the *bèkè* moved their money into tourism, construction, finance, transportation, and import-export. Today economic power remains to a remarkable degree in their hands, plus those of their metropolitan partners. The combination of welfare and consumerism benefits them through their control of finance and imports. As Burton puts it, the island is "essentially a consumer colony parasitically dependent on external funds most of which eventually find their way back to source" (1978: 13). Imported consumer goods include cultural goods—the mass media and the arts—with the result that Martinique is becoming ever more and more *assimilée,* and people worry about losing their identity as Martinicans even as they consume French and global goods and culture. (For more extensive interpretations of Martinique's recent political and economic history, see Burton 1978, 1992, 1993; Cabort-Masson 1992; Constant 1989, 1993; Hintjens 1994; Miles 1986; Réno 1994a, b.)

Ambiguity over politics and identity is reflected in the ideologies of Martinique's major contemporary cultural movements. Césaire's *négritude* privileged blackness and African identity, while criticizing whiteness and Eurocentrism. Quite a number of older Martinicans see *négritude* as the first and most radical break with colonial attitudes. However, as numerous early critics of *négritude* pointed out—among them Sartre (1963) and Fanon (1967: 124–33)—simply inverting the negative value placed on blackness was a weak approach, because it accepted the identity of blacks as Other, and the mutual exclusivity of black and white. It even accepted the prevalent white stereotypes about blacks: if whites saw blacks as irrational, *négritude* celebrated irrationality. Moreover, despite his radical rhetoric about culture and identity, Césaire's political program was primarily accomodationist: autonomy, not independence.

In the 1960s, writer Edouard Glissant broke with Césaire and elaborated an alternative philosophy that he called *antillanité* (Glissant 1989).

Glissant, a member of various underground, quasi-militant *indépendantiste* groups in the 1960s, saw political salvation for Martinique as being possible only through alliance with other independent Caribbean nations. Similarly, believing that Martinique's own culture and identity were already nearly effaced by consumerism and assimilation, Glissant felt that Martinicans could salvage a sense of difference only by seeing themselves reflected in the *diversalité* of other, less assimilated Antilleans.

Whereas Césaire expressed his ideas in a populist manner, Glissant's realm was literary and intellectual. Nonetheless, Glissant influenced a younger generation of writers and activists during the late 1970s. By the early 1980s these individuals coalesced loosely into a movement known as *créolité* (Creoleness). Taking their cue from Glissant's *diversalité,* the *créolistes* saw Martinican identity as a hybrid of races and cultures. As the manifesto *Eloge de la créolité* opens, "Neither Europeans, nor Africans, nor Asians, we proclaim ourselves Creoles" (Bernabé et al. 1989; citation from translation by Khyar 1990: 886.) Most immediately, the name *créolité* refers to the Créole language, which the majority of Martinicans speak along with French—a hybrid language, autochthonous in its *metissage*. Denigrated since its emergence, by the 1970s Créole was felt to be endangered, as more Martinicans became educated (in French) and moved into civil service and professional positions, and as French mass media became more pervasive. Many of the early *créolistes,* notably Jean Bernabé and Félix Prudent, were linguists working toward a revival of the language. Others, such as Patrick Chamoiseau and Raphaël Confiant, were novelists attempting to publish in Créole. Frustrated in this attempt, they turned in the mid-1980s to a French studded with Créole expressions and images, with which they achieved great success in the Francophone literary world.

Créolité celebrates Martinican identity as an "open specificity" (Khyar 1990: 892) and a "constant dynamics" (ibid.: 902). It thus contrasts to *négritude*—quite deliberately—by not repudiating the cosmopolitan European element in Martinican identity, but rather embracing that element, along with any remaining African elements (Bernabé et al. 1989; Burton 1992, 1993, 1995b). Similarly, it embraces modernity along with tradition (although some critics suggest that *créolité* slips from this nuanced position into an essentialist nostalgia for tradition; see Burton 1993, 1995b; Price and Price 1997). *Créolité* thus accepts that being Martinican entails a partial assimilation. It views acceptance of this assimilation as more realistic than *négritude*'s repudiation and, therefore, as potentially more effective.

It is no accident that *créolité* came into public view in the early 1980s, after Mitterand's election and the enactment of decentralization. It was at that point that the PPM, allied with France's new socialist government and given a major dose of the local autonomy it had always sought, clearly became Martinique's political establishment. At the same time, the PPM's success in creating a viable oppositional space, one that the state tolerated rather than overtly repressed, allowed other local political parties to emerge (Burton 1993; Constant 1989, 1993; Hintjens 1994; Réno 1994a, b). The 1980s and early 1990s saw a proliferation of such parties, a phenomenon that economist Fred Réno labeled "the creolization of [Martinican] politics" (Réno 1994a: 13). Réno's phrase illuminates several facets of these parties: they are local, home-grown, and hybrid, embracing a variety of positions from left to right. (The new parties tend toward the Left, but at least one of them, the Mouvement Liberal Martiniquais, is led by a *bèkè* who appropriates *créoliste* rhetoric to argue for increased autonomy for local business.) The parties question Martinique's relation with France and call for varying degrees of increased autonomy (up to and including independence). Yet in practical terms, the new parties' challenge is directed mostly against the local hegemony of the PPM. Finally, the new parties are "creole" in the sense that some of their most visible public supporters and proselytizers are the writers of the *créolité* movement.

The *rapprochement* between *créolité* and Martinique's new political parties can perhaps best be seen through the example of one such party, MODEMAS (Mouvement des Démocrates et Ecologistes pour une Martinique Souveraine). Since 1989 this party has governed the southern tourist center of Ste.-Anne. MODEMAS is sponsored by the environmental action group ASSUAPAMAR (Association pour la Sauvegarde du Patrimoine Martiniquais), founded in 1981 (note the year) by Garcin Malsa, now Ste.-Anne's mayor. "Ecology-conscious" unaffiliated mayors were also elected in 1989 in the tourist centers of Trois-Ilets and Le Diamant (Burton 1992: 73). The emergence of environmental politics in tourist towns is not coincidental. Tourism represents encroaching modernity in, literally, concrete terms: the creeping *bètonisation* ("concrete-ization") of Martinique's landscape. The environmentalists share much of the rhetoric of *créolité,* speaking of Martinique's landscape as its national heritage with the same intensity as the *créolistes* speak of Créole. The environmentalist slogan *sauvegarder et promouvoir* (safeguard and promote) looks, as does *créolité,* both to past and future, tradition and modernity. And in a striking case of intellectual influence, the environmentalists have borrowed from the *créolistes* an image that the latter borrowed from the bowels of French intellectual-ism. This is the image of identity as "rhizomatic"—that is, as intercon-nection and relation—in contrast to the more common image of identity as "roots," which suggests separate, autonomous organisms (Deleuze and Guattari 1980; cf. Burton 1993: 16). *Créolistes* and environmental-ists use the rhizome image when speaking of Martinique's endangered mangrove swamps, where the trees actually are interconnected organ-isms, and the image evokes the interrelations and flexibility of Carib-bean identity.

To date, the new parties have won elected positions mostly in the towns and *communes* outside Fort-de-France, which remains loyal to the PPM. On the cultural front, *créolité* has been successful in instilling Martinicans in all sectors of society with a sense of pride in their Créole language, which is increasingly used in the media, in political oratory, and in everyday public settings (though not in the schools or print jour-nalism). The novelists Chamoiseau and Confiant have between them won most of France's prestigious literary awards. At a less publicly visi-ble level, *créolité* has provoked a revival of Martinique's storytelling tra-dition, *kont kwéyol,* which had been kept alive by only a few old men.

Each of the ideologies described here—*négritude, antillanité, créo-lité,* the new political parties, environmentalism—is pulled between the tendency toward assimilation and the assertion of difference. Césaire's *négritude* was radical in rhetoric, yet political realities forced on him a more moderate position—autonomy, not independence. Glissant, who thought Martinican identity already destroyed, looked for a hybrid dif-ference in Caribbeanness; his major influence was not on the public but on the *créolistes*. The latter, along with the new political parties and the environmentalists, embrace assimilation and modernity within differ-ence and tradition. They posit a flexible sense of identity that allows people to resist, yet also to accommodate to, the dominant realities of modernity, hybridization, and assimilation. Likewise, the political cli-mate of the 1980s and early 1990s—the Mitterand era—allowed a lim-ited localization of power, an alternative that accommodated to the dominant system. *Créolité,* in particular, with its links to the new politi-cal parties, reflects this situation: it is a postcolonial ideology mired in a neocolonial society.

The ambivalence of these ideologies is reflected also in their apparent marginality. *Négritude* has long been the quasi-official philosophy of the PPM, and *créolité* has a certain amount of media exposure. Yet for the most part the arguments of, and between, these ideologies remain the concerns of intellectuals. The pictures of identity that these schools paint may be accurate, and their accomplishments in the realms of language, literature, and local politics may be real, yet they remain limited in their public appeal. Despite ambivalence about change and loss, locality and globality, in their daily lives, most Martinicans seem to negotiate complex identities without too much fuss. A mid-1990s survey of public opinion concluded, "*Négritude* is relegated to secondary importance, and the concept of *créolité* seems to have run out of breath without ever having been important to anyone but a minority of intellectuals" (*France-Antilles* 1994: 4). I agree only partly with this statement: *négritude* and *créolité* have perhaps not mattered to the general public as dogma, but their effects have been broad nonetheless. *Négritude* has had a pervasive impact on Martinican ideas similar to that of the civil rights and black power movements in the United States; *créolité* has changed public acceptance of the Créole language. On the other hand, no common articulated philosophy seems to prevail.[1]

The *Bèlè* Renewal: Tradition as a New Social Movement

How do these ideological issues play out in the world of performance? My research in Martinique focused on *bèlè*, a dance/drum genre with strong rural roots (Gerstin 1996). In the early 1980s, after undergoing a partial eclipse during the previous two decades, *bèlè* was revived by a generation of performers and activists largely from urban Fort-de-France. Within the limited world of *bèlè* the renewal[2] has been successful: the art is performed, taught, and honored to a far greater extent than previously and has been made viable in contemporary urban society, or at least in its margins. The aim of the renewalists is in large part political: to assert Martinican identity through its traditional dance and music. To a large extent, the renewalists explain their goals in the language of *négritude* and *créolité*. Given this ready-made connection, it would seem that the *bèlè* renewal should be a gift to political thinkers, a living example of their ideas. Yet the renewal has been virtually ignored by politicians, the media, and the public. Why?

Martinicans use the term *bèlè* to refer to a number of genres associated with rural life, plantations, and distant African origins. More specifically it refers to a genre of dances from the island's North Atlantic coast, particularly the countryside around the town of Ste.-Marie. A similar set of dances from the south is distinguished as *bèlè du sud*. Other regional dance-drum forms include *lalin klé* (full-moon dances) and *kalenda*, both originally from the North Atlantic area. The martial art/dance *danmyé* (or *ladja*) was traditionally practiced throughout the island, including the cities. Performers and others with specialized knowledge may draw a distinction between the Ste.-Marie *bèlè* dances proper and these others, or may lump them all together as *bèlè*. I will follow this last usage except where I need to be more specific.

These dances share a similar history. They are all "neo-African" styles (Roberts 1972) that developed on plantations during slavery. In Martinique as elsewhere in the diaspora, slaves were allowed their own outdoor dances on Saturday afternoons and nights, after Mass on Sundays, and on holidays. In the 1700s *contredanse* (line dancing) was imported from France, followed by quadrille (square dancing) from the 1780s through the 1820s (Cyrille 1989; Rosemain 1986). Both of these originally elite genres became widely popular, found their way into the Martinican countryside, and developed into regionalized styles. The current Ste.-Marie *lalin klé* dances, which use line and circle choreography, developed from *contredanse*. *Bèlè*, which incorporated quadrille, probably consolidated around 1820–40. In common with a number of Caribbean quadrille traditions, *bèlè* requires specialized knowledge—the complex choreography of the quadrille—and is therefore a prestigious dance, at least in its traditional rural setting (Lafontaine 1982; Rey-Hulman 1986). It is restricted to eight dancers (four couples) at a time. In contrast, *lalin klé* dances employ a simpler choreography, utilize the lead singer as a *koumandé* (caller), and are open to as many couples as wish to dance at one time. However, today both *bèlè* and *lalin klé* are performed at the same events: primarily *swaré bèlè* (*bèlè* evenings), evenings of participatory dancing, drumming, and singing. *Kalenda* (successive soloists), *danmyé* (successive pairs of combatants), and *bèlè du sud* (unlimited couples or individuals) may also be performed at contemporary *swaré bèlè*. From perhaps the mid-nineteenth century until World War II, *swaré bèlè* in the Ste.-Marie area were organized primarily by a network of large rural families that reciprocated host and guest roles and that produced a large portion of the more skilled performers.

Despite the readily apparent European influences on *bèlè* and *lalin klé* choreography, for most urban Martinicans in the departmental era these forms have evoked African origins and their unhappy consequences: rural poverty, plantation life, and racial dilemmas. While the choreography of the dances may be European based, movements (*gestes*) are perceived as African based. Musical accompaniment consists of call-and-response singing, one or more drums, and supporting percussion, all perceived as African in origin. *Bèlè* performers are stereotyped as rural, poor, black, uneducated, and old. Virtually every Martinican has family members living in, or only recently removed from, rural poverty, and most people have no desire to see that life invoked musically. Internal racism may also be a factor; the marginal urban middle classes have little desire to identify with blackness when blackness in turn signifies poverty. Urban Martinicans, who constitute the bulk of today's population, have a long history of indigenous popular genres with which to identify, each of them signifying, in their time, cosmopolitanism: biguine (popular from the nineteenth century until the 1960s), zouk (1980s and 1990s), *ragga* (1990s). In fact, most urban Martinicans view *bèlè* as old-fashioned, in the way that most people in the United States view square dancing. Intellectuals and political activists soured on *bèlè* during the 1950s–1970s because of its demeaning, folkloricized presentation in the tourist troupes that flourished during those years. Musicians involved in the *négritude*-inspired *retour aux sources* of the late 1960s–1970s, many of whom took up drumming as a symbol of Africanity, turned not to the shabby homegrown article but to the more exotic, seemingly authentic *gwoka* drumming of Martinique's sister *département*, Guadeloupe. (To a lesser extent, they turned to French West African *djembe* drumming.) *Gwoka* is now better known in Martinique than *bèlè*, and could be described as an indigenized and resignified tradition (Manuel 1994). Finally, rural life was severely disrupted beginning in the 1950s, sending thousands of Martinicans to the city and from there to metropolitan France and straining the family-based social network that supported *bèlè* performance. This contributed to the urban perception of *bèlè* as an outdated, moribund art.

The *bèlè* renewal that emerged in the early 1980s attempted to change perceptions of *bèlè* and of Martinican identity in general. The renewal's leaders are mostly men in their 30s and 40s. They have grown up and been educated in the city and have established professional careers, yet they are old enough to remember when rural poverty dominated the lives of most Martinicans, and to have been shaped politically by Martinique's active labor and *indépendentiste* movements of the 1960s and early 1970s. In many ways they exemplify what various writers have stated about the role of organic intellectuals in social movements. Organic intellectuals—or grassroots activists—are effective because they are embedded in local social networks and cultural systems. In addition to being organizational foci, they become forgers of new meanings and new ways in which to communicate those meanings (Hannerz 1992: 246–55; Klandermans and Tarrow 1988: 7; Melucci 1988: 343; Touraine 1985: 760–61).

Most of the renewalist groups are organized as *associations de 1901,* roughly equivalent to incorporated nonprofit organizations in the United States. Association status allows the groups to seek certain government funds, although to my knowledge such funds made up, during the period of my fieldwork, only a small part of the income of a single *bèlè* association. A great many Martinican voluntary associations of all types, in fields from sports to retirement clubs to Carnival, are formally organized as *associations de 1901.* The prevalence of voluntary associations in Martinique may recall the mutual aid organizations familiar from the literature on Africa and its diaspora, but the associations are also thoroughly French; *associations de 1901* have played a major role in at least one French grassroots political movement (Alland 1994).

In the 1993–95 period there were perhaps a dozen *bèlè* associations. Their activities included producing tourist shows at resort hotels, performing onstage for Martinican audiences at town fêtes and other celebrations, producing public *swaré* in towns across the island (events open to participation by all), teaching dance and music classes for adults at cultural centers and for children in the schools, publishing texts and instruction books, documenting rural musicians through recordings, recording their own versions of traditional material, producing radio programs on *bèlè* and related traditions, and occasionally performing as entertainment at political rallies. Each *bèlè* association orients itself to certain of these activities. The tourist-oriented troupes do little more than hotel shows, although at least one, Wapa, also offers public dance classes. Several groups—Fleur de Créole, Bel Alians, Maframé, Matchoukann, Rézistans—limit themselves to onstage performances for local audiences, dance classes in schools, and an annual or semiannual *swaré.* They might also play an occasional show at a resort hotel, appear at a political rally, or undertake a short tour to a neighboring island. These groups tend to be organized by younger male performers from the city, around a core of one or two older, traditional performers from the Ste.-Marie area, with younger performers from either Ste.-Marie or Fort-de-France filling the remaining roles. One association, Bèlènou, an offshoot of the Marxist political party APAL (Asé Pléré An Nou Lité, "enough crying, let's fight"), views its primary mission as political activism. Bèlènou was one of the first *bèlè* associations to organize in the early 1980s, and it promoted awareness of *bèlè* by organizing public *swaré* throughout the island, thus expanding beyond *bèlè*'s regional North Atlantic origins.

The largest renewalist association, AM4 (Association Mi Mes Manmay Matinik), covers the widest range of activities: all of those I have listed *except* tourist performance. AM4 views its mission as primarily teaching and promoting a broad range of what it terms "Afro-Martinican" indigenous traditions: the panoply of North Atlantic dances, *bèlè du sud,* and the martial art *danmyé*. It offers the largest selection of dance and music classes of any renewalist group, at several locations throughout the island. AM4's core members are as politically minded as those of Bèlènou, and occasionally AM4 dancers and musicians perform at political events—for example, at an ASSUAPAMAR/MODEMAS environmental rally or in support of a political prisoner. (These are the only occasions in which the group performs onstage for the public.) At the same time, AM4's leaders view their cultural activism as inherently political: "A Martinican culture exists . . . To defend it is to preserve our specificity, to bring forth and stabilize the bases of the new Martinican culture . . . a new culture because it must take into account the sociological givens of the modern epoch" (AM4 1987).

But AM4's leaders see any political realization of their vision for Martinique and Martinicans as far in the future; their immediate work is culturally oriented. They avoid identification of AM4 with any political parties, feeling that blatant advertisement of their political positions could scare off potential students, many of whom are politically unformed urban youth. They also wish to avoid alienating elder rural performers, many of whom are somewhat conservative when it comes to national politics. Finally, while AM4's core members study with and befriend elder rural performers on an individual basis, AM4 as a whole avoids too-close association with any of the recognized elders, in order not to antagonize other elders in that rather cliqueish world.

Although AM4's mission is traditionalist, the group balances traditionalism with adaptations to modernity. Notice that in the quote above the group states its goal as using tradition to "bring forth" a "new Martinican culture," one that takes "into account the sociological givens of the modern epoch." The past will survive only if it can be made relevant to the present and future. This twin aim is reflected in the practices of AM4 and other renewalist groups: updating *swaré bèlè* and holding them in urban settings and in towns outside their original North Atlantic region; offering classes; publishing, documenting, and recording—all activities of the modern world. AM4 even shares the backward-and-forward-looking slogan *sauvegarder et promouvoir* with the environmentalists of ASSUAPAMAR/MODEMAS. As Jocelyne Guilbault writes, local actors in "the global/local nexus" have typically "generated two types of actions, one directed to the protection, the other to the promotion of the local cultural capital and identity" (1993b: 34–35). Contemporary Martinican oppositional movements tend to do both.

Ideologically, the renewalist leaders have been influenced by both *négritude* and *créolité*. Consisting mostly of men now in their 40s (born just after World War II, at the beginning of departmentalization), they are old enough to recognize *négritude*'s impact. As Georges Dru, president of AM4, put it, "Césaire was a point of departure" (interview). The influence of *négritude* is perhaps visible in the renewalists' representation of *bèlè* as a "national" art. Here the term *nation* is both political (a comment on Martinique's ambiguous status vis-à-vis France) and racial, in the sense that "nation" has been used historically throughout the Caribbean as a synonym for "tribe" (e.g., "the Ibo nation," "the Kromanti nation"). As a "national" art, *bèlè* is not limited to the Ste.-Marie region or to the past; yet it is coterminous with a political and racial definition of Martinicans that is somewhat essentialized, as is *négritude*'s. On the other hand, the *créolistes* also use the term *nation* in reference to Martinican identity.

As for connections between *créolité* and the *bèlè* renewalists, AM4 conducts all its business in Créole, a deliberate choice made in support of *créoliste* ideas. More profoundly, both groups have a vision of Martinican identity that embraces the present/future along with the past. Both speak of revitalizing tradition by making it viable in modern life, and of rejuvenating modernity, spiritually and morally, by turning to tradition. Both groups even show similar ambiguities in this regard: although they speak of modernizing tradition, they tend to glamorize a somewhat nostalgic view of the past (see Burton 1993, 1995b; Price and Price 1997), and even a nostalgic, essentialized view of the Créole language (Price and Price 1997; Prudent 1993). The renewalists seem to struggle with this tendency to reify the past, deliberately trying to modernize in many contexts yet, particularly when asserting their authority, falling back on tradition's claim to authenticity. In any case, the similarities between the ideas of the two movements are clear. It is difficult to say whether this is a case of direct influence or parallel evolution, a similar response to the hybrid facts of contemporary Martinican life. I suspect that at times the renewalists intentionally appropriate ideas from *créolité* because the latter's image of tradition-as-relevant-to-modernity helps legitimate *bèlè* to the urban public: to the youth from whom they recruit most of their students, to their sympathizers, and to one another.[3] Nonetheless, the renewalists avoid direct association with the *créolité* movement, just as they avoid association with *négritude,* and for the same reason: so as not to limit their appeal to those who support any one position.

For their part the media, politicians, and the ideologues of both *négritude* and *créolité* all ignore *bèlè*. One reason may be that French culture glorifies literature, and it is no accident that *négritude, antillanité,* and *créolité* have all been authored by poets and novelists. Yet *bèlè* should make a good symbol of Martinican identity, particularly for the *créolistes*. It is clearly an indigenous hybrid: Martinican, not African; sung in Créole on local topics; danced with African-looking movements in a European quadrille format; originally from the country but revived in the city. Consider one choreographic detail: in the *bèlè* dances proper, dancers enter the dance area in a counterclockwise ring before forming their two squares; they exit at the end of each dance in the same way. Whether or not it would be historically accurate, it would be easy to portray the ring as African, framing the European quadrille (cf. Lafontaine's interpretation of Guadeloupean dance sets, 1982). I am further surprised by the fact that, if *bèlè* does not capture the *créolistes'* attention, they seem equally oblivious of other dance/music genres. Martinique's long tradition of urban popular musics (biguine, zouk, *ragga*), its urban populist tradition of Carnival, its Creolized quadrilles *haute taille* and *réjane,* even its recent adoption of Guadeloupean *gwoka*—any or all of these could be portrayed as indigenous hybrids combining tradition and modernity.

Similarly, the majority of the general public ignores *bèlè*. A number of people told me that the public finds the art too old-fashioned. But I never heard anyone offer this as their own opinion, only as something they imagine others think. Media attention to this art, or its appropriation by a political platform, could easily spark public enthusiasm. Why, then, the current situation?

To understand *bèlè*'s continued marginalization it is important to see the *bèlè* renewal in the light of a more general observation: *all* of the realms of oppositional cultural production in contemporary Martinique are limited in their public appeal and isolated from one another. This includes the new political parties, *créolité,* the environmental movement, the *kont kwéyol* revival, and the first stirrings of a women's movement (see Leonard 1997). The general circumscription and fragmentation of Martinican social movements can best be seen as a result of historical and structural factors, the cautious play of resistance and accommodation that has characterized Martinican politics and ideology for the past five decades. But before I venture further thoughts on this topic, I wish to present, briefly, a second case study: the Carnival renewal. The Carnival renewal echoes that of *bèlè* in its history and organization, yet Carnival is even further isolated from Martinican politics.

The Carnival Renewal: Revels without Rebellion

Until recently the anthropology of Carnival has rested on ideas of resistance and subversion. Victor Turner's writings on Carnival (1969, 1974), reinforced by those of Bakhtin (1984), led to a general view of Carnival as a site for liminality, inversion, antistructure, and, by extension, political unrest (see Da Matta 1984). Some writers (Bettleheim 1990; Lafontaine 1983) associate Carnival not so much with resistance as with the co-optation of resistance, as when governments allow Carnival to the masses as a safety valve for their frustrations, or when corporations commercialize Carnival's subversive energy. However, the majority of recent authors view Carnival as *both* subversive *and* co-optable. Because Carnival celebrations are public, massive, intense, and *potentially* disruptive, they become contested ground, with different sides seeking to control and impose meaning on events (Averill 1994; A. Cohen 1980, 1993; Cowley 1996; de Albuquerque 1990; de Oliveira Pinto 1994; Hill 1972; Kasnitz 1992; Manning 1990; Ness 1992; Sommers 1991; Stewart 1986; Treitler 1990). My position is essentially that of these authors, with one nuance: I would warn against assuming that Carnival is necessarily contested ground, that it entails some innate powerful energy that is *there* to be let loose or co-opted. In Martinique I found a Carnival with very little political resonance either way, a Carnival without catharsis.

The early history of Martinique's Carnival is rather like that of many other Caribbean islands. Originating in elite masked balls in the seventeenth and eighteenth centuries, Carnival celebration passed after emancipation (1848) to the affranchised *mulâtres* who formed the upper crust of nonwhite society. The *mulâtres'* glittering Carnival remained separate from that of the masses, which also emerged after emancipation and which was held in the street and periodically suppressed (Julien-Lung Fou 1979; Rosemain 1986). Over time this separation grew less rigid, but it persisted until recently, with wealthy members of society organizing the indoor events such as Carnival song competitions, elections of Carnival Queens, and expensive *soirées* or *zouks* (paid-admission parties). After the complete destruction of Martinique's capital, St.-Pierre, by the eruption of Mt. Pèlè in 1902, the new capital of Fort-de-France became the center of Carnival activity. Both elite and street Carnival waxed and waned through the twentieth century, depending on economic and political circumstances. World War II put a temporary end to Carnival as Martinique fell under Vichy rule, but after the war the celebration was relaunched by *associations de 1901* run by members of bourgeois *mulâtre* society, with aid from the Ministry of Tourism (Bertrand 1965, 1967; Bontemps 1965).

Before World War II and during the first two decades after the war, Carnival music was played by "spontaneous" groups of musicians—the term *spontaneous* encompasses both informally planned, little-rehearsed groups of friends, and groups formed by chance encounters in the streets—and by professional musical groups, usually riding on the backs of trucks. (The *vidé* recorded on Lekis and Lekis 1953 is an example of the latter.) However, according to informants, by the 1970s sound trucks had virtually replaced live bands. Carnival was said to have died.

Then, in 1984, a group of friends from Fort-de-France organized a *group à pied* (marching band) using empty plastic food barrels as drums and calling themselves Plastic System Band. By 1986 Plastic System had become a registered *association de 1901* with standardized, well-made instruments and costumes, tightly rehearsed songs and choreography, sixty-odd percussionists, a brass section with about a dozen players, a dance brigade of about fifty women (*suiveurs,* "followers"), a scaled-down performing unit for paying gigs consisting of a small percussion section and electric instruments (Plastic System Band 1992), and an ambitious program of live appearances in many venues and promotion through the media. Other *groups à pied* quickly followed; there were about two dozen in the 1994 and 1995 Carnivals. Largely due to public interest in the new groups, Martinican Carnival enjoyed a resurgence in the late 1980s and early 1990s. Note that this is the same time period during which the other cultural and political movements I have discussed also emerged.

Most Carnival *groups à pied* are associated with specific localities—for example, Tanbou Bô Kannal consists largely of youths from the impoverished Bô Kannal neighborhood of Fort-de-France. In contrast,

Plastic System—which I joined as a percussionist for the 1994 Carnival season—recruits from the entire Fort-de-France area. Its members identify with one another not by locality but by class, labeling themselves, with a touch of self-mockery, "bourgeois." They are largely what we would call white-collar workers: lycée teachers, lower-level managers, self-employed entrepreneurs. The group raises most of its funds from membership dues, paid performances, and the band's annual *zouk* (paid-admission dance party). In 1995 Plastic System received commercial sponsorship from a fruit juice company, but this constituted only a small portion of its budget. Other Carnival bands are less ambitious than Plastic System but are organized and funded similarly. If bands want corporate sponsorship they must seek it themselves; businesses do not seek them out. Town and *commune* administrations hire bands to play for public pre-Carnival and Carnival events, but this is still not a major source of income. Nor is tourism closely linked with Carnival. A certain number of metropolitan French and Martinicans living in France fly to the island for Carnival, but tourism is nowhere near the level of Trinidad, Brazil, or New Orleans.

The *groups à pied* share the street during Carnival with other forms of expression: massive sound trucks sponsored by radio stations; costume associations, with dozens of people in theme costumes and their own small sound trucks; small semiorganized and unplanned groups of musicians; dozens of nearly derelict cars, heavily decorated and deafeningly loud; traditional masking and cross-dressing; individuals carrying homemade signs on political or sexual themes; and the scapegoat King of Carnival, Vaval, a huge papier-mâché puppet who is burned and tossed into the sea on Carnival's final evening. The various mobile music makers (*groups à pied,* spontaneous bands, sound trucks) attract dozens of followers, dancing and singing behind. These crowds are known as *vidés*—Carnival music is also *vidé*—and there is informal competition between groups to attract the largest, densest, rowdiest *vidé*. Meanwhile, indoor Carnival activity unfolds with a song contest, elections of Carnival Queens, and privately organized *zouk* parties.

The point of this listing is that Carnival expression is quite varied. Correspondingly, Carnival organization is decentralized. In Fort-de-France, representatives of the Carnival associations meet a few times during Carnival season, along with city and police officials, as an umbrella association, Fédération Carnaval Martinique (FECAMA), which discusses such matters as traffic control and the parade route. Otherwise each group is on its own. One association, the Association Carnaval

Foyal (ACF), organizes the major indoor events in Fort-de-France, the Carnival Queen contest and the song competition, and also builds the focal figure of street Carnival, Vaval. Like the *groups à pied,* the ACF is basically a group of lower-middle-class enthusiasts. It receives no government or commercial funds. In 1994 I had a hard time simply locating the ACF, which had no office and no phone listing. When I finally found the house of the association's president, Josiane Trèbeau, just three days before the start of Carnival, I was surprised by the casual atmosphere there. On the veranda, several young women sewed costumes for Mme. Trèbeau's daughter's lycée Carnival Queen competition—the association had not even begun the costumes in which it would accompany Vaval. In an empty, weed-covered parking lot behind the house I met Charly, a welder, reshaping the rusty armature of the previous year's Vaval into a new figure and covering it with cloth, which he would later paint. Charly worked alone. That was the "center" of Carnival. (I should note that the ACF was more casual than some other groups. Plastic System, for example, set up a costume and instrument-building workshop in the garage of one of its core members, where about thirty people worked together every evening for the three weeks before Carnival.)

If centralization were present, it might be linked to government or commercial control, but that is not the case. Political interest in Carnival is scant; politicians do not look to Carnival groups to carry their messages, to appear with them at rallies, or to be used in any of the other ways Carnival groups are frequently used elsewhere. Members of Plastic System pointed out to me that, because they are not sponsored by corporations or the government, they remain free to express themselves as they wish. In fact, however, Carnival groups rarely profess political messages; Carnival participants, unlike the *bèlè* renewalists, do not link their art to ideology. In this the Carnival renewal contrasts sharply to numerous other Carnival-based movements: *blocos Afro* in Brazil (Crook 1993; Crowley 1984), the Carnival resurgence led by the group Akiyo (1993) in Guadeloupe (Martinique's sister island and, like Martinique, effectively a neocolonial outpost of France), and others.

There are limited exceptions to Carnival's general apoliticality. Unaffiliated individuals parade with signs or costumes satirizing politics and politicians. Vaval, the King of Carnival, is represented each year as a different character, and the choice tends toward mild political satire. In 1990 the hit song "Voici les loups" (Dezormo 1990) represented Martinique as a sheep menaced by the Big Bad Wolf of the European Community, due to unify in 1992. Vaval that year was a wolf gobbling a globe. In 1994 Vaval was a generic politician, Lulu Badjol ("Lulu Hot Air"), also taken from a popular hit, Taxikréol's "Special Request" (Taxikréol n.d.). These are rather safe satires. As Josiane Trèbeau of the ACF explained to me, "We can't be too political." In 1992, the quincentenary of Columbus's landing—an event whose interpretation was debated hotly throughout the Caribbean—the ACF decided against representing Vaval as a conquistador, because, according to Trèbeau, associating a conquistador with the scapegoat Vaval "might offend some people."

Nor does Carnival become a site for the expression of class tensions. Again, this diverges from the picture of Carnival painted by most theorists, who either glorify Carnival's inversions as promoting a nonhierarchical *communitas* (Da Matta 1984) or interpret those same inversions as dramatizing "precisely delineated [class] structures and . . . confirming these through performance" (de Oliveira Pinto 1994: 35). In Martinican Carnival, class divisions are obscure. In many Caribbean Carnivals indoor, exclusive events belong to the elite and outdoor, inclusive events to the masses. In Martinique, associations like Plastic System and the ACF—working-class and lower-middle-class groups of friends and Carnival enthusiasts—have largely taken over the former organizing functions of the elite. The bourgeois committees that resurrected Carnival after World War II and filled the society pages of the newspaper with their foibles and bickering (Bertrand 1965, 1967; Bontemps 1965) have disappeared. Many wealthy and middle-class Martinicans no longer attend street Carnival, although they may go to private *zouks*. On the other hand, middle- and working-class people engage in both street and indoor activities; for example, Plastic System, ostensibly a street group, organizes a very expensive annual *zouk* as one of its main fund-raisers.

The obscurity of class divisions in Martinique results partly from the prevalence of government assistance and the continued mutual support of family networks, which make it very difficult to classify people into neat economic brackets. Martinicans avoid being associated with poverty by dressing stylishly and acting in a cosmopolitan manner. As in much of the Caribbean, Martinicans contrast rowdy behavior, poverty, and street life against respectability and middle-class life (Abrahams 1983; Wilson 1973). This may help account for several aspects of Carnival: the popularity of the *groups à pied*—street groups, but with flashy costumes and tight choreography that speak of money and organization; the waning of elite participation; and a general air of restraint in Carnival crowd behavior.

Martinican Carnival crowds are reserved; many if not most people simply watch. Martinicans point out with pride that their Carnival is nonviolent, in contrast to those of Brazil or Trinidad. Public sexual display is muted. Even getting publicly drunk is uncool. In its general restraint, Carnival behavior reflects the atmosphere of everyday Martinican city life, which is more formal, nonaggressive, and nonviolent than elsewhere in the Caribbean or, indeed, than in the United States. At small festive gatherings Martinicans enjoy what they call a sense of fête: a sophisticated, relaxed mingling, extroverted but not aggressive. Settings for this experience include paid-admission *zouk* clubs as well as more casual, intimate groups of friends and family, gathered for parties, meals, or Sunday outings. Carnival seems not to invert this sense of decorous fun, but to focus it.

The sense of decorum found in everyday public life and focused into a sense of fête on festive occasions could be considered a "style" as described by Raymond Williams: a socially constructed, pervasive "structure of feeling" (1977: 128–35). As many ethnomusicologists have argued, performance makes pervasive cultural patterns vivid and convincing through heightened, participatory experience. Writers on Carnival have typically seized on this idea, treating Carnival's massive, heterophonic expressions as necessarily intense and cathartic. But Martinicans themselves do not seem to view Carnival as cathartic.[4] Many claim that Carnival participation is on a long-term decline, despite the surge in interest sparked by the *groups à pied*. They blame this decline on the passive consumerism fostered by *modernité*, on the loss of *spontanéité* (a term that connotes idealized images of premodern authenticity). "We have lost our sense of fête," a friend stated to me. I do not think he is alone in this feeling.

One particular element of the carnivalesque on which many writers focus is the public display of sexuality. Heterosexual activity is carried on openly (inverting the norm of privacy), and cross-dressing inverts or blurs sexual categories. But in Martinican Carnival there is no nudity, and little overt sexual activity (people making out or making love in public). And as Scheper-Hughes points out for Brazil (1992: 480–504), sexual costuming does not imply an egalitarian release from everyday roles; rather, it consists largely of women undressing for men's pleasure, and men dressing as women in ways that demean women. Many Martinican men wear wigs, padded bras, and skirts or tights, but they always leave mustaches or hairy legs showing conspicuously. This may be because they do not want to be mistaken for *makumés* ("fags") (Murray 1996), because they wish to make fun of women, or both. In addition, many of these men carry homemade signs criticizing women and their supposed behavior. Conversely, very few Martinican women dress as men. Even in the traditional *marriage burlesque* costume duo of a bride and groom, one sees more male-male couples (with one partner dressed as the "bride") than male-female partners (with both partners cross-dressed). Whether or not a woman is involved, the "bride" is always much taller than the "groom," and the point of the joke seems to be the inappropriate power of the "woman," the impotence of the man.

Sexuality in Martinican Carnival is, in effect, the public performance of male dominance. Whereas everyday public life may be marked by decorum, in private domestic life abuse, rape, incest, and abandonment are common (Gautier 1995; Leonard 1997; Louilot and Crusol-Baillard 1987). The one public sex act I saw in two years of Carnival was performed by two men, one dressed as a woman, the other pretending to fuck "her" violently; the point of the act seemed to be "her" screams. Martinican Carnival does not invert male and female roles; the inversion consists of the public display of normally hidden tensions.

By portraying Martinican Carnival renewal as nonpolitical, non-cathartic, and sexually nonegalitarian, I have attempted to question the assumptions sometimes made about Carnivals in general. However, this is only a secondary topic within this article, and I now wish to return to the main theme: to consider Carnival along with the *bèlè* renewal as case studies of oppositional cultural movements in Martinique. If these movements are limited, as I believe they are, why is this so?

Limits on Oppositional Social Movements in Martinique

It is always difficult to explain why something does not exist. Ostensibly, it does not exist simply because nothing has caused it to exist. There ought to be stronger opposition in Martinique, many Martinicans feel, but there is not. Perhaps, they continue, if there were more of something missing—more overt poverty, more overt state repression, or a less seductive life of *assistance* making us passive and dependent—then there would be stronger opposition. Yet no one wants this to happen. And perhaps it is too late and we have lost our chance.

This litany is close cousin to the ideology of dependency so familiar to those of us from the United States. It errs in blaming social ills on putative individual psychology. It also errs in attempting to explain a phenomenon on the basis of something that does not exist: *if there were* more of this, *if there were* less of that, then there might be . . . It neglects to look for what *does* exist: a network of constraints on oppositional mobilization, manifest in political and cultural institutions and ideologies. It is easy to recognize these constraints if one traces their development historically. I cannot claim that if these constraints were not there, then oppositional mobilization would be more prevalent. This would be to assume simplistically that opposition ought to be present a priori when people face oppression. But the constraints exist. It is important to examine them, if only to derail the pseudoexplanations that blame Martinicans as individuals for large-scale social problems.

Césaire's long administration, spanning the entire postcolonial, departmental era since 1946, successfully struggled for a degree of autonomy within the French state. But this led to the establishment of the PPM-dominated administration as a "political class." Moreover, the political establishment exercises power largely in one limited domain, the administration of funds, themselves largely drawn from the French state. The election of a socialist government in 1981 opened a space for increased local autonomy, which led to two contrasting developments: the further entrenchment of the existing establishment and the proliferation of new political parties and cultural movements. The latter, in turn, have been pulled in two directions: on the one hand their ideologies and rhetoric question Martinique's relationship to France, the global capitalist system, and modernity in general; on the other hand their practical efforts go into small-scale challenges to the local political establishment and to prevailing cultural trends.

Thus the contemporary movements operate within highly circumscribed fields: within a space of actions tolerated by the state, against specific local political institutions, and toward the revival of specific traditions (e.g., the Créole language, Créole storytelling, *bèlè*). Such circumscription helps explain why each contemporary movement seems preoccupied with establishing its own legitimacy, carving out its own sphere of action; why they do not ally with one another; and why they appeal only to the small portion of the public that is inclined to pay attention to their particular spheres of action (literature, language, music, etc.). *Créolité* and the new political parties have received a fair amount of public recognition and media attention, and *créolité* has been able to capitalize on the high prestige of literature in the French world. *Bèlè,* on the other hand, enjoys no such advantages. This, to me, explains more about the limited appeal of the *bèlè* renewal than does the (putative) fact that people perceive *bèlè* as "old-fashioned."[5]

A more particular limit on Martinican oppositional movements may be found in their internal organization, typically as *associations de 1901* or political parties led by a handful of organic intellectuals. Alland (1994) draws attention to the proliferation of *associations de 1901* within the Larzac movement, a 1980s French regional movement for the preservation of land rights, ecology, and rural traditions. The multiplication of associations focused on related but differing goals allowed individuals to mobilize according to their predilections (162). As in Martinique, associations coalesced around small cores of organic intellectuals; Alland describes associations in the Larzac movement as "a particularly strong form of social structure, invented by strong individuals" (158).

However, this form of organization is decentralized and can become fragmented. If key individuals fail to perform, or if outside circumstances cause difficulties, followers may drift away, and there is no backup. For example, just before the 1995 Carnival I returned to the Trèbeau's house to observe the ACF's preparations. I found the house empty and boarded up. The Trèbeau family seemed to have fallen on hard times, nobody filled the gap, and there was no song contest, Carnival Queen competition, or Vaval in Fort-de-France that year.

Martinique's political, economic, and cultural history and current circumstances generate a pervasive emotional ambivalence. On the one hand there seems to be widespread resentment of dependence and assimilation, of modernity and all it implies—passive consumption, the loss of traditions, the dissolution of community. On the other hand there is a fear of independence and an attraction to French/global culture, material goods, and sophistication. This ambivalence is reflected in the complex ideologies of Martinique's oppositional cultural movements. It helps explain their limited appeal. However, it seems self-defeating and reductionist to lament, as many Martinicans do, that opposition has been entirely tamed. Despite the reality of ambivalence, there persists a tenacious sense of racial and cultural difference. As one observer puts it, Martinicans engage in a "continuous balancing" (Réno 1994a: 8) between two inconclusive, compromised positions: a resented dependence and an ambiguous opposition. The flexibility with which they negotiate these positions is itself part of their "style," their *créolité*.

Is the personal political? Can art be politics? Are NSMs effective? I cannot hope to answer such questions, other than to say that the answers are probably not either/or. Martinican oppositional social movements refute easy generalizations about terms such as *resistance, opposition,*

containment, or *co-optation.* They accommodate, yet are still oppositional. Rather than debate such abstractions abstractly, I have turned to
what ethnography does so well: it opens a window into the lived experience of history, of relations of power and relations between people. I
have attempted to show the particular historical and organizational circumstances that have shaped Martinican social movements and the ways
in which they have responded, why they might simultaneously resist and
accommodate, and how they operate in the spheres of both politics and
expressive culture. In interpreting this ethnographic material, I have
found NSM theory particularly valuable, with its close attention to the
flexible workings of power and symbol in everyday life. In return, the
ambiguities of Martinique's contemporary political and cultural scenes
generate rich possibilities for exploring social movements.

Acknowledgments

Versions of portions of this essay have been presented to the Society for
Ethnomusicology, October 1996, the American Anthropological Associ-
ation, November 1996, and the Latin American Study Group, Wesleyan
University, December 1997. Research was undertaken with the aid of
the J. W. Fulbright Foundation, Wenner-Gren Foundation for Anthropo-
logical Research, and University of California, Berkeley. For discussion
and criticism of ideas I would like to thank Gage Averill, Ilesa Barbash,
Kathleen Chen, Vévé Clark, Dominique Cyrille, Alan Dundes, Marius
Gottin, Nelson H. H. Graburn, Jocelyne Guilbault, Adam John, Jill
Leonard, Fred Réno, Aletha Stahl, John Stiles, Lucien Taylor, Bonnie
Wade, and all of the Martinican performers and commentators involved,
especially Daniel Bardury, Loulou Boislaville, Félix Casérus, Paco
Charley, Georges Dru, Pierre Dru, Alan Genviéve, Eric Grenet, Nico
Grenet, Charly Labinsky, Malou Mongis, Patrick Mongis, Siméline
Rangon, Paulo Rastocle, Josiane Trèbeau, Victor Treffre, and the mem-
bers of Association Mi Mes Manmay Matinik, Bel Alians, Maframé,
Plastic System Band, and Tanbou Bô Kannal.

Notes

[1]The *France-Antilles* survey found most young people, when queried about
their beliefs, mixing together in a somewhat undefined, not-yet-ideological manner

négritude's idea of racial, pan-diasporic links, *créolité*'s acceptance of hybridity and modernity, plus a general identification with African culture, or, more precisely, Africa as represented by North American consumer culture in music videos, sports, and fashion. The survey dubbed this mixture *blackitude* (ibid. 1994: 4). I never heard anyone actually use this anglicism, but it seems to capture a prevalent attitude. The music that appears to express this attitude is *ragga* (or *raggamuffin*), a mixture of Jamaican dancehouse, African American rap, and localized touches: the stick rhythm *tibwa* that is common to *bèlè*, biguine, and zouk, plus singing in Créole. In the 1980s zouk, then a new genre, created a wave of excitement, signifying contemporary French Antillean identity in its biguine- and *vidé*-based rhythms, Créole lyrics, and sophisticated production values (Guilbault 1993a). In the 1990s zouk has already come to seem the music of the middle-aged mainstream, and ragga represents youth's self-identity (Yerro 1993).

[2]I prefer the word *renewal* to the more obvious choice, *revitalization,* because in anthropology *revitalization* refers specifically to movements arising in tribal societies (or marginal groups within the global world system) that are religious and apocalyptic, and that draw rigid lines between insiders and outsiders (lines with ethnic or nationalist connotations) (Wallace 1956). These characteristics are not necessarily true for oppositional cultural movements in Martinique. For example, Martinique can be considered marginalized within and by the world system, but none of its cultural movements are religious.

[3]The *bèlè* community includes a still sizable number of performers from small towns and the countryside. These performers are stereotypically thought of as *les anciens*, "elders"; as older, poor, and uneducated. The elders take little interest in the intellectual world of the city and the political ideas of the renewalists, although they appreciate the renewalists' work in reviving *bèlè*. The renewalists tend to deemphasize their ideology in situations that involve the elders—which include most performance situations. Here, renewalists almost universally defer to the elders' aesthetic knowledge and moral authority. For a closer look at relations between these sectors as manifested in representations of tradition and the phenomenon of reputation, see Gerstin (1998).

[4]Perhaps at the paid-admission zouk parties, which many people attend at night after daytime Carnival events in the streets, people find sexual or other consummations. As Guilbault (1993a) makes clear, part of the appeal of zouk music is that it replicates the rhythms and participatory cues of Carnival *vidé*. Zouk is danced by couples while *vidé* is danced by individuals in crowds; however, both take place in crowds of strangers. As one of Guilbault's informants puts it, the ideal experience of zouk is "couples, in the midst of a crowd, all doing the same thing, together" (ibid.: 4). Perhaps the zouk experience brings together the carnivalesque crowd of strangers, the couple and their intimacy, and a setting sanctioned by being indoors and costly (as were former elite Carnival activities). Zouk also elicits the "sense of fête": individuals experiencing themselves in an outgoing, casual way within groups. According to Guilbault's informants, when zouk is played at family rituals, communions, baptisms, and so forth, it engenders this feeling (ibid.: 4).

[5]An article by Grenier and Guilbault (1997) raises issues similar to mine about constraints on cultural production. The article describes two musical movements, zouk and the Québéçois musical mainstream, which are both hybrid cultural manifestations crossing national, ethnic, and artistic boundaries and appealing to various

specific audiences. They also cross economic boundaries, disrupting some of the dominant currents of international commodity circulation; for example, zouk circulates in a "polylateral" market in the Caribbean and its diaspora. Yet Grenier and Guilbault warn that the same "strategies of valorization through which these musics are produced and marketed are monitored, controlled" (230). The blurring of boundaries does not give these musics universal appeal, rather an eclectic appeal to limited audiences. Paths of production and distribution are also circumscribed.

References

Abrahams, Roger D. 1983. *The Man-of-Words in the West Indies: Performance and the Emergence of a Creole Culture.* Baltimore: Johns Hopkins University Press.

Akiyo. 1993. *Mouvman.* Déclic 066–2.

Alland, Alexander, Jr., with Sonia Alland. 1994. *Crisis and Commitment: The Life History of a French Social Movement.* Yverdon, Switzerland: Gordon & Breach Science Publishers.

AM4 (Association Mi Mes Manmay Matinik). 1987. "Des Connections Fondementales." Fort-de-France: unpublished paper.

Averill, Gage. 1994. "Anraje to Angaje: Carnival Politics and Music in Haiti." *Ethnomusicology* 38(2): 217–48.

Bakhtin, Mikhail. 1984. *Rabelais and His World.* Bloomington: Indiana University Press.

Bernabé, Jean, Patrick Chamoiseau, and Raphaël Confiant. 1989. *Eloge de la créolité.* Paris: Gallimard.

Bertrand, Anca. 1965. "Images de Carnaval à Fort-de-France." *Parallèles* 4: 5.

———. 1967. "Carnaval à la Martinique et à la Guadeloupe." *Parallèles* 21: 4–15.

Bettleheim, Judith. 1990. "Carnaval in Cuba: Another Chapter in the Nationalization of Culture." *Caribbean Quarterly* 36(3 & 4): 29–41.

Blérald, Alain-Philippe. 1981. *Négritude et Politique aux Antilles.* Paris: Editions Caribeennes.

Bontemps, Grazielle. 1965. "Les Souvenirs de Grazielle Bontemps." *Parallèles* 4: 12.

Burton, Richard D. E. 1978. *Assimilation or Independence? Prospects for Martinique.* Montreal: Centre for Developing-Area Studies, McGill University.

———. 1992. "Toward 1992: Political-Cultural Assimilation and Opposition in Contemporary Martinique." *French Cultural Studies* 3: 61–86.

———. 1993. "Ki Moun Nou Ye? The Idea of Difference in Contemporary French West Indian Thought." *New West Indian Guide/Nieuwe West-Indische Gids* 67(1&2): 5–32.

———. 1995a. "The French West Indies *à l'heure de l'Europe*: An Overview." In *French and West Indian: Martinique, Guadeloupe, and French Guiana Today,* edited by Richard D. E. Burton and Fred Réno, 1–19. Charlottesville: University Press of Virginia.

———. 1995b. "The Idea of Difference in Contemporary French West Indian Thought: Négtitude, Antillanité, Créolité." In *French and West Indian: Martinique, Guadeloupe, and French Guiana Today,* edited by Richard D. E. Burton and Fred Réno, 137–66. Charlottesville: University Press of Virginia.

Cabort-Masson, Guy. 1992. *Les Puissances d'Argent en Martinique: le Nouveau Leadership Bèkè 1981–1991*. St.-Joseph, Martinique: Laboratoire de Recherches de l'A.M.E.P./Editions La V.d.P.

Cohen, Abner. 1980. "Drama and Politics in the Development of a London Carnival." *Man* 15(1): 65–87.

———. 1993. *Masquerade Politics: Explorations in the Structure of Urban Cultural Movements*. Berkeley: University of California Press.

Cohen, Jean L. 1985. "Strategy or Identity: New Theoretical Paradigms and Contemporary Social Movements." *Social Research* 52(4): 663–716.

Constant, Fred. 1989. "Les usages politiques de la décentralisation dans les D.O.M.: le cas de la Martinique." *Cahiers de l'Administration Outre-Mer* 2: 43–65.

———. 1993. "The French Antilles in the 1990s: Between European Unification and Political Territorialization." *Caribbean Studies* 26(3–4): 293–310.

Cowley, John. 1996. *Carnival, Canboulay and Calypso: Traditions in the Making*. Cambridge: Cambridge University Press.

Crook, Larry. 1993. "Black Consciousness, *Samba Reggae*, and the Re-Africanization of Bahian Carnival Music in Brazil." *World of Music* 35(2): 90–108.

Crowley, Daniel J. 1984. *African Myth and Black Reality in Bahian Carnaval*. Los Angeles: UCLA Museum of Cultural History.

Cyrille, Dominique. 1989. "Quadrilles Nègres: Contribution à l'Étude des Musiques et Danses Introduites à La Martinique entre 1780 et 1840." Master's thesis, Université Paris Sorbonne.

Da Matta, Roberto. 1984. "Carnival in Multiple Planes." In *Rite, Drama, Festival, Spectacle: Rehearsals Toward a Theory of Cultural Performance*, edited by John J. MacAloon, 208–40. Philadelphia: Institute for the Study of Human Issues.

de Albuquerque, Klaus. 1990. " 'Is We Carnival': Cultural Traditions under Stress in the U.S. Virgin Islands." In *Caribbean Popular Culture*, edited by John Lent, 49–63. Bowling Green, KY: Bowling Green State University Popular Press.

de Certeau, Michel. 1984. *The Practice of Everyday Life*. Berkeley: University of California Press.

Deleuze, Gilles, and Félix Guattari. 1980. *Mille plateaux*. Paris: Editions de Minuit.

de Olivero Pinto, Tiago. 1994. "The Pernambuco Carnival and Its Formal Organisations: Music As Expression of Hierarchies and Power in Brazil." *Yearbook for Traditional Music* 26: 20–38.

Dezormo, Djo. 1990. *Voici les loups (Europe des EEC)*. CocoSound 88031/CS525.

Epstein, Barbara. 1990. "Rethinking Social Movement Theory." *Socialist Review* 20(1): 35–65.

Eyerman, Ron, and Andrew Jamison. 1998. *Music and Social Movements: Mobilizing Tradition in the Twentieth Century*. Cambridge: Cambridge University Press.

Fanon, Frantz. 1967. *Black Skin, White Masks*. New York: Grove.

France-Antilles. 1994 (15 Jan.). "Quête d'identité." P. 4.

Frasier, Nancy, and Linda Gordon. 1994. "Dependency Demystified: Inscriptions of Power in a Keyword of the Welfare State." *Social Politics* (Spring): 4–29.

Garofalo, Reebee, ed. 1992. *Rockin' the Boat: Mass Music and Mass Movements*. Boston: South End Press.

Gautier, Arlette. 1995. "Women from Guadeloupe and Martinique." In *French and West Indian: Martinique, Guadeloupe, and French Guiana Today*, edited by Richard D. E. Burton and Fred Réno, 119–36. Charlottesville: University Press of Virginia.

Gerstin, Julian. 1996. "Traditional Music in a New Social Movement: The Renewal of *Bèlè* in Martinique (French West Indies)." Ph.D. diss., University of California, Berkeley.

———. 1998. "Reputation in a Musical Scene: The Everyday Context of Connections Between Music, Identity, and Politics." *Ethnomusicology* 42(3): 385–414.

Glissant, Edouard. 1989. *Caribbean Discourse: Selected Essays.* Charlottesville: University Press of Virginia.

Grenier, Line, and Jocelyne Guilbault. 1990. " 'Authority' Revisited: The 'Other' in Anthropology and Popular Music Studies." *Ethnomusicology* 34(3): 381–97.

———. 1997. "*Créolité and Francophonie* in Music: Socio-Musical Repositioning Where It Matters." *Cultural Studies* 11(2): 207–34.

Guilbault, Jocelyne. 1993a. *Zouk: World Music in the West Indies.* Chicago: University of Chicago Press.

———. 1993b. "On Redefining the 'Local' through World Music." *World of Music* 35(2): 33–47.

Hannerz, Ulf. 1992. *Cultural Complexity: Studies in the Social Organization of Meaning.* New York: Columbia University Press.

Hill, Errol. 1972. *The Trinidad Carnival: Mandate for a National Theatre.* Austin: University of Texas Press.

Hintjens, Helen. 1994. "Evolution Politique et Constitutionnelle des Antilles Françaises Depuis 1946." In *Les Antilles-Guyane au rendez-vous de l'Europe: le grand tournant?* edited by Richard Burton and Fred Réno, 19–35. Paris: Economica.

Julien-Lung Fou, Maire-Thérèse. 1979. *Le Carnaval aux Antilles.* Fort-de-France: Editions Désormeaux.

Kasnitz, Philip. 1992. *Caribbean New York: Black Immigrants and the Politics of Race.* Ithaca: Cornell University Press.

Kauffman, L. A. 1990. "The Anti-Politics of Identity." *Socialist Review* 20(1): 67–80.

Khyar, Mohammed B. Taleb. 1990. "In Praise of Creoleness." Translation of Jean Bernabé, Patrick Chamoiseau, and Raphaël Confiant, 1989, *Eloge de la créolité. Callaloo* 13(4): 886–909.

Klandermans, Bert, and Sidney Tarrow. 1988. "Mobilization into Social Movements: Synthesizing European and American Approaches." In *From Structure to Action: Comparing Social Movements across Cultures,* edited by Bert Klandermans, Hanspeter Kriesi, and Sidney Tarrow, eds., 1–38. International Social Movement Research Annual, Vol. 1. London: JAI Press.

Klandermans, Bert, Hanspeter Kriesi, and Sidney Tarrow, eds. 1988. *From Structure to Action: Comparing Social Movements across Cultures.* International Social Movement Research Annual, Vol. 1. London: JAI Press.

Laclau, Ernesto, and Chantal Mouffe. 1985. *Hegemony and Socialist Strategy: Towards a Radical Democratic Politics.* London: Verso.

Lafontaine, Marie-Céline. 1982. "Musique et Société Aux Antilles: 'Balakadri' Ou le Bal de Quadrille au Commandement de la Guadeloupe: un Sense, une Esthétique, une Mémoire." *Présence Africaine,* special edition *Présence Antillaise,* no. 121–22: 72–108.

———. 1983. "Le Carnaval de l' 'Autre.' " *Les Temps Modernes,* nos. 441–42: 2126–73.

Lekis, Walter, and Lisa Lekis. 1953. *Caribbean Dances.* Folkways FP 6840.

Leonard, Jill Autumn. 1997. "Martinican Women and the French State: Race and Gender in the Construction of the Colonial Relation." Ph.D. diss., University of Illinois at Champaign-Urbana.

Louilot, Germaine, and Danielle Crusol-Baillard. 1987. *Femme Martiniquaise: Mythes et Réalités*. Fort-de-France: Editions Désormeaux.

MacAloon, John, ed. 1984. *Rite, Drama, Festival, Spectacle: Rehearsals Towards a Theory of Cultural Performance*. Philadelphia: Institute for the Study of Human Issues.

Manning, Frank. 1990. "Overseas Caribbean Carnivals: The Art and Politics of a Transnational Celebration." In *Caribbean Popular Culture*, edited by John Lent, 20–36. Bowling Green, KY: Bowling Green State University Popular Press.

Manuel, Peter. 1994. "Puerto Rican Music and Cultural Identity: Creative Appropriation of Cuban Sources from Danza to Salsa." *Ethnomusicology* 38(2): 249–80.

Melucci, Alberto. 1985. "The Symbolic Challenge of Contemporary Movements." *Social Research* 52(4): 789–816.

———. 1988. "Getting Involved: Identity and Mobilization in Social Movements." In *From Structure to Action: Comparing Social Movement across Cultures*, edited by Bert Klandermans, Hanspeter Kriesi, and Sidney Tarrow, 329–48. International Social Movement Research Annual, Vol. 1. London: JAI Press.

Miles, William F. 1986. *Elections and Ethnicity in French Martinique: A Paradox in Paradise*. New York: Praeger.

Murray, David. 1996. "Homosexuality, Society and the State: An Ethnography of Sublime Resistance in Martinique." *Identities: Global Studies in Culture and Power* 2(3): 249–72.

Ness, Sally Ann. 1992. *Body, Movement and Culture: Kinesthetic and Visual Symbolism in a Philippine Community*. Philadelphia: University of Pennsylvania Press.

Plastic System Band. 1992. *Itinéraire*. Rhythmo-Disc AD40143.

Pratt, Ray. 1990. *Rhythm and Resistance: Explorations in the Political Uses of Popular Music*. Media and Society Series. New York: Praeger.

Price, Richard, and Sally Price. 1997. "Shadowboxing in the Mangrove." *Cultural Anthropology* 12(1): 3–36.

Prudent, Félix. 1993. "Political Illusions of an Intervention in the Linguistic Domain in Martinique." *International Journal of the Sociology of Language* 102: 135–48.

Réno, Fred. 1994a. "Repenser le Changement: Universalisme et créolisation aux Antilles et a la Guyane." In *Les Antilles-Guyane au rendez-vous de l'Europe: le grand tournant?* edited by Richard Burton and Fred Réno, 5–17. Paris: Economica.

———. 1994b. "Politique et Société à la Martinique." In *Les Antilles-Guyane au rendez-vous de l'Europe: le grand tournant?* edited by Richard Burton and Fred Réno, 69–83. Paris: Economica.

Rey-Hulman, Diana. 1986. "Faiseurs de Musique a Marie-Galante." In *Les Musiques Guadeloupéennes dans le Champ Culturel Afro-Américain au Sein des Musiques du Monde*, edited by Marie-Céline Lafontaine, 115–39. Paris: Editions Caribéennes.

Roberts, John Storm. 1972. *Black Music of Two Worlds*. New York: William Morrow.

Rosemain, Jacqueline. 1986. *La Musique dans la Société Antillaise, 1635–1902*. Paris: L'Harmattan.

Sartre, Jean-Paul. 1963. *Black Orpheus*. Paris: Présence Africaine.

Scheper-Hughes, Nancy. 1992. *Death without Weeping: The Violence of Everyday Life in Brazil*. Berkeley: University of California Press.

Scott, James C. 1990. *Domination and the Arts of Resistance: Hidden Transcripts*. New Haven, CT: Yale University Press.

Seeger, Anthony. 1987. *Why Suya Sing: A Musical Anthropology of an Amazonian People*. Cambridge Studies in Ethnomusicology. Cambridge: Cambridge University Press.

Sommers, Laurie Kay. 1991. "Inventing Latinismo: The Creation of 'Hispanic' Panethnicity in the United States." *Journal of American Folklore* 104(411): 32–53.

Stewart, John. 1986. "Patronage and Control in the Trinidad Carnival." In *The Anthropology of Experience*, edited by Victor Turner and Edward M. Bruner, 289–315. Urbana: University of Illinois Press.

Taxikréol. n.d. *Special Request*. Debs TKD 001-4.

Touraine, Alain. 1985. "An Introduction to the Study of Social Movements." *Social Research* 52(4): 749–87.

Treitler, Inga. 1990. "A Case Study in Political Resistance: Antigua Carnival '87." In *Caribbean Popular Culture*, edited by John Lent, 37–48. Bowling Green, KY: Bowling Green State University Popular Press.

Turner, Victor. 1969. *The Ritual Process*. Chicago: Aldine.

———. 1974. "Liminal to Liminoid in Play, Flow, and Ritual: An Essay in Comparative Sociology." *Rice University Studies* 60(3): 53–92.

Wallace, Anthony F. C. 1956. "Revitalization Movements." *American Anthropologist* 58: 264–81.

Waterman, Christopher Alan. 1990. " 'Our Tradition Is a Very Modern Tradition': Popular Music and the Construction of Pan-Yoruban Identity." *Ethnomusicology* 34(3): 367–80.

Williams, Raymond. 1977. *Marxism and Literature*. London: Oxford University Press.

Wilson, Peter J. 1973. *Crab Antics: The Social Anthropology of English-Speaking Negro Societies of the Caribbean*. New Haven, CT: Yale University Press.

Yerro, Phillipp. 1993. "Stars in the Night: Société, reggae, ragga en Martinique." *Tyanaba 3: Harmonies du Desordre: Musiques et Sociétés d'Afrique et d'Amérique*, 87–92.

CHAPTER 11

Art Blakey's African Diaspora

Ingrid Monson

> It's just that I feel that African thing: it has a good beat and something that gets to the soul. There's nothing wrong with technique, but I like to keep it swinging, do something that moves an audience.
>
> ART BLAKEY 1961 (JONES 1961)

> Jazz is known all over the world as an American musical art form and that's it. No America, no jazz. I've seen people try to connect it to other countries, for instance to Africa, but it doesn't have a damn thing to do with Africa.
>
> ART BLAKEY 1971 (TAYLOR 1993)

> Of course, I'd get a tremendous kick out of taking the group to Africa. When I was there [in West Africa] ten years ago, I didn't play at all. Kind of like to make up for that now.
>
> ART BLAKEY 1957 (TYNAN 1957)

Art Blakey's enigmatic statements about Africa have long been a source of puzzlement and speculation. Blakey's dismissive comments about the connection between jazz and African music have often been invoked to undermine the position more commonly taken in the post–civil rights era that jazz is deeply connected to Africa. Yet Art Blakey was one of the first jazz musicians to travel to Africa (in the late 1940s) and did so not as a musician on tour but in order to study religion and philosophy. Blakey's music, moreover, tells a different story than his words, especially his recordings in collaboration with Afro-Cuban musicians at the time of Ghana's independence in 1957. Unraveling Art Blakey's relationship to the African diaspora necessitates exploration of three contexts pertinent to understanding the relationship of African American music and culture to Africa in the mid-twentieth century: (1) anticolonialism, pan-Africanism, and Islam from the 1920s through the 1940s; (2) African independence, Afro-Cuban music, and religion in the 1950s; and (3) the indefinite nature of music signification. A rather extended historical discussion is required.

Anticolonialism, Pan-Africanism, and Islam

From the Pan-Africanism of W. E. B. Du Bois to the black nationalism (and internationalism) of Marcus Garvey and Malcolm X, African American leaders have consistently looked beyond America's borders for solutions to domestic racism. The look toward Africa and other regions of the non-Western world has been primarily political for some and essentially cultural and spiritual for others. The 1940s witnessed a peak of internationalism in the African American political consciousness and a growing interest in Islam, especially the multiracial version of the Muslim faith propagated by the Ahmadiyya movement. Art Blakey and several other jazz musicians, including Ahmad Jamal, Yusef Lateef, McCoy Tyner, Dakota Staton, Rudy Powell, and Sahib Shihab, were members of the Ahmadi community (Turner 1997: 139; McCloud 1995: 20).[1] Musicians in the 1940s were also affected by the towering presence of Paul Robeson, whose anticolonialism and antiracism was combined with a deep interest in Africa. Blakey was surely shaped by both the political and religious interests of his peer group, company that included Charlie Parker, Dizzy Gillespie, Thelonious Monk, Mary Lou Williams, and Billy Eckstine.

In politics, a left-leaning internationalism emerged among African Americans in the early 1940s through the combined efforts of W. E. B. Du Bois, Paul Robeson, and the Council on African Affairs (CAA). African Americans viewed the domestic struggle for civil rights as obviously connected to the anticolonial and nationalist aspirations or the colonized regions of the globe, which intensified in the wake of World War II. This broadly anticolonialist perspective earned the support not only of leftists but also of more mainstream African American leaders such as Adam Clayton Powell Jr. (then a New York City councilman), Walter White, executive director of the NAACP, and Mary McLeod Bethune of the National Council of Negro Women (Von Eschen 1997: 73–74). The pages of African American newspapers, such as the Pittsburgh *Courier,* the Baltimore *Afro-American,* and the Chicago *Defender,* regularly reported international events such as the independence struggle in India, labor strikes in the Gold Coast (now Ghana), and the working conditions of gold miners in South Africa. African American leaders routinely linked the domestic fight against racism to an anti-imperialist perspective similar to the following position taken by Walter White in 1945: "the struggle of the Negro in the United States is part and parcel of the struggle against imperialism and exploitation in India, China, Burma, Africa, the Philippines, Malaya, the West Indies, and South America" (Von Eschen 1997). This alliance of leftists and liberals, as Penny Von Eschen has convincingly shown, was only possible before the postwar bipolar division of the world into communist and anticommunist spheres of influence, after which criticism of American foreign policy by African American leaders became tainted with the suspicion of communist influence.

Paul Robeson was the figure through which many jazz musicians came to know this perspective. Robeson had become interested in African culture and politics while in London in the mid-1930s, where he met several future leaders of the African independence movement, including Kenya's Jomo Kenyatta, Ghana's Kwame Nkrumah, and Nigerians Nnamdi Azikiwe and K. O. Mbadiwe (Von Eschen 1997: 54–56).[2] In London he also became acquainted with Jawaharlal Nehru's sister Vijaya Lakshmi Pandit, who informed him of anticolonial efforts in India (29). In 1937 Robeson and Max Yergan founded the International Committee on African Affairs, which was reorganized in 1942 as the Council on African Affairs (CAA). The organization had as its purpose educating the American public about Africa and facilitating study by African students in the United States (17–20).

Robeson's prestige cannot be overestimated as an inspiration to many in the entertainment industry. Robeson's highly successful appearance as Othello on Broadway in 1943–44 was viewed as a watershed event, and many jazz musicians took notice, including Dizzy Gillespie, who attended opening night (Gillespie 1979: 288). For the first time a black man had been cast in a major production of what was considered one of the greatest roles in theater. When Ben Davis Jr., a Communist party member, ran for a seat on the New York City Council in late 1943, Robeson performed a scene from *Othello* at a victory rally organized by Teddy Wilson. Among other performers participating in the all-star show were Coleman Hawkins, Billie Holiday, Pearl Primus, Hazel Scott, Mary Lou Williams, and Ella Fitzgerald. Not long after, twelve thousand people turned out for a 46th birthday celebration for Robeson on 16 April 1944 at the Armory at 34th street and Park Avenue in New York City. Among the performers were Count Basie, Duke Ellington, and Mary Lou Williams (Duberman 1988: 283–85). Another enthusiastic admirer of Robeson was Charlie Parker, who was known to go out of his way to hear any Robeson performance. In 1951, after Robeson's passport had been revoked by the State Department, Parker even sought Robeson out at Chicago's Pershing Hotel because he wanted to shake his hand and tell him personally, "you're a great man"(397).[3] Robeson was also one of the most prominent voices in the 1940s directing the attention of mainstream civil rights leaders to African struggles against colonialism.

The popular legitimacy of an anticolonial internationalist perspective was also encouraged by the founding of the United Nations in 1945, whose organizing conference included much debate over how colonial subjects should be represented. Within six months of the conference (which opened on 25 April), two major gatherings were held dedicated to the rights of African colonial subjects and developing a means for representing them in the United Nations. W. E. B. Du Bois organized a meeting of several organizations to discuss proposals that had originated at the Pan-African Congress held in Manchester, England, in 1945, and the African Academy of Arts and Research (AAAR) held another. The AAAR was headed by Kingsley Ozoumba Mbadiwe,[4] a Nigerian who had been encouraged to study in the United States by activist newspaper editor Nnamdi Azikiwe. Dizzy Gillespie met Mbadiwe in New York in the mid-1940s and later gave a benefit concert for the AAAR at the Diplomat Hotel with Max Roach, Charlie Parker, and a group of African and Cuban drummers. Gillespie (1979: 290) spoke about doing several concerts for the organization in his autobiography: "Those concerts for the African Academy of Arts and Research turned out to be tremendous. Through that experience, Charlie Parker and I found the connections between Afro-Cuban and African music and discovered the identity of our music with theirs. Those concerts should definitely have been recorded, because we had a ball discovering our identity."

Gillespie's well-known collaborations with Chano Pozo in 1947, including George Russell's "Cubana Be, Cubana Bop" (Russell 1947), consequently took place during a peak of anticolonialist discussion in the African American press. Although the seeds of Gillespie's interest in

Cuban music had been sown much earlier (when Gillespie befriended Mario Bauza in Cab Calloway's band), the blossoming of Cubop came to fruition just after political interest in the African diaspora on the streets of New York had come to a head. While 1947 and 1948 saw many collaborations between Machito's Afro-Cubans and various jazz musicians, including Dexter Gordon, Stan Getz, Harry "Sweets" Edison, Johnny Griffin, Buddy Rich, Lee Konitz, Chico O'Farrill, and Zoot Sims, these experiments seemed to dry up as the cold war set in, not to be revived until Art Blakey's work with Afro-Cuban drummers at the time of Ghana's independence in March 1957 (Roberts 1985: 115–18; Machito 1947).

If Robeson represented a Marxist-oriented argument for internationalism, Marcus Garvey's Universal Negro Improvement Association articulated a more redemptive notion of international black unity based on nationalism, reclaiming the glories of Africa, black pride, and economic self-determination. The goals of the pan-Islamic movement were sufficiently similar (uniting Muslims in Asia, Africa, Europe, and the United States in a spiritual community) that there was a considerable Muslim presence in Garvey's organization. Although the prominence of the Nation of Islam in the late twentieth century has resulted in the strong association of racial separatism and Islam in African American consciousness, a brief review of Islam in early twentieth century African American communities provides an alternative story. The history of the Ahmadiyya movement, as Richard Turner (1997) has argued, reveals a more complicated relationship among Garveyism, Islam, and the cultural politics of racial pride and self-determination.[5]

The Ahmadiyya movement, which has its roots in late nineteenth-century India, was founded by Ghulam Ahmad, who aroused Orthodox wrath by claiming to be a prophet of Islam. Since Orthodox Islam considers Muhammad to have been the last prophet, the Ahmadis are viewed as a heretical sect (Turner 1997: 112–14). The Ahmadiyya movement, which established proselytizing missions to Europe, West Africa, and North America, published the first English translation of the Qur'an available in the United States and established the first Muslim newspaper in the United States, the *Moslem Sunrise,* in 1921. By 1940 the Ahmadis had between five thousand and ten thousand members in the United States, with principal centers in Chicago, Cleveland, Kansas City, Washington, DC, and Pittsburgh (137). Although Mufti Muhammad Sadiq, the first of the Ahmadi proselytizers, had envisioned a broadly multiracial Islamic movement, Jim Crow frustrated the abilities of Indian missionaries to convert Americans across racial lines. Sadiq's own experiences with racism, including difficulties with white immigration officials and white Christian congregations, embittered him soon after his arrival in 1920. As the intractability of racial segregation emerged, the Ahmadis concentrated their conversion efforts on the African American community (124).

The Ahmadis argued that Islam was a better religion for black people worldwide than Christianity, since Islam was without caste and color prejudice.[6] The linking of spiritual stance with the politics of racial liberation and identity, of course, has a long tradition in African American thought. Spirituals such as "Go Down Moses" bear witness to the capacity of enslaved African Americans to shape Christian symbols to their own liberatory aims. Marcus Garvey stressed that followers of the UNIA (Universal Negro Improvement Association) should no longer worship a white God (Cronon 1968). Garvey was closely associated with the founder of the African Orthodox Church, George Alexander McGuire, who advocated the formation of a new Negro religion that would worship a black God while retaining the fundamental principles of Christianity (178–79). Although McGuire sought to have this new religion declared the official religion of the UNIA, the delegates to the Fourth International Convention of Negroes of the World in 1924 thought it unwise to declare Christianity the official religion of the organization. Garvey likewise turned down a request that Islam be declared the official religion of the movement (Turner 1997: 83, 88).

Garvey had encountered Islam in London (1912) through his friendship with the Sudanese-Egyptian (and pan-Africanist) Duse Mohammed Ali. Ali was associated with an Ahmadi mosque outside London and later wrote for the UNIA's *Negro World* (Cronon 1968: 43). While writing for the *Negro World,* Ali included much coverage of Islam, and some contributors to the newspaper likened Garvey himself to the prophet Muhammad (Turner 1997: 88–89). From 1912 to 1920 Ali published the *African Times and Orient Review,* an influential pan-Africanist journal with circulation in the Caribbean, Europe, West and East Africa, Turkey, Egypt, Japan, India, and Ceylon (Turner 1997: 83). Ali's journal serves as a reminder of the broad scope of early twentieth-century pan-Africanism, which frequently linked African and Asian nationalist concerns, a theme later taken up by the Nation of Islam.

The Moorish Science Temple of America was also an important religious presence in the African American community from the 1920s through the 1940s and beyond. Borrowing ideas from Islam, theosophy, freemasonry and pan-Africansm, its founder, Noble Drew Ali (Timothy Drew), established a "Moorish community" in Newark, New Jersey, in 1913. During the following ten years he increased membership to thirty thousand and established temples in several American cities, including Detroit, Pittsburgh, Chicago, and Baltimore. The popular association of Spain and Africa in African American newspapers of the 1950s may have some relationship to the presence of the Moorish Science Temple in African American communities (Walker 1955). Followers of the Moorish Temple carried identification cards identifying their "Moorish American" nationality (Turner 1997: 99). According to Turner (92): "they claimed that they were not Negroes, blacks, or colored people, but instead an olive-skinned Asiatic people who were the descendants of Moroccans." By a similar logic and by using their Arabic names, some Muslim jazz musicians, including Idrees Sulieman and Kenny Clarke (Liaqat Ali Salaam), were able to get the New York police to issue cabaret cards indicating their race as white (W) rather than colored (C). According to Gillespie (1979: 291), this led to some musicians converting to Islam for social rather than religious reasons.[7]

Islamic groups came under repression from the FBI during the early 1940s for their expression of sometimes pro-Japanese sympathies (based on the African Asian alliance in their spiritual views) and opposition to the draft during World War II. In 1942 members of the Moorish Science Temple and the Nation of Islam were arrested in several cities for failing to register with the Selective Service and encouraging others to avoid the draft (Turner 1997: 103). Elijah Muhammad of the Nation of Islam was incarcerated in Michigan from 1942 to 1946 for these reasons. (103, 168). In the New York of the 1940s, then, the Ahmadiyya movement, with its multiracial philosophy, had a greater presence than the Nation of Islam.

Art Blakey's African Travels

It is clear that members of the New York jazz community of the 1940s demonstrated awareness of both the anticolonialist internationalism of Robeson and Du Bois, as well as the more cultural and spiritual pan-Africanism and pan-Asianism of Islam. Art Blakey emerged in the New York modern jazz scene through his work with the Billy Eckstine band from 1944–1947 (Charlie Parker and Dizzy Gillespie were his bandmates in 1944) and his recordings with Thelonious Monk in 1947. He had come to New York from Pittsburgh with Mary Lou Williams in 1938 and worked with the Fletcher Henderson orchestra from 1939–1941. Blakey's first recordings as a leader were four sides for Blue Note in December 1947 with the 17 Messengers, a band conceived as a training band for young musicians. Its members included Sahib Shihab and Musa Kaleem (Orlando Wright). Blakey, whose Muslim name was Abdullah ibn Buhaina, dated his conversion to Islam at about this time. Blakey never publicly explained his path to conversion to the Ahmadiyya movement, but Dizzy Gillespie reports that a Mulsim missionary named Kahlil Ahmed Nasir converted many New York musicians to the faith (Gillespie 1979).[8]

Blakey's choice of the name Messengers for his short-lived group of 1947 and for the more enduring group from 1954 onward signifies in several directions. From an Islamic perspective, the word invokes the Islamic belief in Muhammad as the messenger of Allah; from a more broadly African American cultural context, the word implies the common cultural belief that African American music has a message, that it "says something" of deeper cultural significance. Since the Ahmadiyya movement believed in a continuous prophetic tradition (i.e., that there were prophets after Muhammad), the name of the later group, the Jazz Messengers, implies a prophetic view of the music itself. After the failure of the 17 Messengers in 1947, Blakey was unable to secure regular work and decided to travel to Africa to pursue religious studies by working his way over on a ship. Although Blakey later remembered going to Africa for two years beginning in 1947, he likely spent only one year in Africa.[9]

Blakey consistently denied that he ever played music while in West Africa. In one of the most detailed accounts of his African sojourn, Blakey told two French interviewers in 1963: "For two years, I immersed myself solely in philosophers, religion, and Hebrew and Arab languages. I do not remember having played an instrument even one time during that entire period" (Clouzet and Delorme 1963).[10] Blakey's denials later became even more emphatic: "I didn't go to Africa to study drums—somebody wrote that—I went to Africa because there wasn't anything else for me to do. I couldn't get any gigs, and I had to work my way over on a boat. I went over there to study religion and philosophy. I didn't bother with the drums, I wasn't after that. I went over there to see what I could do about religion" (Nolan 1979: 19).

Implying that his religious quest was somehow incompatible with music (a remarkable assertion when considering religion in West Africa), Blakey always stressed that his main interest in Africa was religion.

Although Orthodox Islam disapproves of music, particularly instrumental music, Islam in West Africa has long blended the celebration of Islamic festivals and beliefs with traditional animist worship practices that are deeply musical. In West Africa Blakey is likely to have encountered Muslim groups who made considerable use of drumming. He is also likely to have encountered Akan, Ewe, and Yoruba religious ideas, practices, and music, as well as secular urban popular music in his travels. In 1963 Blakey explained African American interest in Islam to his French interviewers: "Islam brought the black man what he was looking for, an escape like some found in drugs or drinking: a way of living and thinking he could choose freely. This is the reason we adopted this new religion in such numbers. It was for us, above all, a way of rebelling" (Clouzet and Delorme 1963: 38).[11]

Although Blakey traveled to Nigeria, he spent the majority of his time in Accra, Ghana (then Gold Coast). There he is likely to have encountered the drumming traditions of the Southern Ewe and Akan peoples and the anticolonialist fervor of Kwame Nkrumah, who in 1949 had founded the Convention People's Party, the organization through which Ghana was to gain independence in 1957 (July 1970: 530).

African Independence and Afro-Cuban Collaborations

As Norman Weinstein (1993) has suggested, for someone disinclined to identify with Africa, Blakey recorded a lot of African-sounding music. Several of Blakey's musical projects, including "Message from Kenya" (1953), *Ritual* (1957a), *Drum Suite* (1957b), *Orgy in Rhythm* (1957c), *Holiday for Skins* (1958), and *The African Beat* (1962) demonstrate an active interest in African diasporic musical connections, expressed primarily in quasi-Afro-Cuban and Afro-Caribbean terms. Blakey's playing on these recordings shows a more than passing awareness of African and Afro-Cuban means of rhythmic variation and musical development, and their timing suggests Blakey's active knowledge of independence events in Ghana. Although Blakey later dismissed these recordings, saying that "a lot of people said they liked it but as far as I was concerned it never came off," these relatively overlooked recordings, I believe, are important in understanding how African diasporic rhythmic conceptions contributed to the shaping of an expanded idea of the jazz rhythm section in the early 1960s.

Ritual was recorded three weeks before Ghana's independence celebrations with a band including Jackie McLean on alto saxophone, Bill

Hardman on trumpet, Sam Dockery on piano, and Spanky DeBrest on bass. On the album's title track the band was refigured into a quasi-Afro-Cuban percussion section to accompany Blakey's extended drum solo. McLean played lead cowbell; DeBrest, supporting cowbell; Dockery, maracas; and Hardman, claves. Blakey's (1957a) recorded introduction to the title track of *Ritual* is at odds with his later claims to have never touched a drum while in West Africa:

> In 1947, after the Eckstine Band broke up, we took a trip to Africa. I was supposed to stay there three months, and I stayed two years, because I wanted to live among the people and find out just how they lived and about the drums, especially. We were in the interior of Nigeria. And I met some people they call the Ijaw people, who are very, very interesting people. They live sort of primitive. The drum is the most important instrument there. Anything that happens that day that is good, they play about it that night. This particular thing caught my ear for the different rhythms. The first movement is about a hunter . . ."

What are we to make of Blakey's contradictory statements? The recorded message on the track "Ritual" is his first public pronouncement about the trip to Africa, a decision perhaps motivated by the impending independence of Ghana. Is this version of events more likely to be true than his later denials of ever having touched a drum? Was Blakey caught up in the excitement of Ghana's independence, as the African American press seemed to be? If so, why did he mention Nigeria rather than Ghana? The *Pittsburgh Courier* published a thirty-two-page special supplement to commemorate independence that included feature stories about Ghana's history, personal profiles of Nkrumah, and many ads and editorials congratulating Ghana on its triumph (Nations Cheer Africa's Ghana 1957). Ghana's independence was taken as a harbinger not only of the demise of colonialism on the African continent but also as a beacon of hope and challenge to the American civil rights movement.

Why did Blakey mention the Ijaw people rather than the Ewe, Akan, or Yoruba groups he is more likely to have encountered? The Ijaw (or Ijo) live on the Niger River delta (Port Harcourt is the nearest city), many in areas accessible only by water transport, and are known more for fishing and farming than for hunting (Hollos and Leis 1989: 4–6). Given Blakey's many contradictory and enigmatic statements about his experiences in Africa, it is hard to take the programmatic description of

"Ritual" he provides very literally. When asked why Blakey verbally denied Africa, Randy Weston (1999) emphasized that Art was a legendary "storyteller" whose words were less important than what he played. "Art was the one," Weston emphasized, who inspired his musical explorations of African music in the 1950s.

Following Weston's advice, an examination of three performances illustrates the musical means through which Blakey invoked African diasporic connections at the time of Ghanaian independence and his active collaboration with Afro-Caribbean musicians. "Ritual" (1957a) begins with an out-of-time introduction featuring Blakey's signature press rolls and horn cries in call and response. Blakey then establishes a bell pattern that is picked up by the accompanying percussion section. McLean's lead cowbell pattern is a common Brazilian tamborim pattern used in samba.[12] Blakey combines this rhythm with a 2–3 son clave pattern from Afro-Cuban music played by trumpeter Bill Hardman (Figure 11-1). Like West African master drummers, who lead from the lowest pitched instrument, Blakey introduces riff patterns on low toms that "cut" the texture established by the accompanying percussionists. As these rhythms stabilize, Blakey introduces soloistic variations and elaborations of the pattern. As the accompanists continue their relatively fixed supporting patterns, Blakey continues soloing by introducing a repeating pattern, allowing it to center, and then varying it.[13] Although Hardman plays a son clave pattern, the ensemble is not really "thinking" in clave, for clave direction shifts haphazardly, and Blakey plays many patterns that "cross clave"—that is, violate the accentual pattern set up by the clave rhythm. One of Blakey's solo riff patterns crosses clave by playing rhythms that fit the "two side" of the pattern on the "three side" (Figure 11-2). Blakey's purpose, however, was not to keep clave but to invoke the notion of Africa and ritual. To do this he tells a story about the Ijaw people, combines a Brazilian and an Afro-Cuban rhythm to create a hybrid groove, and solos almost exclusively in the lower register on toms and bass drum as an Ewe master drummer might do.

FIGURE 11-1. Art Blakey, "Ritual," 0:35.

Figure 11-2. Art Blakey, "Ritual."

However admirable the percussion efforts of McLean, Hardman, De-Brest, and Dockery may be, they are not "tight" (by a long shot) by the standards of Afro-Cuban percussion. Perhaps this is why the *Orgy in Rhythm* session held a few weeks later on the day after Ghana's independence ceremonies (7 March) includes a true Afro-Cuban percussion section organized by Blakey's friend Sabu Martinez: Sabu on bongos, timbales, and vocals; "Patato" Valdez and Jose Valiente on congas; Ubaldo Nieto (a veteran of the Machito's Afro-Cubans) on timbales; and Evilio Quintero on cencerro, maracas, and tree log. Herbie Mann plays African wooden flutes on the recording, with Wendell Marshall on bass and Ray Bryant on piano. Arthur Taylor, Jo Jones, and "Specs" Wright join Blakey on drumset. As Blakey recalled later, "I was trying to prove to the drummers that they could do something if they cooperate" (Nolan 1979: 21).

"Toffi" (Blakey 1957c) features Art Blakey singing call-and-response chants with a chorus in "several African dialects, including Swahili." The bass enters first playing a one bar tumbao-like[14] pattern that sets up the expectation of a 3/4 or 6/8 meter. The meter is redefined as 4/4 when the conga enters playing a pattern related to the rumba guaguancó (3–2 clave). The piano then enters introducing the melody of the chant harmonized in parallel perfect fourths (Figure 11-3). After the vocal call and response, Ray Bryant takes a dexterous solo centering on a C blues scale. Toward the end of Herbie Mann's flute solo, the meter shifts to a 12/8 feel when the "long bell" (or Congolese) variation of the classic Ewe 12/8 gankogui pattern enters (Figure 11-4).[15]

The percussionists then solo against this texture: Jo Jones with Patato

Figure 11-3. Art Blakey, "Toffi," 4/4.

Figure 11-4. Art Blakey, "Toffi," 12/8.

Valdez[16] on conga, Arthur Taylor on drumset in dialogue with "Specs" Wright on tympani, followed by Sabu Martinez on bongos, and Art Blakey. The Afro-Cuban percussion section affords the jazz drummers a chance to take extended solos against an interactive accompaniment, rather than solo alone, as is more usual in jazz bands. Even with the Afro-Cuban percussion section, however, clave is not maintained to the strictness of Afro-Cuban standards. This is not surprising. Clave as a structural principal involves phrasing in two-bar units that are internally differentiated into a call-and-response relationship (3–2 or 2–3). The swing ride cymbal beat, by contrast, is a symmetrical time-keeping pattern that can be phrased in many different units, including two-bar phrases. Art Blakey plays his hi-hat on 2 and 4 during his solo, phrasing symmetrically against the clave feel established by the percussionists. This is an interesting amalgam of an African American feel and a Cuban one. This is not to say that there are not considerable stretches when clave is maintained, but that it is likely that Blakey "picked up on it" rather than studied its rules.

The use of chants not only gives the album a heavily African flavor but also invokes the religious songs of Santería (Lucumí). A year later on *Holiday for Skins* (1958), Blakey included a piece entitled "Dinga" that includes a chant sung to Elegua, the Yoruba *orisha* of the crossroads, the messenger mediating between the deities and the human world, who, it is believed, opens the door for all possibilities (Thompson 1983: 19). In Santería ceremonies, Elegua is the first *orisha* to be saluted in the *oro del igbodu,* a series of musical rhythms to honor the *orishas* (Amira and Cornelius 1992). This is not the first time a Blakey recording saluted the *orishas,* for on "Message from Kenya" (1953), in a duet with Sabu Martinez, both Changó and Ogun are invoked. Blakey's interest in religion, it seems, extended to the Afro-Caribbean.

In "Dinga," a brief out-of-time introduction is followed by a bass line that sets up the expectation of a 3/4 or 6/8 meter (Figure 11-5, entrance 1), similar to what occurred in "Toffi." When the cowbell enters, it establishes a two-against-three feel against the bass (entrance 2). After this pattern stabilizes, the bell player enters with the Afro-Cuban 6/8 clave pattern (entrance 3). Soon a conga rhythm enters, which invokes *bembé* (entrance 4), the flowing rhythmic feel associated with the central public ceremony in Santería of the same name. A second conga rhythm enters (entrance 5), which soon becomes a soloing pattern. The chant to Elegua enters over this composite texture; later on, Changó is invoked in the lyrics. Although the bass continues centered on G, the singer's principal sustained note in the first phrase of the song is A♭. When Martinez returns to singing at the end of the piece, the principal sustained note moves up to A. Solos follow on bongo and drumset. When the drumset enters, the bass and clave fade out, leaving the first conga rhythm as the sole accompaniment. Martinez subsequently returns on bongos to play in dialogue with Blakey until the chant, along with bass and clave rhythms, returns to complete the piece.

Figure 11-5. Art Blakey, "Dinga."

Blakey's rejection of these recordings has obscured their significance in jazz history. Blakey claimed that the musicians' egos and competitiveness got in the way of achieving the musical experience he was seeking: "On my record date I called all these drummers. You would tell one, 'Take a solo here and we will play background.' Well, the first drummer would take a solo and it would be so damn long the next guy would have no chance to play. He'd be trying to show the other drummers how much he knew. But put us all together and we knew nothin'. It was a novelty at the time, but it just didn't happen" (Nolan 1979: 21).

Critics were also ambivalent about these recordings. Dom Cerulli (1957), writing for *Down Beat,* gave *Orgy in Rhythm* three and a half stars, finding "the effect . . . more that of a travelog sound track than of a jazz session." He found the album halfway between "religious and/or tribal music" and jazz and argued that the latter selections were the most valid. Don Gold (1957), on the other hand, praised *Ritual* highly, saying the album witnessed "Blakey firing more intercontinental missiles than the Russians dreamed existed." He nevertheless drew on common Western images of Africa at the time, exclaiming: "it's all quite fascinating, in its savagery." *Metronome*'s reviewer, continuing on the trope of African backwardness, found volume two of *Orgy in Rhythm* "less bloody than his first." He thought that drummers would be particularly interested in the record. In what would become a common inference later on, he heard hostility in the African sound: "the main reservation we have about this album is the wild and frightening hostility Blakey and Taylor show as they seem intent upon beating heads in and the rumble filled background" (Maher 1957). *Holiday for Skins* was given two and a half stars by *Down Beat*'s reviewer, who found it a "scant offering indeed" and asked "how many Africanesque chants can one stand?" He noted in a somewhat sarcastic tone that fans of drum solos would nevertheless probably find it the "apotheosis of everything" (review of Art Blakey, *Holiday for Skins* 1959) None of the reviewers mentioned Ghana's independence as a context for Blakey's recordings, but then these predominantly white writers were not likely to have been avid readers of the *Pittsburgh Courier* or the *New York Amsterdam News*.[17]

Despite Blakey's disappointment in *Ritual, Orgy in Rhythm,* and *Holiday for Skins,* his use of densely layered percussion ensembles to showcase the soloing capacities of drummers, and his comfort with Afro-Cuban textures, nevertheless demonstrated an awareness of African diasporic drumming that surpassed his contemporaries. Blakey's use of pitch-bending techniques (usually his elbow), in evidence in his solo on Horace Silver's "Safari in 1952" (Blakey 1953), recall the pitch shaping accomplished on West African pressure drums including the Yoruba *dundun* and Dagbamba *luna* ("talking drums," hour-glass shaped, held under the arm and squeezed to mimic the tonal contours of speech). Blakey's ride cymbal patterns on "Latin" tunes had long shown familiarity with Afro-Cuban timbale patterns such as the mambo pattern used on "Split Kick" (Blakey 1954) (Figure 11-6). Ride cymbal patterns like this one later become standard in "Afro-Latin" feels in the early 1960s, especially in the work of Elvin Jones. Although Blakey's percussion-only albums generated a small audience, live performances of "A Night in Tunisia" often witnessed him modeling the way an Afro-Cuban jazz feel should be done. Indeed, the introduction to the 8 April 1957 recording of the piece (Blakey 1957d) includes all of the Africanized stylistic invocations mentioned so far: pitch shaping, Afro-Cuban timbale patterns, open tom patterns, which articulate the open tones of conga rhythms, and solo tom patterns cutting across the texture. Like on

Figure 11-6. Art Blakey, "Split Kick," second B section.

"Ritual," the remaining band members simulate an expanded Afro-Cuban percussion section.

The significance of Blakey's invocations of African and Afro-Cuban diasporic patterns do not lie in their authenticity. As the playing of Blakey and his collaborators indicates, it is quite possible to borrow rhythmic patterns that are "in clave" without fully internalizing clave as a structural principle of phrasing and rhythmic combination. Rather, Blakey and many other jazz drummers took salient rhythms from African and Afro-Cuban rhythmic composites and adapted them to the time-keeping principles of jazz improvisation, where the ride cymbal pattern is the functional equivalent of a bell pattern. Borrowing one layer of an Afro-Cuban timbale pattern (as in Blakey's mambo pattern on "Split Kick" or Elvin Jones's ride pattern on John Coltrane's "Africa"), jazz musicians invented new feels with appropriate bass lines, comping patterns, and vamps—free of the obligation to keep clave—that enriched the rhythmic resources of the early 1960s rhythm section (Coltrane 1961).

As Christopher Washburne (1997) has documented, the influence of Afro-Cuban phrasing principles on jazz is more frequent in early jazz. Louis Armstrong's phrasing on "Come Back Sweet Papa," for example, observes clave phrasing for a considerable stretch of time. Citing riffs and phrases from performers such as Bennie Moten, Jelly Roll Morton, Duke Ellington, and King Oliver, Washburne has argued that the relationship of jazz musicians to Africa has frequently come through Afro-Cuban and Afro-Caribbean sources. Although Washburne ends his consideration of the "Latin tinge" with Dizzy Gillespie, Art Blakey's recordings in the 1950s illustrate that the Afro-Caribbean music continued to be a source of innovation in the jazz of the 1950s and the development of an African diasporic sensibility.

Art Blakey as Trickster, or, Musical Signification Revisited

Art Blakey's African and Afro-Cuban musical explorations have been frequently overlooked in assessments of his otherwise "straight ahead" musical legacy. Blakey's own dismissals of these recordings and his many contradictory statements about Africa provide one explanation of this oversight. Blakey's opposition to the racial separatist politics of the Nation of Islam and the black power movement offer an additional factor. In the early 1960s he characterized the Nation's version of Islam as "fascist" and accused the organization of serving itself rather than Islam (Clouzet and Delorme 1963: 38), a position consistent with the multiracial teachings of the Ahmadiyya movement. Blakey's advocacy of a multiracial Islam, however, coexisted with a fierce pride in the black American roots of jazz. A third explanation lies in the greater understanding of differences between the United States and Africa that Blakey gleaned during his sojourn in Africa. A closer analysis of Blakey's statements denying the relationship between jazz and Africa reveals two interrelated points: (1) Blakey's desire for African Americans to take credit for the culturally hybrid musical synthesis in jazz, without the need to claim Africa as a better place of origin than African America, and (2) Blakey's stress on the great differences between African music and jazz based on his better understanding of the musical and spiritual mastery necessary to seriously undertake African and Afro-Cuban drumming.

Blakey's statement that jazz "doesn't have a damn thing to do with Africa" (quoted in the epigraph to this essay) continued:

> We're a multiracial society here, there are no black people in America who can say they are of pure African descent . . . So what difference does it make? We are here, we are the most advanced blacks, and jazz comes from us. When we heard the Caucasians playing their instruments, we took the instruments and went somewhere else . . . This is our contribution to the world, though they want to ignore it and are always trying to connect it to someone else. It couldn't come from anyone but us. (Taylor 1993: 242)

Blakey's emphasis on the difference between musical traditions was based on a healthy respect for the distinctiveness of diasporic musical traditions: "I've had African drummers in my band—they've toured with me—but they have nothing to do with what we are doing. You have to respect the African for what he is doing, and the Latin for what *he* is doing. You know what I mean? You respect the Japanese folk musicians for what they are doing—that's a very drum-conscious country—but they have another thing going rhythmically. You have to respect each one and have the wisdom to know the difference" (Taylor 1993: 242). Blakey seemed to see a danger in jumbling everything into an undifferentiated African diaspora, which is not the same as denying the shared interests of people of color in fighting racism, or the existence of musical continuities. His acceptance of the idea that African Americans are "the most advanced blacks," however, also reveals an apparent belief in a hierarchy of value within the African diaspora, with modernized and urbanized populations at the top.

When discussing the avant-garde in jazz, Blakey lamented the stylistic move away from a hard driving beat: "Swinging is our field, and we should stay in it. The Latin people have never left their thing. The Africans have never left their thing. So why the hell should we give up our thing when we've got the greatest thing in the world? We're going out there messing with something else which has no beat . . . Our thing is to swing, and it's nothing to be ashamed of. It's something to be proud of" (Taylor 1993: 249–50).

These statements from Blakey are largely from what James Scott (1990: 2) calls the "public transcript"—the open record of interaction between subordinates and those who dominate, in this case predominantly white journalists taking statements from Blakey for publication in magazines that have an effect on the performer's career. The "hidden transcript," by contrast, is more "offstage," beyond the observation of holders of power (4), or communicative only to a more restricted community of people "in the know" (14). Scott's framework is designed to emphasize the role of "disguise" in power-laden relationships, the way in which statements and symbolic practices both conceal and reveal, mediating between the powerful and the powerless constantly "pressing against the limit of what is permitted on stage" (196). These attributes also describe a trickster figure, able to play with the ambiguities between general cultural understanding and subgroup specific meanings and understandings. Whether conceived as the *orisha* Elegua or the Signifying Monkey (Gates 1988), the trickster cleverly mediates between the understandings of the hegemonic and the subaltern.

Blakey's statements about his travels and Africa and the significance of his Afro-Cuban musical explorations seem to disguise his sense of belonging to an African diaspora community, while his drumming at the same time points to a deeper understanding of diasporic connection. Music nevertheless remains a "hidden transcript" in Scott's sense, because (despite its public visibility) it takes an insider audience to map the indexical relationships among the sound patterns, the specific historical circumstances to which they respond, and their specifically black cultural and spiritual implications. Reviewers for major jazz publications in the 1950s and 1960s completely missed the connections between Blakey's sojourn in Africa, Ghanaian independence, and the salutes to the *orishas* in *Orgy in Rhythm* and *Holiday for Skins*. But as Blakey told a St. Louis audience in 1957: "the Jazz Messengers are very serious about getting the message across to you. If you don't want to listen, maybe the person sitting next to you does" (Frost 1957: 26).

That "message" does not lie simply in the sonic form itself but is dependent on the aural and cultural experience that various audiences bring to the performance (and the use to which they put them). Hence, the mode of signification is not denotational but indexical. The 6/8 Afro-Cuban bell pattern does not "stand for" for "Africanness" or any other object or concept so much as it "points to" or "connects" the listener to a broader context of interpretation. This context may presuppose particular cultural knowledge (e.g., that the listener recognizes a sound as a component of Afro-Cuban religious music and/or additional stylistic, political, emotional, and spiritual associations) or may actually create context in performance, by providing a musical framework over which various kinds of culturally significant musical participation and interaction take place—improvisation, hand clapping, dancing, singing, flirting, and showing off, to name only a few.[18] There is, in other words, a large interpretive space around musical signs, both in time and over time, that contributes to the emergence of its ambiguous yet powerful cultural meaning. The indirectness of sound, the deniability of any connection indexically made, yet the obviousness of the cultural messages to the initiated are very much a part of the pleasure and symbolic power of African diasporic musics.

Conclusion

This article has endeavored to illuminate the principal political, religious, and musical contexts through which Art Blakey's travels to Africa and his African diasporic musical explorations of the 1950s might profitably be interpreted. The importance of internationalism to both politically oriented and spiritually oriented modes of pan-Africanism has been noted, as well as Art Blakey's historical connections to persons within the jazz community with known relationships to both perspectives. The examination of the Ahmadiyya movement has demonstrated that the common presumption that African American Islam has always been associated with racial separatism is not true. There is, rather, a more complicated relationship between ideologies of pan-African unity, economic self-determination, and religion. Finally, the masterful disjunction between what Art Blakey said about his relationship to Africa and African music and what he actually played reveal the complex pathways through which music has mediated and continues to mediate African diasporic experience.

Notes

[1] I thank John Work for alerting me to the importance of the Ahmadiyya movement in the African American community.

[2] Nkrumah became the first president of an independent Ghana in 1957. Jomo Kenyatta became prime minister of Kenya in 1963. Nnamdi Azikiwe was the editor of a chain of newspapers in Nigeria and West Africa and played a prominent role in the struggle for Nigerian independence. See Von Eschen (1997: 54–56).

[3] Duberman refers to the "Persian Hotel." He cites a newspaper that may have misspelled the name.

[4] Gillespie's autobiography spells the name "Azumba" (Gillespie 1979: 289). Elsewhere it is reported as K. O. Mbadiwe and K. Ozoumba Mbadiwe. He later became Nigeria's central minister of communications and aviation. ("Overseas Datelines," *Pittsburgh Courier* 47 [19: 12 May 1956]: 9. See also the Institute for Jazz Studies' clippings files, "U.S. State Department.")

[5] My account of the Ahmadiyya movement is drawn from Turner (1997: 109–46) and McCloud (1995: 18–21).

[6] Turner (1997: 13–14) argues that Islam's reputation for lack of color prejudice is not entirely true, especially in the years before the Atlantic slave trade.

[7] The FBI considered the Moorish Science Temple of America a potentially subversive organization by virtue of its "racial sympathy" for the Japanese. In an extravagantly paranoid fantasy, the FBI viewed the Moorish group as part of a worldwide plot by the "darker races" to take over the United States while white soldiers were fighting World War II abroad (Turner 1997: 101).

[8] Gillespie was rumored to be a Muslim in the 1940s but was never a convert, despite *Life* magazine's 1948 report to the contrary. Gillespie (1979: 287–93) explains his relationship to Islam in his autobiography.

[9] Art Blakey's recording history precludes a two year stay in W. Africa. Blakey recorded with Billy Eckstine on October 6, 1946; as a leader on December 22, 1947;

with James Moody on October 19, 1948; and with Sonny Stitt on February 17, 1950. Blakey likely spent his year in Africa from late 1946 to late 1947.

[10]My translation: "Pendant deux ans, je me suis plonge uniquement dans les philosophes, les religion et les langues hebraique et arabes et je n'ai pas le souvenir d'avoir joue une seule fois d'un instrument pendant toute cette periode" (Clouzet and Delorme 1963: 37).

[11]"L'Islam a apporté a l'homme noir ce que celui-ci cherchait, une porte de sortie que certains ont trouvée dans la drogue ou la boisson: une manière de vivre et de penser qu'il puisse choisir en tout liberté. C'est la raison pour laquelle nous avons été si nombreux à adopter cette nouvelle religion. Ce fut pour nous, avant tout, une façon de nous rebeller" (Clouzet and Delorme 1963: 38).

[12]My understanding of the African diasporic connections in the following musical examples owes much to Elizabeth Sayre and Julian Gerstin, who reviewed the recordings and transcriptions for me and contributed analytical observations.

[13]For a description of West African aesthetics of musical variation, especially those of the Dagomba, see John Chernoff (1979).

[14]*Tumbaos* are repeating patterns played by bass and congas in Afro-Cuban music.

[15]The strokes of the pattern can be conceived in terms of longs (L = quarter note) and shorts (S = eighth note). The "long bell" is LLLSLLS, while the "short bell" is LLSLLLS. The "short bell" version is the equivalent of the 6/8 Afro-Cuban clave used in sacred music especially (see Figure 11-5). I thank Elizabeth Sayre for introducing this term to me. I thank Julian Gerstin for identifying the secular conga patterns in these examples.

[16]The name is misspelled "Potato" on the recording.

[17]See Weinstein (1993: 51–53) for a more sympathetic account of these recordings.

[18]For more on indexicality and jazz see Monson (1996: 185–91). For a very clear explanation of the semiotic theory and linguistic anthropology on which these assertions are made, see Duranti (1997: 17–20; 37–38).

References

Amira, John, and Steven Cornelius. 1992. *The Music of Santería: Traditional Rhythms of the Bata Drums.* Crown Point, IN: White Cliffs Media Co.

Blakey, Art. 1953. "Message from Kenya." *Horace Silver Trio.* New York: 23 November. Blue Note CDP 81520 2.

————.1954. *A Night at Birdland, vol. 1.* New York: 21 Feb. Blue Note CDP 7 46519 2.

————. 1957a. *Ritual.* New York: 11 Feb. Blue Note CDP 7 46858 2.

————. 1957b. *Drum Suite.* New York: 22 Feb. Columbia CL 1002.

————. 1957c. *Orgy in Rhythm, Vols. 1 and 2.* New York: 7 Mar. Blue Note CDP 7243 8 56586 2 4.

————. 1957d. *Theory of Art.* New York: 8 Apr. BMG 09026-68730-2.

————. 1958. "Dinga." *Holiday for Skins, Vol. 2.* New York: 9 Nov. Blue Note BST-84005.

———. 1962. *The African Beat.* New York: 24 Jan. Blue Note BLP-4097 (BST 84097).

Cerulli, Dom. 1957. Review of Art Blakey's *Orgy in Rhythm. Down Beat* 24 (18: 5 Sept.): 22.

Chernoff, John Miller. 1979. *African Rhythm and African Sensibility: Aesthetics and Social Action in African Musical Idioms.* Chicago: University of Chicago Press.

Clouzet, Jean, and Michel Delorme. 1963. "Entretien: Les Confedences de Buhaina." *Jazz Magazine* 9 (6: June): 35–42.

Coltrane, John. 1961. "Africa." *Africa Brass.* New York: 23 May. Impulse! MCAD-42001.

Cronon, Edmund David. 1968. *Black Moses: The Story of Marcus Garvey and the Universal Negro Improvement Association.* Madison: University of Wisconsin Press.

Duberman, Martin Bauml. 1988. *Paul Robeson.* New York: Knopf.

Duranti, Alessandro. 1997. *Linguistic Anthropology.* Cambridge: Cambridge University Press.

Frost, Harry. 1957. "In Person: Art Blakey in St. Louis." *Metronome* 74 (2: Feb.): 26, 35, 42.

Gates, Henry Louis, Jr. 1988. *The Signifying Monkey: A Theory of African-American Literary Criticism.* New York: Oxford University Press.

Gillespie, Dizzy. 1979. *To Be or Not to Bop: Memoirs of Dizzy Gillespie with Al Fraser.* New York: Da Capo Press.

Gold, Don. 1957. Review of Art Blakey's *Ritual. Down Beat* 24 (22: 31 Oct.): 24.

Hollos, Marida, and Philip E. Leis. 1989. *Becoming Nigerian in Ijo Society.* New Brunswick, NJ: Rutgers University Press.

Jones, Max. 1961. "Get Inside Drums! Says Art Blakey." *Melody Maker.* Rutgers University, Institute for Jazz Studies. Clippings File: "Art Blakey."

July, Robert W. 1970. *A History of the African People.* New York: Scribner's.

Machito. 1947. *Afro-Cuban Jazz.* New York: 1947, 1950, 1957, 1958. Saludos Amigos CD 62015.

Maher, Jack. 1957. Review of Art Blakey's *Orgy in Rhythm, Volume 2. Metronome* 74 (12: Dec.): 25, 28.

McCloud, Aminah Beverly. 1995. *African American Islam.* New York: Routledge.

"Nations Cheer Africa's Ghana." 1957. *Pittsburgh Courier* 48 (10: 9 Mar.): 1.

Nolan, Herb. 1979. "New Message from Art Blakey." *Down Beat* (Nov.): 19–22.

Review of Art Blakey's *Holiday for Skins.* 1959. *Down Beat* 26 (17: 20 Aug.): 55.

Monson, Ingrid. 1996. *Saying Something: Jazz Improvisation and Interaction.* Chicago: University of Chicago Press.

Roberts, John Storm. 1985. *The Latin Tinge: The Impact of Latin American Music on the United States.* Tivoli, NY: Original Music.

Russell, George. 1947. "Cubana Be/Cubana Bop." On *Dizzy Gillespie: The Complete RCA Victor Recordings.* New York: 22 Dec. Bluebird 07863 66528-2.

Scott, James. 1990. *Domination and the Arts of Resistance: Hidden Transcripts.* New Haven, CT: Yale University Press.

Silver, Horace. *Horace Silver Trio.* New York: 9 and 20 Oct. 1952 and 23 Nov. 1953. Blue Note CDP 7 81520 2.

Taylor, Arthur. 1993. *Notes and Tones: Musician-to-Musician Interviews.* Expanded edition. New York: DaCapo.

Thompson, Robert Farrris. 1983. *Flash of the Spirit: African and Afro-American Arts and Philosophy*. New York: Vintage.

Turner, Richard Brent. 1997. *Islam in the African American Experience*. Bloomington: Indiana University Press.

Tynan, John. 1957. "The Jazz Message." *Down Beat* 24 (21: 17 Oct.): 15.

Von Eschen, Penny M. 1997. *Race against Empire: Black Americans and Anticolonialism, 1937–1957*. Ithaca, NY: Cornell University Press.

Walker, Charles. 1955. "African Imprint in Spain." *New York Amsterdam News* 46 (32): 17.

Washburne, Christopher. 1997. "The Clave of Jazz: A Caribbean Contribution to the Rhythmic Foundation of an African-American Music." *Black Music Research Journal* 17 (1: Spring): 59–80.

Weinstein, Norman C. 1993. *A Night in Tunisia: Imaginings of Africa in Jazz*. New York: Limelight Editions.

Weston, Randy. 1999. Personal communication. Cambridge, MA, 13 Apr.

Contributors

Gage Averill is an Associate Professor of Ethnomusicology at New York University. His book *A Day for the Hunter, A Day for the Prey: Popular Music and Power in Haiti* (1997) won an award for "Best Research in Folk and Popular Music in 1997" from the Association of Recorded Sound Collections, and he co-edited *Making and Selling Culture* (1996). He is currently working on *Four Parts, No Waiting: A Social History of American Barbershop Harmony* (Oxford, forthcoming). His major areas of research are in Caribbean popular music, North American vernacular musics, the music industry, carnival, and music and politics. He has also been a columnist for *Beat* magazine and has directed steelbands and Afro-Cuban ensembles.

Eric Charry is an Associate Professor of Music at Wesleyan University. He is the author of *Mande Music: Traditional and Modern Music of the Maninka and Mandinka of West Africa* (forthcoming). He studied in Africa for several years, researching Maninnka musical traditions, and has regularly organized summer institutes on jembe drumming in the United States.

Steven Cornelius is an Associate Professor at Bowling Green State University in Ohio. He is co-author (with John Amira) of *The Music of Santeria: Traditional Rhythms of the Bata Drums* (1992). His research interests include the Caribbean, West Africa, and the classical music industry.

Lucy Durán is a Lecturer in Music in the Department of African Languages and Cultures at the School of Oriental and African Studies, University of London. She is the author of "Stars and Songbirds: Mande Female Singers in Urban Music, Mali 1980–99" (Ph.D. University of London, 1999) and of several articles on Malian, Guinean, and Senegalese music appearing in such venues as the *British Journal of Ethnomusicology, Popular Music,* and *Folk Roots*. Durán has also written liner notes for African and Cuban releases by Globestyle, Stern's Africa, Hannibal, and World Circuit, and has produced several albums of music for Hannibal and Globestyle featuring Malian musicians, including *New Ancient Strings* (Toumani Diabate) and most recently *Kulanjan* (Taj Mahal and Toumani Diabate).

Veit Erlmann is Professor of Ethnomusicology and Anthropology, and holds the Endowed Chair of Music History at University of Texas at Austin. He has done fieldwork in Ecuador and in several African countries such as Cameroon, Niger, Ghana, South Africa, and Lesotho. His most recent publications include *Music, Modernity, and the Global Imagination: South Africa and the West* (1999) and *Nightsong: Performance, Power, and Practice in South Africa* (1996). His theoretical interests include globalization, modernity, media, world music, diaspora, and history of sound.

Akin Euba is the Andrew W. Mellon Professor of Music at the University of Pittsburgh and founder and Director of the Centre for Intercultural Music Arts, London. He is the author of four books, including *Yoruba Drumming: The Dundun Tradition* (1990). The CD of his opera *Chaka* (from an epic poem by Leopold Sedar Senghor), performed by the City of Birmingham Touring Opera, United Kingdom, conducted by Simon Halsey, was published by the Music Research Institute in March 1999.

Julian Gerstin earned his M.A. at the University of Chicago with work on avant-garde jazz drummer Milford Graves, and his Ph.D. at University of California, Berkeley with research on traditional music and social movements in Martinique. Along the way he has studied and performed in situations ranging from Ghanaian dance to Afro-Cuban religious drumming, from salsa to Afrobeat to mbaqanga, from jazz to punk. Julian currently lives in Oakland, California, teaching music and anthropology at San Jose State University, the California Community College system, and in the traveling workshop-demonstration group Ka Bô Kay.

Jerome Harris is a New York-based jazz and new-music guitarist/bass guitarist. After studying psychology and social relations at Harvard University (A.B. 1973), Harris majored in jazz guitar at New England Conservatory, graduating with honors in 1977. He has recorded and/or toured with Sonny Rollins, Jack DeJohnette, George Russell, Ned Rothenberg,

Bobby Previte, Julius Hemphill, Ray Anderson, Oliver Lake, and Bill Frisell, among many others. His recordings as leader include *Rendezvous* (Stereophile) and *Hidden in Plain View* (New World).

Travis Jackson is Assistant Professor of Musicology (Ethnomusicology) and Jazz & Improvisational Studies at the University of Michigan. His research on jazz and rock, filtered through critical race theory, cultural anthropology, and Marxist urban geography, focuses broadly on issues of meaning and interpretation. He is the author of *Blowin' the Blues Away: Performance and Meaning on the New York Jazz Scene* (forthcoming). A guitarist and songwriter, his spare time is devoted to recording in his home studio.

Lansiné Kaba is Professor of History and Dean of the Honors College at the University of Illinois at Chicago. He witnessed *Mamaya* celebrations as a child growing up in Kankan in the 1940s as well as the 1952 recordings of Gilbert Rouget. He has written on various aspects of Guinean history and is completing a monograph on Kankan.

Ingrid Monson is an Associate Professor of Music at Washington University in St. Louis. She is the author of *Saying Something: Jazz Improvisation and Interaction*, winner of the Sonneck Society's Irving Lowens award for the best book published on American music in 1996. She is currently working on *Freedom Sounds: Jazz, Civil Rights, and Africa, 1950–1967* (forthcoming). She has published articles in *Ethnomusicology, Critical Inquiry, World of Music, Journal of the American Musicological Society, Women and Music,* and the *Black Music Research Journal.* Her research interests include jazz, the African diaspora, and cultural theory. She is also a trumpet player.

Yuen-Ming David Yih has a Ph.D. in Ethnomusicology from Wesleyan University. His dissertation is entitled "Music and Dance of Haitian Vodou: Diversity and Unity in Regional Repertoires." His field recordings appear on *Rhythms of Rapture* (Smithsonian Folkways), and he co-produced another Vodou music CD, *Angels in the Mirror* (Ellipsis Arts). A pianist and percussionist, David creates and performs music for dance and drama productions and is in demand as pianist and arranger for Latin dance orchestras. As a member of various musical ensembles, he has performed at Carnegie Hall, Lincoln Center, and Symphony Space in New York City, and on television and radio programs.

Index

Abercrombie, John, 42
Abrams, Muhal Richard, 110
Acculturation, theory of, 26
Adderley, Cannonball, 42
Adderley, Nat, 44
Adorno, Theodor W., 87
Aesthetics, canon versus process,
    120–122
"Africa," 345
African Academy of Arts and Research
    (AAAR), 332
African American culture, role of,
    42–46
African Beat, The, 337
African Times and Orient Review, 334
Agbeli, Godwin, 13, 245–260
Ahmad, Ghulam, 333
Ahmadiyya movement, 333–334, 335
Ajíṣafé, A. K., 210
Akínyanjú, Akin, 230
Akiyo, 315
Alajobi, 217
Alárìnjò, 208–209
Alberts, Arthur S., 198
Ali, Duse Mohammed, 334
Ali, Nobel Drew, 335
Alland, A., Jr., 320
Amen, 147
American classical music, 54–55
American Jazz Music (Hobson), 113
AM4 (Association Mi Mes Manmay
    Matinik), 309–310
Àmọ̀ọ́, Àyàntúnjí, 230

Anderson, Ray, 110
Anti-antiessentialism, 4
Anticolonialism, 330–332
Antiessentialism, 4
Antillanité, 301–302, 304
Apollo, 201
Apter, Andrew, 12
Aristide, Jean-Bertrand, 267
Armstrong, Louis, 109, 110, 345
Art Ensemble of Chicago, 110
Association Carnaval Foyal (ACF),
    314–315, 316
Association des artistes du Mali, l'Am-
    biance, 201
Associations de 1901, 308, 313, 320
Avant, 110
Averill, Gage, 14–15
Àyánṣọlá, Làìsì, 230

Bajourou, 201
"Balakonininfi," 152, 175–176
Balancing different musical parameters
    in performance, 38–40
"Bambougoudji," 174
Baraka, Amiri, 26–27, 29
Barber, Karin, 9–10
Barretto, Justi, 69
Barth, Bruce, 36, 38, 40, 44
Basie, Count, 8, 332
*Batteries et Sonneries de l'Infanterie
    Française* (Melchior), 273
BBC (British Broadcasting Company),
    111

357